THE RADICAL THREAD

Political Change in Scotland. Paisley Politics, 1885–1924

SCOTTISH HISTORICAL REVIEW

MONOGRAPHS SERIES

No. 7

Scottish Historical Review Monographs are major works of scholarly research covering all aspects of Scottish history. They are selected and sponsored by the Scottish Historical Review Trust, in conjunction with Tuckwell Press

CURRENT AND FORTHCOMING VOLUMES

1 Helen M. Dingwall — *Physicians, Surgeons and Apothecaries: Medicine in Seventeenth-Century Edinburgh*

2 Ewen A. Cameron — *Land for the People? The British Government and the Scottish Highlands, c.1880–1925*

3 Richard Anthony — *Herds and Hinds: Farm Labour in Lowland Scotland, 1900–1939*

4 R. Andrew McDonald — *The Kingdom of the Isles: Scotland's Western Seaboard, c.1100–c.1336*

5 John R. McIntosh — *Church and Theology in Enlightenment Scotland: The Evangelical Party, 1740–1800*

6 Graeme Morton — *Unionist-Nationalism: Governing Urban Scotland, 1830–1860*

7 Catriona M. M. Macdonald — *The Radical Thread: Political Change in Scotland. Paisley Politics, 1885–1924*

8 James L. MacLeod — *The Second Disruption: The Free Church in Victorian Scotland and the Origins of the Free Presbyterian Church*

THE RADICAL THREAD

Political Change in Scotland. Paisley Politics, 1885–1924

CATRIONA M. M. MACDONALD

TUCKWELL PRESS

First published in Great Britain in 2000 by
Tuckwell Press Ltd
The Mill House, Phantassie, East Linton, East Lothian, EH40 3DG
Scotland

ISBN 1 86232 141 8

British Library Cataloguing-in-Publication Data. A catalogue record for this book is available on request from the British Library

Typeset in 10/12 Baskerville by
Aligra Lancaster
Printed and bound in Great Britain by
The Cromwell Press, Trowbridge, Wiltshire

Contents

Illustrations vi
Acknowledgements vii
Abbreviations viii
Map: Locating Paisley in central Scotland x

1 'The Weavers Knew': The Theory and Historiography of Liberal Decline 1

2 Interests and Industry, Politics and Paternalism 36

3 'A Motley and Ill-Assorted Group': Paisley Politics, 1885–1900 74

4 'Mild Liberalism and the Divine Rights of Capital': Paisley Politics, 1900–1914 149

5 'There are no new Liberals being born': Paisley Politics, 1914–1924 207

6 Conclusion: The Radical Thread 267

Appendices (1–7) 283

Bibliography 297

Index 320

Illustrations

between pp. 150 and 151

Plate 1 Map: Paisley in the 1890s

Plate 2 Anchor Mill, Paisley

Plate 3 Cartoon: Peter Coats

Plate 4 Cartoon: George A. Clark

Plate 5 Anchor Boy Scouts (est. 1915)

Plate 6 Bowling Club Fête Day (1916)

Plate 7 Thread works outing (1913)

Plate 8 Girls' hockey team and the Anchor Recreation Club

Plate 9 Weaving looms, Paisley Co-operative Manufacturing Society, Colinslee (*c.*1880s)

Plate 10 Neilston strike (1910)

Plate 11 Cartoon: 1885 general election

Plate 12 Cartoon: 1891 Paisley by-election

Plate 13 Boer War victory parade, Paisley

Plate 14 The Prince of Wales' visit to Paisley (1921)

Plate 15 Street oratory, County Square, Paisley (*c.*1900)

Plate 16 Sma' Shot Day parade, Gauze Street (1890s)

Plate 17 Thread-mill workers, World War One

Plate 18 Munitions workers, World War One

Plate 19 Willie Gallacher

Acknowledgements

I owe a lot to a great number of people who helped and supported the research from which this book emerged. The encouragement, wisdom and friendship of Professor W. Hamish Fraser and Dr Richard J. Finlay, my supervisors as a postgraduate student at the University of Strathclyde, helped me direct and focus my thoughts and research endeavours. Likewise, the assistance and advice of Professor Thomas M. Devine, Dr Arthur McIvor, Dr Elaine W. McFarland and Dr I. G. C. Hutchison were invaluable. Finally, looking back, I owe much to my undergraduate tutors at the University of St Andrews whose enthusiasm and teaching remain a significant influence.

The financial support of the Carnegie Trust for the Universities of Scotland warrants my particular appreciation, as does the backing of the Scottish Historical Review Trust. I hope my efforts reflect in true measure, my gratitude to these remarkable Scottish institutions and their faith in this project.

Numerous individuals and institutions gave practical assistance over the past few years. My thanks are extended to David Roberts and Maureen Lochrie of Paisley Museum, the staff of Paisley Central Library, Peter and 'the gang' at the Coats Observatory, Audrey Canning of the Willie Gallacher Library and the staffs of Glasgow City Archives, the Mitchell Library, the National Library of Scotland, Glasgow University Library, Glasgow University Archives and Business Records Centre, Edinburgh University Library, the British Library (Colindale) and the Bodleian Library. Due acknowledgement is also accorded to those named for permission to quote from the following manuscript collections: Asquith MSS (Jane Bonham Carter and the Bodleian Library); Elibank MSS (Trustees of the National Library of Scotland): Gilbert Murray MSS (Alexander Murray and the Bodleian Library); Haldane MSS (Trustees of the National Library of Scotland): Harcourt Papers (Hon. Mrs E. A. Gascoigne and the Bodleian Library); ILP Archives (ILP and the British Library of Political and Economic Science); J. & P. Coats MSS (Coats Viyella, Paisley Museum and Art Galleries and University of Glasgow); McCallum Scott MSS (Glasgow University Library, Department of Special Collections); Muirhead MSS (Trustees of the National Library of Scotland); National Party MSS (Bodleian Library); Parker Smith MSS (Glasgow City Archives); Rosebery MSS (Trustees of the National Library of Scotland); SCUA MSS (Scottish Conservative and Unionist Party and the Trustees of the National Library of Scotland); SLA Archives (Scottish Liberal Democrats and Edinburgh University Library); Sir Donald Maclean MSS (A. D. Maclean and the Bodleian Library).

I have made all efforts to obtain necessary permission with reference to copyright material; however, I apologise should there be any omissions in this respect.

Finally, numerous personal debts must be acknowledged. Without the guidance of my parents and their encouragement, the research would have been far harder. Their joy in learning, their passion for their Gaelic heritage and the calm simplicity of their love and patience will, I hope, forever guide my attitude to my work. To Mairi and Murdo, I extend the thanks of a grateful sister. I greatly appreciated their confidence in me and this project. To Martyn my debts are both intangible and material. His patience, forbearance and sound good sense in escaping to the Scottish mountains when things seemed to go wrong; his understanding of my preoccupation with my work, and his commitment to the intrinsic worth of education have proved a genuine support.

C. M. M. M.

Abbreviations

AEU	Amalgamated Engineering Union
ASE	Amalgamated Society of Engineers
AHR	*American Historical Review*
ARA	Advanced Radical Association
BJS	*British Journal of Sociology*
BLO	Bodleian Library, Oxford
BSP	British Socialist Party
BWL	British Worker's League
CDC	Co-operative Defence Committee
CP	Co-operative Party
CSSH	*Comparative Studies in Society and History*
CWC	Clyde Workers Committee
EHR	*English Historical Review*
EUL	Edinburgh University Library
GCA	Glasgow City Archives
HJ	*Historical Journal*
ILP	Independent Labour Party
INL	Irish National League
IRSH	*International Review of Social History*
JBS	*Journal of British Studies*
JCH	*Journal of Contemporary History*
JPC	J. & P. Coats
LSE	London School of Economics
ML	Mitchell Library
NDP	National Democratic Party
NGL	National Guilds League
NLS	National Library of Scotland
NSA	*New Statistical Account for Scotland*
NSDF	National Society of Dyers and Finishers
NUCAS	National Union of Conservative Associations for Scotland
OSA	*Old Statistical Account for Scotland*
P&P	*Past and Present*
PAEU	Paisley Amalgamated Engineering Union
PCA	Paisley Conservative Association
PCL	Paisley Central Library
PDE	*Paisley Daily Express*
PLA	Paisley Liberal Association
PLRUA	Paisley Liberal and Radical Unionist Association
PM	Paisley Museum
PP	*Parliamentary Papers*
PRG	*Paisley and Renfrewshire Gazette*

PTPA	Paisley Tenants' Protection Assocation
PWEC	Paisley Workers' Elections Committee
PWMEC	Paisley Workers' Municipal Elections Committee
PWPEC	Paisley Workers' Parliamentary Elections Committee
SCUA	Scottish Conservative and Unionist Association
SCWS	Scottish Co-operative Wholesale Society
SDF	Social Democratic Federation
SH	*Social History*
SHMA	Scottish Horse and Motorman's Association
SHR	*Scottish Historical Review*
SHRA	Scottish Home Rule Association
SLA	Scottish Liberal Association
SLHA	Scottish Labour Housing Association
SLP	Scottish Labour Party
STUC	Scottish Trade Union Congress
SUTCLP	Scottish United Trades Council Labour Party
SWPEC	Scottish Workers' Parliamentary Elections Committee
SWRC	Scottish Workers' Representation Committee
TCBH	*Twentieth Century British History*
TLC	(Paisley) Trades and Labour Council
UGABRC	University of Glasgow Archives and Business Records Centre
UIL	United Irish League
WEC	War Emergency Committee
WSLUA	West of Scotland Liberal Unionist Association

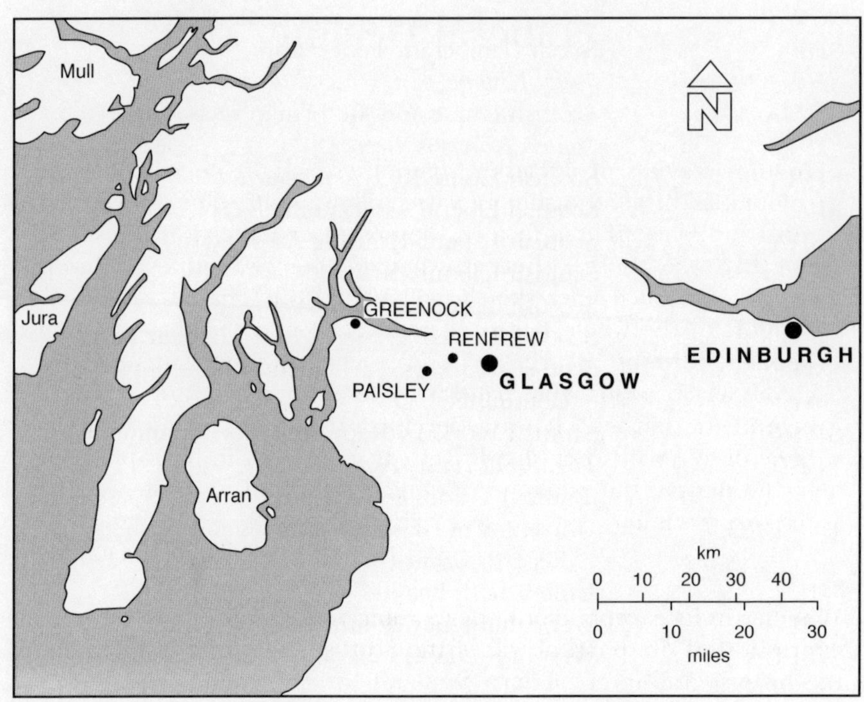

Map: *Locating Paisley in central Scotland*

CHAPTER ONE

'The Weavers Knew': The Theory and Historiography of Liberal Decline

> In the weaving of a Paisley shawl there might be six or seven colours, all of good cashmere yarn, yellow, white, blue, green, red, pink and black. These formed the design or pattern of the shawl. but there was another shot thrown across the web with every bridle ... It was a much finer shot, usually of cotton. That was the main support of the whole fabric. It was woven into the shawl by four heddles, forming a three-and-one twill quite independent of the cards which made the pattern. These heddles were mounted behind the harness. It was, therefore, the ground-work or back-bone of every plaid or shawl. But you never saw it. Not appearing in the design, the public were quite ignorant of its existence. But the weavers knew.
>
> William McQuilkin[1]

Whether in its exceptionalism or its coincidence with British norms, the expression of the political will of the Scottish electorate has dominated the historiography of modern Scotland for generations and has been considered indicative of wider socio-economic and cultural 'difference'. However, given the diversity of the regional experience within Scotland itself, it is debatable whether the national is the most appropriate vantage point from which to hear the voice of the body politic.

Explaining 'difference' through appeals to national electoral results encourages a self-perpetuating logic which confuses votes cast during a period of heightened political awareness with the expression of popular politics which develop beyond the restrictions of electoral registration and the timing of the ballot. Such politics evolve through the 'social contexts within which people live their lives', on a scale far removed from the national – in neighbourhoods and communities.[2] Such 'organic' politics are only partially translated and expressed in elections

[1] W. McQuilkin, 'Sma' Shot Day', *Paisley and the Trade Union Movement* (unpublished manuscript, 1930).

[2] J. A. Agnew, *Place and Politics: The Geographical Mediation of State and Society* (Boston, 1987), p. 108.

(both parliamentary and municipal), through the party labels and programmes which often restrict rather than reflect the political choices available. There is therefore something beyond and within the national patterns made when votes are cast which determines the character and longevity of trends revealed in the results of ballots – something which supports and grounds the pattern but is seldom revealed in the overall design. Like the cotton 'shot' in a Paisley shawl, it supports the threads which together determine the pattern, but is hidden to the casual observer.

The manner in which the politics of community sought expression in the formal institutions of party and state dominates this study of the politics of Paisley in the period from 1885 to 1924. It is by no means suggested that Paisley was either indicative or representative of trends evolving elsewhere (or indeed that the burgh was exceptional), but that Paisley's experience usefully highlights how 'what is possible politically is defined by the evolving cultures of specific places'.[3] As John Agnew has emphasised:

> For most of its modern history, Scotland has been able to exist with benign multiple identities. Class-consciousness, Britishness and Scottishness have coexisted. But they have coexisted in different ways in different places.[4]

Going beyond the 'national', however, also necessitates going beyond 'party'. Changing socio-economic interests are seldom simplistically absorbed into existing political identities and interest groups, and party programmes seldom encompass the complex and frequently conflicting interests and beliefs of individual actors. Revealing what 'the weavers knew' thus requires an insistence on the discontinuities between aim and action, between motive and expression: an acceptance that what is revealed in the pattern of politics is always a partial truth.

Text and Subtext: The Fragments of Political Inquiry

Writing in 1978, E. P. Thompson reflected:

> In the old days, vulgar Political Economy saw men's economic behaviour as being *lawed* (although workers were obtuse and refractory in obeying these laws), but allowed to the autonomous individual an area of freedom, in his intellectual, aesthetic or moral choices. Today, structuralisms engross this area from every side; we are *structured* by social relations, *spoken* by pre-given linguistic structures, *thought* by ideologies, *dreamed* by myths, *gendered* by

[3] J. A. Agnew, 'Place and politics in post-war Italy: a cultural geography of local identity in the provinces of Lucca and Pistoia', in K. Anderson and F. Gale (eds.), *Inventing Places: Studies in Cultural Geography* (Cheshire, 1992), p. 58.

[4] Agnew, *Place and Politics*, p. 160.

> patriarchal sexual norms, *bonded* by affective obligations, *cultured* by mentalités, and *acted* by history's script. None of these ideas is, in origin, absurd, and some rest upon some substantial additions to knowledge. But all slip, at a certain point, from sense to absurdity, and, in their sum, all arrive at a common terminus of unfreedom.[5]

Thompson's criticism of Althusserian structuralism and his fear of the alienation of the individual in the writing of history are today echoed in the fears of historians who view with concern the 'linguistic turn' which many social historians are taking through their adoption of linguistic and post-structural methodologies and approaches, much influenced by Derrida.[6] The new concern with language and the text has caused many to fear that the 'logic' of a class-based philosophy of economic determinism and cultural materialism will be replaced by an equally uncompromising linguistic determinism in which words will take the place of historical agents.[7] This, they argue, will make intention and responsibility meaningless concepts in the historical context as linguistic theory substitutes empirical historical inquiry. In Scotland, our academic journals have been curiously silent on this theoretical debate and indeed one could be excused for thinking that recent forums on the future of the historical profession point us backwards rather than forwards in developing methodologies for the next millennium.[8] Are we to assume

5 E. P. Thompson, 'The poverty of theory: or an orrery of errors', in E. P. Thompson, *The Poverty of Theory and Other Essays* (London, 1978), p. 345.

6 The recent debate in the journal *Social History* concerning the work of Gareth Stedman Jones is characteristic of the issues being contested. See D. Mayfield and S. Thorne, 'Social history and its discontents: Gareth Stedman Jones and the politics of language', *SH*, xvii (1992), pp. 165–88; J. Lawrence and M. Taylor, 'The poverty of protest: Gareth Stedman Jones and the politics of language – a reply', *SH*, xviii (1993), pp. 1–15; P. Joyce, 'The imaginary discontents of social history: a note of response to Mayfield and Thorne, and Lawrence and Taylor – a comment', *SH*, xviii (1993), pp. 81–5; D. Mayfield and S. Thorne, 'Reply to "The poverty of Protest" and "The imaginary discontents"', *SH*, xviii (1993), pp. 219–33. The debate has broadened in recent years to highlight the competing positions of a variety of historians: see J. Vernon, 'Who's afraid of the "linguistic turn"? The politics of social history and its discontents', *SH*, xix (1994), pp. 81–99; R. Gray, 'Class, politics and historical "revisionism"', *SH*, xix (1994), pp. 209–21; N. Kirk, 'History, language, ideas and post-modernism: a materialist view', *SH*, xix (1994), pp. 221–4; P. Joyce, 'The end of social history?', *SH*, xx (1995), pp. 73–93; G. Eley and K. Nield, 'Starting over: the present, the post-modern and the moment of social history', *SH*, xx (1995), pp. 355–65; P. Joyce, 'The end of social history? A brief reply to Eley and Nield', *SH*, xxi (1996), pp. 96–9; M. W. Steinberg, 'Culturally speaking: finding a commons between post-structuralism and the Thompsonian perspective', *SH*, xxi (1996), pp. 193–215. Further important works, relevant to the current debate include: P. Joyce, *Visions of the People: Industrial England and the Question of Class, 1840–1914* (Cambridge, 1991); P. Joyce, *Democratic Subjects: The Self and the Social in Nineteenth-Century England* (Cambridge, 1994); J. W. Scott, *Gender and the Politics of History* (Columbia, 1988); B. D. Palmer, *Descent into Discourse: The Reification of Language and the Writing of Social History* (Philadelphia, 1990); and K. Jenkins (ed.) *The Post-modern History Reader* (1997).

7 See M. Savage and A. Miles, *The Remaking of the British Working Class, 1840–1940* (London, 1994), p. 17; and Steinberg, 'Culturally speaking', pp. 202–3.

8 See T. C. Smout, '"Writing Scotland's history": preface', *SHR*, lxxvi (1997), pp. 1–3.

that we have been able to solve the debate's many paradoxes and philosophical challenges, or, rather, are we resting content in the academic *cul de sac* of narrative and self-satisfied empiricism? The argument that Scottish history, a discipline in its infancy, should stay clear of such controversy cannot hold for long if the discipline is to maintain its position in the academic world.[9] Moreover, it is surely damaging to the quality of our study if worn conventions are not tested against new methodologies.

In this study of Paisley, the writings of historians who have experimented with new linguistic and post-structural approaches have influenced the work by framing an approach which establishes a theoretical context in which the historical 'building blocs' of 'experience', 'meaning' and 'identity' have been shown to have discursive rather than given historical qualities. At its most basic, the approach follows much of post-modernist thought by questioning the apparently unproblematic distinction between representation and the 'real'. Its consequences for historical inquiry are to de-stabilise 'sacred categories' common to much social history – 'experience', 'class', 'society', 'identity' – and to make such categories themselves the focus of discussion.[10]

Joan Wallach Scott, a leading proponent of post-structural approaches in women's history, has questioned the theoretical legitimacy of accepting experience as the foundation of historical explanation:

> When experience is taken as the origin of knowledge, the vision of the individual subject (the person who had the experience or the historian who recounts it) becomes the bedrock of evidence on which explanation is built. Questions about the constructed nature of experience, about how subjects are constituted as different in the first place, about how one's vision is structured – about language (or discourse) in history – are left aside.[11]

The evidence of experience therefore reproduces more than the experience itself. Experience, once articulated, becomes intentionally or otherwise, 'infected' with meaning. The experience is refracted through a host of ideological systems both implicit and explicit in the evidence itself, in its author and in the historian concerned. Scott concludes:

> Experience in this definition then becomes not the origin of our explanation, not the authoritative (because seen or felt) evidence that grounds what is known, but rather that which we seek to explain, that about which knowledge is produced.[12]

[9] T. C. Patterson, 'Post-structuralism, post-modernism: implications for historians', *SH*, xiv (1989), p. 84.
[10] See Vernon, 'Who's afraid of the "linguistic turn"?', p. 88.
[11] J. W. Scott, 'The evidence of experience', *Critical Inquiry*, xvii (Summer, 1991), p. 777.
[12] Ibid., pp. 779–80.

The *woman*, the *worker*, the *bourgeoisie*, the *socialist* (and so on) have, over the years, become the essentialised identities of human agency in many historical narratives. Used as fixed 'subjects' of inquiry, they make invisible the processes through which such categories emerged and mask the characteristics they seek to compose. It is at this point that history touches language. As we seek the history of each identity (or subject) we seek to historicise the language through which it is or has been articulated. Historical explanation cannot separate the two.[13]

Scott has clearly shown the folly of accepting an unmediated linear relationship between language and experience and indeed has gone one step further and suggested that 'subjects are constituted discursively and experience is a linguistic event (it doesn't happen outside established meanings) but neither is confined to a fixed order of meaning'.[14] Yet what becomes of historical explanation if the originary status of experience is questioned and the reflective power of language called into question? Gareth Stedman Jones has suggested a way forward:

> Language disrupts any simple notion of the determination of consciousness by social being because it is itself part of social being. We cannot therefore decode political language to reach a primal and material expression of interest since it is the discursive structure of political language which conceives and defines interest in the first place. What we must therefore do is to study the production of interest, identification, grievance and aspiration within political languages themselves. We need to map out these successive languages of radicalism, liberalism, socialism etc., both in relation to the political languages they replace and laterally in relation to rival political languages with which they are in conflict.[15]

In terms of the political changes under way in Paisley in the late Victorian period, an emphasis on language proves enlightening. In a local setting the deconstruction of an emerging class awareness of politics allows us to move beyond the economic determinism of traditional Marxist accounts of political change to uncover the mechanisms of change itself. By making class that which needs to be explained, rather than that which need only be described, the political changes of the late nineteenth century and the Edwardian period are more readily understood as changes in the political identity of the area and its classes, rather than functions of that identity. The period in question was one of tremendous political upheaval when established party boundaries were re-defined, party programmes re-assessed and political allegiances questioned. Within this context, change altered that

[13] Ibid., pp. 792–3.
[14] Ibid., p. 793.
[15] G. S. Jones, 'Introduction', in *Languages of Class: Studies in English Working-Class History, 1832–1982* (Cambridge, 1993), pp. 21–2.

upon which it acted (local political identity), and, as a corollary, local identity influenced the pace at which change would occur. As Scott has made clear, changing one's focus to the language of discourse means

> assuming that the appearance of a new identity is not inevitable or determined, not something that was always there simply waiting to be expressed, not something that will always exist in the form it was given in a particular movement or at a particular historical moment.[16]

Yet, should 'class' be abandoned so easily to its fragmented elements? Abstracted in such a manner, can class retain any meaning, beyond the coded expression of its conflicting component discourses? Are we discontented with class analysis because class in reality is 'less than' its theoretical definition? Is class to be discarded as history fails to live up to its philosophical heritage?[17] Both Jones and Scott see 'class' – in its 'pure' sense – as existing *outwith* its textual expression and with it the 'truth' of historical experience. The realm of material life is therefore closed to historical inquiry as it exists beyond the text. Yet, in this manner, we surely arrive at the reification of discourse at the expense of lives lived beyond the text or excluded from literary form.

Laura Lee Downs, in an article of 1993, voiced a common criticism. She wrote that:

> the fragmentation of both subject and knowledge, as well as the concomitant collapse of social relations into textual ones, diverts our attention from the operation of power in the social sphere and fixes our gaze upon its metaphorical manifestations in the text.[18]

Since the early '80s, many critics have echoed similar concerns and challenged that ironically, instead of something 'new', post-structural approaches guide us back to the concerns of an old 'antiquarian' age in history during which history's voice was exclusively that of the literate elite and the voice of politics was devoid of a social context.[19] They also challenge that far from liberating the historian in the search for competing voices to represent, there is an inherent de-politicising

16 Scott, 'Evidence of experience', p. 792.

17 Savage and Miles have suggested that the definitions of class used by Joyce and Stedman Jones have been 'unduly restrictive' and argue that there are 'many sentiments and values which may express feelings relating to the existence of class divisions in an indirect or oblique way': Savage and Miles, *Remaking of the British Working Class*, p. 17. See also Kirk, 'History, language, ideas and post-modernism', p. 229.

18 L. L. Downs, 'If "Woman" is just an empty category, then why am I afraid to walk alone at night? Identity politics meets the post-modern subject', *CSSH*, xxxv (1993), p. 420.

19 Kirk, 'History, language, ideas and post-modernism', p. 237; M. Savage, 'Urban history and social class: two paradigms', *Urban History*, xx (1993), p. 65.

dynamic in post-modern perspectives which seek to justify the voice of the oppressor as much as the oppressed.[20]

Although Scott has qualified her commitment to the textuality of history by emphasising that a focus on language need not dismiss the *effects* of the identities it constructs, nor deny the potential of explaining behaviour in terms of their operation, the danger inherent in the *textualisation* of political experience is that material action (experience) will become lost in 'discursive sets of symbolic systems or codes' and 'context' will be meaningless if language in and of itself is prefigurative.[21]

Thus, although discourse theory and linguistic methodologies have proved useful in this study, most especially in deconstructing political identities such as 'Radical', 'Liberal', 'Working Class' and 'Unionist', the ontological limitations of the approach in determining human agency have resulted in only a qualified adoption of its wider philosophical implications. Clearly a close consideration of language is critical in appreciating political change, and the questioning of its reflective properties encourages a healthy scepticism. Foucauldian perspectives which emphasise the determination of 'meaning' (knowledge) as a source of social power, moreover, further clarify the hegemonic basis of language in operation. However, few would deny that, taken to extremes, discourse theory tends to epistemological confusion when the boundary between fact and fiction is not so much blurred as made irrelevant.[22]

In the revised introduction to *Keywords*, Raymond Williams noted:

> New kinds of relationship, but also new ways of seeing existing relationships, appear in language in a variety of ways: in the invention of new terms ... in the adaptation and alteration (indeed at times reversal) of older terms ... in extension ... or transfer. But ... such changes are not always either simple or final. Earlier and later senses co-exist, or become actual alternatives in which problems of contemporary belief and affiliation are contested.[23]

Whilst qualifying Williams's perspective by emphasising the potential *constructive* power of language in addition to its conventional representative role and its power to limit as well as empower historical actors, in methodological terms, this ultimately encapsulates the approach towards language adopted in this study of political change in Paisley. In this sense, it follows Steinberg in his attempt to mould an integrative approach through which 'the social' and 'the textual' are thoroughly grounded in one another and echoes Mayfield and Thorne in emphasising that: 'Political language ... necessarily conditions social

20 R. Evans, *Times Higher*, 12 Sep. 1997.
21 L. Stone, 'History and post-modernism', *P&P*, cxxxi (1991), p. 218.
22 A. Easthope, 'Romancing the stone: history-writing and rhetoric', *SH*, xviii (1993), p. 239.
23 R. Williams, *Keywords: A Vocabulary of Culture and Society* (rev edn, London, 1983), p. 22.

identities of mobilisation such as class, rather than being epiphenomenal to identities pregiven by social structure.'[24]

Yet, although this perspective deals adequately with the components of political change in general, it reveals little of our wider concerns – the grand theme of the decline of Liberalism – nor its place in the continuum of the perpetual re-formation of political cultures.

Order, Organic Change and the Articulation of a Meta-narrative

'Any historical moment', wrote E. P. Thompson, 'is both a result of prior process and an index towards the direction of future flow.'[25] Thus, the elements of change which we hope to deconstruct – 'local identity', 'class', 'politics', 'radicalism' etc. – are themselves part of a larger 'process', a process of continual metamorphosis, in which the identity of each is relational to that of the others and is in a perpetual process of 'becoming'. In adopting such a perspective, the stasis which is inevitably reached if discourse theory is taken to its ultimate bounds may be contained by placing textual analysis within a wider concept of change over time: by 'moving beyond the formal analyses of languages' to the 'social situations which mediate their production and reception'.[26] That has been attempted in this study through the adoption of Gramsci's concepts of hegemony and organic change. In this way texts are re-invested with the responsibility associated with human agency within the context of social power relations, and political change over time is seen as something more than the re-definition of established terminologies. Gramsci acknowledged

> A certain socio-historical moment is never homogenous. On the contrary, it is rich with contradictions. It acquires 'personality', it is a 'moment' of development because a certain fundamental activity of life predominates over the others, represents an historical 'peak'. *But this presupposes a hierarchy, a contrast, a struggle.*[27]

In essence, he points to reasons external to the text why, at a certain time and in a certain context, one interpretation will transcend others or exert a dominant influence.

Here it is useful to turn to just what is meant by Gramsci's concept of 'hegemony', the framework of 'struggle'. Although Gramsci never gives a precise definition of cultural hegemony, Gwyn Williams outlines a useful working model when he writes:

24 Steinberg, 'Culturally speaking', pp. 200–1.
25 Thompson, 'Poverty of theory', p. 239.
26 Savage and Miles, *Remaking of the British Working Class*, p. 18.
27 A. Gramsci, *Quaderni del carcere*, as quoted in A. S. Sassoon, *Gramsci's Politics* (London, 1987), p. 180 [my italics].

> By 'hegemony' Gramsci seems to mean a socio-political situation ... in which the philosophy and practice of a society fuse or are in equilibrium; an order in which a certain way of life and thought is dominant, in which one concept of reality is diffused throughout society in all its institutional and private manifestations, informing with its spirit all taste, morality, customs, religious and political principles, and all social relations, particularly in their intellectual and moral connotation.[28]

Translated into the political culture of Paisley during the period under consideration, this framework provides a useful context within which to place the dominance of the Liberal ethos in the town in the late nineteenth century and the ethico-political power of the small 'caucus' of manufacturers who guided the Liberal party and indeed the political life of the burgh. It furthermore provides the means whereby one may link the power relations of the factory to those in the 'outside world'. According to this formulation, work-place culture and liberal politics mesh into a 'world view' where economic power is legitimated and a liberal morality is dominant, and both are mutually supporting. In this way, the political can no longer be separated from the economic, and the ethical or cultural becomes an integral part of power relations. Language is thus reinforced as a site of political battles.

Yet, whilst through a concept of 'hegemony' we can side-step simplistic Marxist models of a direct transference of power from base to superstructure, where economic power is translated unproblematically into political might without recourse to cultural relations, we still need to engage with the processes through which 'consent' is given to the Liberal hegemony. Are we to assume that power is maintained through an active commitment on the part of subordinates to the legitimacy of elite rule? Does power or coercion maintain the hierarchy? Or do apathy and resignation counter the impulse to resistance? Gramsci has framed the processes whereby hegemony is maintained as a duality – force married to consent.[29] Fundamentally, however, the hegemonic relationship has its basis in economic activity. Thus, although Liberal manufacturers could not establish or maintain their hegemonic power through merely occupying their position in the capitalist power chain, the origins of the relationship were firmly rooted in the economic sphere.

However, the overall picture which Gramsci presents to us is far from 'static', where capital, by its very nature, will always dominate. Rather, society is seen 'in constant process, where the creation of counter-hegemonies remains a live option'.[30] What impulses therefore influenced

28 G. Williams, 'The concept of "Egemonia" in the thought of Antonio Gramsci', *Journal of the History of Ideas*, xxi (1960), p. 587, as quoted in Sassoon, *Gramsci's Politics*, p. 232n.

29 Sassoon, *Gramsci's Politics*, p. 115.

30 T. J. Jackson Lears, 'The concept of cultural hegemony: problems and possibilities', *AHR*, xc (1985), p. 571.

Paisley's working classes to participate in this Liberal culture rather than to adopt more radical alternatives? In their commitment to a Liberal politic do we see in action the effects of 'false consciousness'?

Gramsci's concept of hegemony proves flexible enough to accommodate the 'difference' which conventional Marxist approaches disregard as mistaken acts of deviant behaviour and which post-structuralists consider the actions of 'others' denied in conventional historiography. Rather, the hegemonic concept acknowledges that 'subordinate groups may participate in maintaining a symbolic universe, even if it serves to legitimate their domination'. As Lears has explained, 'they share a kind of half-conscious complicity in their own victimisation'.[31] This formulation does not deny that subordinate groups may have a personal interest in maintaining the hegemonic base, but rather, by co-operating in its legitimation, they undermine their own power to establish an alternative hegemony. However, contradictions and internal divisions in the producer ideology point simultaneously to co-operation with and resistance to the dominant hegemony. Consciousness, therefore, is 'divided' or 'contradictory' rather than 'false' and the line between dominant and subordinate cultures is seen more in sympathy with the perpetual processes of political change – 'a permeable membrane' rather than 'an impenetrable barrier'.[32] Change thus comes about as a form of discourse *through* rather than *across* lines of difference and as such continuity rather than dramatic fracturing emerges as the key to explaining how change happens. Both change and continuity are negotiated in a perpetual process of conflict rather than the end result of conflict.

In the *Prison Notebooks*, Gramsci wrote that in studying 'a structure' – for our purposes this 'structure' is defined as the political identity of Paisley:

> it is necessary to distinguish organic movements (relatively permanent) from movements which may be termed 'conjunctural' (and which appear as occasional, immediate, almost accidental) ... When an historical period comes to be studied, the great importance of this distinction becomes clear. A crisis occurs, sometimes lasting for decades. This exceptional duration means that incurable contradictions have revealed themselves (reached maturity), and that, despite this, the political forces which are struggling to conserve and defend the existing structure itself are making every effort to cure them, within certain limits, and to overcome them.[33]

The distinction here outlined between organic and conjunctural movement is one which is both pertinent and appropriate as a model of

[31] Ibid., p. 573.
[32] Ibid., p. 574.
[33] A. Gramsci, *Selections from the Prison Notebooks of Antonio Gramsci*, ed. and trans. Q. Hoare and G. N. Smith (London, 1971), p. 177.

political change in Paisley between 1885 and 1924.[34] In these terms, during this period we are looking at a series of conjunctural crises – when the conventions and dominant principles of the Liberal hegemony which reached prominence in the Gladstonian period were called into question by the 'oppositional forces' of the new Labour movement. As such they are part of the 'organic' shift whereby Labour 'replaced' Liberalism as the dominant political force in Paisley, thus altering the identity of the community in a fundamental fashion.

Such a framework has proved necessary as a key determinant in distinguishing between and ordering the long-term and immediate causes of change. This formulation undermines approaches which seek a 'turning-point' when the fate of Liberalism was sealed, and likewise cautions against an approach which seeks in the mists of time the initial and inevitable steps in Liberalism's decline. As political parties are seen to form identities in opposition to their rivals in a continually changing political equilibrium where dominance is not unassailable nor power absolute, the approach forms an appropriate context for the utilisation of new linguistic approaches which re-invest power in ideology.

Yet perhaps most important here is the concept of the unity of history as a continuously developing process.[35] Taken on board, traditions and historical antecedents to contemporary political change thus become *effective* phenomena. As a vestige of the power of the dominant elite and an element of a history through which its power is validated, tradition becomes an active force – that which oppositional parties seek to re-form and possess as their own.

It is at this point that the potential for the coalescence of 'post-modern' and Gramscian theories becomes most evident. Whilst there are undeniable epistemological difficulties in marrying these two traditions, the benefits of such a dual approach overwhelm the difficulties.

The linguistic parallel of the experiential realm of tradition is to be found in the 'post-modern' concept of the meta-narrative. Recent work by Joyce, Vernon and others has highlighted how the history of political change is as much the history of how individuals 'narrativised' (historicised) themselves as 'unified acting subjects' as how they acted.[36] Harnessing the tropes of contemporary popular fiction and theatre, political actors made sense of the world by deploying the familiar narrative schemes of romance and melodrama to structure and interpret

[34] Ashcraft has recently highlighted how it was during periods of 'extensive social conflict' that the 'structural instability of the belief system' of Liberalism became apparent: R. Ashcraft, 'Liberal political theory and working-class radicalism in nineteenth-century England', *Political Theory*, xxi (1993), p. 249.

[35] Ibid., p. 201.

[36] Vernon, 'Who's afraid of the "linguistic turn"?', p. 91. See also J. Vernon, *Politics and the People: A Study in English Political Culture, c.1815–1867* (Cambridge, 1993); Joyce, *Democratic Subjects*; and A. Callinicos, *Theories and Narratives: Reflections on the Philosophy of History* (Cambridge, 1995).

change. Custom, tradition and precedent, moreover, reinforced these governing narratives by offering historical exemplars of contemporary dilemmas and drawing on a sense of continuity with the past. Appreciating historical change in this manner has the benefit of avoiding narrow materialist arguments based on economic self-interest and takes us further in appreciating the evolution of historical 'subject positions' which at once permitted access and restricted the voice of the individual in the body politic.

In relation to Paisley politics, this study identifies the town's radical tradition as the meta-narrative within which political change was appreciated, and follows Vernon in recognising the ability of individuals and groups in society to narrativise politics in this way as a source of power only partly founded on their position with regard to the means of production.[37] In this way, 'ownership' of the meta-narrative was a critical component of the cultural and political foundations of the Liberal hegemony in the town. The ability to articulate and defend its governing premises would, in turn, be a fundamental factor in the survival of the governing elite.

However, notwithstanding the dynamic for change which re-interpretations of the meta-narrative imply, a framework through which the *process* of change can be appreciated is still absent from this formulation. As Stedman Jones has made clear, 'a theory', or in our case a ruling ideology, 'however ultimately inappropriate, is more likely to be stretched and forced to take account of new phenomena than to be abandoned'.[38] How then do identities change, and with them their ruling ideologies?

Gramsci, in considering class politics during a period of conjunctural crisis, noted:

> At a certain point in their historical lives, social classes become detached from their traditional parties. In other words, the traditional parties in that particular organisational form, with the particular men who constitute, represent and lead them, are no longer recognised by their class (or fraction of a class) as its expression ... [This] is the crisis of the ruling class's hegemony, which occurs either because the ruling class has failed in some major political undertaking for which it has requested, or forcibly extracted, the consent of the broad masses (war, for example) or, because huge masses (especially of peasants and petit bourgeois intellectuals) have passed suddenly from a state of political passivity to a certain activity, and put forward demands which taken together, albeit organically formulated, add up to a revolution. A 'crisis of authority' is spoken of: this is precisely the crisis of

[37] Vernon, 'Who's afraid of the "linguistic turn"?', p. 93.
[38] G. S. Jones, 'Engels and the genesis of Marxism', *New Left Review*, cvi (1977), p. 104.

> hegemony, or general crisis of state ... The traditional ruling class, which has numerous trained cadres, changes men and programmes and, with greater speed than is achieved by the subordinate classes, reabsorbs the control that was slipping from its grasp.[39]

In this formulation of crisis, our subject proves a ready, if minor, exemplar of the processes under consideration. The decline of the Liberal elite in Paisley and its attempts to maintain political power over a changing electorate which was growing increasingly aware of its class composition and identity follow, as we shall see, Gramsci's model of 'general crisis'. The attempted re-formulation of policy and leadership in the Paisley scenario contained the Labour threat for many years, yet ultimately attempted reform proved insufficient in the light of the altered political identity of the mass of Paisley voters – the final organic transformation. As Gramsci made clear, one of the most important questions concerning political parties concerns their 'capacity to react against force of habit, against the tendency to become mummified and anachronistic'. He continued:

> Parties come into existence, and constitute themselves as organisations, in order to influence the situation at moments which are historically vital for their class; but they are not always capable of adapting themselves to new tasks and to new epochs.[40]

Paisley's radical tradition was both cause and consequence of Liberal transcendence in the nineteenth century and the source and expression of the rootedness of the Liberal elite in the burgh. By the 1920s, however, it similarly posed as cause and consequence of Labour ascendance and the source and expression of a transformation in social relations.

The Historiography of Decline

The continuing debate on the decline of the Liberal Party in the years 1886 to 1924 has moved from allusions to a 'strange' inevitability to counter factual assertions positing various alternative outcomes had war and the creation of a new democracy not transformed the character of the electoral 'game'. Over 100 years after Gladstone opted for Home Rule, even the basic chronology of decline is as much open to controversy as ever, and indeed is an integral part of the debate. *When* one says decline began, it appears, remains as crucial as *why*. What follows seeks to trace the development of the debate rather than judge the respective cases.

39 Gramsci, *Selections from the Prison Notebooks*, p. 210.

40 Gramsci, *Selections from the Prison Notebooks* (ed. and trans. Hoare and Smith), as cited in D. Forgacs (ed.), *A Gramsci Reader: Selected Writings, 1916–1935* (London, 1988), p. 219.

Essentially, the history of the debate may be seen as incorporating five elements, not necessarily sequential in their evolution, yet together interacting to produce the current 'position' – one hesitates to call it the orthodoxy – as represented in the works of G. R. Searle and Duncan Tanner.[41] The first of these elements – the appeal to inevitability – owed much to Dangerfield's work and the reminiscences of gloomy Edwardians looking back after 1918 to the decay of a 'Golden Age'. Moving away from this position, the concept of class invaded the debate, most notably in the works of P. F. Clarke, although this position has recently been resurrected and adapted in the work of Laybourn and Jarvis.[42] As a qualified counter attack on such determinism, Matthew, McKibbin and Kay may be seen as epitomising the third element in the on-going debate in their article of 1976 which took a pragmatic look at the parameters within which political opinion was expressed, most notably in terms of franchise restrictions before 1918.[43] Almost simultaneously, however, the debate at this stage was becoming fragmented. In the works of Thompson and Clarke, and later with Savage and Joyce in the early 1980s, the regional dimension was being stressed, undermining earlier national generalisations.[44] Integral to the

41 See G. R. Searle, *The Liberal Party: Triumph and Disintegration, 1886–1929* (Basingstoke, 1992); and D. Tanner, *Political Change and the Labour Party, 1900–1918* (Cambridge, 1990).

42 See P. F. Clarke, *Lancashire and the New Liberalism* (Cambridge, 1971); P. F. Clarke, 'Electoral sociology of modern Britain', *History*, lvii (1972), pp. 31–55; P. F. Clarke, 'Liberals, Labour and the franchise', *EHR*, xcii (1977), pp. 582–9; K. Laybourn, 'The rise of Labour and the decline of Liberalism: the state of the debate', *History*, lxxx (1995), pp. 207–26; and D. Jarvis, 'British Conservatism and class politics in the 1920s', *EHR*, cxi (1996), pp. 59–84. See also: J. Belchem, *Class, Party and the Political System in Britain, 1867–1914* (Oxford, 1990); and K. D. Wald, 'Class and the vote before the First World War', *British Journal of Political Science*, viii (1978), pp. 442–57.

43 See: J. P. D. Dunbabin, 'British elections in the nineteenth and twentieth centuries: a regional approach', *EHR*, xcv (1980), pp. 241–67; also, N. Blewett, 'The franchise in the United Kingdom, 1885–1918', *P&P*, xxxii (1965), pp. 27–56; H. C. G. Matthew, R. I. McKibbin and J. A. Kay, 'The franchise factor in the rise of the Labour Party', *EHR*, xci (1976), pp. 723–52.

44 See Clarke, *Lancashire*. See also K. Laybourn and J. Reynolds, *Liberalism and the Rise of Labour, 1890–1918* (London, 1984); M. Coneys, 'The Labour Movement and the Liberal Party in Rochdale, 1890–1906' (Huddersfield Polytechnic, M.A. thesis, 1982); R. Hawarth, 'The Development of the Bolton ILP, 1885–1895' (Huddersfield Polytechnic, M.A. thesis, 1982); J. Hill 'Manchester and Salford politics and the early development of the Independent Labour Party', *IRSH*, xxvi (1981), pp. 171–201; J. Holford, *Reshaping Labour: Organisation, Work and Politics. Edinburgh in the Great War and After* (London, 1988); Jones, *Languages of Class*; P. Joyce, *Work, Society and Politics: The Culture of the Factory in Later Victorian England* (London, 1980); P. Joyce, 'The factory politics of Lancashire in the later nineteenth century', *HJ*, xviii (1975), pp. 525–53; Joyce, *Visions of the People*; A. McKinlay, 'Labour and locality: Labour politics on Clydeside, 1900–1939', *Journal of Regional and Local Studies*, x (1990), pp. 48–59; A. McKinlay and R. J. Morris (eds.), *The ILP on Clydeside, 1893–1932: From Foundation to Disintegration* (Manchester, 1991); I. McLean, *The Legend of Red Clydeside* (Edinburgh, 1983); K. O. Morgan, 'The New Liberalism and the challenge of Labour: the Welsh experience, 1885–1929', *Welsh History Review*, v (1972), pp. 288–312; R. J. Morris and J. J. Smyth, *Paternalism as an Employer Strategy, 1800–1960* (ESRC Pamphlet, London, 1989); A. W. Purdue, 'The Liberal and Labour Parties in north-east politics,

arguments of these regional studies were appeals to the political impact of the workplace, earlier highlighted by Burgess, Bulmer Thomas, Poirier and Cole, and, most importantly, the role of the trade unions.[45] Now, however, organised Labour was being looked at 'from the bottom up' on a scale much reduced and thus more attentive to divergent local phenomena. In these regional studies the concept of community was stressed, both as a challenge and a qualification to the earlier class models.

Throughout, secondary debates underlay the dominant narrative themes, forming something of a subplot, as historians weighed up the relative importance of 'breaks' and 'turning-points' in the overall political continuum. Historians seeming to adopt similar positions overall frequently took differing stances on such issues as Gladstone's support for Home Rule in 1886, the Boer war, the Ulster question, the franchise, industrial militancy, the reform of the Lords and the impact of World War One, thus preventing any easy division of individuals into 'schools'. By the end of the 1980s, however, the historical debate had been divided into two apparently distinct groupings: those arguing from a national position and those working more specifically on regional issues, hesitating to derive from their work any overtly national conclusions.

The fifth element in the debate has been recent attempts to bring these two spheres together, arguing, as Tanner has argued, for a review of the argument so far and the acknowledgement that 'the political system was an elaborate jigsaw'.[46] Differences of opinion, however, are hardly reconciled by a simple acknowledgement that they exist.

In 1935, Dangerfield identified pre-1914 Britain as a society of rebels. 'The Tory Rebellion', 'The Women's Rebellion', 'The Workers' Rebellion'

1900–1914: the struggle for supremacy', *IRSH*, xxvi (1981), pp. 1–24; M. Savage, 'Capitalist and patriarchal relations at work: Preston cotton weaving, 1890–1940', in L. Murgatroyd, *et al.* (eds.) *Localities, Class and Gender* (1985), pp. 177–94; M. Savage, *The Dynamics of Working-Class Politics: The Labour Movement in Preston, 1880–1940* (Cambridge, 1987); J. Smith, 'Commonsense Thought and Working-Class Consciousness: Some Aspects of the Glasgow and Liverpool Labour Movements in the Early Years of the Twentieth Century' (Edinburgh University, Ph.D. thesis, 1980); J. Smith, 'Labour tradition in Glasgow and Liverpool, 1880–1914', *History Workshop Journal*, xvii (1984), pp. 32–56; J. Smith, 'Class, skill and sectarianism in Glasgow and Liverpool, 1880–1914', in R. J. Morris (ed.) *Class, Power and Social Structure in British Nineteenth-Century Towns* (Leicester, 1986) pp. 157–215; J. J. Smyth, 'Labour and Socialism in Glasgow, 1880–1914: The Electoral Challenge Prior to Democracy' (Edinburgh University, Ph.D. thesis, 1987); P. Thompson, 'Liberals, Radicals and Labour in London, 1880–1900', *P&P*, xxvii (1964), pp. 73–101; P. Thompson, *Socialists, Liberals and Labour: The Struggle for London, 1885–1914* (London, 1967).

45 See K. Burgess, *The Challenge of Labour* (London, 1980); I. Bulmer Thomas, *The Growth of the British Party System*. vol. I: *1640–1923* (London, 1965); P. P. Poirier, *The Advent of the Labour Party* (London, 1958); G. D. H. Cole, *British Working-Class Politics, 1832–1914* (London, 1946).

46 Tanner, *Political Change and the Labour Party*, p. 420.

are the chapter heading coffin nails which mark *The Strange Death of Liberal England*. Dangerfield saw in the militancy of the suffrage movement, the violence of the Ulster crisis, the apparent 'Red Threat' of Syndicalism in the industrial unrest of 1911–14, and the unconstitutional leanings of the Tory Party, a society on the brink of collapse, a government without sufficient power of control and a Liberal party dying 'from a poison administered by its conservative foes, and from disillusion over the efficacy of the word "Reform"'.[47] The 'crises' of the pre-war years were thus both cause and consequence of the Liberal decline.

Dangerfield described a society in 1910 'about to get rid of its Liberalism'. He emphasised: 'The war hastened everything – in politics, in economics, in behaviour – but it started nothing.'[48] In the faces of the ministers on the Liberal front bench Dangerfield detected 'a spirit dangerous and indefinite, *animula vagula blandula*, the Spirit of Whimsy, which only afflicts Englishmen in their weakness'.[49] Under such circumstances Dangerfield saw the death of Liberalism as an inevitable consequence of the age. ('Sir Henry's political faith had been a noble one in its day, but that day was over.'[50]) As he concludes, Liberalism 'was killed, or killed itself in 1913'.[51]

In the 1940s and 1950s historians came to concentrate on specific elements of the so-called 'crisis' in Liberalism, yet ultimately failed to abandon the idea that in the Edwardian era there were distinct premonitions of impending doom or signs of rot, proving that decline had already set in.[52] The ontological validity of the argument from inevitability thus remained unchallenged. Although significantly now focused on a level of political culture below that of cabinet politics, no real alternative to the 'Strange Death' scenario had been delineated. At this time, G. D. H. Cole and Philip Poirier singled out the trade unions, as the representatives of the labouring classes, as prime movers in the decline of the Liberal Party. As Poirier noted in 1958: 'Above all it was the channelling of trade union discontent into political action that paved the way for a Labour Party.'[53] Both writers stressed the importance of the legal wrangles surrounding the Taff Vale dispute and the Osborne Judgement as crucial incentives which encouraged a move away from the Liberal fold. Yet, still no direct alternative had been suggested to the concept of inevitable decline. Granted, the terms of the debate were changing but essentially the task remained the same. Evidently, the overall agenda was to stack more and more factors against the possibility

47 G. Dangerfield, *The Strange Death of Liberal England* (London, 1935), p. 69.

48 Ibid., pp. 20, 14.

49 Ibid., pp. 70–1.

50 Ibid., p. 27.

51 Ibid., p. 14.

52 See, e.g., J. F. Glaser, 'English nonconformity and the decline of Liberalism', *AHR*, lxiii (1958), p. 352.

53 Poirier, *Advent of the Labour Party*, pp. 10, 12.

of Liberal renewal or survival. These issues and others, such as the importance of the Home Rule question, have since become the 'unit variables' of the debate. However, it was not until Clarke's work on Lancashire that a new overall theory would posit an alternative framework of interpretation and a refutation of the standing orthodoxy of steady irreversible Liberal decline.

In his study, *Lancashire and the New Liberalism,* published in 1971, P. F. Clarke argued that:

> for all the variations in party fortunes in the late nineteenth century, popular attitudes as expressed in elections were rooted in a political temperament which was fundamentally stable; whereas change in this temperament itself was the most significant aspect of the Liberal revival after 1906.[54]

No longer was the Liberal party cast in the role of the 'sick man' of Edwardian politics; rather it was seen as the manifestation of a popular view of society, both in moral and economic terms, and a powerful electoral force.

In national terms Clarke's argument seems valid. The Liberal party on the eve of the war had a sizeable electoral mandate.[55] How then did Clarke explain the Liberal decline? Clarke focused on what he saw as a 'qualitative change' in the character of party politics in the Edwardian period. From the 'status-group' and 'value-orientated' character of the Victorian party system, Clarke identified a change by 1910 which, although neither universal nor complete, involved a transformation to class-based politics. Yet Clarke argued that the Liberals initially *gained* from this process by winning working-class votes. Liberalism's decline was placed *after* World War One. The dynamics of the change, however, are not investigated. Clarke's agenda was to emphasise that 'during the late nineteenth century the struggle for power was institutionalised by the pre-existing parties', and in this system Liberalism proved strong.[56] Clarke succeeded in pushing the 'time of death' of the Liberal Party forward and, by introducing the concept of class, added much to an

[54] Clarke, *Lancashire*, p. 14.

[55] General Election Results (1900–1910), MPs Elected:

	1900	**1906**	**1910[J]**	**1910[D]**
Liberal	184	400	275	272
Conservative	402	157	273	272
Labour	2	30	40	42
Irish Nationalist	82	83	82	84
Other	–	–	–	–

[56] Clarke, *Lancashire*, p. 402.

increasingly stale historical debate. However, in order to complete the picture, an account of the dynamics of war and post-war change would have had to have been tackled. Without this Clarke's argument hangs uneasily at the edge of a more profound dilemma. He has answered when without really tackling how or why.[57]

Kenneth O. Morgan, writing in 1971, pointed to 'the obscene tragedy of the first world war, which mocked at every moral value that Liberalism embodied' and identified as a result of the war 'the growing cohesion and class consciousness of Labour'.[58] Agreeing with Clarke, Morgan stressed that although 'it cannot be disputed that the Liberals were a struggling party in 1914 ... they were very far from being a dead one'.[59] The implication is that after 1918 the Liberals failed the test of a politicised and truly class-conscious electorate. Class politics according to this model worked against Liberal survival *after* the war.

Writing in the 1960s, Paul Thompson, however, had timed the beginning of class-conscious politics much earlier – after 1885. He pointed to the Liberal revival in the years after 1906 as an 'illusion', and although his views coincide with Clarke and Morgan in that he places the 'eclipse' of Liberalism after 1918, he maintained that the battle had been all but lost before 1914.[60] The 'class argument' thus presents us with an ambiguous chronology of decline. It is rootless and thus of dubious merit in suggesting a way forward other than that of chasing another 'time of death' made irreversible by a sectional political consciousness.

Despite sociological works such as those of Richard Rose which have contested the theory of the class basis of the party system, the class argument lives on in many guises.[61] Recently, Belchem has argued that for the period from 1867 to 1914, 'Religion and regionalism were reduced to the residual as class emerged as the decisive variable' in voting patterns.[62] He claims:

> In adjusting to working class politics, Liberals still denied the very validity of class; progressive Liberals hoped to prevent class polarisation, to eradicate the contentious issue of class itself.[63]

57 Whilst Clarke goes some way to addressing these concerns in his later work: P. F. Clarke, *Liberals and Social Democrats* (Cambridge, 1978), the emphasis on the biographical histories of key Liberal figures (Wallas, Hobhouse, Hobson and the Hammonds) fails to elaborate how and to what extent, 'grass-roots' Liberals adjusted to post-war change.

58 K. O. Morgan, *The Age of Lloyd George: The Liberal Party and British Politics, 1890–1929* (London, 1971), pp. 109, 75–6.

59 Ibid., p. 51.

60 See Thompson, 'Liberals, Radicals and Labour'; and Thompson, *Socialists, Liberals and Labour*. In his view on the Liberals' inability to adapt to class changes, Thompson is joined by H. Pelling, *Social Geography of British Elections, 1885–1910* (Aldershot, 1967).

61 R. Rose, 'Class and Party divisions: Britain as a test case', *Sociology*, ii (1968), pp. 129–62. The role of class is crucial to the regional studies of Joyce, Stedman Jones and Savage.

62 Belchem, *Class, Party and the Political System*, p. 16.

63 Ibid., p. 45.

However, he concludes, 'class politics eradicated the Liberal Party'.[64] In denying the possibility of a successful Liberal populism, Belchem presents us with a Liberal Party which becomes the victim of irresistible societal change.

In response to such class interpretations of Liberalism's decline, the main challenge has come from those who see in the pre-1918 franchise the predominant obstacle to Labour's rise. This ought not to be seen as incompatible with a class interpretation, and indeed has been used to enhance it.[65] However, stated as an alternative to it and one in which cabinet politics, ideology or social change have no necessarily determining impact, the 'franchise argument' served to highlight the restrictions on political freedom and the limits of previous approaches to Liberal decline.

In 1965, Neal Blewett drew attention to the limited parliamentary franchise in the United Kingdom after the Franchise Act of 1884. In 1911, after the new franchise had been operational for around twenty five years, Blewett maintained that 40% of all adult males were not on the electoral register.[66] The combined restrictions of qualification and registration meant that for thirty three years, the 'will of the people' expressed itself through an 'intricate mesh'.[67] Although pointing to the greater efficiency of the Scottish system of registration, Blewett stressed the inadequacies and bureaucratic fumblings in the administration of registration and provided a caution for historians who sought in the election results of these years, a true reflection of the nation's will.

J. P. D. Dunbabin in his 'Psephological Note' of 1966, however, focused on the voting patterns revealed in the elections of the pre-1900 period and found in them 'many indications of the existence of a considerable body of radical feeling' which if 'tapped', he felt, might have tipped the balance against the 'stagnant' Liberal share of the vote.[68] In 1976 the combined influences of Blewett's caution and Dunbabin's 'what might have been' found articulation in a study by Matthew, McKibbin and Kay. In explaining the 'rise and fall of the Liberal Party', they maintained that 'changes in the structure of British politics were at least as significant as chronological developments; in other words, that the changes in the franchise were at least as significant as the effects of the First World War.'[69]

They further suggested that:

> the Liberals were wedded to the forms of the 1867–1914 political community as their opponents were not, that the ideologies of both

64 Ibid., p. 88.
65 Ibid., pp. 9–10.
66 Blewett, 'Franchise in the United Kingdom', p. 27.
67 Ibid., p. 56.
68 J. P. D. Dunbabin, 'Parliamentary elections in Great Britain, 1868–1900: a psephological note', *EHR*, lxxxi (1966), p. 96.
69 Matthew, McKibbin and Kay, 'Franchise factor', p. 723.

> the Labour and Conservative parties made them better to exploit a fully democratic franchise, and that these things were true before 1914 as well as after the war.[70]

They argued that instead of Labour merely being the beneficiary of the Liberal break-up, Labour in the post-war years drew on a 'latent source of support which had not been available to the other two parties'.[71] They continued to deduce that there was evidence of a Labour vote in the pre-war electorate which could have been mobilised by more candidates and that the 'substantial post-war growth in Labour's relative strength must in large measure be attributable to the franchise extension and registration reform of 1918'. [72] Aside from gross electorate numerical changes, Matthew *et al.* claimed that the 1918 act transformed the character of the electorate by 'significantly lowering its political awareness', making it – it is implied – even less likely than the pre-war voters to support sophisticated New Liberal ideas.[73]

On first appraisal the argument is convincing. In 1906 the electorate numbered 7,264,608; in 1918 it stood at 21,392,322.[74] One would be surprised if such a dramatic change had no impact. However, P. F. Clarke has challenged the authors' emphasis and assumptions. He stated in an article in 1977 that:

> before 1914 the Labour Party was the party of trade unionists; and these were the one section of the working class who were overwhelmingly likely to be already enfranchised. It is clearly necessary to make good the implied claim that before 1914 the Labour vote had a strongly working class character but that the Liberal vote did not.[75]

Amongst many other criticisms of the position taken by Matthew *et al.* was that offered by Michael Hart in 1982. He openly contradicted the 'franchise school' and stated that 'the war was the most important single cause of the Liberal decline and that this is true of the party both inside and outside parliament'.[76] Hart illustrated the *strength* of the Liberals until 1923, their decline progressing rapidly after this date. The franchise factor was held to be of secondary importance.[77] It was the Liberals' move to the right and their internal wranglings that were held

70 Ibid., p. 723.
71 Ibid., p. 739.
72 Ibid., p. 740.
73 Ibid., p. 749.
74 D. Butler and J. Freeman, *British Political Facts, 1900–1968* (3rd edn, London, 1969), p. 141.
75 Clarke, 'Electoral sociology of modern Britain', p. 582.
76 M. Hart, 'The Liberals, the war and the franchise', *EHR*, xcvii (1982), p. 821.
77 John Turner has emphasised this view when he writes: 'the relationship between the new electorate and the rise of labour is too contradictory to be reconciled with the 'franchise theories' first expounded by Matthew, McKibbin and Kay': J. Turner, *British Politics and the Great War: Coalition and Conflict, 1915–1918* (London, 1992), p. 434.

as being responsible for their loss of the progressive vote, essential for their survival. Hart implied that the franchise reform of 1918 would have been worth much less to Labour, but for the experience of the First World War, and that after 1918 Labour gained from internal Liberal divisions and the party's lack of a definite programme. Hart thus pushes the 'time of death' forward into the 1920s, the major cause being fatal injuries sustained during the war.[78]

Addressing electoral shifts and changes, Dunbabin has questioned how far one can discuss electoral change without looking at its component elements – the results of regional and individual constituency elections.[79] By looking at election results in different regions over a length of time Dunbabin has found local differences 'surprisingly durable'. Such a regional approach casts further light on the limits of class-based approaches. Dunbabin states:

> Class make-up entered into these regional differences – in some areas working class (and especially mining) communities acquired an electoral hegemony in the late nineteenth and early twentieth centuries, and as they went so went the seats; in other areas there was sufficient isolation, diffusion or admixture of classes to prevent such automatic identification between working class and community, and to make the displacement of Liberal by Labour a far more difficult process.[80]

The franchise and class arguments when based purely on national statistics thus fail to illustrate the complexity of divergent regional experiences – the components and crucibles of change itself.[81]

The Scottish Dimension

Scottish historians have contributed greatly to this historiography of regional 'difference', and though few attempts have been made to deconstruct Scotland further to a sub-regional level – beyond a plethora of works on Glasgow's experience – there has evolved a Scottish agenda with which any new local study must engage.

Between 1832 and 1918, the Liberals gained a majority of seats in Scotland in every general election with the sole exception of 1900, and even then they held the majority of votes cast.[82] Of this era, therefore, it

78 Hart, 'Liberals, the war and the franchise', p. 832.
79 See Dunbabin, 'British elections in the nineteenth and twentieth centuries'.
80 Ibid., p. 264.
81 Recently, historians have taken electoral analysis one step further and focused on the micro-levels of political expression, namely contrasting ward results in municipal elections and 'neighbourhood' politics. See D. Tanner, 'Elections, statistics, and the rise of the Labour Party, 1906–1931', *HJ*, xxxiv (1991), pp. 893–908; also, Savage, 'Urban history and social class', p. 72.
82 J. G. Kellas, *Modern Scotland* (London, 1980), p. 130.

would be very hard to prove the case for a dying party. However, for some historians, the ingredients of disaster were apparent by the 1880s. In the 1960s, in the works of Kellas and Urwin, the emphasis was on a decaying Liberal Party organisation, debilitated by internal dissension and split on the Home Rule question after 1886.[83] As Urwin noted in 1965: 'the general theme of the history of the Liberal Party during this period is that of an unwieldy alliance undergoing a process of secession and disintegration, following internal dissension'.[84]

However, since the 1960s, historians of the Scottish experience have generally tended to focus on the early twentieth century as the period of perceivable Liberal decline and the rise of the Labour challenge, splitting into two schools over whether decay had taken root before or after the First World War, and showing varying degrees of commitment to a class model of political change. In 1981, Christopher Harvie noted that in Scotland 'the idea of politics as social drama was ... deeply entrenched', more so, he claims, than in England. 'Parliamentary politics were about status, citizenship, religious equality and, less sublimely, patronage.'[85] Similarly, the point made by Howell, that 'Scottish Liberal candidates tended to be men of local standing rather than iconoclast critics', emphasises the status- rather than class-based character of nineteenth-century Scottish politics.[86] Yet, though most agree that status politics eventually gave way to class-determined voting patterns, no consensus has emerged on the time of death of the old political model.

In his 1982 study of Clydeside industrialists during the First World War, Joseph Melling noted that:

> During the two decades before the war, there was a clear drift of previously Liberal families such as the Dennys of Dumbarton from Radicalism to Conservatism. At the same time a significant number of professionals ... left the ranks of Liberalism and joined with lower middle class and artisan voters in support of the cause of Labour at a local level.[87]

In this atmosphere of 'shifting class relations', the Liberal party fell between two stools in the pre-war years, losing support from both left and right as politics took on a more secular character.[88]

83 J. G. Kellas, 'The Liberal Party in Scotland, 1876–1895', *SHR*, xliv (1965), pp. 1–16; D. W. Urwin, 'The development of the Conservative Party Organisation in Scotland, until 1912', *SHR*, xxxviii (1965), pp. 89–111.

84 Urwin, 'Development of the Conservative Party Organisation', p. 95.

85 C. Harvie, *No Gods and Precious Few Heroes: Scotland, 1914–1980* (London, 1981), p. 6.

86 D. Howell, *British Workers and the Independent Labour Party, 1888–1906* (Manchester, 1983), p. 137.

87 J. Melling, 'Scottish industrialists and the changing character of class relations in the Clyde region, *c.*1880–1918', in T. Dickson (ed.), *Capital and Class in Scotland* (Edinburgh, 1982), p. 100.

88 Ibid., p. 101.

Accounts of both the English and Scottish experience share in a concern with the influence of reformist religion. Emphasised by Kellas and Urwin in the 1960s, Keating and Bleiman reiterated the Liberals' debts to the Free Church in Scotland in their study of nationalism in 1979. Although since then the disestablishment question has taken a back seat to considerations of the political impact of the Irish Catholic community, it is now widely accepted that Liberalism in the late nineteenth century owed much to the religious fervour for disestablishment and presbyterian democracy, although at times this proved a cause for division.[89] Kellas has made clear that the passion for democracy and freedom of conscience characteristic of many Presbyterian churches was paralleled in the traditions of Gladstonian democracy.[90] Yet how and whether this element of political religiosity lost the Liberals support in the pre-war society, increasingly ignoring the call to worship, is a question much in need of serious consideration.

Nevertheless, religious concerns were clearly only one element mitigating against a Liberal accommodation of new societal changes. In 1992, Christopher Harvie commented that 'Scottish Liberalism did not handle the transition to welfare and interest group politics well',[91] though he avoided any overt references to class politics, locating the ultimate 'death' of the 'individualist moralism' of the Liberals *after* the 1914–18 war.[92]

By way of contrast however, Iain Hutchison has emphasised the relevance and power of the Liberals in Scotland in the pre-1914 years in accommodating new progressive and interventionist sentiments. According to Hutchison, far from being regressive in their involvement in new welfare politics, Scottish Liberals were committed to the emerging social ideals of the new century. He concludes:

> It seems likely, then, that most of the rank and file Liberals were not reluctant followers of the new social radical policies enacted by the Liberal movement, implying that the adjustment to twentieth

89 M. Keating and D. Bleiman, *Labour and Scottish Nationalism* (London, 1979), p. 27. See also W. W. Knox, 'The political and workplace culture of the Scottish working class, 1832–1914', in W. H. Fraser and R. J. Morris (eds.) *People and Society in Scotland*, vol. II: *1830–1914* (Edinburgh, 1990), pp. 154–6. Highlighting the potential for division in the disestablishment debate, Hutchison refers to disestablishment as 'by far the most profound factor making for disunity in Scottish Liberalism before the Home Rule Crisis'. See I. G. C. Hutchison, *A Political History of Scotland, 1832–1924: Parties, Elections and Issues* (Edinburgh, 1986), p. 157.

90 Kellas, *Modern Scotland*, pp. 130–1.

91 C. Harvie, 'Scottish politics', in A. Dickson and J. H. Treble (eds.), *People and Society in Scotland*, vol. III: *1914–1990* (Edinburgh, 1992), p. 243.

92 Note, however, that in another article: C. Harvie, 'Before the breakthrough, 1888–1922', in I. Donnachie, C. Harvie and I. S. Wood (eds.), *Forward! Labour Politics in Scotland, 1888–1988* (Edinburgh, 1989) pp. 10–11, he acknowledges dissension in the Liberal ranks and a falling away in support in the pre-1900 period.

> century politics had been achieved before 1914 without breaking up the party.[93]

Hutchison's position has not been shared by everyone, however. Harvie noted in 1981 that in Scotland 'the New Liberalism seemed distant' and in his essay of 1989, he developed this idea, stating that: 'The "New Liberalism" appears to have made little impact in the north. Party activity was limited, doctrine stagnant, and the electorate seemingly uninterested in positive legislation.'[94]

More local studies need to be tackled to clarify these national impressions. Nevertheless, it seems clear that in Scotland one needs to look beyond the barometer of 'progressivism' and interventionist Liberalism to gauge the potency for survival of the Liberal vote in the years of an emerging class-based politic. Gordon Brown has suggested an alternative perspective on Liberal decline by stressing the perpetuation of the concerns of Victorian politics in the Edwardian period. He writes:

> There can be no doubt that the Labour Party suffered from the apparent radicalism of local Liberal candidates and the fact that the traditional issues of 'classical Liberalism' remained at the centre of the political stage ... the key issues remained those of constitutional reform, free trade and land.[95]

The de-stabilising impact of the Great War is a critical feature of many historical narratives of this period which seek the causal factors of Labour's success, and one which often unites historians who otherwise disagree on the legacy of the progressivism of the Edwardian years. Hutchison comments of the post-1918 Liberal Party:

> The party had been badly split during the war, its ideals and policies were outmoded in the post war world, its organisation had become hopelessly dilapidated. In sum, it represented a past political tradition which had little appeal to young people. Its eclipse was therefore steady, as politics naturally polarised between the other two parties.[96]

A similar viewpoint has been taken by other historians who have commented on the 'disenchantment' with the Liberals after the First World War.[97] Michael Fry attributes to the effects of the war the

93 Hutchison, *Political History of Scotland*, p. 238.

94 Harvie, 'Scottish politics', p. 8; Harvie, 'Before the breakthrough', p. 11.

95 G. Brown, 'The Labour Party and Political Change in Scotland, 1918–1929: The Politics of Five Elections' (Edinburgh University, Ph.D. thesis, 1981), p. 43.

96 Hutchison, *Political History of Scotland*, p. 309.

97 W. W. Knox, 'Whatever happened to radical Scotland?: the economic and social origins of the mid-Victorian political consensus in Scotland', in R. Mason and N. Macdougall (eds.), *People and Power in Scotland: Essays in Honour of T. C. Smout* (Edinburgh, 1992), p. 234.

undermining of the 'national consensus' on which Liberalism had nourished itself.[98] At the 'advent of class politics' he describes a Liberal Party losing the support of the bourgeoisie as the working classes 'go it alone'. Yet Fry concentrates more on the consequences of Liberal decline than on the causes when he writes:

> People and politicians alike found Liberal ethics impossible of application to the immense social and economic problems of the post-war period. Reduced to a tiny faction at Westminster, the Liberals could offer no hope of fulfilling anyone's moral imperatives or political aspirations.[99]

Here the facilitating elements which made war a truly social phenomenon are lost and the mechanisms of change surrendered to the drama of the consequences. Here, most importantly, the true impact of the 1918 franchise legislation is lost to the rhetoric of disillusion.

The Matthew, McKibbin and Kay hypothesis regarding the necessary impact of the 1918 Franchise Act has, however, caused much debate in Scotland. In his thesis of 1987, Smyth outlined the restrictive powers of the pre-1918 franchise, and warned against 'taking the 1918 Reform Act for granted or simply giving a cursory nod in its direction'.[100] Although he further makes clear the importance of considering both war and reform as parts of the same whole, Liberalism, he claims, 'could only have survived under the nineteenth century franchise system'.[101] Ian Wood, however, has approached the 1918 Act more cautiously, stating:

> Important though electoral reform was, it cannot be viewed in isolation from overall trends like the break-up of the historic working class, or at any rate a vital element within it, who turned away from the Liberals in the belief that they were 'no longer the party of the working class', but that in some perceived if undefinable way, the Labour party was.[102]

If on any point, consensus seems to exist on the timing of eventual irreversible decline in the inter-war years. Evidence from the late Victorian and Edwardian periods of dissension in party ranks or unpopularity at the polls may be acknowledged, but most hesitate in awarding them *causal* – as opposed to contextual – status, even as a long-term influence. The choice of date – 1918, 1922, 1924 – in a way is irrelevant, as historians trace the same features at various stages of

98 M. Fry, *Patronage and Principle: A Political History of Modern Scotland* (Aberdeen, 1991 edn), p. 119.
99 Ibid., p. 148.
100 Smyth, 'Labour and Socialism in Glasgow', p. 336.
101 Ibid., pp. 348, 341.
102 I. S. Wood, 'Hope deferred: Labour in Scotland in the 1920s', in Donnachie, Harvie and Wood, *Forward! Labour Politics in Scotland*, p. 32.

debilitating maturity. However, Michael Lynch has sounded a cautionary note by stressing the strength of Liberal resilience even in these years:

> The continuing ability of Liberalism – in its various disguises – to attract Scottish voters, despite its own organisational disorders and with little new in the way of policy except a growing nostalgia for the pre-1914 world, blunted the new politics of class.[103]

A legacy of the Scottish Edwardian scene which took a long time in succumbing to the imperatives of a class-based politic was the Irish Catholic vote.[104] The impact and determining influence of the Irish Catholic vote has been seen as a fundamental factor in the timing, and to a lesser extent, the character, of the rise of the Labour movement and the death of popular Liberalism in Scotland.[105] Labour's capture of the Irish Catholic vote from the Liberals in the 1920s has been seen by some as evidence of the point at which the Irish in Scotland finally began voting on class as opposed to ethnic lines. However, others see in this late departure from the Liberal fold the ultimate bankruptcy of Liberalism once the Irish 'mission' had been accomplished. Ultimately, as a monocausal explanation for the final success of Labour, the Irish factor is inadequate. By treating the Irish community too much in isolation, Scottish historiography has placed too much weight on flimsy ethnic arguments, instead of incorporating this factor in a wider analysis of the mechanics of change.[106]

The historiography of Liberal decline in Scotland has thus shared many of the national concerns which have framed the English debate and has similarly failed to reach any overall consensus on either the timing or character of decline itself. Yet the Scottish debate has been handicapped in recent years by a lack of local studies through which national concerns may be viewed from the grass-roots level. The exception to this rule is the coverage of Glasgow's experience during this period, yet on occasion this focus on Clydeside has hampered rather than encouraged innovative analyses of other regions, as Glasgow has become the core testing ground of national generalisations and thus the apparent exemplar of political Scotland in miniature.

103 M. Lynch, *Scotland: A New History* (London, 1992), p. 432.

104 S. Gilley, 'Catholics and Socialists in Glasgow, 1906–1912', in K. Lunn (ed.), *Hosts, Immigrants and Minorities: Historical Responses to Newcomers in British Society, 1870–1914* (Folkestone, 1980), pp. 160–200. On p. 166, Gilley notes: 'Catholics thought of themselves as Catholics first, not as members of the wider working class, and their sense of need for local community was fulfilled by the parish church.'

105 See Howell, *British Workers and the Independent Labour Party*, pp. 163–7; also Kellas, *Modern Scotland*, p. 140; Harvie, 'Before the breakthrough', p. 21; I. S. Wood, 'Irish immigrants and Scottish radicalism, 1880–1906', in I. MacDougall (ed.) *Essays in Scottish Labour History: A Tribute to W. H. Marwick* (Edinburgh, 1978), pp. 65–89; and Smyth, 'Labour and Socialism in Glasgow', p. 88.

106 Brown, 'Labour Party and Political Change in Scotland', p. 40. Here Brown contests the emphasis placed on the Irish vote as a determining factor by disputing its size, the extent of Irish enfranchisement and its poor organisation.

As a feature of the Glasgow experience, the evolution of class politics has been a key determinant of many of the theories regarding Liberal decline. In his article on 'Glasgow working-class Politics', Hutchison noted:

> Here the First World War and the post 1918 developments, particularly in Ireland, paved the way for the fusing of that powerful working class solidarity and class-consciousness which were to be the prevailing feature of Glasgow politics in the next phase.[107]

In recent years, however, labour historians have come to question the importance of the First World War as a decisive 'turning-point' in Glasgow's political profile. Joan Smith has focused on the economic slump of 1908 as the key period when the 'internal contradictions' in the Liberal Party undermined its electoral potential. Denying the impact of New Liberalism in Glasgow, she sees in 1908, evidence to prove that at this point 'Old Liberalism' 'could not lead a progressive movement against unemployment and poverty'.[108] In addition, for Smith, it was the years before 1914 which were crucial in establishing the Independent Labour Party [hereafter ILP] as a potent political alternative to Liberalism through the medium of 'ethical socialism'.[109] In this concern, Smith's perspective has been echoed in the writing of Alan McKinlay. Along with Smith, McKinlay has stressed the importance of socio-political networking in the labour ranks in Glasgow before 1914. He writes:

> Before 1914 the ILP had become the organisational intersection of a series of progressive social networks, the hub of radical activity from the shop floor, the teeming tenements of the Glasgow communities, to the Council Chambers.[110]

Admirably, both authors have attempted to refocus the debate on Liberal decline on the minutiae of local change, seeking in *local* parties the key determinants of the chronology of decline. Yet the plethora of Glasgow studies, by addressing political change in a self-referential manner, have generally failed to tap the potential of local studies as a means of re-constructing the Scottish experience as the sum of its often contradictory parts.[111]

107 I. G. C. Hutchison, 'Glasgow working-class politics', in R. A. Cage (ed.), *The Working Class in Glasgow, 1750–1914* (London, 1987), p. 134.

108 J. Smith, 'Taking the leadership of the Labour movement: the ILP in Glasgow, 1906–1914', in McKinlay and Morris, *ILP on Clydeside*, p. 70.

109 Ibid., p. 56.

110 A. McKinlay, '"Doubtful wisdom and uncertain promise": strategy, ideology and organisation, 1918–1922', in McKinlay and Morris, *ILP on Clydeside*, p. 123. See also McKinlay, 'Labour and locality'. For a similar approach, see also M. Savage, 'Whatever happened to Red Clydeside?', in J. Anderson and A. Cochrane (eds.), *A State of Crisis* (London, 1989), pp. 231–43.

111 See Smyth, 'Labour and Socialism in Glasgow'; R. K. Middlemass, *The Clydesiders: A*

Regrettably, little work has been carried out on the political changes of these years in individual constituencies outwith Glasgow and its immediate environs. Yet although little attention has been paid to the small body of work which does exist, such works have already thrown up some interesting questions as well as parallels with national concerns.

In his study of 1973 of the politics of Kincardineshire, M. C. Dyer illustrated an 'independent political culture' in this area, one which was 'in marked contrast to the party politics with which most people in Britain are familiar'.[112] Here, where the Labour Party proved a significant electoral property only after 1945, a Liberal dominance was achieved in the late nineteenth century through skilful alliances of 'tenant farmers, fishermen, the urban population ... sections of the small town businessmen and ... the backing of the Free Church'.[113] For Dyer, it was the imperatives of twentieth-century politics which 'undermined' this alliance and the Liberal dominance which rested on its strength. National generalities regarding the instrumental power of the Labour Party in the process of Liberal decline are thus seen as significant, though non-essential, factors in Liberalism's decline in this area. Similarly, in his article of 1982 on Asquith's defeat at East Fife in 1918, Stuart Ball emphasised the importance of the local challenge from the right, often ignored in conventional discussions of Liberalism's post-war crisis, by considering decline in a rural setting. He wrote: 'The theme of Conservative popularity is at least equal in importance to that of the rise of the Labour Party in any realistic appraisal of the decline of the Liberal Party.'[114] The composition of, and local challenges to, the Liberal Party are thus seen as critical determining factors in the fate of Liberalism – two factors often lost by more general narratives which concentrate to an overwhelming degree on the dichotomy of Liberal decline and Labour success.

In the studies of Aberdeen by Kenneth Buckley in 1955 and, more recently, C. W. M. Phipps in 1980, further national orthodoxies are called into question. Both Buckley and Phipps conclude that the Eight Hour Day question, rather than concerns with working-class representation, determined the trade unions' split with the Liberal Party. Phipps notes:

> The failure of the Aberdeen Liberal Association to endorse the Eight Hour Day proposal was a major impetus for the Trades

Left Wing Struggle For Parliamentary Power (London, 1965); and McLean, *Legend of Red Clydeside*. The exception to the overwhelming focus on Glasgow in isolation has been Joan Smith's work on Glasgow and Liverpool (see above) where, through comparison, Glasgow's experience is placed in a broader context, and the extent of its representativeness assessed.

112 M. C. Dyer, 'The Politics of Kincardineshire' (Aberdeen University, Ph.D. thesis, 1973), p. 285.

113 Ibid., p. 411.

114 S. R. Ball, 'Asquith's decline and the General Election of 1918', *SHR*, lxi (1982), p. 48.

> Council to break with that body and seek an independent Labour organisation to forward the claims of the working men.[115]

However, both Phipps and Buckley stress the lasting influence of the Liberal Party in the early twentieth century and most importantly diverge from the recent 'Glasgow revisionism', which gives a leading role to the ILP in the story of Labour advancement, by stressing the power of the trades council in local politics.[116] As Phipps maintains: 'In Aberdeen, any viable Labour Party organisation had to be centred on the Trades Council. This had proved to be true before 1914 and continued to be the case after 1918.'[117]

The evidence from these localities, whilst not disproving the validity of conclusions regarding the experience of Glasgow, nor indeed seriously undermining any of the key features of the national debate, presents us with alternative patterns of change which ought to be constitutive of wider generalities rather than exceptions which seek to prove a grander rule.

William Walker's study of the 1922 General Election in Dundee clearly shows the potential for local and national studies operating in association, rather than at a distant remove, when he seeks to contribute to the debate between Henry Pelling and Trevor Wilson on their respective evaluations of the First World War as a factor in the decline of the Liberal Party.[118] Walker here qualifies the impact of the war on Dundee politics by highlighting that it succeeded only in activating 'latent dangers to Liberalism' pre-existent in Dundee before 1914.[119] He further contextualises the impact of the 1918 reform legislation which increased the electorate of Dundee three-fold, by crediting it only with permitting the 'electoral expression of a political character already formed'.[120] Wider generalisations are thus tested against local experience and are found wanting.

Yet, if national debates are continually to set the agenda of local studies, the potential for imaginative and theoretical inquiry within the context of local history will undoubtedly be surrendered to the search for contradictory examples of national conventions. Similarly, the recent works of Robert Duncan on Wishaw and Motherwell clearly highlight

115 C. W. M. Phipps, 'The Aberdeen Trades Council and Politics, 1900–1939: The Development of a Local Labour Party in Aberdeen' (Aberdeen University, M.Litt. thesis, 1980), p. 5.

116 Ibid., p. 8.

117 Ibid., p. 111.

118 W. M. Walker, 'Dundee's disenchantment with Churchill: a comment upon the downfall of the Liberal Party', *SHR*, xlix (1970), p. 85. See also T. Wilson, *The Downfall of the Liberal Party, 1914–1935* (London, 1966); and H. Pelling, *Popular Politics and Society in Late Victorian Britain* (London, 1979), esp. pp. 101–21.

119 Ibid., p. 86.

120 Ibid., p. 97.

the limiting nature of narrative accounts.[121] His breadth of detail and much needed focus on municipal and parish politics are indeed to be applauded. However, the absence of a theoretical foundation and failure to place the studies in a national context warn us that the push towards deconstructing the national Scottish perspective *could* result in the unintegrated fragmentation of the historiography of change. The more we know about what change meant at a local level need not result in greater knowledge of *how* change happened in the first place. Local studies, if they are to be of use to the wider concerns of the historical discipline, need to move beyond the restrictive bounds of narrative and self-referential concerns to wider theoretical and politico-historical debates.

Of works currently in print, Holford's 1988 study of Edinburgh labour politics in the inter-war period suggests an imaginative way forward.[122] Here, empirical data and theoretical perspectives, combined with a close attention to the language of protest and patriotism, interact to produce a detailed investigation of local labour relations and politics. Holford's work moves beyond the conventional elaboration of a class-based analysis of Labour success to highlight the competing voices of labour in this period of economic and political dislocation and the complex legacy of the Great War. Yet, whilst Holford's detailed analysis of labour relations and changing management styles provides a useful counter-weight to more recent local histories in England which prioritise the political and ideological roots of change, the focus on the work-place tends towards a certain economic determinist perspective in which the voices of religion, female workers and the middle classes are only seldom heard. The development of independent labour politics was determined as much by the restrictions placed on it by the broader socio-cultural context in which it emerged as by the organisations which it spawned. In this regard we must look outwith the work-place as well as within to analyse the means and motives of the labour ascendancy.

The Regional Perspective

A new perspective is urgently required in the realm of local political studies in Scotland which, if they are to prove their potential as windows on a wider political past, must look beyond the *cul de sac* of narrative for a way forward. As a critical new contribution to the debate on Liberalism's decline, recent local studies of English constituencies suggest a possible means of releasing the potential of local history in Scotland. By looking briefly at three authors – Patrick Joyce, Gareth Stedman Jones and Michael Savage – and their works on Lancashire,

121 R. Duncan, *Wishaw: Life and Labour in a Lanarkshire Industrial Community, 1790–1914* (Motherwell, 1986); R. Duncan, *Steelopolis: The Making of Motherwell, c.1750–1939* (Motherwell, 1991).

122 Holford, *Reshaping Labour*, p. 2.

London and Preston respectively, it is clear that their studies have called into question the conclusions of the national debate and forced historians to look at the dynamics at work within the constituencies.

In 1980 Joyce identified a 'transition from cultural to class politics [which] involved a change of consciousness' as the foundation of the rise of an independent labour voice in Lancashire.[123]

> Because the old politics was *not* a matter of political consciousness but of community, deference and influence, the new politics of the Labour Party involved a leap from one kind of consciousness to another.[124]

From the competing and conflicting paternalisms of Tory and Liberal factory and land owners, Joyce sees hegemonic control being broken down by a locally defined concept of 'class' in which the factory acted as a cultural and economic catalyst of political change: 'The factory had a direct, unmediated role in political life. More than this, indeed, urban politics at large was in considerable degree shaped in the matrix of factory life.'[125] Factory culture moved from being a stabilising and integral element in paternalist control to the focus of radical sentiment when, through organisation, labour appropriated the medium and its rituals for its own purposes. In this way, Joyce presents us with a sense of class emerging prior to the First World War which was 'locally (and regionally) conscious'.[126] Unlike those adherents of a national 'class' argument, however, he observes how such a sense of class did not inevitably lead to the decline of Liberalism and the rise of the Labour Party:

> this ambiguous sense of class ... was made up of strong ties between workers and employers ... The rootedness of the sense of class in particular communities could therefore serve to work in different directions, enabling a larger inter-regional, inter-trade solidarity, but as often emphasising tendencies of an opposite sort.[127]

Loyalties to religion and the ethos of free trade could just as easily mean that class consciousness – as Joyce defines it, at this time – bolstered rather than undermined Liberal power. Class as a determinant of electoral performance thus becomes regional and time specific and not entirely a factor intimating Liberal decline and the betterment of Labour. Moreover, this formulation escapes the charges levelled at attempts to use the class model on a national scale by tightening definitions and being more disciplined in the method of application.

123 Joyce, *Work, Society and Politics*, p. 332.
124 Ibid., p. 332.
125 Ibid., p. 204.
126 Joyce, *Visions of the People*, p. 138.
127 Ibid., p. 139.

Since 1980, however, Joyce's 'celebrity' status as one of the major voices of postmodernism in British social history has tended to overwhelm his significant innovative contributions to regional research. Through his application of linguistic and post-structural theories, Joyce in *Visions of the People* and *Democratic Subjects* has pushed the discipline to acknowledge the significance of tensions, explored at a local level, in the individual and collective identities of political actors, and has pointed to the importance of the cultural construction of politics as a key determinant of the timing of change.

Stedman Jones, in his earlier studies of London, likewise cautioned historians to beware of automatically investing working-class groupings with a distinct, institutionally defined political consciousness. In *Outcast London* he maintained that: 'At a political level, the most striking characteristic of the casual poor was neither their adherence to the left, nor yet their adherence to the right, but rather their rootless volatility.'[128] Stedman Jones, by denying the mobilising impact of New Unionism on the labouring poor, stressed the case for a closer look at casual labour. Unlike the studies of the labour 'aristocracy' and industrial proletariat of the north of England and the west of Scotland, Stedman Jones presents us with a working-class culture characterised by an 'enclosed and defensive conservatism' – a 'culture of consolation' epitomised by the escapism of the music hall.[129] In the period 1870 to 1900 Stedman Jones sees Labour as a party of stasis – one which accepted the class hierarchy and made the most of its position in it. Liberalism, in this model, declined because it failed to see this shift from power to welfare politics early enough to absorb the electoral force of a 're-made' working class. Stedman Jones's emphasis on culture, moreover, has further enhanced our appreciation of the context and cultural influences on electoral politics. Yet this model of change, by concentrating on 'the mass', has taught us little regarding *individual* motive forces and responses to the readjustments in the party system beyond a perceived politico-cultural inertia among the unskilled born of a de-industrialised metropolis.

His seminal piece of 1983, 'Rethinking Chartism', however, imaginatively addressed this dilemma. Sharing with Joyce, a 'new-found' interest in the dynamics of the language of political expression, Stedman Jones challenged the materiality of political interest by positing that whilst 'matter' determined the development of the form of political expression, 'form condition[ed] the development of the matter'.[130] In this way,

128 G. S. Jones, *Outcast London: A Study in the Relationship between Classes in Victorian Society* (Oxford, 1971), p. 343.

129 Jones, 'Working-class culture and working-class politics in London, 1870–1900: notes on the remaking of a working class', *Languages of Class*, pp. 183, 237.

130 Jones, 'Rethinking Chartism', *Languages of Class*, p. 95.

Stedman Jones sought 'a more precise relationship between ideology and activity' and reinvested power in the voice of the masses.[131]

In stark contrast, Michael Savage appeals to the complex material interests of the working class of Preston to uncover a working-class 'practical politics' which articulated the needs and interests of a class seeking to reduce the insecurity which came from their separation from the means of their subsistence.[132] Savage thus looks below the regional political character of Preston to discern the motive forces behind voting and the meanings evidenced therein. He insists that: 'It is important to separate out formal political organisation from the "practical political struggles" which, while present in the strategies of local Labour movements, may also be articulated outside them.'[133] Unlike Joyce and Jones, Savage has maintained a commitment to a class model of political analysis which, whilst more nuanced than those of his contemporaries, has persisted in prioritising the socio-economic context of politics over its cultural forms. He writes: 'In Preston, the Conservatives did *not* attempt to play down class divisions but merely harnessed them to their own ends ... The Liberals' weakness was due to their reluctance to come to terms with these same forces.'[134] However, Savage, unlike Morgan or Belchem, emphasises that Liberal weakness did not necessarily intimate Labour strength. Savage stresses that attempts by the ILP to change the issues of local politics away from economistic concerns failed in the years before 1906. In agreement with Joyce, he highlights that: 'One of the major developments of the decade before 1914 was the emergence of the neighbourhood in working class life and the steady development of capacities for collective action based upon it.'[135] Yet this did *not* necessarily boost the Labour vote. As Savage makes clear: 'The Labour Party's reliance on union-based and work-based capacities left it unable to mobilise at the neighbourhood level.'[136] Labour broke through in Preston only after it secured a neighbourhood base during the war. Here, the inter-connectedness of class and community point again to the locality as the principle 'space' in which change happened.

Regional studies, by looking at municipal and county voting patterns in addition to parliamentary elections and analysing change on a more restricted scale, have shattered the fallacy that Liberal decline was either caused by or necessitated the rise of Labour. Historians have begun to abstract from election figures the agency of the voter and have significantly pointed to the roles of industry, community, language and gender as crucial determinants of political change. They have shown that it is not enough to accept blindly the oratory of the articulate few

131 Ibid., p. 95
132 Savage, *Dynamics of Working-Class Politics*, pp. 17, 18.
133 Ibid., p. 37.
134 Ibid., p. 143.
135 Ibid., p. 156.
136 Ibid.

and have come to question the validity of an undifferentiating national approach to Liberal decline.

Searle and Tanner, however, have attempted to reconcile the national and the regional in their recent works. Searle's *The Liberal Party: Triumph and Disintegration, 1886–1929* is based solely on secondary sources and lines up the arguments which compose the overall debate on the Liberal decline, offering 'only a few observations' in the concluding pages. He contends that Liberal attempts to be a populist party were incompatible with a political system drawn increasingly on class lines. In that he says nothing new. Yet in his foremost hypothesis – that the Liberals 'seem to have been slower to have grasped the *political* implications of the emergence of the rise of the corporate economy' – he reveals the potential of looking beyond the working-class vote to the commercial classes for an explanation of Liberal failure, rooted in a complex appreciation of the economic climate.[137] Ultimately unsatisfying as a method of explaining the decline of Liberalism, his study is worth while as a recapitulation and reassessment of former orthodoxies, yet as a way forward it holds little hope. Tanner, however, appeals for a new approach to political change following the plethora of studies comprising 'the debate so far'. He writes:

> New information has to be put in a new framework if it is to make sense of the complex pattern of change revealed in these and other studies. It is more instructive, I will argue, to treat the competing ideas of a class-based Liberal party powered by New Liberal ideas on the one hand, and a class-based Labour party powered by a limited 'cultural' class consciousness on the other as equally inappropriate guides to the political realignment of 1900–1918. The question is essentially how to reconstruct and rephrase these debates in a manner which will explain the electoral changes and the changes in the parties themselves.[138]

Tanner maintains that politics in the period from 1900 to 1918 were neither class based nor class specific. Neither were politics nationalised: expectations were local, not national.[139] He stresses that: 'The 1918 election marked the end of a formative stage in some areas. It marked a sharp, unheralded electoral breakthrough in others.'[140] The whole is thus seen by Tanner as the sum of its parts and is, therefore, divested of any inherent overall identity other than the common ground shared by its component elements.

137 Searle, *Liberal Party*, p. 173.
138 Tanner, *Political Change and the Labour Party*, p. 10.
139 Ibid., pp. 419–20.
140 Ibid., p. 431.

The historical debate is now at the stage where we must accept political change as a 'fragmented' process chronologically, geographically and theoretically. Only by accepting change as such can we hope to reach closer to the totality of the experience and understand in greater depth the complexity of the dynamics involved in the process of political realignment. It is as a consequence of this changing perspective that any new history of Liberalism's decline must engage not merely with the evidence of change and its consequences but also, most importantly, with the dynamics of change itself and those identities upon which it acted. It must consider the inherent complexities of the political entities it seeks to trace through time and explore their 'constructed' natures and contextual existence. Altogether, the agenda is a challenging one.

CHAPTER TWO

Interests and Industry, Politics and Paternalism

'Community'

In his study of the north-east of Scotland of 1981, Robert Turner has argued that 'individual identity presupposes the existence of an identifiable community, which generates a cultural language, or code, rendering individual expressions of identity meaningful'.[1] Taking such a perspective on board, it seems reasonable to conclude that in our study of Paisley, local identity is not merely created as a sum of its economic, social, cultural and political components, but exists as that which gives these components 'meaning'. How we define community is in this way critical to how we evaluate political expression.

'Community', as an ordering concept in sociology, anthropology and indeed recent local history has had a long lineage.[2] Consensus, however, has not been reached even on the definition of the term, thus making inter-disciplinary comparisons problematic and the search for a common methodology fraught with difficulty. In the light of such problems, therefore, it seems essential that before we consider the political experience of Paisley in the years of Liberalism's decline, we first decide what it is we are considering when we look at local political identity.

First Paisley, in the context of 'community', is here considered to be spatially located within the old burgh boundary of Paisley *and* its suburbs, located within the old Abbey and Paisley parish boundaries as set before 1895.[3] The *political* community, though admittedly mobile, is

1 R. Turner, 'Gala day as an expression of community identity', in A. Jackson (ed.), *Way of Life and Identity*, SSRC, North Sea Oil Panel Occasional Paper, no. 4 (London, 1981), p. 63.

2 For a useful summary, see A. Macfarlane, 'History, anthropology and the study of communities', *SH*, v (1977), pp. 631–52. Here Macfarlane questions the efficacy of continuing to use 'community' as an ordering concept in historical investigation. However, for an alternative approach, see D. B. Clark, 'The concept of community: a re-examination', *The Sociological Review*, xxi (1973), pp. 397–416; C. J. Calhoun, 'Community: toward a variable conceptualization for comparative research', *SH*, v (1980), pp. 105–27. For a historical perspective, see E. and S. Yeo, 'On the uses of "community": from Owenism to the present', in S. Yeo (ed.), *New Views of Co-operation* (London, 1988), pp. 229–58.

3 In 1895, the Abbey and Paisley parishes were united, along with a portion of Renfrew parish located in the boundaries of Paisley burgh, to form one parish – the parish of Paisley.

seen as being located *within* the parliamentary constituency boundaries or residing in the suburbs of the burgh and immediate neighbouring districts, whilst concentrating all or most of its political activity in Paisley or in relation to Paisley in a regional or national political context.[4] The parameters of the study, therefore, though limited by geography, are determined, appropriately, by contemporarily defined constitutional limits and the changing historical and geographical profile of the area's political 'activists'. Change over time in the location and composition of the political milieu is thus accommodated within a flexible definition of *where* we locate the political community.

Secondly, who and, abstractly, what processes define the transformations which determine the altering composition of the political community are critical in our broader concerns of how changes in political involvement have affected and effected different definitions of Paisley as an identifiable political entity, from the 'Liberal capital of Scotland' to a safe Labour seat after 1945. As a prominent and developing industrial town, consideration must thus be given to patterns in location over time of manufacturing industry in Paisley, the consequential transformation of the labour force and the impact such developments necessarily had on regional class structure. Through such an investigation it will become clear that, contrary to convention, national economic development in these years, although tending ultimately towards the homogenisation of local and regional cultural differences, also had the contrary – ultimately, short-term – effect of encouraging specialisation in certain areas, thus supporting separate local identities, and contributing towards the survival of regional voting patterns.

Using Doreen Massey's geological metaphor, the altering industrial profile of Paisley, from weaving town to 'threadopolis', and the transformation of the labour market of the textile industry in the town to a predominantly female concern may be considered as consequences of cycles of accumulation which deposited layers of industrial sediment and produced 'spatially uneven effects as a result of historically prior social uses of space'.[5] As a way of considering the consequences which Paisley's contemporary industrial profile had on the community's political identity, this paradigm has the advantage of perceiving the present as a combination of all its 'pasts', moving one step beyond more static sociological formulations. However, by isolating and concentrating solely on the industrial, we run the risk of appealing to economic determinism as an explanation of local political identity and creating

4 Exceptions to this general rule will include parliamentary candidates and MPs who, although not residing in the Paisley area, were obviously a critical part of the political community.

5 For a detailed account of Massey's explanation of uneven regional development, see A. Warde, 'Spatial change, politics and the division of labour', in D. Gregory and J. Urry (eds.), *Social Relations and Spatial Structures* (Basingstoke, 1985), p. 195.

restrictive models which seek to locate in the historical continuum a periodisation in which phases of development are anticipated by that which has gone before, without any recourse to non-economic, non-class specific factors existent in the wider community. Models which seek to draw a structural explanation of political identity from historical investigations of the industrial landscape impose a very even logic on a very uneven development.[6] Such models are destabilised when one introduces cultural factors or indeed the problematics of gender and the household economy into their format, and are thus found wanting.[7]

Local political identity, isolated spatially, and resulting partially from economic imperatives, must therefore finally be located in the processes which evolve and transform local tradition. Likewise tradition should be appreciated as a concept which, being rooted in the associational life of the community, has the power to legitimise change and accredit authority to its exponents, whether through implicit means of identification with an idealised or actual past, or materially, by absorbing change through secular rituals, local institutions, or what Turner has referred to above as a 'cultural language'. 'Community', as C. J. Calhoun has emphasised, 'was far more than a mere place or population'.[8]

In these terms, Tonnies's *Gemeinschaft/Gesellschaft* dichotomy, by setting in opposition the 'communal relationship', based on subjective emotive responses (the realm of tradition), and the 'associational relationship', composed of rationally determined exchanges, appears an artificial partitioning of collective interaction. Rather, as Calhoun again has made clear: 'the experiential dimension is not independent of the structural; the sense of belonging to a community is directly founded on the social relationships through which one does belong to a community.'[9] In this way, tradition, founded on a social structure which is in a constant process of formation, often proves malleable, adapting to the needs of new associational groupings as and when they are formed. 'Actual social practice and tradition are constantly interrelated and mutually determining.'[10]

In adopting such a perspective, this study dissociates itself from the definition of an 'invented tradition' utilised by Hobsbawm in *The Invention of Tradition*, in favour of a more fluid, metaphysical and less material, interpretation. It also rejects his contestable and, at times, arbitrary distinction between 'custom' and 'tradition' and the ease with

6 Ibid., p. 203.
7 Ibid., pp. 207–9.
8 Calhoun, 'Community', p. 106.
9 Ibid., p. 109. Note, Savage and Miles make a similar point with regard to the language which expresses tradition: 'Rather than discourse being contrasted with material forces, or culture juxtaposed to social structures, we would insist on their inseparable and mutually dependent character': Savage and Miles, *Remaking of the British Working Class*, p. 18.
10 Calhoun, 'Community', p. 116.

which it is assumed the generation (or invention) and application of the legitimising force of tradition can be distinguished. Whilst in sympathy with the attempt to contextualise the utility of tradition in the politico-economic frame in which it emerges, what follows will contest Hobsbawm's focus on the 'national' as the most appropriate 'window' on the elaboration of nineteenth-century political traditions. Rather, by emphasising the ways in which the experience of the individual was mediated through family, work-place, neighbourhood, locality, constituency, regional and sub-national milieu, this study contests the extent to which politics 'was essentially nation-wide politics'.[11]

In the context of our study of Paisley, the inter-relationship between the social and the communally determined traditions of the political community proves a potent force as we seek to explain the resilience of Liberalism under the pressures of the post-1918 franchise when 'the loyalties and habits of neighbourhood feeling' proved sufficiently compelling to cut across the imperatives of a developing class consciousness.[12] However, tradition, custom and cultural responses can only contribute to our appreciation of change – they cannot encompass it – and in this manner, the industrial profile of the town reasserts its power as a critical explanatory category.[13]

Industrial Structure and Political Tradition, Paisley: 1790–1850

Paisley's growth to industrial maturity, reflected in the demographic history of the area from the late seventeenth century to 1931, is one marked by steady expansion up to 1911 with an 'easing off' thereafter, with only one period of serious contraction in the mid-nineteenth century, as Appendix 1 illustrates. The population growth of the early decades of the nineteenth century fostered by the booming textile industry was, after a period of economic crisis in the 1840s, matched after 1861 by a steady increase supported by the emergent cotton thread industry. The relationship between industrial prosperity and population growth, however, is a far from simple one, being determined by the composition of the local labour market, the skill resources of the population, and the relative availability of local capital as well as by the whims of national market forces. Paisley's growth was thus dependent

11 E. Hobsbawm, 'Mass-producing traditions: Europe, 1870–1914', in E. Hobsbawm and T. Ranger (eds.), *The Invention of Tradition* (Cambridge, 1983).

12 For an enlightening account of the importance of community in late nineteenth-century politics, see Joyce, *Work, Society and Politics*, esp. pp. 53–7, 93, 116–18.

13 In this perspective, I echo the concerns of Robert Gray who has stressed that 'to invoke the tradition was to claim support in a process of political mobilisation, and its meaning was conditioned by the historical context': Gray, 'Class, politics and historical "revisionism"', p. 218. See also G. Rose, 'From "Locality, politics, and culture: Poplar in the 1920s", 1988', in C. Hamnett (ed.), *Social Geography: A Reader* (London, 1996), p. 251, where she states: '"Culture" ... is not a simple solution to the problems of geographic variation in social and political action.'

on the favourable interaction of all these forces and the manner in which redevelopment built on the legacy of an industrial heritage of long-standing.

Maturing from the small market town which it had been in the days before the Union, Paisley by 1790 was a prominent manufacturing centre in the west of Scotland, dominated by the textile industries, the roots of which can be located in the mid-seventeenth century. During the first half of the eighteenth century, textile manufacture in the town was concentrated on 'coarse checkered linen cloth ... bengals ... [and] checkered linen handkerchiefs', these being later displaced by lighter fabrics of a higher quality.[14] By 1760, the manufacture of linen thread had become a considerable interest in the town, silk gauze had been introduced and white sewing thread had been established as a growing concern for over fifty years.[15] Paisley thus entered the nineteenth century as something of a 'boom' town; the value of the manufactures of silk, lawn and linen gauze and white thread alone being valued at around £600,000 in 1784.[16]

Such a transformation had complex and dramatic consequences for the town's social structure. Yet perhaps more important than the impact of this period of success were the implications that the subsequent period of decline in the weaving industry had on the character of intra- and inter- class relationships in the burgh. The dominant historians of this period of upheaval in Paisley have been Anthony Dickson, along with his collaborators W. Speirs and Anthony Clarke, who sketch a picture of a society in transition.[17]

In their studies in the 1980s these three historians focused on the potential dangers which were inherent in the weaving industry in Paisley in the early part of the nineteenth century and which were realised in the catastrophe of the 'Hungry Forties'. They focused on the small-scale nature of the manufacturing units in the town and the low level of technology which facilitated numerous relatively low-capital investors to enter the industry. In addition, they pointed to the nature of the industry in this period as one becoming increasingly dominated by the manufacture of distinctive Paisley shawls – a product which proved unable to weather the vagaries of a fickle fashion industry.[18] In 1841, therefore, when a general depression in the domestic British market for textiles was met by a collapse in the demand for shawls and local over-

14 *OSA* vol. VII (1793), p. 826; *NSA*, vol. VII (Edinburgh, 1845), pp. 261–2.

15 *OSA*, vol. VII, p. 826; see also: *NSA*, vol. VII, pp. 262–3.

16 Ibid., pp. 827–8.

17 A. Dickson and W. Speirs, 'Changes in class structure in Paisley, 1750–1845', *SHR*, lix (1980), pp. 54–72; T. Clarke and T. Dickson, 'Class consciousness in early industrial capitalism: Paisley, 1770–1850', in T. Dickson (ed.), *Capital and Class in Scotland* (Edinburgh, 1982), pp. 8–60; and T. Dickson and T. Clarke, 'Social concern and social control in nineteenth-century Scotland: Paisley, 1841–1843', *SHR*, lxv (1986), pp. 48–60.

18 *NSA*, vol. VII, pp. 264–7.

production, few Paisley weavers were able to diversify and invest in other more profitable branches of the textile trades. By 1843, a total of 77 of the town's previous 112 manufacturing firms were declared bankrupt, and 7,000 were out of work in 1848.[19]

Such a general industrial catastrophe clearly had profound economic consequences for the burgh. However, for our concerns these must be related to the impact the economic collapse of the 1840s had on the profile of the local labour market, and the dominant political culture of the town.

That the key period of dramatic growth in Paisley's cotton thread industry can be located in the years immediately following the collapse of the weaving industry is no coincidence. As Matthew Blair wrote in his history of the shawl trade in 1904: 'One of the controlling causes ... which made the [thread] business settle in Paisley in preference to other places, was the cheap labour thrown upon the market by the decay of the shawl trade.'[20] Yet the labour-force requirements of the new leading industry were neither simply nor largely supplied by unemployed weavers. Clarke and Dickson in their work of 1982 noted a resistance among male weavers in the 1830s to enter the cotton mills, even in periods of extreme hardship.[21] The resistance was motivated by the skilled weavers' sense of their superiority in the industrial hierarchy as independent or semi-independent producers, leading to Clarke and Dickson identifying a lasting 'sectionalism' among Paisley's working classes in the mid-century decades, militating against the development of local class consciousness. The cotton spinning and thread factories employed a high percentage of women and children and relied heavily on the increasing immigrant work-force from the Central Highlands and, in the 1830s, from Ireland. Indeed, in one Paisley spinning mill in 1834, of the 279 hands, 199 were Irish.[22] Although, as Brenda Collins has shown, 'the in-movement of Irish families decreased sharply during the depression years of the 1840s', in Paisley their early involvement in the thread industry contributed towards a process of differentiation between workers in the thread and weaving trades.[23]

The development and labour profile of the thread industry in the town, instead of having a homogenising impact on the local working-class population, contributed in this period to the intensification of sectional barriers to class unity, by sustaining a process whereby occupational differences were closely associated with gender, cultural

19 Dickson and Speirs, 'Changes in class structure in Paisley', p. 71.

20 M. Blair, *The Paisley Shawl and the Men who Created and Developed It* (Paisley, 1907), p. 32.

21 Clarke and Dickson, 'Class consciousness in early industrial capitalism', p. 22.

22 Ibid., p. 24.

23 B. Collins, 'Irish emigration to Dundee and Paisley during the first half of the nineteenth century', in J. M. Goldstrom and L. A. Clarkson (eds.), *Irish Population, Economy and Society* (Oxford, 1981), p. 200.

and – in the case of the Catholic Irish – religious divisions.[24] In an essay of 1806, William Carlile distinguished the highly educated, independent weaver from the cotton operatives. He wrote:

> The Cotton Spinning trade now established in this part of the country is highly valuable, on account of such numbers of poor children and women as are employed in its various operations, but it appears to have no tendency to improve the morals of the country. The numbers collected in large cotton mills, from families immersed in ignorance and vice, spread the contagion among such as have been more regularly educated, and profligate conduct is the natural result.[25]

The labour market which was thus structured around the demands of the new thread industry had as its key resource, therefore, not the skilled male weaving sector, but a plentiful supply of predominantly unskilled female and child operatives whose presence evidently threatened to de-stabilise the social relations which were at the basis of the traditions of the weaving community.

In considering a viable conceptualisation of the Paisley community we have already determined that tradition, as a social component partially founded on a distinctive social structure, is malleable, adapting to accommodate the needs of new associational groupings and, necessarily, changes in the industrial structure. Yet a crucial question remains to be asked, namely what happens to this process if the labour market is segmented and an identity of interests between the primary (skilled, male) and secondary (unskilled, female) sectors of the labour market can no longer be safely assumed?[26] In this regard, the components of local custom and culture and their validity in the 'new social order' are two key determinants of the fate of tradition.

In 1828, a pamphlet detailing a *Short Account of the Town of Paisley* noted that 'the inhabitants of Paisley are ingenious and among the working classes, there is a degree of intelligence and a taste for literature seldom met with'.[27] Earlier, in his *General Description of the Shire of Renfrew,* George Robertson had commented that

> There is [a] ... very prominent trait in the character of the Paisley weavers, and that is, a pretty general taste for books. If you enter into conversation with them, you will find many of them well-

24 Ibid., p. 25.

25 W. Carlile, 'A short sketch of the improved state of Paisley', *Scots Magazine* (Jul. 1806), pp. 17–18, as quoted in Dickson and Speirs, 'Changes in class structure in Paisley', p. 64.

26 Warde, 'Spatial change, politics and the division of labour', poses this problematic in a theoretical sense, yet posits no general conclusion.

27 As quoted in R. L. Crawford, 'Literary Activity in Paisley in the Early Nineteenth Century' (Glasgow University, B.Litt. thesis, 1965), p. 57.

informed on several subjects, particularly general history, natural history, religion, and, of late, politics.[28]

This love of learning and taste for knowledge are key features of the culture associated with the male weavers. Such men, it is maintained, fostered a tradition of self-education and a social life based on a multitude of improving societies and clubs. The Paisley Trades Library, the Paisley Literary Institution, the Literary and Convivial Association, the Baron Club and the Burns Club all emerged as potent associational groupings in the years when the weaving industry dominated the economy of the town.[29] Alongside this intellectualism, the poetry of Robert Tannahill, Alexander Wilson and William Motherwell further enhances the image of a vibrant cultural heritage developing in these years among the artisan elite.

Clarke and Dickson have shown that in the 1830s these traditions of the weaving community proved useful to Paisley's new employing class. 'Many employers' they maintain, 'saw the fancy weavers as a strategically placed group *vis-à-vis* their concern to maintain work discipline and social acquiescence within the labour force.'[30] Local employers feared that the culture of the weaver, with its strong commitment to education, sobriety, religiosity and respectability, would descend into the mire of intemperance and immorality. Likewise the weavers, threatened by the demands of new economic imperatives after 1841, feared their sublimation into the growing army of factory 'hands'. Tendencies towards class collaboration between the artisan elite and the employer classes thus, according to Clarke and Dickson, strengthened sectional impulses between workers.

Questions, therefore, have to be asked regarding the extent to which the weaving culture penetrated the habits of the new industrial proletariat and in this way remained the property of the workers rather than a tool of the employers. Similarly, the extent to which the fostering of this culture, in the long term, led to permanent division at a grass-roots level must be assessed. An important feature of the Clarke and Dickson argument rests on the case that class barriers in the first decades of the nineteenth century were fluid due to the relative ease of social mobility facilitated by domestic production and low-cost capital investment in industry. Just as many weavers with few capital reserves entered independent business, so many thread employers in the mid-century 'derived from relatively humble social origins'.[31] They also point

28 G. Robertson, *General Description of the Shire of Renfrew* (1818), as quoted in ibid., p. 57.

29 Crawford, 'Literary Activity in Paisley', pp. 66–84.

30 Clarke and Dickson, 'Class consciousness in early industrial capitalism', p. 25. Note also this comment from Patrick Joyce, regarding the 'artisan tradition' in Lancashire: '[the pre-factory link and the artisan tradition] could be powerful sources of integration in the system of authority to which factory production gave rise': Joyce, *Work, Society and Politics*, p. xviii.

31 Clarke and Dickson, 'Class consciousness in early industrial capitalism', p. 29.

to the relative absence of a 'big bourgeoisie' in Paisley as a feature which encouraged the strength of the appeal to both the employers and the weaving classes of a set of 'common interests'.[32]

This concentration on 'common interests' Clarke and Dickson have seen as critical in determining the predominantly reformist nature of radicalism in Paisley in the early nineteenth century. In particular

> these two groups worked together to oppose those interests which they saw as being mainly responsible for Paisley's troubles. These were the inadequate representation of the people in Parliament and the domination of the landed interest, particularly in relation to the Corn Laws. Over such issues as the Reform Bill it was almost a 'natural' alliance of working class leaders and local employers who spearheaded the enormous popular enthusiasm in Paisley for change.[33]

From the activities of the Friends of the People in the 1790s and the creation of the Scottish Conventions through the Reform agitations of the 1830s to the moral-force Chartism of the 1840s, Clarke and Dickson draw a picture of a continuing tradition of employer radicalism which found its echo in the concerns of the skilled working classes.

However, in their formulation, in contrast to the weavers who tended towards co-operation with middle-class moderates, the spinners, with their different experience of 'class conflict' in the exploitative conditions of factory production, are seen to adopt more radical and confrontational forms of protest. Yet such activity, they highlight, was not the sole preserve of the spinners. Clarke and Dickson emphasise that even before the emergence of the thread industry, more 'covert' forms of proletarian action in Paisley were evident. Participating in the activities of the United Scotsmen, many workers – including some weavers – operated independently of the town's employers.[34] In the period of economic crisis following the Napoleonic Wars and the weavers' strike of 1812, leading into the local rioting following the Peterloo massacre and the 'Radical War' of 1820, when 'Paisley's operatives came out solidly in support of the revolutionary general strike for a Scottish Republic', Clarke and Dickson highlight a pattern of local political expression which 'oscillated'

> between demands for reform of the system (which brought together sections of the working class with the 'advanced' Whigs of the local

32 Ibid., p. 31.

33 Dickson and Clarke, 'Social concern and social control in nineteenth-century Scotland', pp. 55–6.

34 See also R. Brown, *The History of Paisley From the Roman Period Down to 1884* (Paisley, 1886), pp. 424–7. Here Brown describes local rioting between 1835 and 1868, associated with Parliamentary elections, weavers' wages and the price of foodstuffs in which various trades were represented.

employers and professions) and more directly oppositional forms of action (which tended to frighten away local manufacturers).[35]

Yet this dichotomy of interests and protagonists was far from a simple or conclusive one. Clarke and Dickson have shown the political culture of the artisan elite to have contained 'contradictory tendencies', encompassing antagonistic demands for radical change, reformist strategies and restrictive inter-class alliances.[36]

In the long term it was these conflicting susceptibilities which, by promoting incompatible interpretations of Paisley's radical tradition, led to the subsequent assimilation of many of its elements in the doctrines of Gladstonian democracy and, later, Edwardian Liberalism; determined its reformulation after 1886 as a feature of popular Unionism; and led after 1920 to its rehabilitation as the exclusive heritage of the local Labour Party.[37] The changing nature of capital accumulation and the increasing capital investment required to compete successfully in the textile industries contributed to this process of cultural reformulation, dictating the ultimate decline of the independent small manufacturer and the clarification of the parameters of 'capital' and 'labour'. In addition, the increased status and number of skilled engineers and the consequent re-location of the prominent craft elites from the workshops to the factory flats and shop floors, re-moulded the dominant work-place culture of the artisan to resemble more closely that of the factory operative. Such changes in industry and in the occupational profile of Paisley did not, in themselves, determine the timing or character of Liberalism's eventual decline, but contributed in large part to the nature of the challenge from the left which would eventually replace the party of Gladstone as the guarantor of the radical tradition.

The manner in which Paisley radicalism survived such mid-century industrial and political changes was substantially determined by the restricted nature and operation of the franchise, the growth of industrial paternalism, the development of the trade-union and Co-operative movements and the growing stability of the local labour market.[38] The inter-relation of these factors contributed to the subsequent 'closure' which was effected in the public political community – the marginalis-

[35] Dickson and Clarke, 'Social concern and social control in nineteenth-century Scotland', p. 56.

[36] Clarke and Dickson, 'Class consciousness in early industrial capitalism', p. 53. See also A. Leitch, 'Radicalism in Paisley, 1830–1848, and its Economic, Political, Cultural Background' (Glasgow University, M.Litt. thesis, 1993).

[37] Richard Ashcraft has recently commented that liberalism was 'an unstable compound of radical and conservative elements': Ashcraft, 'Liberal political theory and working-class radicalism', p. 249.

[38] See J. Saville, 'The ideology of Labourism', in R. Benewick, R. N. Berki and B. Parekh (eds.), *Knowledge and Belief in Politics: The Problem of Ideology* (London, 1973), pp. 213–26.

ation of women, the unskilled and revolutionary radicals.[39] Such closure, however, also had ideological roots. An elite-sponsored Liberalism was elevated to the status of a meta-narrative which determined the political identity of the community, by the absorption of the 'legend of the prosperous handloom weaver' as its own.[40] In electoral terms, this manifested itself in the steady and unbroken Liberal representation of the burgh from 1832 onwards, the development of restrictive party structures, and changes in the 'dynamics of political communication which gradually afforded individuals less and less power in the creation of their own political languages and identities'.[41]

Whilst Liberal MPs were returned for Paisley unopposed on six different occasions between 1832 and 1884, however, they frequently faced challenges from more radical candidates. In 1841, for example, the sitting Liberal member – Archibald Hastie, a London merchant – faced William Thomason, a Chartist from the Vale of Leven. The power of the established Liberal elite proved potent, however, when, after a show of hands at a public meeting indicated Thomason as the 'people's favourite', a subsequent poll demanded by Hastie recorded him the victor with 157 votes. The ideological division between those entitled to vote and those without the franchise was marked.[42] Yet, as the polls of the 1870s and 1880s make clear, even after the extension of the electorate towards the end of the century, the ruling Liberal ethos proved transcendent. As Hutchison has shown, the dominance of the Church question up to 1881 goes some way to explaining this state of affairs, as does the charismatic leadership of Gladstone after that time, but – in local terms – the return of industrial prosperity also played a significant part.[43]

Change and Continuity: Industrial Development: 1850–1914

The eclipse of the shawl industry as a dominant industrial concern of the burgh of Paisley provoked dramatic changes in the character of the local economy. However, though 'the Hungry Forties' ultimately proved a death-blow to the industry, it took a considerable time before it actually succumbed to its fate – in 1860 there were still 71 shawl manufacturers in the town.[44] In 1861, while 746 weavers in Paisley were unemployed, 800 were still working. In 1880, 946 weavers are recorded of whom 107 were unemployed. By 1901, however, the number of weavers had dropped to 90.[45]

39 See Vernon, *Politics and the People*, p. 9.
40 Leitch, 'Radicalism in Paisley', p. 13.
41 Vernon, *Politics and the People*, p. 9. See below, Appendix 4.
42 Leitch, 'Radicalism in Paisley', p. 206.
43 Hutchison, *Political History of Scotland*, pp. 65, 82, 149.
44 M. McCarthy, *A Social Geography of Paisley* (Paisley, 1969), p. 163.
45 Ibid., p. 162.

By the late nineteenth century, Paisley, supporting a relatively small middle class, illustrated in its occupational profile a diverse yet overwhelmingly 'working class' population which may be defined, almost exclusively, as 'industrial'.[46] Yet perhaps more significant than the industrial cast of the occupied population were the types of industry in which these workers were employed. As one would expect, textiles, and most notably the cotton thread industry, was a dominant feature; with the level of its dominance changing over time, in line with international economic imperatives. The Coats combine employed the majority of these workers, their factories in addition demanding the services of other subsidiary concerns and skilled (predominantly male) operatives in trades such as finishing, dyeing and engineering. Primarily, however, textiles were an employer of women and of these, the majority were young and single.[47]

Employee registers for this period, and for the early inter-war years, highlight a significant number of young women leaving the thread mills to be married. Yet as the circumstances of a worker's departure are not always given in these records, and, further, as these records do not specify the conjugal status of the employees, we need to look to census statistics for an impression of the low level of married female employment in the thread mills. When we do, we find that Paisley followed the national pattern whereby in 1911 the census recorded only 4.1% of married women in Scotland as working – a figure around 6% below the English average.[48]

From the figures in Table 1.7 of Appendix 1, we may conclude that textile employers (and here there is no reason to doubt the dominance of the Coats combine in determining this pattern) hired the vast majority of their female labour from an age group in society whose level of marriage was very low. In 1885, the average age of women taken on full time and noted in an employment register of J. & P. Coats was 16.9 years.[49] In 1895, of the 213 female workers noted, the average age was 15.36 years.[50] A general pattern of female employment was thus established in Paisley, almost exclusively centred on the single woman.

Cultural testimony strengthens this impression, implying social conventions operating against the continuation of women in employment upon marriage. In Lennox Kerr's novel, *Woman of Glenshiels*, a work based on Kerr's home town of Paisley, Mary goes back to work in the inter-war period to the meat factory where she had worked before marriage. The 'table' greeted her with suspicion; Kerr recounts:

46 See below, Appendix 1, Table 1.4.
47 See below, Appendix 1, Tables 1.5 and 1.6.
48 E. Gordon, *Women and the Labour Movement in Scotland, 1850–1914* (Oxford, 1991), p. 20.
49 PM, JPC Collection, 1/5/41, 'Register of Female Employees, 1859–1908'.
50 Ibid.

> Why should any married woman leave her home? Single girls worked, and widows worked, but women with husbands and children didn't work. There was an extravagance, a rebellious defiance against established laws in Mary working. She was taking the bread from the mouth of some single girl. If other women could stay at home and manage on their dole why should this woman not submit to her lot?[51]

For the majority of women, therefore, the work-place would not provide a long-term locus for political interaction.

Textiles remained the dominant employer for women throughout the period, consistently 'beating' domestic service by a large majority as the premier employer of women in Paisley (see Appendix 1, Tables 1.5 and 1.8). It was not until the 1920s that textiles in Paisley came to employ less than half of the female population in work. Yet even before this date, the level of diversification in the Paisley economy was marked. Professional occupations and commercial secretarial work challenged the more traditional categories of dress-making and 'food and lodging' as the third largest employer of women in 1911.[52]

For male workers, the image of a diverse industrial base also holds. Although textiles proved the major employer of males until the turn of the twentieth century, the industry never directly employed more than 20% of the working male population. The key feature in the changing occupational profile of Paisley males between 1881 and 1931, was the rise to prominence of the metal work and engineering industries (see Appendix 2, Graph 2.3). The skill bias among Paisley workmen thus moved further and further from the loom sheds to the shop-floors, away from the thread mills and into the ship-yards and the new engineering concerns in Paisley, Renfrew and Clydeside.

In Paisley itself, the engineering firm of Fullerton, Hodgart & Barclay of the Vulcan Foundry and Engineering works on the Renfrew Road was one of the largest concerns, building large-scale engines and hydraulic machinery. The Caledonia Works of A. F. Craig & Co., established in 1868, was another major employer, as were Bow, McLachlan & Co., Marine Engineers of Abbotsinch; James Boyd & Sons, heating engineers; William Christie & Sons of the Underwood Iron Works; the Seedhill Works of Eadie Bros., manufacturing engines and parts for the thread industry; Beardmore's at Underwood; Thomas Reid & Sons of Thread Street; the Albion Works of Walter McGee & Son; Fisher & Co. at the St Mirren Works in McDowall Street; and Thomas White & Sons at Laigh Park. Furthermore, the White Cart river came to support a small yet notable number of ship-building firms – John Fullerton & Co. of Merksworth (est. 1867), manufacturers of steam

51 L. Kerr, *Woman of Glenshiels* (London, 1935), p. 202.
52 See below, Appendix 2.

vessels; Hanna, Donald & Sons at the Abercorn Works, who, alongside trading vessels, specialised in other forms of engineering, including bridges; Fleming & Ferguson, manufacturers of dredgers at the Phoenix Works on the Inchinnan Road; and J. McArthur & Co., manufacturers of light stern and side wheel steamers. Beyond the bounds of the parish, Paisley engineers could be found in Babcock & Wilcox and Lobnitz & Co. in Renfrew, and many, if not most, of the Clydeside ship-yards – commuting to work on the early morning 'workers' trains into Glasgow.[53]

Yet Paisley's economic recovery after the 1840s was dependent on a wider range of industries than the above may imply. Many of the new companies which grew out of the chaos of the mid-century depended not just on the abundant supply of labour available in Paisley in these years, but on the town's natural resources, most notably water. The chemical works and finishing and dyeing industries which grew alongside the Coats empire were key concerns in the diversification of Paisley's economy; William Fulton & Sons of the Glenfield Dyeing and Finishing Works employed nearly 1,000 workers in 1896.[54] Just outside the burgh at Carriagehill, the firm of Brown & Polson emerged after 1840 as a prominent manufacturer of cornflour, their brand-name becoming famous world-wide, as did the 'Glenfield Starch' produced at William Wotherspoon's at Maxwellton.[55] Locally, smaller companies competed with these larger concerns – William MacKean at the St Mirren Works on MacDowall Street, MacKenzie Brothers, Robert Wilson & Co. at the Adelphi Starch Works, and William Caldwell's of Murray Street.[56]

Soap manufacture also became a key industry – the firms of Robin & Houston, the Gleniffer Soap Company at Lonend, and Isdale & McCallum of the Caledonia Soap Works, together with other smaller factories, producing in excess of fifteen million pounds of soap per annum at the close of the nineteenth century.[57] The food industry also spawned some household names, most notably the 'Home Made' Marmalade and meat extracts produced by Alexander Cairns & Sons and their competitors, James Robertson of the Thrushgrove Preserve Works, manufacturer of 'Golden Shred' marmalade.[58] With a tannery, a

[53] Out of 60 engineers joining Branch 7 of the AEU (previous to Aug. 1920, the Society of Amalgamated Toolmakers, est. 1882) in Paisley during the period 14 Oct. 1919–8 Mar. 1921, one Paisley screwer gave Kincaid & Co. of Greenock as his place of employ; a planer and slotter cited the North British Locomotive Company at Springburn. An apprentice fitter from Simons at Renfrew also joined, as did a miller from Melvin & Sons of Glasgow: PAEU Offices, Society of Amalgamated Toolmakers (Paisley) Minute Book, 1919–1920.

[54] *Guide to Paisley and Surrounding Districts with Fifty Photographic Views of Places and Persons of Interest* (Paisley, 1896), p. 91.

[55] PCL, 664.2 Ren–1, Pam PC9252, Misc. File.

[56] Ibid., 664.2 Ren–1, Pam PC7916, Misc. File.

[57] *Guide to Paisley*, p. 93.

[58] Growing out of a small grocer's business, Robertson's emerged as a major concern; in 1891 it opened its first English factory in Manchester. Thereafter another was opened

number of fire-clay works,[59] timber merchants, box makers, rope manufacturers,[60] electrical contractors,[61] distilleries, breweries, mines, carpet manufacturers,[62] bakeries, printing works, and a strong commercial and mercantile core focused on the High Street, Paisley was clearly *not just* a mill town.

Paternalism and the Evolution of the Liberal Hegemony

On the eve of the twentieth century, Paisley had come a long way since the days of the shawl industry. Yet although the town's economy was no longer precariously balanced on the health of just one commercial enterprise, Paisley's diverse industries still had much in common. By the end of the nineteenth century and well into the Edwardian period and beyond, the industrial base of the town was dominated by local family businesses, the owners of which resided locally, were often educated locally and, as well as providing employment, provided Paisley with a distinctive middle class financed by the profits of local industrial manufactures.

Looking first at the soap and starch industries, the dominance of the local family firm is apparent. William MacKean, owner of the St Mirren Starch Works, born near Paisley Cross, was introduced into business by his uncle, the local soap manufacturer, William Sim, with whom he worked initially. MacKean became the provost of the burgh in 1879 and a prominent local political figure. His sons continued in the family business following their father's retiral in 1882 and subsequent death in 1894. One of them, William Muir MacKean, became the president of the Starch Trade Association and a local councillor for the fifth ward, dying in office in June 1913 at his home in Lansdale Road, Paisley.[63]

The MacKeans's main competitors, Brown & Polson, were also a local concern. The initial partners in the firm, established in 1840, were William Brown and his son John (who had both previously been in the muslin business in Glasgow), and John Polson and his younger brother William, both natives of Paisley. Having introduced 'Powder Starch' in 1843, the direction of the firm changed after 1854 when John Polson's son, John Polson (Jr), patented his process of cornflour manufacture from maize. Though moving outwith the burgh to the estate of Castle Levan, John Polson (Jr), later a JP for the counties of Renfrew and Haddington, proved an influential figure locally during his lifetime

in London in 1900, and a further factory in Bristol in 1914. The factory in Paisley remained, though on a much smaller scale than the English concerns, employing around 340 workers (of these 75% were women) in 1954: *PRG*, 16 Jan. 1954.

59 PCL, 738 Ren–1, Pam PC 8519, Doulton & Co. File.

60 PCL, 677 Ren–1, PC 3430, o/s, William Peacock (High Street) File.

61 PCL, PC939, 621.31, o/s, 'The Story of Kilpatrick of Paisley' (Pamphlet).

62 PCL, A. F. Stoddard & Co. of Elderslie File.

63 *PRG*, 6 Oct. 1894; 7 May 1913.

(1825–1900), encouraging the local artistic, poetic and musical life of the burgh, writing his own poetry and contributing towards the restoration of the Abbey. [64] John Brown's son, John Armour Brown, joined the firm in 1861. Though born in Glasgow, he received part of his education in Paisley and lived in the Paisley district at Moredun. A member of Paisley School Board, and a JP for the burgh, Brown was also a director and vice-president of the local Royal Alexandra Infirmary, and conductor of the Tonic Sol-fa Institute and local Choral Union.[65]

In 1868, two employees of the local soap manufacturers Messrs Robin & Houston, Ralph Isdale (head soap boiler) and John M. McCallum (commercial traveller), founded a household soap manufacturing business in the Sneddon district of Paisley – Isdale & McCallum. After 1895 soap-powder became their main concern, marketed as 'Al' powder, alongside their other brand, 'Thistle Soap'. Isdale, born in Leith, entered the employ of William Sim & Co., as had William MacKean, before becoming manager of MacKean's St Mirren Soap Works. Then, following a period as manager at Messrs Jamieson & Sons' soap works, he entered the same position with Robin & Houston. A prominent member of the local United Free Church for over fifty years, Isdale died at his home at Sunnyside, Paisley in 1910, and was followed into the business by his son James and son-in-law Charles Pollock. It was, however, John Mills McCallum who, from a position of local industrial eminence, came to influence, more than his partner, the social life of the Paisley community. Born in Paisley in 1847, the son of John (Sen.), partner in a firm of dyers, and originally from Kintyre, John M. McCallum attended Allan Glen's School in Glasgow to pursue studies in chemistry. Returning to Paisley, he was for many years the president of the Young Men's Christian Association, a member of the Philosophical Society, a director of Paisley Museum and Art Gallery, a director of the Poor Association, and later a town councillor (1899), magistrate (1900), Justice of the Peace and MP for the Burgh (1906–20); he received a knighthood in 1912. McCallum resided in Paisley throughout his commercial and political life, moving from his residence in Garthland Street to Carriagehill and then to Castlehead.[66]

This pattern of local family business evidenced in the examples above is readily duplicated when attention is turned to other Paisley firms at this time. One could continue. However, before considering Paisley's

64 Note that John Polson (Jr) was married in 1859 to Mary Barclay Shanks (1832–1911), daughter of Thomas Shanks, first provost of Johnston and owner of a major local sanitary ware business. Also, Polson's daughter, Alice Mary married Mr Cameron Corbett, MP for the Tradeston Division of Glasgow (later Baron Rowallan) in 1887.

65 W. S. Murray, *Captains of Industry* (Glasgow, 1901), pp. 203–8; for further details on Brown and Polson, see PCL, 664 Ren–1, PC 62, o/s, Brown and Polson File; Ernest Gaskell, *Renfrewshire and Ayrshire Leaders* (published for private circulation, *c.*1908); and PCL, Paisley Pamphlets Collection, vol. 73/371, vol. 71/970.)

66 Ibid., pp. 251–6.

ultimate exemplars of the local family firm – J. & P. Coats and J. & J. Clark – it is essential to explore the character of authority perpetuated within such concerns in Paisley which at root coloured the political vision of the community – paternalism.

The dynamics involved in social organisations based on 'paternalism' and 'deference' have had a long academic history, both in sociology and, though more recently, in the historiography of our period.[67] Recent debate has succeeded in problematising paternalism as a simple explanation for certain forms of apparently deferential behaviour, whether in the voting booth or on the shop floor. Deference, in the work of Newby, has been re-cast as a 'form of social *interaction*' involving the exercise of traditional authority, encompassing both 'types' of behaviour and 'a set of beliefs about the nature of society'.[68] Stability, Newby has stressed, is the keynote of the deferential relationship, and thus paternalism is a functional tool, facilitating this essential constancy through its resolution of the inherent tensions in the relationship which simultaneously calls for identification with and differentiation from the source of power.

Morris and Smyth have suggested that paternalism was suited 'to large scale industry, dominated by family owned businesses, exposed to fluctuations in demand and using large amounts of low paid labour'.[69] The Coats's and Clarks's thread mills in Paisley fall neatly into this formulation, yet the importance of paternalism as a *locally* based form of authority is missing from this model.[70] Norris has highlighted the interactive and mutually sustaining association between localism and paternalism. He writes:

> Historically the power of the ideology of localism lay in its emphasis on the way in which the potentially separate interests of the dominant and subservient groups are unified by their subordin-

[67] E.g., H. Newby, 'The deferential dialectic', *CSSH*, xvii (1975), pp. 139–64; H. Newby, 'Paternalism and capitalism', in R. Scase (ed.) *Industrial Society: Class, Cleavage and Control* (1977), pp. 59–73; also G. M. Norris, 'Industrial paternalist capitalism and local labour markets', *Sociology*, xii (1978), pp. 469–89. For a recent debate on deference and paternalism, based especially on the work of Joyce in *Work, Society and Politics*, see M. Huberman, 'The economic origins of paternalism: Lancashire cotton spinning in the first half of the nineteenth century', *SH*, xii (1987), pp. 99–109, the response from M. Rose, P. Taylor and M. Winstanley, 'The economic origins of paternalism: some objections', *SH*, xiv (1989), pp. 89–99, and the subsequent response from Huberman: 'The economic origins of paternalism: reply to Rose, Taylor and Winstanley' in the same volume (pp. 99–103). Also fascinating for the 20th-century perspective in Scotland is Morris and Smyth's 'Working Paper', *Paternalism as an Employer Strategy*, which focuses on the industries of Kirkcaldy.

[68] Newby, 'Deferential dialectic', pp. 142–3.

[69] Morris and Smyth, *Paternalism as an Employer Strategy*, p. 9. Successive Parliamentary reports highlighted that Scottish textile operatives were consistently paid at a lower rate than their English counterparts during the period under review: *PP*, 1909, LXXX, Cd. 4545.

[70] Norris, 'Industrial paternalist capitalism', p. 473.

> ation to a common interest in the welfare of a particular area. This ideology was sustained by the existence of some degree of personal interaction between subordinate groups and a personally identifiable traditional elite.[71]

The perpetuation of a local middle class, residing within the area of industrial production, located paternalism as a feature of community identity in Paisley in the late nineteenth century. In this way paternalism became *part of* the process through which local identity was translated into the wider realm of politics, colouring the outlook of voters and determining a certain character of local industrial relations.

However, hindsight highlights the inherent danger in this symbiotic relationship in an age of emerging *national* concerns, *national* culture and *class* rather than *local* politics. As Norris makes clear:

> The survival of paternalism in a particular area rests ... on the ability of the elite to maintain this historically local tradition against the claims of democratic capitalism which specifically deny the relevance of local ties by emphasising universalistic criteria of resource allocation and the determination of priorities by a central government body.[72]

The future of Liberalism and the character of paternalistic management were thus connected, though by no means did the latter create or determine the fate of the former. Both were made meaningful only in relation to *local interests* – phenomena which, by the early twentieth century, could no longer be relied upon to coincide with those of the middle-class elite.

As the principal exemplars of paternalism in Paisley, the political consequences of the strategies of the Coats combine and the Coats and Clark families illustrate key factors which contributed to the decline of Liberalism in the constituency. Cairncross and Hunter referred to J. & P. Coats as 'above all a typical family concern with an abundance of thrifty brothers and sons', yet one which by the end of the nineteenth century 'had become the largest manufacturing enterprise in the United Kingdom ... [with] associated or subsidiary companies in several countries, besides selling depots or agencies in many more'.[73] The histories of J. & P. Coats and its competitors (later partners), J. & J. Clark & Co., are full of paradoxes.

James Coats, born in Paisley in 1774, the son of a weaver, was the first of the family to embark in the thread industry. A weaver to trade, his main concern initially was in the manufacture of Canton crepe shawls, before turning his attention to thread in the early 1820s, as a sleeping

71 Ibid., p. 473.
72 Ibid.
73 A. K. Cairncross and J. B. K. Hunter, 'The early growth of Messrs J. & P. Coats, 1830–83', *Business History*, xxix (1987), p. 157.

partner in the firm of Messrs Ross & Duncan, twiners. In 1826, however, he established his own independent thread concern, building a small mill at Ferguslie. Retiring in 1830, he left his thread business to his sons, James (1803–45) and Peter (1808–90), the business shortly after becoming known as J. & P. Coats.[74]

Eighteen years earlier, however, the brothers James (1783–1865) and John Clark (1791–1864), following in their father's footsteps, had opened a small factory in Seedhill, using the name J. &. J. Clark.[75] Among the first to sell their thread on wooden spools rather than in hanks, the company prospered, soon moving into the national market and then abroad. In 1853, on their retiral, having taken into partnership Kerr of Underwood, the brothers left the business in the hands of the next generation in the person of James Clark of Ralston (1821–81), John's son, who had entered the mill as an accountant as a young boy. Thereafter, James's brothers, John (1827–94) and Stewart (1830–1907), entered the family business. J. & J. Clark continued to expand under their control, with mills in New Jersey. Another brother, George A. Clark (1823–73), having gained a great deal of experience in Canada in the employ of Kerr & Company, returned to Paisley in the 1840s to manufacture shawls – a venture which he soon abandoned, setting up the Linside Mill in 1851 with his brother-in-law, Peter Kerr, a manufacturer of heddle twine, under the name Kerr & Clark. In 1866 the two branches of the 'family' concern were united as Clark & Co. The amalgamation of various family interests proceeded apace in the latter decades of the nineteenth century, drawing in Kerr & Co. of Underwood, the Mile End Mill of John Clark (Jr) and the business of J. & R. Clark at the new Burnside Mill, established by the sons of James Clark, who had died in 1865. By 1880, the capital concerns of Clark & Co. were estimated at over £320,000, Paisley's Atlantic Mill having been built in 1872 and the town's Pacific Twisting Mill in 1875. Together, as the Anchor Mills, by 1880 the Paisley concern was running over 230,000 spindles and employing over 3,500 male and female workers.[76]

At Ferguslie, the Coats's enterprise followed a similar pattern of expansion to that of the Clarks. The founders' brother Andrew, a lawyer, had been sent to the States in the 1840s to develop sales there and the first American mill was built in the 1870s at Pawtucket, Rhode Island. In 1890, Coats, Clarks and the firm of Jonas Brook of Huddersfield established the Central Agency to facilitate co-operation in the overseas markets into which they were expanding. That same year J. & P. Coats became a limited liability company, declaring capital of

74 PCL, 366 Ren–1; 600 Ren–1; 941.41 Ren B/COA, Coats Files (Secondary Sources).

75 Their father, James (b. 1747) and uncle Patrick, had both been involved in the production of silk twine used in the manufacture of loom 'heddles', working from a small house at 10 Cotton Street. They diversified their production after silk supplies were interrupted by Napoleon's Berlin Decree of 1806 by using cotton.

76 PCL, 941.41 Ren; 677 Ren–1; Coats Files (Secondary Sources).

£5.75 million. Clark & Co. followed suit in 1896, and in that same year amalgamated with J. & P. Coats, Jonas Brook & Brothers Ltd. of Meltham, Huddersfield and James Chadwick & Brother of Eagley, Bolton under the name J. & P. Coats Ltd. 'Such is the result', wrote Andrew Coats, 'of an enterprise inaugurated by a humble weaver who first saw the light in a humble cottage.'[77]

The survival of industrial paternalist capitalism well into the twentieth century in a company with such international concerns and operating through such large industrial units, seems on a first impression somewhat bewildering. Studies by prominent sociologists have alerted us to the potential inverse relationship between plant size and worker attachment or commitment to a company. Yet, more recent studies have called into question the structural consequences of increased plant size on the mode of control, calling for the implied effects of plant size to be related to the range of influence of the employer in key areas outwith the workplace.[78] When viewed in this manner, we return to the need for stability in the perpetuation of the deferential dialectic and are forced to deconstruct the tool of paternalism into its component factors. After all, deference and status are the *consequences* of an existing relation of dominance, the origins of which must be sought elsewhere.[79]

With this in mind, Norris's five implied 'essential characteristics of industrial paternalist capitalism' will be employed to locate the processes through which the Coats and Clarks exercised social control in Paisley in the late nineteenth century. These are:

> (1) the existence of a personally identifiable ownership class with a shared background and ideology, (2) the occupation of positions of political power by the members of this same class, (3) a significant level of involvement of the local economic elites in directly alleviating the deprivations visited upon the subordinate groups through the operation of market forces ... (4) the underpinning of this structure of relationships by an ideology which emphasizes local ties ... [and] fifthly [the existence] of a deferential workforce.[80]

This model clarifies the manner in which power in the workplace translated into the political arena as a potent tool in the perpetuation of the local Liberal hegemony. In subsequent chapters, it will become apparent that, likewise, the interrelation of these two factors and the decline of both in the twentieth century acted as important influences on the timing of Labour's rise to prominence within the Paisley electorate.

By the 1880s, Paisley's middle and upper classes had established their residences outwith the centre of the burgh. In the 1840s Thomas Coats

77 PCL, 366 Ren–1; 'J. & P. Coats – History', p. 21.
78 Newby, 'Paternalism and capitalism', pp. 62–3.
79 Newby, 'Deferential dialectic', p. 148.
80 Norris, 'Industrial paternalist capitalism', p. 474.

acquired the site for Ferguslie House, to the west of the town, Peter Coats built Woodside House and in 1873 Stewart Clark moved into his new mansion of Kilnside House. To the south, a villa suburb had emerged in the area of Castlehead between the 1860s and 1880s, and in the east, the elegant homes of Garthland Street drew the 'middling ranks' and managerial classes away from the old weavers' wynds.

Though no longer residentially close to their workers, however, the Coats and Clark families remained a personally recognisable power grouping in Paisley, their residential segregation possibly working to their advantage by emphasising their differentiation from their employees and the smaller employers of the burgh. Through the use of workers' soirées, works' excursions and the metaphors and ceremonies associated with family ownership, however, the tensions inherent in the hegemonic relationship – between identification and differentiation – were controlled.

In 1887, the eighth annual soirée of the half-time workers at Coats's Ferguslie Mills was described in the *Paisley Daily Express*. The columnist commented:

> It says much for the firm to take such a deep interest in promoting the happiness of their little half time workers, and shows they are possessed of charming humanity in stepping down from the lofty pinnacle of commercial eminence to mingle with, and participate once a year in the simple pleasures of the youngest and perhaps the fairest of their most numerous and fair toilers.[81]

From the moment even the youngest of the operatives entered the mill, the presence and person of the owners was unmistakable. The tendency in large manufacturing units towards the formation of work-place sub-cultures, 'promoting interaction among fellow workers, while removing the opportunities for interaction between employer and employee', was thus impeded.[82]

It would appear, however, that divisions within the work-force necessitated by the mode of production, and determined by the sexual composition of the employees, were also exploited by Coats. In this manner, they attempted to influence the parameters within which potential sub-cultures could be formed in a manner most suitable to their own interests. Separate soirées were frequently held for foremen, the unskilled workers, the engineers, workers grouped by their geographical location in the factory, the dyeing and finishing flats and so on. On 17 February 1888, for example, the annual supper for the male workers of the spooling department was held at the Globe Hotel, at which Alexander Lyle, a long-standing employee of the company, addressed those present. He encouraged his fellow workers:

81 *PDE*, 17 Mar. 1887.
82 Newby, 'Paternalism and capitalism', p. 61.

> [always to go] with ready hands, cheerful face and contented spirit to any job we may get. When the bugle sounds, the good soldier asks no questions, but shoulders his knapsack, fills his canteen, and listens for command of 'March'. Do not get the idea that your interests and those of your employer are antagonistic – their success will be your honour.[83]

The rhetoric of 'service', the imagery of the loyal soldier and the legitimation of traditional authority in the person of the employer show the paternalist ideology in action. Two years later, at the fourth annual supper of the male workers of the finishing department, Alex Lyle recapitulated his message in similar terms:

> Whether it is on the tennis ground, bowling green, cricket or football field, or at a social gathering you will find the firm of J. & P. Coats keeping in touch with their employees ... Are not our interests and the interests of our employers bound up together? We rise and fall with one another.[84]

The association of interests and the differentiation evidenced in respect for the status of the Coats family as employers are combined and are shown to have an impact beyond the factory gates, into even the leisure pursuits of the workers. Similar speeches were delivered at numerous soirées, suppers, smoking concerts, dances, balls and charity events attended by the workers of the Coats combine throughout our period. Frequently the presence of the employers was supplemented by that of other local notables, and particularly the clergy. The Rev. Dr Flett, on the platform party with Colonel Thomas Glen Coats at a soirée for the workers of the north side departments of the Ferguslie works in 1886, cautioned:

> The consequences of a firm having careless workers is that the goods manufactured are not in demand, and that means that employment becomes scarce, hands require to be paid off, and they all knew what that meant.[85]

Raising the ghost of the 1840s, such platform orations were instrumental in directly associating the person of the employer with the prosperity of the locality – the personification of a recognisable set of shared *local* interests. Community, as Joyce has made clear, did not in itself *make* deference, yet deference is 'inexplicable without a sense of its imbrication in community'.[86]

83 *PDE*, 21 Feb. 1888.
84 Ibid., 17 Feb. 1890.
85 Ibid., 18 Dec. 1886.
86 Joyce, *Work, Society and Politics*, pp. xxi–xxii; also note: 'the integration of the factory workforce in an industrial system characterised by factory paternalism and deference took place in community terms': ibid., p. 111.

That such occasions were duplicated in the experiences of other Paisley firms is easily proved. At the Glenfield workers' soirée at the Town Hall in February 1887, the audience listened to an oration which concluded that 'for the present at all events, the fruits of labour are about as equally distributed among all classes in this country as would be possible under any system whatever', and later that same year the workers of Whitehill & Sons were addressed by Councillor David Wilson – an employee of the firm – who encouraged them to:

> be always courteous, civil and obliging. Do unto others as you would wish others to do unto you. Never do a mean thing; always be straightforward in all your dealings. Ever strive to do justly, to love mercy, to walk humbly, and should it not be your good fortune to reach worldly success, you will at least have that inward satisfaction, that comfort and happiness, that worldly honours or wealth cannot purchase.[87]

Echoes of biblical teachings, couthy good sense, and a stress on good works were framed in a structure of status relationships modelled within the work-place yet through which a shared ideology of thrift, respectability, moral integrity, temperance and conscientiousness was developed which attempted to draw together the potentially antagonistic exponents of 'capital' and 'labour' and justify evident inequalities in the distribution of the profits of industry.

Such an ideology was reinforced in a positive and substantive manner by what Newby has termed 'the gift'.[88] This took many forms, one of the most important, in a symbolic sense, being the annual works excursion. Although Coats's and Clarks' workers contributed towards this event, it was heavily subsidised by the companies themselves, female workers in the immediate pre war years contributing less than 10d. for the Coats's 'Young Workers' excursion, and the company paying around 3/6d. per head towards the costs.[89] The day contained many elements of ritual – the walk from the mill gates to the railway station behind the works brass band, the prayers of thanksgiving before the picnic lunch, the sports activities and presentation of prizes. In 1889, the Ferguslie workers visited Girvan, leaving in three trains from Paisley. Arriving in Girvan, the gathering of around 4,000 workers was led behind a flute band to a field south of the pier where 'a flag was conspicuously unfurled, bearing the familiar name of J. & P. Coats'.[90] Such a 'ritual' procession from Paisley was repeated every year until the war of 1914–18 – each year a new location, but the same customary events.

87 *PDE*, 19 Feb. 1887; 9 Dec. 1887.
88 Newby, 'Deferential dialectic', p. 161.
89 PM, JPC Collection, 1/5/72, 'Notes on Welfare of Workers' (1920), p. 5.
90 *PDE*, 1 Jul. 1889.

Several other companies and institutions in Paisley held similar annual excursions. Though not on the same scale as those of the Coats combine, they clearly fostered a general local tradition whereby the excursion as 'gift' became absorbed as a local 'institution'.[91] Significant in this sense, was the day usually chosen for these annual events – 'Sma' Shot Saturday' – the first Saturday in July.[92]

The historical origins of this local holiday, established in 1856, are rooted in a dispute in the weaving industry. The 'shot' or binding thread was an essential feature of a length of fabric, ensuring its durability when being worked on the loom and was paid for by the weaver himself, the cost estimated at around one day's work. When, in 1856, the weavers demanded that the cost of the shot should be covered by their employers (threatening to strike on 1 July if their demands were not met), the employers relented, and the first Saturday of July emerged as a local holiday in commemoration of their 'moral as well as material triumph'.[93]

By the late nineteenth century, this commemoration of protest had been transformed into a day of ritualised frivolity and a feature of a distinctly different philosophy to that which had spurred the weavers on to their industrial victory. 'Sma' Shot Day' was now part of a wider employer-fostered hegemonic creed whereby its celebration was a key exemplar of the 'gift' relationship which underpinned a wider paternalistic code.

Such stage-managed ritual, furthermore, proved a highly compatible supplement to the images of family ownership which Coats and Clarks attempted to foster, lending apt reinforcement to frequent celebrations of various rites of passage of many family members.[94] Morris and Smyth have found that in the context of paternalism, 'the family' was important as 'a set of metaphors and authority structures for both community and workplace relationships', encouraging at once co-operation with and respect towards a recognisable (male-dominated) hierarchy. At times the apparent patriarchal concern of the employer was explicit, as when Thomas Glen Coats encouraged the female workers of Ferguslie not to have 'anything to say to a young man till he can prove he is in a position to keep a wife – (Applause.) – and unless you know his character to be all

91 Note the statement: 'The gift celebrated and reaffirmed the bond of master and man': Joyce, *Work, Society and Politics*, p. 169.

92 On Sma' Shot Day 1889, the Provident Co-operative Society sent 2,300 of its workers and members to Largs; the Equitable Co-operative Society sent 1,200 to Ardrossan; Oakshaw Free Church took 300 of its members to Howwood; 700 members of the Free South Sunday School went to Miliken Park; 250 workers from the Nethercommon Carpet factory went to Millport; 700 from the Wallneuk Mission; the Christopher North Branch of the Good Templars sent 150 of its number to Inverkip; and Fairlie proved the destination of 65 workers from the firm of Smith Brothers: *PDE*, 6 Jul. 1889.

93 *PDE*, 7 Jul. 1906.

94 A similar phenomenon is highlighted by Joyce, 'Factory politics of Lancashire', p. 545.

that it should be; and, lastly, ask your mother's advice before you say "Yes".'[95] Yet the importance of the family metaphor as a functional and motivating dynamic in paternalism is most clearly appreciated in the celebrations of the births, marriages and deaths within the Coats family circle.

On 28 April 1886, Stewart Clark's daughter Annie married Mr Bryce Allan of the Allan Line Steamer Company. In honour of the marriage, several vessels of the Allan Line docked at Glasgow and Greenock were decked with flags, and in Paisley:

> the Anchor Thread Mills were profusely decorated with bunting & c., The clock-tower and upper portion of the buildings of the George A. Clark Town Hall were also gaily festooned with flags. Between two and three o'clock, while the marriage ceremony was being performed, the bells of the Clark Town Hall played merrily. A grand triumphal arch of evergreens crowned the entrance gate at Seedhills to the Kilnside demesne. Large crowds assembled at the gates, and when about three o'clock the happy pair, united in the bonds of wedlock, drove away on their honeymoon, they were greeted with enthusiastic cheers.[96]

Three years later, Miss Jeanie Coats, the youngest daughter of Thomas Coats, was married to Mr George Barclay of the local engineering firm, Messrs Fullerton, Hodgart & Barclay, at Ferguslie House. The guests at the wedding included the

> principal members of the leading *families* of Paisley and District ... The works of both the firms were decorated with flags, and during the day cannons were fired at short intervals from the works of Messrs Fullerton, Hodgart & Barclay.[97]

In 1890, news of the death of Sir Peter Coats was greeted in Paisley by solemn scenes of public mourning. Following the funeral, which took place at the family home at Woodside, the course of the procession through the streets of the town was 'thickly lined with spectators, and from the windows of most of the houses the mournful procession was viewed by groups of people'.[98]

Thirty two years later, in 1922, such scenes were repeated at the funeral of Sir Thomas Glen Coats. 'All functions of any consequence in the town were postponed, business premises were closed, and the traffic of the main thoroughfare discontinued for the time.'[99] The funeral procession passed through streets 'densely crowded with townspeople in

95 *PDE*, 8 Feb. 1890: Colonel Thomas Glen Coats addressing a soiree for Ferguslie thread workers on the 7th February 1890.
96 *PRG*, 1 May 1886.
97 Ibid., 19 Jan. 1889 [my italics].
98 *PDE*, 22 Mar. 1890.
99 *PRG*, 22 Jul. 1922.

respectful silence ... a living mass of rich and poor, old and young ... a high tribute in itself, for they all claimed him as a friend'.[100] On the Sunday following the funeral, a queue system had to be employed to cope with the numbers wishing to visit Sir Thomas's grave.

The sheer numbers and spectacle involved in each of these events highlight the potent power of ceremony, and its associated links with family as important factors in the translation of paternalist ideologies into living experiences and elements of local identity.

The rhetoric of many Paisley employers in the late nineteenth century evidenced a pride in their success as 'self-made men', who had worked their way up to positions of authority and respectability in the town. In the Paisley which Lennox Kerr fictionalises as 'Glenshiels', the factory owner Sam Mcfarlane is admired 'because he had risen from a grocer's message boy to one of the most successful men in the town.'[101] 'All the women admired their employer ... because he worked harder than even they worked. He was in the factory from five in the morning until ten at night. No task was too menial for him.'[102] Reflecting on the early years of his family's business, Peter Eadie described his initial venture into manufactures in Galashiels in the family home – a room measuring fifteen feet by twelve.[103] The Coats themselves similarly drew strength from an image of an 'Empire' which had emerged from 'a room and kitchen in Paisley'.[104] Casting themselves, therefore, as a meritocracy, the shared (and often mythologised) working-class background of the Paisley middle class formed a part of a wider ideology of respectability and hard work and was a key characteristic in the processes by means of which their position in society and politics was legitimated.

At a Liberal Party meeting in 1886, Provost Robert Cochran, a prominent activist of Paisley's Chartist past, rose to voice his concern and bitterness regarding 'a class in Paisley known as the "upper ten" [who] ... thought they had only to put their foot down and they were obeyed'.[105] From a survey of the occupations of members of Town Councils, School Boards, and political associations in the 1890s, it is clear that local political power in Paisley rested in the hands of a very small, and relatively privileged elite of local employers, fulfilling Norris's second imperative of elite occupation of positions of political power.[106]

Three critical features are apparent when one considers the occupational profile of Paisley's political elite. First and foremost, the

100 Ibid., 22 Jul. 1922.
101 Kerr, *Woman of Glenshiels*, p. 25.
102 Ibid., p. 30.
103 *Eadie Brothers, 1871–1971* (Glasgow, 1971), p. 20.
104 A. Sinclair, *Sewing it Up: Coats Patons Multinational Practices* (Scottish Education and Action for Development, Edinburgh, 1982), p. 3.
105 *PDE*, 9 Sep. 1886.
106 See C. M. M. Macdonald, 'The Radical Thread: Political Change in Scotland: Paisley Politics, 1885–1924' (Strathclyde University, Ph.D. thesis, 1996), Appendix 4.

narrow range of occupations represented, dominated by small merchants, manufacturers and the business and legal professions, is obvious. The fluid class barriers which Clarke, Dickson and Speirs observed in the early nineteenth century had by the 1890s apparently hardened, at least in so far as they encouraged a co-operative inter-class political establishment. Only rarely does the skilled man appear on the committees of local government and the local branches of the established political parties. The mercantile and manufacturing interest is predominant. Secondly, emphasising the permanency of this hierarchy, the stability of the elite is shown in the slow and sluggish manner in which 'new blood' enters its ranks. Using 1890–1 as a base year, only three new members had entered the committee of the Liberal Unionist Association by 1895–6. Moreover, when new figures do enter the ranks, it is clear that they are of the same social class as their predecessors. The elite shows, in this manner, a critical ability to re-create itself, thus ensuring the stability essential to the perpetuation of its hegemonic influence.

Finally, and perhaps most interestingly – given our overall focus on political change over time – is the apparent reluctance of the larger manufacturers to become involved in local government after 1890. Exceptions to this 'rule' are found in the presence of the starch manufacturers on the School Board, and, as we shall see, John M. McCallum, the soap manufacturer, on the Town Council. Yet the consequence of this recession into the political associations (and increasingly the *honorary* duties and titles of the local associations) with hindsight had, perhaps, crucial implications for the survival of the Liberal hegemony in Paisley – local government being the first target of the emergent Labour forces. However, for the moment, it is sufficient that we acknowledge the early signs of this drift from local government in the late nineteenth-century context of a still strong and, for the large part, stable local political elite.

In 1949, C. Stewart Black in his *Story of Paisley*, reflected that the Coats and Clarks had been 'Paisley's most generous benefactors ... [having given] lavishly to the town' and treating their workers with 'patriarchal care and kindliness'.[107] This combination of municipal philanthropy with industrial welfare was by no means unique to the Coats combine. Dunn Square, opposite the town hall, and the Brough Educational Institute emphasise that other 'names' contributed to the evolution of Paisley's civic identity. Likewise a brief glimpse at the company ledgers and committee minute books of other Paisley companies highlights that, in a less public manner, the 'secondary' members of Paisley's elite also showed consideration for the interests and concerns of the Paisley populace, and, importantly, their own

107 C. S. Black, *The Story of Paisley* (Paisley, 1949), p. 137.

workers. In 1898, for example, William Fulton & Sons recorded contributions to the Paisley Poor Association and the local Eye Infirmary; in 1910, Fullerton, Hodgart & Barclay were still making an annual subscription to the Paisley Total Abstinence Society; and in 1919 both these companies, along with A. F. Craig & Co. and other engineering concerns in the town, contributed to a Boys' Welfare Scheme.[108] Such represent only a small fragment of the total local input of the other employers in Paisley who, during these years, can be found on the Boards of Poor Associations, the Breakfast Mission, Missionary Societies and a host of philanthropic concerns. Yet, the contributions of the Coats and Clark families tower above them all both in their scale and diversity.

Within the factory walls, paternalist strategies were notable in both the financial and cultural provision which the thread companies made for their workers. From an early stage in the company's development, pensions were frequently 'granted' to long-time 'servants' of the company as the table in Appendix 3 illustrates. Additions were consistently being made to the list of pensioners: the company's commitment to the old employee evident until his/her death, when Coats were frequently called upon to pay funeral expenses. Other one-off payments and supplements also pepper the company records; the following is merely a selection of a much larger collection of cases:

> A letter was read from Mr Murray as to the case of Margaret Brown who had been a worker for 14 years and was now suffering from consumption. On consideration it was agreed to ask Mr Murray to allow her from the funds of the Company 5/- per week and such assistance as he thought necessary.
>
> It was agreed to supplement the 2/6 a week agreed to be paid by the Parochial Board to Cath Shordin (?), a worker of 12 or 13 years standing to enable her to get into the Paisley Incurable Home.
>
> ... it was agreed to put Widow Townshend, the mother of Robina Townshend (who was killed at No. 9 Yarn Store on 17th September) on pension list at 6/- per week and to give donation of £25 to the father and mother of Mary Crawford who was killed at cylinder of frame in No. 8 Mill on 8th September.
>
> ... [£100 is to be set by] to be applied by the Superintendent of the Poor Association in assisting workers recommended by the Directors who are in ill health but who have not been sufficiently long in the service to warrant their being put on the pension list or otherwise helped by the Company.[109]

108 UGABRC, Fullerton, Hodgart & Barclay Collection, UGD 120/1/1/4, Minute Book 1908–1910, 13 Sep. 1910; A. F. Craig & Co. Collection, UGD 173/1/1, Minute Book 1895–1921, 10 Oct. 1919 (p. 402); William Fulton & Sons Collection, UGD 273/1/1, Minute Book 1896–1902, 17 Oct. 1898.

109 UGABRC, JPC Collection, UGD 199/1/1/1, Minute Book 1884–1890; UGD 199/1/1/2 Minute Book 1890–1902, 7 Feb. 1887, 2 Apr. 1888, 29 Sep. 1891, 25 May 1896.

Although after 1908 Coats decided to reduce the pensions paid to old workers by the amount they would be entitled to claim from the government, by this time they had already introduced a company pension scheme for the salaried employees on their books. Furthermore, in 1920 they established the Women Thread Workers Benefit Fund – a pension scheme which guaranteed members 30/- per week when they were 56 and 40/- per week at 60 years.[110] Even after 1908, Clark & Co. were still paying out a considerable amount through their 'Workers' Assistance Scheme'.[111]

When one then adds to their 'Scheme' contributions, their pensions expenditure, averaging around £3,000 per annum in the pre- and immediate post-war years, the personal charity donations of the thread families as private individuals and the companies' contributions to charities and other donations considered below, it is clear that the Liberal governments' welfare reforms in the Edwardian period did not kill the paternalistic impulse of Paisley's thread industry.[112] Added to these figures the ledgers show constant annual payments throughout the period 1897–1928 made for the upkeep of the Anchor recreation ground, evening classes, workers' excursions, compensation payments and bonuses. Taken altogether, these payments represent a considerable commitment to workers' welfare in an era of supposed growing alienation between employer and employed.

More material needs and interests were, furthermore, far from ignored – educational and health provision and leisure pursuits for workers being financed and instituted by both the local thread companies from their early beginnings. Although, after the 1890s, both companies apparently stopped building houses for their employees – the Maxwellton and Meikleriggs developments being the key projects of earlier years – their other contributions to the welfare of their employees were profound.[113]

In 1887 J. & P. Coats's 'show-case' Half Timers' School was officially opened by Peter Coats Jr, chairman of the company's school committee,

110 UGABRC, JPC Collection, UGD 199/1/1/3, Minute Book 1903–1918, 29 Oct. 1908 (pp. 143–4); UGD 199/1/2/1 (Letter Book), 'J. & P. Coats Pension Scheme'.

111 See below, Appendix 3, Table 3.2.

112 See below, Appendix 3, Table 3.3.

113 In 1887, the Minute Books of J. & P. Coats record plans being made for a house-building programme on Corsebar Road, the developments to be entitled 'Thistle Terrace' and 'Thistle Street' and let to sub-managers and workmen. Buildings were to be of two classes, estimated cost per unit being £308.3.2 and £195.17.2, to be let at a weekly rate of 7/6 and 5/- respectively. This is the last recorded company housing development I have been able to locate in the Coats records: UGABRC, JPC Collection, UGD 199/1/1/1 Minute Book 1884–1890. Knox has highlighted Coats's increased ownership of domestic properties over the period from 1871 to 1891, which were rented predominantly to supervisory and managerial staff as a reward for 'loyal service', but emphasises that 'ownership of domestic property was never large enough for the threadocracy to use it as the main thrust of a paternalist policy': W. W. Knox, *Hanging by a Thread: The Scottish Cotton Industry, c.1850–1914* (Preston, 1995), p. 127.

and operated as the company's concern until 1904 when it was taken over by the Paisley Education Board. As chairman of the School Board, Thomas Coats had earlier donated £4,000 for the building of four new schools in the burgh, and Coats's commitment to local education was further shown in 1885 in their donation of the George Street site and £3,000 to assist in the establishment of a local technical college. Eleven years later, moreover, as a consequence of a £5,000 bequest from John Clark, a new dining room, gym and swimming bath was built for the industrial school on Albion Street.

Within the works themselves, both the Coats and Clarks encouraged attendance at company-sponsored evening classes. The classes ranged from dance and sports to domestic sciences, health lectures and millinery, apart from the more usual academic disciplines. The Girls' Club, based in the Girls' Home (est. 1901) on the north side of Coats's Ferguslie Works provided the focus for many of these events in the early twentieth century.[114]

From the early 1880s, ambulance and first aid instruction was given to all J. & P. Coats's male employees and around 1885 their first ambulance service began. The following year, James Coats Jr presented the town with a 'thoroughly modern ambulance carriage'. Apart from contributions to local hospitals, inside the works health education and welfare were key priorities of management. In 1911, the No. 24 Voluntary Aid Detachment of the Red Cross was established in the Anchor Mills and the Ferguslie Mills followed this lead during the war years. In 1911, Coats established a Fresh Air Home at Peesweep in Renfrewshire for female workers suffering from TB; in 1921 new medical facilities were constructed at both Anchor and Ferguslie sites, replacing older out of date equipment; and that same year 'Lady Visitors' were hired to visit sick employees and pensioners. In 1924 a full-time dentist was appointed for Anchor and Ferguslie employees, although it was not until 1952 that the mills' first full-time Medical Officer was appointed. Specific 'Welfare Departments' were established after the 1914–18 war, though concern for employees' general welfare was clearly evident in earlier years in the setting up of canteen facilities as far back as the 1880s and hot baths, constructed by 1914, for male and female employees at Mid and East Lane respectively.

Yet though such provision, as an element of the paternalistic 'gift relationship', was clearly important in the fostering of employee dependence and deference, it is in the leisure clubs and activities that we see most clearly the active absorption by the Coats's and Clarks' workers of a 'factory-centred' group identity. By providing facilities which encouraged the geographic and conceptual separation of work and leisure – a development already established in the early decades of

114 See below, Appendix 3, Table 3.4, following survey emerging from PCL, 366 Ren–1.

the nineteenth century with the move away from domestic production – employers revalued leisure, and in doing so defined it's 'other'. Work was 'redeemed' and 'moralized'.[115]

Ferguslie Football Club was established in the 1880s and the Anchor Club was set up just over twenty years later. Only employees of the firms could play for the teams, and tournaments were arranged between the mills and other company teams. The companies provided all the kit in company colours and undertook the washing of the same for their players, in addition contributing to any contingent expenses which were incurred. Ferguslie Bowling Green was opened for play in June 1883, the event being commemorated by the presentation of a silver 'jack' to Peter Coats Jr. Additions were subsequently made to the greens, and further facilities were provided by the company, most notably the new club-house built in 1922 when the club membership was around 250. Anchor Bowling Club was established in June 1896, its first presidents being Messrs Stewart and William Clark – the first of whom opened the club's green the following month and donated a trophy first competed for in 1897. Fourteen years before, Ferguslie workers had founded a tennis club, playing on a site next to the company's bowling green before moving to new courts at Meikleriggs in the early 1900s. Anchor tennis club evolved rather later, in 1923, during which year a cricket club was also established in the works – thirty six years after the Ferguslie cricketers had begun play. Swimming clubs were also established in both mills in the 1900s, company bosses again providing cups and trophies to encourage the competitive spirit. Hockey and badminton teams evolved in the 1920s and '30s in both works, receiving a terrific boost in 1923 when the Anchor Recreation Club was established, with extensive grounds and facilities. Finally, annual sports galas were popular in both works in the early Edwardian period, providing, like the annual excursions, excellent opportunities for speeches and ceremonial. Dressed alike in company 'kit' and uniform, competing for company trophies, identified as a group by the company name, and playing with and on company property, such sports clubs encouraged a 'working-class' identity which was far from the stuff of 'class war' models. Rather, through simultaneous identification with one another and with the company, a sectionalism between workers was encouraged, defined by company ties.

Beyond the sports field both mills had their own musical bands – the Ferguslie Brass and Reed band, known originally as the J. & P. Coats Limited Military Band, being set up in 1856 and the Anchor Mills Pipe Band being established in 1920, kitted out by the company in Hunting McPherson tartan with grey doublets – the colour of J. O. M. Clark's dress uniform in the Guards. There were also mill choirs, the Ferguslie

[115] See Yeo, 'On the uses of "community"', p. 241.

male voice choir being established in the 1880s. Scout, Guide and Brownie groups were established during and after the 1914–18 war, the necktie colours of the Coats 14th Paisley Scout Troop being royal blue and red – the colours of a Coats spool ticket. Again the employers' families became involved: Katherine Coats, a great granddaughter of Sir Peter Coats, was the first captain of the Ferguslie Girl Guide Company, founded in 1915.

In such financial, welfare and cultural endeavours the Coats combine clearly displayed a concern to alleviate directly 'the deprivations visited upon the subordinate groups through the operation of market forces', as per Norris's third characteristic of paternalist capitalism. As we have seen, they were not alone in such concerns for their own employees. Yet for the paternalistic metaphor to prove a potent factor in political change, we have seen that it must exert an influence beyond the factory gates: it must neither be restricted by industrial parameters nor defined merely by the concerns of management.

That the concerns of the Coats combine invaded the locality is clear.[116] Members of both the Coats and Clark families occupied prominent posts in numerous committees and societies, ranging from the School Board to the Philosophical Institution, the Deaf and Dumb Institution to the Abbey Parochial Board, the Association for Improving the Condition of the Poor to the Artizans Association, the Ladies Sanitary Association to the Society for the Reclamation of Fallen Women, and Paisley Infirmary to the Board of Directors of the Royal Alexandria Infirmary. Yet, in terms of lasting emblems of their wider social and civic concerns, it is as the benefactors of many of Paisley's civic buildings and monuments that they are best remembered. Peter Coats announced his gift of the Free Library and Museum in 1867 – a promise which was fulfilled when it opened to the public in 1871 – and from this date until the end of the nineteenth century the gifts of the thread magnates began to dominate the social geography of Paisley. The Town Hall (opened in 1882), the Observatory (1892), Gleniffer Home for Incurables (1885), The Nurses' Home of the Royal Alexandria Infirmary (1896), the Fountain Gardens (1868), Oakshaw Free Church Sunday School (1873), the organ of St George's Church (1874), and the Thomas Glen Coats Memorial Baptist Church (1894) as gifts from the Coats and Clark families, stand as living reminders of Paisley's industrial history. More importantly, however, they stood as elements of a civic identity created under the influence of paternalistic capitalism. They not only supplied a need, they created a new Paisley in the image of their creators, one which reinforced the cultural hegemony of a local elite whilst simultaneously inhibiting the growth of conflicting counter-

[116] PCL, 366 Ren–1; 600 Ren–1; 941.41 Ren B/COA. The characteristics of paternalism outwith the factory have their parallel in Patrick Joyce's account of Lancashire mill towns: see Joyce, 'Factory politics of Lancashire', pp. 546–53.

hegemonic civic forms.[117] In this manner, 'civic virtue' – in the sense recently outlined by Biagini – was a problematic notion for the labour radicals of late nineteenth-century Paisley to absorb, rather than their natural expression. [118] Indeed, Savage has suggested that it was not until the 1920s that the 'working class began to occupy the wider urban scale' by taking over 'spatial bases' left vacant by a retreating middle class.[119]

As a consequence, rather than a pre-condition, Norris's final characteristic of paternalist capitalism – the existence of 'a deferential work-force' – is one which must be qualified by a re-statement that deference is a relationship formed through the favourable interaction of forces encouraging identification and differentiation between employer and employee. As such it is in a constant state of re-negotiation. That Paisley citizens responded to the style of social engineering we have analysed above, however, was clearly evident both in personal displays of commitment to the company and public displays of appreciation by the town.

On 8 March 1910, 'Fairplay', a worker for J. & P. Coats, wrote to the management as follows:

> Dear Sir,
> Just a note to let you know that their is a woman callad Maggie Provan in the Cop-winding department who does not need to work as her husband is a packer in the mill with 30/- a week and she has a girl working and a boy her income is about seven pounds in the fortnight and she makes tablet and sells it in the mill and gets girls to sell it in other departments when wee shops trying to make a living cant make one as too much tablet is getting sold in the mill and other woman with small familys cant get work when they go to look for it who needs it more than she does so I hope you will see justice done and oblige yours
>
> fairplay.[120]

This letter highlights three significant points in the silent working out of the deferential dialectic. First, the author frames the charges against Maggie Provan in line with the dominant ideology on marriage and work, on greed and on trade – married women shouldn't work; earning more than you need to survive is wrong; and (less convincingly) small businesses should be encouraged. Secondly, there is the assumption that the bosses, knowing these facts should act upon them – that is, that the

117 See Yeo and Yeo, 'On the uses of "community"', p. 237.

118 E. F. Biagini, 'Introduction: citizenship, liberty and community', in E. F. Biagini (ed.), *Citizenship and Community: Liberals, Radicals and Collective Identities in the British Isles, 1865–1931* (Cambridge, 1996), p. 1.

119 Savage, 'Urban history and social class', pp. 72–3; Savage and Miles, *Remaking of the British Working Class*, pp. 68, 73, 82.

120 UGABRC, JPC Collection, UGD 199/1/2/1, Letter Book 1905–1911, Letter, 8 Mar. 1910.

author and the boss share the same concerns. To the extent that Coats actually investigated these claims, 'Fairplay' was right in this assumption, throwing up the third feature of this drama – Coats's ability and perceived 'right' to enter the private family relationships of their workers.

On the reverse of the letter, an anonymous management representative wrote the following to E. S. Coats:

> For your satisfaction I have made an enquiry about this case and find.
> Husband – packer at Shields W.hse, wife cop-winder 3 ...
> Family all married less one boy just left school, and not yet working.
> Married sons and daughters have all enough to do in keeping their own house.
> The daughter and a baby stays with her and keeps house thus enabling her to come to work. This daughter is parted from her husband who is lazy and drunken.
> The woman stoutly denies making or selling sweets to workers.
> Altogether I am of opinion the writer of this letter has some spiteful spleen to vent.[121]

The employer's access to private and personal family information is unchallenged and his concerns investigated, even though the allegations threaten neither his profitability nor his industrial interests. Instead the accusations made refer to threats to the cultural basis which underpins the industrial environment. Class unity is thus usurped by cultural concepts of 'rights', respectability and 'fairplay'.

Two months later 'A.a.L.' wrote to Messrs Coats Ltd:

> Dear Sir
> I was astonished today when visiting in West end at the talk and stories being circulated by one Mrs MacPherson who they say goes abroad with all haste because she went to the works and told some person that *they must send her away*. She appears to be able to talk of matters such as should not be carried out of any Public Works. it seems this lady has friends and by that she is able to speak of *purely Works Business*. Indeed from what can be heard she speaks much against the firm and work people making much annoyance and excitement.[122]

The letter is signed, 'A.a.L. not wishing to harm her'.

Here, what is most important to note is A.a.L.'s apparent commitment to 'the firm' both within and outwith the workplace. Clearly the author considers '*Works Business*' an inappropriate focus of gossip outwith the factory – the inference being that its reputation must be guarded from such outbursts.

121 Ibid. (verso side).
122 UGABRC, JPC Collection, UGD 199/1/2/1, Letter Book 1905–1911, Letter, 17 May 1910.

Quietly, silently, the deferential dialectic was operating, assumptions of rights being met with acknowledgements of responsibilities. Yet, again, the relationship must flourish beyond the parameters of the mill for it to be a motivational influence on political culture – it must be a force beyond the locus of production.[123]

In 1882, the George A. Clark Town Hall was inaugurated. To commemorate the 'auspicious day', a procession was organised through Paisley's streets:

> The various streets through which the demonstration passed were everywhere lined with spectators, and every window was filled with sight-seers, who at times greeted with hearty cheers the appearance of the various devices and models carried by the trades ... In front of the portico to Kilnside House, the senior members of the Clark family and relatives were assembled in a group, and returned the salute of the different bodies in the procession as they passed.[124]

Following the Grand Master on horseback, at the front of the procession, the Carters, Fleshers, the Pipers of the Renfrewshire Militia and the local Volunteers, the Anchor workers, led by the Works' Fire Brigade, held banners announcing:

> Long may Paisley's sons inherit
> The Clarks' and Coats's public spirit[125]

Behind them, other banners had the mottoes:

> Our Lives are hung upon a thread,
> And yet it gives us daily bread
>
> Famous once for Paisley shawls,
> Now for thread and Public Halls
>
> It well becomes the Brothers Clark
> To leave behind them such a mark
>
> Clark supplies the 'Anchor',
> Coats supplies the 'Chain',
> That keeps the trade to Paisley –
> And long may it remain!

123 William Knox has highlighted a critical feature of Paisley's demographic character in this regard. By tracing the birth-place of household heads employed by Paisley textile firms over the period from 1851 to 1891, he has shown that even at the end of the nineteenth century, there existed in Paisley 'a core of worker households whose roots in Paisley were long established and might be expected to respond to paternalistic overtures from management'. The relatively low level of geographical mobility was essential in fostering a stable community identity which owed much to the demands of local industry: Knox, *Hanging by a Thread*, p. 124.

124 *The Inauguration of the George A. Clark Town Hall, Paisley* (Paisley, 1882), pp. 61–2.

125 Ibid., p. 64.

Whenever the Town Hall chimes do ring
The Donors to our minds they bring

Long live the Brothers one and all,
The Donors of the New Town Hall

The Clarks have cast their hearts on their
fellow townsmen[126]

At Kilnside House:

> where there was an evident desire on the part of the several bodies to linger a moment and acknowledge the salutations of the members of the Clark family and friends there assembled, the time occupied in passing was quite an hour and a half.[127]

Over the course of two evenings, conversaziones were held for the Anchor Thread workers. At the first of these, an address was presented to Stewart Clark by Robert Balderston, the head manager of the works. It read:

> Many of us have been in your service for a long series of years, and can speak from experience of the many good deeds, the kind consideration, and the happiness and comfort we have enjoyed at your hands.
>
> Your action towards us as Employees has been such that peace and concord have always reigned through every department of your works. The sick and aged have been attended to, and the widow and fatherless have not been forgotten ...
>
> When we look at the enormous mills erected by your enterprise and ability, the three thousand workers directly employed therein, and consider the great benefits thereby conferred on the community, we are right in regarding you as great public benefactors.
>
> It has been gratifying to us to know that our Employers, in their liberality, have given so freely and so largely of the fruits of their industry to their native town. This noble Hall in which we meet tonight is a princely gift, and one that will speak the name of CLARK to many future generations.
>
> We honour the names and revere the memory of your worthy and respected Mother and Brothers, who have passed away without being permitted to see the full fruit of their labour, and we sympathise with you in your great loss. Yet we rejoice that many younger members of the family are fast coming to manhood; and we trust they may see it to be their duty to emulate their Fathers and Uncles,

[126] Ibid., pp. 64–5.
[127] Ibid., p. 74.

> and ever keep the name of CLARK an honoured and unsullied name.[128]

In response to the address, presented in printed form on white satin, Stewart Clark took the stand. 'So far as lay in our power', he declared that:

> we have endeavoured to discharge the duties devolving upon us as employers of labour; and, as in the past, so shall we continue to do in the future, for I would have you to remember that there are duties devolving upon us, as your employers, which we hope, so far as God gives us strength, faithfully to perform. (Applause.) If we have, as we have endeavoured to do, discharged the trust placed in our hands, – if we have faithfully carried out our intention towards you in that respect; if we have, in short, done that which we ought to have done, – we consider we have done no more than our duty towards you. (Applause.)[129]

The following evening, at a second conversazione, Stewart Clark spoke of the 'mutual respect' which he and the work-force 'mutually bore', thus stressing the relationship of compromise which underpinned the paternalistic ethos.[130]

In this patchwork of language, rhetoric and the written word, the elemental components of paternalism are to the fore, interacting in this public display of deference: the capitalist family group at the doorway of their local mansion, whose family titles later appear in a printed address as capitalised representatives of the ultimate 'Family'; the rhyming couplets and clever phrases using the imagery of the thread industry and local history; the emblems of the company products and examples of the generosity of the 'Brothers' appearing on banners in the crowd; the printed address, emphasising the 'service' of the work-force, the 'good deeds' and 'liberality' of the employers and the importance of the family name; and finally the response of the employer, whose rhetoric is dominated by the language of deference. 'Duty', 'respect', 'trust' – combine in this explosion of paternalist ritual as the public incantation of the Liberal hegemony, too big to be contained within the factory walls.

Local identity was, in this way, re-created in the crucible of industrial and cultural imperatives. It did not abandon its weaving and radical past but invested them with new meaning. For the moment, it seemed that the local elite had the power and sanction to contain and interpret this

128 Ibid., p. 120.
129 Ibid., p. 121.
130 Ibid., p. 123; note Joyce, *Visions of the People*, p. 121: 'interpretations of the labour process have viewed matters solely in terms of resistance and conflict. Yet, tendencies towards compromise and co-operation between capital and labour have in fact been just as visible.'

heritage, infusing new life into it through civic forms and welfare measures when it seemed to grow tired. Yet, as their retreat from local government has shown, the elite's possession of the past was not always constant in form nor stable throughout its duration. It was conditional rather than consistent. Resting on a delicate community of interests and an ideology, the internal dynamic of which was open to contradictory renderings and bolstered by deferential forms which were perpetually seeking equilibrium, the hegemony had been formed only to be broken from within.

CHAPTER THREE

'A Motley and Ill-Assorted Group': Paisley Politics, 1885–1900

1885: Heralds of Change

> On Thursday night – the night of the last day of 1885 – when the Town Clock struck ten, the old established Coffee Room ended its career as a public resort and news room. Only the following subscribers happened to be in the room at the time: Ex-Provost MacKean; Ex-Provost Clark; Mr William Abercrombie, banker; Mr John Fullerton, ship-builder; Mr D. S. Semple, writer: Mr James Gardner, writer; Mr William Muir MacKean, chemical manufacturer; Mr John Anderson, accountant; Dr Thomas Graham; Mr John Murray, late dyer; Mr James Cook, printer and Chief Constable Robert Hunter. When the ten o'clock bell began to toll, the company rose from the seats they had occupied to take their final departure, but before they left, a call was made on Ex-Provost MacKean to say a few farewell words ... [He proceeded] 'As the president of the Ancient Scots Parliament said when that body rose for the last time – "This is the end of an auld sang." To many of us, too, this is as it must be the end of another chapter in the history of Paisley ... This room used to be the resort of the old magnates of our Burgh, and in the evenings, it was crowded with readers.' [In response, ex-Provost Clark continued] 'In the closing of this reading room, another nailmark has been made in the door of our town's history, and changes are taking place that sadden me to witness.'[1]

In symbolic terms, the closure of the town's Coffee Room, which had reached its eightieth year, with hindsight represented more than the sentimental passing of a perceived golden era of gentlemanly social exchange, but rather an example of the destructive impulses of the social, economic and political processes which, even in 1885, were threatening the hegemonic power of Paisley's industrial elite with erosion and ultimate extinction. Just as the Coffee Room, echoing with the whispers of generations of Paisley industrialists, had no place in a society poised on the eve of an era of powerful counter-attractions and

[1] *PRG*, 2 Jan. 1886.

the vogues of 'modernity', so the social inheritance of the elites themselves – their determining powers over local politics, education, religion, labour and welfare – and their unity as a commanding force, capable of interpreting and articulating the voice of the community, were being challenged both from within and from outwith their restrictive bounds.

By 1886, the stability necessary for the perpetuation of paternalist control could no longer be assumed to exist, nor could it be easily recreated when political division undermined the unqualified communication of its 'message'. The extent of division and its lasting character were at once clarified and created in the crucible of Home Rule politics, yet the roots of Liberal disharmony pre-dated Gladstone's gamble of 1886. Although the defection of the Liberal Unionists into the Tory hinterland was indeed national in scale, closer inspection reveals that it was frequently, to a certain extent, local in motivation. Paisley's Liberal elites were a fractured body even in 1885 and, as the guardians of a local political tradition, were already being taken to task as an unrepresentative clique on the verge of losing the mandate of the politically conscious rank and file.[2]

Liberal rhetoric was turned against the elite by both Tory political opponents and local Radicals who challenged the reforming credentials of the key exponents of party Liberalism in the town and accused them of being, to adapt Lawrence's phrase, 'a closed and static sect'.[3]

Re-modelling the national attack on Liberalism, epitomised by the reformist impulse of 'Tory Democracy', Paisley Conservatives, by focusing attention on the definition of the term 'Liberal', sought to deny the 'historical continuum' of local Liberalism, insisting that it had 'lost its direction and purpose'.[4] During a speech to the local Conservative Association in Paisley in March 1885, it was noted that the Liberal government of the day was 'disgracing its name' and that although 'Liberalism had the good fortune to have an attractive name; that was the best of it, for behind the name they found only the whitened sepulchre.'[5] Attacking 'the mass that called itself by name Liberal', Conservatives sought to recreate political battle lines and re-form the political agenda by highlighting the meaningless divisions symbolised by party labels which had ceased to have a true bearing on reality.[6]

2 This should be seen alongside earlier broader Liberal dissatisfaction in the 1870s with the 'caucus' system which seemed to advantage the party's wealthy patrons at the expense of the grassroots. See J. Lawrence, 'Popular radicalism and the socialist revival in Britain', *JBS*, xxxi (1992), p. 173.

3 J. Lawrence, 'Class and gender in the making of urban Toryism, 1880–1914', *EHR*, cviii (1993), p. 636.

4 Ibid.

5 *PRG*, 28 Mar. 1885.

6 *PDE*, 21 Apr. 1885.

Many Radicals and Liberals clearly shared the same concerns: the *Renfrewshire Independent,* challenging the parliamentary candidature of James Parker Smith in West Renfrewshire, wrote thus:

> Are we to take a man because he chooses to call himself a Liberal, but who has no sympathetic voice with the masses of the people on the questions that are pressing for settlement ... Those of us who have been lying under political disabilities for years are not going to give votes to men who temporise with great principles of justice.[7]

Perceived as failing to live up alike to name, inheritance and 'rank and file' opinion, local Liberalism, on the eve of the Home Rule crisis, was clearly a power already under threat. In 1885 three events coincided to confirm fears regarding the unrepresentative nature of Paisley's Liberal elite in local politics. In the events surrounding the passage through parliament of the Cart Navigation Bill, the fiasco of the School Board 'elections' and the evident decay of the Paisley Liberal Association [PLA], local concerns became focused on apparent abuses of power and position in municipal affairs.

Overshadowed by the Clyde, both in terms of navigable potential and industrial profitability, Paisley's local waterway – the White Cart – had, since at least 1875, been the focus of local entrepreneurial plans for transport and trade reform in the burgh. When, at a meeting of ratepayers in October 1884 the local community had supported an increase in taxation of 3d. for 12 years to finance the improvements proposed by the embryonic Cart Trust, Paisley's challenge to her neighbour 'upstream' seemed only a matter of time. By February 1885, however, the *Paisley Daily Express* had detected a distinct 'lukewarmness' towards the plans by some prominent local industrialists on the Town Council, and a petition against the Cart Navigation Bill was already being circulated throughout the burgh.[8] On 9 March, the *Express* reported that a memorial against the scheme, signed by thirty local firms, had been presented to Lord Redesdale, and by the 11th, John Clark of Gateside (at this time provost of Largs) had proposed that he, along with thirty-eight other gentlemen, should invest £2,000 each in the scheme to prevent the need for an increase in local taxation.[9] Later that night, John Clark, along with ex-Provost McKean and other major starch manufacturers in the town (including Messrs Brown & Polson), formed a deputation to the Town Council against the bill, arguing that the improvement of the river would do little to improve the starch trade and should be opposed as a measure too costly on the public purse and posing the threat of a perpetual tax on local ratepayers. The *Express* reacted angrily to this protest:

7 *Renfrewshire Independent,* 19 Sep. 1885.
8 *PDE,* 26 Feb. 1885.
9 Ibid., 9 Mar. 1885; 11 Mar. 1885.

> This means, of course, that Paisley's prosperity is to be 'starched up' by one class of manufacturers who, while we are still glad to have their industries in our midst, do not employ high paid labour, and pay wages not at all akin to the shipyards and engineering shops they would decry.[10]

Meanwhile, of the four prominent ship-builders in the area – Hugh McIntyre & Co., Abercorn Shipbuilding Co., Messrs John Fullerton & Co., and Messrs McArthur & Co. – three were members of the Cart Trust and Joseph Bow of Bow & McLachlan, engineers, was the largest individual stock-holder in the scheme. On 1 May, Hugh McIntyre, at the launch of the 'William Eccerts', the largest vessel built, at that date, by any of the Cart yards, made the case for improvement:

> Situated as Paisley was, with her railway connection, if the river was deepened, Paisley would become an emporium for goods from other countries, and the vessels that brought these goods would take other cargoes away.[11]

Clearly, the picture is one of an elite divided against itself, as each group promotes the interests of their individual trade and frames such as being in the best interests of the community. The unity of purpose and the public display of stability essential to the perpetuation of the hegemony of the industrial elite was thus shaken, as communal ties seemed to give way to self interest. Yet beyond this, local commentators drew from the Cart fiasco a warning for local democracy:

> [The petitioners against the Bill] represent not one tenth of the valuation [of the burgh] and only a five hundred and sixty fifth part in point of householding population. This is the deadweight that is hanging like a millstone round the neck of our river – 29 persons representing £24,000 of the town's rental will not allow the remaining 13,471 people paying on over £200,000 of rental to have their way.[12]

Local resentment was rife towards the 'obstructive tactics' of the 'auld-farrant and auld-ware starch manufacturers ... opposing *a people's aspirations*'.[13] The petitioners, who had raised the ghost of the 1840s and the potential threat the Navigation Bill posed to the burgh's financial health, were attacked as reactionary.[14] 'The blame', according to the *Express* editorial of 24 March 1885, 'rests with the impecunious-minded

10 Ibid., 12 Mar. 1885.

11 Ibid., 1 May 1885.

12 Ibid., 13 Mar. 1885.

13 Ibid., 16 Mar. 1885 [my italics].

14 Such appeals to the memory of the 'Hungry Forties' have been identified as a characteristic response by Liberals to challenges from the right over issues such as tariff reform. See A. Howe, 'Towards the "hungry forties": free trade in Britain, *c.*1880–1906', in Biagini, *Citizenship and Community*, p. 199.

fossils that have outlived the age we live in, and take delight in retarding progress and thwarting *a community's just aspirations*.'[15] The Cart drama clearly had implications beyond immediate taxation concerns.

On 16 April, the Town Council debated the future of the Cart Bill in the light of recent protests and a new petition from ratepayers in favour of the improvements. Bailie McGown raised his fears regarding local democracy, stating that he supported the bill as 'the will of the people ... not the will of the few, however influential'.[16] The council, by a one-vote margin, however, decided to consult the Cart Trust before making its decision. Following a meeting with the Cart Trust, it was agreed that the council would support the bill in its second reading in the House of Lords.

Reaching the committee stage of the House of Lords on 15 June, the Navigation Bill faced strong opposition by many Paisley representatives who travelled to London to make their views known to the earl of Belmore's committee, among them ex-Provost MacKean, John Clark and Bailies Weir and MacKenzie. Despite such protests, however, an amended bill which limited the period of taxation to twenty five years passed the committee stage and went thence to its third reading in the House of Lords on 25 June. In August the bill became law.

For the moment, the Cart scheme appeared secure. Yet its passage had engendered suspicions and hostilities which would seek to manifest themselves through further outlets. Even in the middle of the Cart controversy itself, fears were manifest of divisive cliques, similar to those identified among the starch interests, threatening the representative role of the School Board.

On 8 April sixteen candidates were proposed for the nine vacant seats on Paisley's School Board, among them Thomas Glen Coats, Provost James Clark and John Armour Brown. One day earlier, the local press had commented on the public apathy surrounding the proposed contest and so it was that, on 11 April, despite a notable divergence of opinion regarding whether the contest should take place, a meeting was held of all the candidates and their nominators, chaired by Sheriff Cowan. Votes were taken on the most popular candidates who would (if no protests were made) become the *de facto* new School Board members. Jointly, at the top of the poll came Thomas Glen Coats and Provost James Clark and thereafter (excluding the usual clerical presence) came John McGown, an accountant; Robert Cochran, the former Chartist and local draper; Mrs Arthur a well-known local figure and previous School Board member; and John Armour Brown. The unsuccessful candidates were William McGee, an engineer; Andrew Ross, a teacher; John MacDonald, a Roman Catholic clergyman; T. J. Melvin, a printer; James Mclean, a clothier; and the Rev. F. Mills, a Protestant clergyman.[17]

15 *PDE*, 24 Mar. 1885.

16 Ibid., 17 Apr. 1885. McGown became burgh Treasurer later that year.

17 Note that Brown and Arthur later withdrew and Melvin and McGee took their places.

Though the decisions made at the meeting stood and were not met by a general public outcry, the protests against this procedure were immediate and uncompromising; the *Express* described the meeting as 'a Mutual Admiration and Pulse-Feeling Association'.[18] Focusing on what he/she termed 'secret diplomacy', 'Ratepayer' wrote to the local press:

> That the inhabitants should have displayed so much apathy and indifference at this time in connection with School Board matters is perfectly astonishing, and can only be accounted for, I think, by their sheer disgust at the system of jobbery which has been going on in certain quarters which I need not name ... We have had presented to us the spectacle of public men professing to be true Liberals in *thought* and *action* combining together for the purpose of denying to the electors their legitimate rights.[19]

Recalling Paisley's radical past, 'Citizen' asked: 'What have our forefathers and Radical Paisley fought for? ... Are we becoming careless of rights and liberties now that we have got them?'[20]

Clearly, some citizens in 1885 were beginning to question the extent to which present-day Liberals were living up to their radical antecedents. The Liberal hegemony was being threatened by the principles it proposed to represent – most especially, representative rule. Increasingly, allegations arose regarding cliques and caucus control on local municipal and political bodies, culminating by December in explicit attacks on the PLA.[21]

In July 1885, the Liberal Club resolved to hold a meeting of the town's Liberal electors with a view to forming a new Liberal Association for Paisley. A meeting was subsequently held on 22 September, some weeks before the general election. Encouraged by the prominent local clergyman and disestablisher, Rev. Dr Hutton, that 'The do-nothing, stand-still, or mere rest-and-be-thankful is no present day Liberal', the September meeting agreed to form a new association, which was constituted on 2 November.

The following week, 'Independent Liberal' wrote to the *Express*, warning that the Liberals who proposed to join the new association were 'giving their consent to the establishment in their midst of a form of oligarchy which may prove a most dangerous instrument for the destruction of that independent action in political matters which has hitherto been enjoyed by the Liberals of this Burgh'.[22] Echoing such

18 *PDE*, 13 Apr. 1885.

19 Ibid., 16 Apr. 1885.

20 Ibid., 16 Apr. 1885.

21 Hutchison has highlighted elite domination of local Liberal party organisation in Scotland from as early as the 1830s and the subsequent growth of dissent within local committees as the disestablishment issue became more vexing after mid-century: Hutchison, *Political History of Scotland*, chaps. 2, 5.

22 *PDE*, 10 Nov. 1885.

concerns, whilst reflecting on this period from the perspective of 1886, the *Paisley Chronicle* identified a significant 'Whig element' in the new association which 'soon developed itself'.[23] Local support for the Liberal elite was thus of a clearly qualified nature and was, even in 1885, seeking justification for its perpetuation in sources of legitimation quite alien to the realms of the deferential dialectic – majority rule and radical precedent. Cracks appearing in elite ranks over industrial and political questions were duplicated in suspicions 'from below' as the inability of the Liberals to contain the contradictory impulses of the radical tradition became increasingly evident.

The 1885 general election in Paisley distilled local concerns, more than national issues, from the confusion of personalities into the rhetoric of perceived rights and radical sentiments, thus preparing the ground for the cleavage of the following year. To a certain extent the outcome dictated future Liberal policy which, marked as it was by hesitation and compromise, by the 1890s had forced local radical sentiment to seek articulation outwith established institutions, and Whiggish sympathies to move further to the right. Echoing Howell, it is probable that, in Paisley, the Home Rule crisis of 1886 represented less the cause than the mere occasion for the defection of many Liberals.[24]

When, on 22 September, Paisley Liberals heralded the inauguration of a new association, their member of parliament, Stewart Clark, the thread manufacturer, declared that he would not be standing for re-election due to the pressure of his business commitments. From all accounts, Clark's retiral was wholly unexpected and left the Liberals in a difficult position on the eve of a general election.[25] Clark, the first resident townsman to represent the burgh in parliament, had been elected at a by-election the previous February, standing against the Conservative, Lord Ernest Hamilton. The competition had been marked, initially, by Liberal division as the former Chartist, Robert Cochran, and W. B. Barbour, a prominent Paisley-born merchant, both contended for the Liberal nomination. 1885 also found the Liberals divided. The day after Clark's retiral, two names had already appeared as potential candidates: Provost James Clark, the retiring MP's cousin and W. B. Barbour, who had stepped down in favour of Stewart Clark in 1884. A week later, Robert Cochran (at this time, burgh treasurer) appeared again as a possible contender.

By 28 September both James Clark and W. B. Barbour had issued their electoral addresses, Clark's speedy entrance into the nomination race arousing significant suspicion of Clark family collusion. The *Gazette* noted on the 26th: 'The promptitude with which Provost Clark entered the field as a candidate for the seat from which his cousin proposes to

23 *Paisley Chronicle*, 24 Jul. 1886.
24 Howell, *British Workers and the Independent Labour Party*, p. 139.
25 *PRG*, 26 Sep. 1885.

retire, led to a rumour that it had been an understood arrangement between the two'.[26] Though the *Gazette* was quick to deny any substance to the rumour, others were not, and Thomas Glen Coats was to raise the subject again later in Barbour's campaign.[27] He noted:

> there were some of them who did not see why, having had one Mr Clark they should have another. (Applause and slight hisses.) He thought they had a right to exercise their own judgement to say who was to be the member for Paisley. (Applause and slight hisses.)[28]

Such suspicions of corruption echoed prominent concerns in local politics during the year and were further exacerbated when, on 21 October, Cochran made known his retiral from the Liberal nomination contest and on the 23rd declared his support for James Clark, his bitter opponent in the Cart negotiations, and the man whom he would succeed as provost on 9 November (Clark having intimated his intention not to seek re-election to that office at the beginning of October).

James Clark and W. B. Barbour thus approached October as the two major contenders for the Liberal nomination. Clark, as provost and local industrialist, was well known to the Paisley electorate. Yet, his high local profile was not of unqualified benefit to him in the contest, as the *Gazette* made clear; in comparison, Barbour 'had no antipathies or dislikes to overcome'.[29] In the midst of the parliamentary contest, the local election focused attention on Clark's municipal record and his apparent inconsistency over the Cart Bill which he had initially supported, then opposed when the taxation clauses had been drawn up. On the question of policy, however, there was little to choose between the two candidates. Both supported free elementary education, both were in favour of land reform, both were fervent free traders, both backed McLaggan's Local Option Bill and both supported limited Home Rule for both Ireland and Scotland. On the important question of the disestablishment of the Church of Scotland, however, whilst both shared in a commitment to ultimate religious equality, Barbour articulated his views in a more conciliatory manner. At a meeting in the Good Templar Hall on 12 November, Barbour declared his 'adhesion to Disestablishment':

> though not to any particular measure or any particular bill, and when the time does come for giving effect to this, then I shall be found certainly on the side of those who are wishful to bring it about in a way that is at once just and liberal, and on such terms as

26 Ibid., 26 Sep. 1885.

27 Ibid., 10 Oct. 1885. Here it is recorded that James Clark met allegations made by a Mr Alexander Smith that he and his cousin had attempted to make Paisley 'a pocket burgh' with outright denial.

28 Ibid., 14 Nov. 1885.

29 Ibid., 21 Nov. 1885.

will evoke no unpleasant feeling on the part of our brethren in the Church.[30]

Following very much the party line established by Gladstone at the Free Church Assembly in Edinburgh the day before, Barbour clearly had no intention of alienating local Liberal Churchmen by making disestablishment a 'test question' at the coming general election. Meanwhile, the previous month, Clark had been adamant in his declaration: 'I am and always have been, opposed to the existence of a State Church.'[31] The choice was therefore not a simple one of establishment versus disestablishment, as Kellas seems to imply of the twenty-seven constituency contests which hosted rival Liberal candidates in 1885.[32] But this did not make the Paisley contest any less bitter.

Local agendas permeated the Church question in 1885 just as they were to invest the Home Rule Question in 1886 with a local sub-plot. When, on 14 November the Liberal electors of the five Paisley Wards went to the polls to decide on their Liberal candidate, they did so conscious of *local* political imperatives and in the context of a *local* political history upon which one of the players at least could be judged.

At the Liberal poll on 14 November, Barbour was elected as Liberal candidate for the burgh, beating his opponent by 2,215 votes to 1,463 to face the Conservative candidate, Major McKerrell of the 1st Ayrshire Rifles, at the general election the following week.[33] An embarrassing episode for Paisley Liberals was thus over, but it had highlighted divisions both in the party and in the local industrial elite, most notably in the thread interest, where Clark faced Coats on opposing sides. The disunity in Paisley was, in a way, symptomatic of divisions in Scottish Liberalism, as the disestablishers of the Federation fought the 'battle ecclesiastic' against an immovable Scottish Liberal Association. Yet, here, the impulse behind division was local in both origin and character, fuelled by local concerns and ultimately decided upon the basis of local fears regarding unpopular elite domination and corruption.

On 25 November, William Barbour, the 'week-old' Liberal candidate, faced Major McKerrell at the polls to decide Paisley's parliamentary representation. The Liberal campaign was a fractured one. Until the final week of campaigning, the Liberals fought themselves as much as their Conservative opponent, reinforcing Machin's recent perceptive comment that 'no political party could be the perfect medium for realising [nonconformist aims]'.[34] Both candidates, however, conducted

30 *PDE*, 13 Nov. 1885.

31 *PRG*, 10 Oct. 1885.

32 Kellas, 'Liberal Party in Scotland', p. 9; also J. G. Kellas, 'The Liberal Party and the Scottish Church Disestablishment Crisis', *EHR*, lxxix (1964), p. 36.

33 Yet, the turn-out at the polls to decide the Liberal candidate was small – only 54.75% of the potential Liberal electorate turned out to vote: *PRG*, 21 Nov. 85.

34 I. Machin, 'Disestablishment and democracy, *c.*1840–1930', in Biagini, *Citizenship and Community*, p. 133.

energetic campaigns, speaking at work-gate meetings and soliciting the support of special interest groups; the Liberals courting the Temperance movement, and the recalcitrant Irish National League [INL] and the Conservatives, the Orange lodges, the publicans and most importantly, the Liberal Churchmen and newly formed Church Defence Committees.

The question of disestablishment dominated the contest. McKerrell cast the election as a local referendum on disestablishment from the first, warning 'if they voted for a Radical candidate, they were adding one more nail to the coffin of the Established Church'.[35] On 21 October a crowded meeting of established churchmen and prominent local Conservatives met in the Town Hall to voice their protest against the disestablishment and disendowment of the Church of Scotland. The following evening a Church Defence Association was established in the Abbey Parish. By early November, associations had been established in the Low, Martyr's and North parishes and were being condemned by disestablishers for making the Church 'a den of Tories'.[36] Campaigning to secure the Liberal Church vote for McKerrell, the task of the Church Defence associations was blighted somewhat by Gladstone's Free Church Declaration on 11 November. Yet, as a campaigning force, their influence was significant in the Tory interest, though ultimately insufficient to secure the seat for McKerrell.

Barbour won the seat for Liberalism by 3,390 votes to 2,523, in a contest which had attracted a turn-out of almost 88% and saw a comparative increase in the Conservative vote. Despite Parnell's diktat to Irish voters to vote for the Conservative candidate, it is doubtful whether the entire Catholic vote 'went Tory'. Yet, clearly, the impact of the estimated defection of around 200 Liberal Churchmen assisted in the rise in the Conservative vote and posed as an omen of continued Liberal discord.

Looking to the national stage, local publisher T. J. Melvin, proprietor of the progressive *Paisley Chronicle*, supported the view that 'Hitherto the party of progress has been mainly political and economic. Henceforth it must become social and moral ... [appealing] to the better self of all citizens.'[37] In February 1886, the *Chronicle* identified such zeal in the new Gladstonian cabinet – 'a Radical Cabinet' – which, it concluded, exemplified the 'principles for which the Radicals of 1822, assembled in Meikleriggs Moor and for which the Martyrs of Peterloo and of Bonnymuir suffered and died'.[38] This pressure of the past consequently weighted Gladstone's subsequent Home Rule declaration with the complex legacy of a radical tradition which amplified existing divisions in Paisley Liberalism and determined the composition of new power

35 *PRG*, 10 Oct. 1885.
36 Ibid., 7 Nov. 1885.
37 *Paisley Chronicle*, 9 Jan. 1886.
38 Ibid., 6 Feb. 1886.

groupings in local party elites, as both Unionists and Gladstonians sought the position of guarantor of Paisley's Liberal heritage.

1886: The Fragmentation of the Master Narrative

On 26 April the Paisley Liberal Club debated the Government of Ireland and Irish Land Purchase Bills, presented to the commons by Gladstone earlier that month. On a division, it was agreed by seventy-five votes to forty to support the motion of local soap manufacturer, and future MP, J. M. McCallum: 'That the Paisley Liberal Club thanks Mr Gladstone for his noble attempt to settle the Irish grievances, and trusts that the Government proposals will form a satisfactory basis for legislation'.[39]

In terms of unqualified support for Gladstone, the resolution is somewhat ambiguous, yet its implications for local Liberal unity proved decisive. Almost immediately, the Liberals divided into two oppositional groups over the Home Rule bills. Prominent on the Gladstonian 'side' were W. B. Barbour MP; Provost Cochran; Thomas Glen Coats; J. M. McCallum; Treasurer McGown, Councillor Wilson, Bailie Andrews and Bailie Weir (all of whom had supported the Cart Bill); Bailie Wills, who had opposed the bill; J. Parlane, proprietor of the *Paisley Daily Express*; John Millar, president of the Paisley Liberal Club; Peter Eadie of Eadie Bros, engineers; and Andrew Fisher of Fisher & Co., engineers. Though failing to retain all their previous support among the local business community, the high profile of local employers in the Liberal ranks in Paisley undermines McCaffrey's bold assertion that 'nationalism in the sense of Home Rule for Ireland made little appeal to west of Scotland businessmen'.[40] Among those forming the Unionist body were Stewart Clark of Kilnside, the former MP; his cousin, ex-Provost James Clark; Archibald Coats; Hugh Smiley of Kerr & Son, thread manufacturers; ex-Provost Macfarlane and ex-Bailie Caldwell; John Polson, the starch manufacturer; John and Alexander Fullerton; Matthew and John Hodgart and James Barclay, the engineering employers; James Barr, who moved a motion in opposition to Gladstone's bills at the Liberal meeting in April; and William Muir and J. A. D. MacKean, starch manufacturers. The Liberal elite was clearly fractured.

On 30 April Rt. Hon. G. J. Goschen MP and Lord Hartington, two of the most prominent 'Unionist Liberals', addressed a huge demonstration in Edinburgh against the new Gladstonian measures. The following day, Goschen spoke to the discontented Liberals of Paisley at a meeting in the Town Hall chaired by Stewart Clark. The meeting approved a resolution which questioned the 'principle of a measure which erects a separate and

39 *PRG*, 1 May 1886.

40 J. McCaffrey, 'The origins of Liberal Unionism in the West of Scotland', *SHR*, l (1971), p. 67.

independent Parliament for Ireland ... [and provides] rights for minorities which are inconsistent with Liberal principles'. It also attacked the Land Bills, as 'the expropriation of Irish landlords' – of which Stewart Clark was one. Rev. Dr Brown (a key player in the previous year's disestablishment debate in Barbour's interest) then attacked the Gladstonian myth which had apparently gripped his erstwhile Liberal brothers:

> To bow to the decision even of ... a leader with a united cabinet, would be *sheer popery* in politics; but to bow to a leader who spoke *ex cathedra* without the authority of his united cabinet would be that *Vaticanism* against which Mr Gladstone so earnestly and eloquently appealed.[41]

The Unionists thus defended their dissent in terms of traditional Liberal principles and in the rhetoric of radicalism. As Graham Goodlad has made clear:

> Irish Home Rule was not a policy which automatically commended itself to the average Liberal. The Parnellites' record of obstruction in the 1880–5 parliament and their opportunism in directing Irish voters to reject the Liberals in the 1885 general election; the long-standing anti-Catholic strain in English Nonconformity; the association of Nationalism with violence and illegality in Ireland: these factors scarcely pre-disposed rank and file Liberals in favour of such a policy departure.[42]

Meanwhile, however, the Gladstonians defined in explicit terms their support for Irish Home Rule as 'just and reasonable' at a demonstration on 15 May. Here Peter Eadie attacked the Unionists as blinkered bigots: 'He never could see the loyalty of playing 'Boyne Water' to annoy their fellow men. He never could see any Christianity in smashing chapel windows when their fellow creatures were at prayer.'[43] The Gladstonian speakers defended Home Rule in terms of 'responsible Government', as 'the *natural* sequence and corollary of past Irish legislation' and, adopting the religious imagery used by the Unionists, announced their intentions to 'atone' for periods of 'plunder and rapine'.[44]

The radical tradition of the burgh infused into the Home Rule debate over the next months would be pulled by both sides in attempts to illustrate their case as the 'truer' and 'purest' form of Liberalism. In this process the tradition itself did not cease to be meaningful, but proved

41 *PDE*, 3 May 1886.

42 G. Goodlad, 'Gladstone and his rivals: popular Liberal perceptions of the party leadership in the political crisis of 1885–6', in E. F. Biagini and A. J. Reid (eds.), *Currents of Radicalism, Organised Labour and Party Politics in Britain, 1850–1914* (Cambridge, 1991), pp. 163–4.

43 *PDE*, 17 May 1886.

44 Ibid., 17 May 1886.

flexible enough to absorb new meanings, malleable enough to adapt to the creation of new arguments and powerful enough to contain new mythologies.

In more theoretical terms, this metamorphosis of the radical tradition is a clear illustration of its operation as a 'meta-' or master narrative, or, to use Patrick Joyce's phrase – 'a single tale tying together a diversity of representations'.[45] Here, the 'single tale' common to both Liberal groupings was a shared commitment to a local radical sensibility, and a concept of 'Union' which could be encompassed within it – two phenomena which, in this period of conjunctural crisis in the evolution of British Liberalism, separated and demanded mutual re-composition in accordance with contemporary imperatives. As Lee has illustrated: 'Similar ideological foundations may result in different party affiliations, especially when the ideological distance between the parties is perceived not to be great.'[46]

In his attempt to delineate a *national* 'dominant tradition' in a re-conceptualisation of 'class', Joyce has stressed the importance of 'variation and conflict within bodies of national myth and narrative'.[47] Whilst the political processes associated with the elaboration, definition and adaptation of Paisley's radical tradition have ultimate meaning only in their local sense, in their creation of an interface between the local and the national, they re-assert the creation of political identity at the constituency level as a key determinant of the character and chronology of national trends. The manner in which the radical tradition was conceived by different parties mutated in accordance with national events, yet, likewise, the radical tradition formed a critical part of the historical sense through which contemporary events were perceived and made meaningful for the Paisley electorate.

This being the case, a sense of continuity emerges through the crisis of 1886, party labels being seen as subordinate to an over-riding core of principles, the definition of which was the critical element in determining political re-alignments. As Lawrence has made clear:

> democratic political parties are invariably broad-based coalitions, within which one can identify a wide range of ideological traditions. At particular historical conjunctures one of these traditions may capture the levers of power within a party, but even then its political success is likely to rely in part on the survival (and mobilizing ability) of other ideological traditions.[48]

45 Joyce, *Visions of the People*, p. 331.

46 A. J. Lee, 'Conservatism, traditionalism and the British working class, 1880–1918', in D. E. Martin and D. Rubinstein (eds.), *Ideology and the Labour Movement: Essays presented to John Saville* (London, 1979), p. 95.

47 Joyce, *Visions of the People*, p. 332.

48 Lawrence, 'Class and gender', p. 634.

Accommodating this formulation in a Gramscian appreciation of this period of Liberal crisis is relatively straightforward and has the advantage of emphasising the inherent instability of hegemonic local political elites in a democratic state, whose power depends on their ability to justify, in popular terms, their position of superiority in a manner which also illustrates their commitment to an ideology shared with the general electorate. National events impacting on such an ideology can and do frequently undermine elite power and cohesion at certain conjunctural periods and, in this instance, had a lasting legacy in the movement towards the organic change away from party Liberalism.

Planning for the creation of a West of Scotland Liberal Unionist Association began in Glasgow soon after the Home Rule bills were introduced and on 11 June 'satisfactory progress' was being reported in Paisley.[49] Archibald Coats was one of the earliest members of the executive committee of the new association and was joined in November by Stewart Clark. In June, it was reported that already negotiations were proceeding between Conservatives and Liberal Unionists with the view to arranging a candidate to champion their united interests in Paisley. A private meeting had been held in Glasgow on the 11th, at which Archibald Coats represented the local Liberal Unionists and William Abercrombie, president of Paisley's Beaconsfield Club, and ex-Provost Brown, a notable local Tory, represented the Conservatives. Rumours soon circulated that Stewart Clark and H. H. Smiley of Gallowhill had been requested to contest the seat as Unionists and Major McKerrell had intimated his readiness to fight the seat for the Conservatives again, yet for most, James Parker Smith of Jordanhill, the former Liberal candidate for West Renfrewshire in 1885, seemed the likely compromise choice, the Liberal Unionists having intimated their reluctance to accept a Conservative.[50]

On 18 June, Parker Smith was adopted as Paisley's Unionist candidate at a meeting chaired by ex-Provost Brown at the Beaconsfield Club. As Urwin has made clear, and as the experience of Paisley confirms, co-operation between Conservatives and Liberal Unionists began relatively quickly at constituency level.[51] On 3 June, the annual report of Paisley's Beaconsfield Club had detailed the directors' hopes that 'an arrangement may be come to, whereby the solid 'Unionist' vote may be cast against the sitting member'.[52] Their honorary president, Col. Sir

49 NLS, SCUA, Acc. 10424/19, WSLUA, Minutes 1886–1894, vol. I, 11 Jun. 1886 (p. 23).

50 *PRG*, 12 Jun. 1886.

51 Urwin, 'Development of the Conservative Party Organisation', pp. 95–6. Note, however, the comment in the *PDE* editorial of 17 Jul. 1886: 'Our local Conservatives are in a bit of a quandary. The "young bloods" of the Beaconsfield Club do not, we hear, like the idea of deserting Major McKerrell, who made such a gallant stand for them at the last election; while the older hands are willing that he should get the go-bye, in order that Mr Parker-Smith, the Whig, should be supported on what is called the "Unionist" platform.'

52 *PRG*, 5 Jun. 1886.

Archibald C. Campbell of Blythswood, would later write to Parker Smith of his pleasure in finding himself 'at last in cordial accord with so many men who for too long [he had] respected ... but one thing kept us apart a mere Political difference [which he felt sure would] eventually melt away'.[53] Indeed, as early as 1 June, the Scottish Conservative Association had written to the West of Scotland Liberal Unionist Association, offering its support for Liberal Unionist candidates and its willingness to discuss further co-operation.[54]

The new political 'union' attracted the scorn and satire of its opponents. The *Paisley Chronicle* described the platform party at one of Parker Smith's meetings as:

> truly a motley and ill-assorted group; old fashioned Tories; Tory Democrats from the Beaconsfield Club; and Liberal Churchmen, the pillars of the Church Defence Associations ... the Paisley adherents of Mr Goschen ... and the members of the Which school who worship Lord Hartington ... two or three renegade Radicals ... [The platform] was very 'respectable' and painfully 'influential'. Certainly the interests of 'Capital' were well represented, whatever lack there was of the popular element or of the working men of Paisley. It was thoroughly typical of the character of the struggle all over the country – 'the classes' *versus* the nation.[55]

The popular mythology that Unionism succeeded only in attracting former Whigs is here contradicted, although the commentator clearly agrees with many current historians that '1886' assisted in the formation of a distinct class basis in British party politics, by preparing the ground for Whigs to cross the final party barrier into Conservative ranks, leaving the Liberals the classic party of the shopkeeper, artisan and urban middle classes. Yet the realignment in Liberal politics was neither as simple nor as immediate as John McCaffrey's depiction of the evolution of class-differentiated political behaviour in the West of Scotland suggests, with, as he puts it, 'the Gladstonians enjoying the support of the labouring masses as the Liberal Unionists drew closer in practice and spirit to the Conservatives'.[56] Just as some Whigs remained in the Liberal Party – such as Rosebery, Tennant and Elgin – so some Radicals came out against Gladstone – such as Fraser MacKintosh, the Crofters' MP, J. B. Kinnear of East Fife and Cameron Corbett of Glasgow, for example.[57] Thus, though perhaps 'creaming off' a large number of Whigs, Unionism, as it appeared after 1886, further confused party differences, falling heir as it did to some volatile Radicals – on the

53 ML, GCA, Parker Smith Collection, TD/1/311, Colonel Sir Archibald C. Campbell to Parker Smith, Jun. 1886.

54 NLS, SCUA, Acc. 10424, WSLUA, Minutes 1886–1894, vol. I, 1 Jun. 1886 (p. 16).

55 *Paisley Chronicle*, 26 Jun. 1886.

56 McCaffrey, 'Origins of Liberal Unionism', p. 71.

57 Hutchison, *Political History of Scotland*, pp. 163–4.

national stage, most notably Chamberlain.[58] In Scotland, this radical influence has been seen by Hutchison as critical in determining the positive social policies established by the Unionists in the 1890s.[59]

In June 1886, Gladstone was defeated by thirty votes on the second reading of the Home Rule (Ireland) Bill and an immediate dissolution of parliament was announced. In the contest which resulted, the question of Home Rule dominated the campaign platforms, with the rhetoric of radicalism meeting the eloquence of 'Union' as the competed ground of Liberalism came under assault. The debate in Paisley, though utilising the conventional fears of Rome Rule and Imperial dislocation on the Unionist side and the moral crusading for representative rule and notions of 'justice' on the Liberal platforms, focused largely on the emergence of a new form of local party as the most direct manifestation of the crisis that had entered Paisley politics. Critical here was the figure of the 'Liberal Unionist'.

At Parker Smith's campaign meeting on the 23rd, a member of the audience greeted his arrival on stage with the shout: 'A Tory with a new name'.[60] A week later, Barbour reflected on Paisley's candidates: 'They had before them now two candidates, one of one colour only and the other what might be termed piebald – like the clown in the circus, all dark coloured on the one side and light on the other.'[61] To Barbour, Parker Smith fitted none of the established 'types' upon which party politics were structured: 'He could not be all Liberal or all Tory. The name that he preferred himself was Unionist, and he might be said to represent the Tories and Liberals in an equal degree.'[62] Provost Cochran commented on Unionist strategy: 'They said they could not put in a Conservative and they would try Parker Smith, who was next door to a Tory. (Cheers.) They were trying to gain the seat for the Tory party under the care of Parker Smith.'[63] Meanwhile the *Chronicle* judged that 'any so-called Liberal, who is the nominee of the Beaconsfield Club and the choice of Mr Goschen's Paisley Committee has no right to the name of Liberal'.[64] Parker Smith, however, grasped the mantle of Liberal sentiment, insisting on the rights of the people of Ulster against the 'dynamite, intimidation, crime, treason [and] blood' of the proposed Home Rule settlement. It was not the Liberal Unionists, he claimed, who had changed their position: they 'were not deserting Liberalism'.[65]

The rhetorical emphasis of the language which could legitimately be used to describe the new phenomenon of Unionism, the questioning of

58 See J. Belchem, *Popular Radicalism in Nineteenth-Century Britain* (Basingstoke, 1996), p. 142.
59 Hutchison, *Political History of Scotland*, pp. 199–200.
60 *PDE*, 24 Jun. 1886.
61 Ibid., 29 Jun. 1886.
62 Ibid., 29 Jun. 1886.
63 Ibid., 30 Jun. 1886.
64 *Paisley Chronicle*, 12 Jun. 1886.
65 *PDE*, 24 Jun. 1886.

definitions and the conflicting interpretations of 'Liberal', highlight the importance of language on the political stage in 1886. Words clearly did not merely represent a crisis going on elsewhere, they themselves at once embodied and created that crisis, imparting confusion into the party structure as existing words and definitions seemed ill-suited to emergent new interests. Definitions were thus re-created, interpretations modified to accommodate aroused sensibilities, and local precedents sought for the attribution of new labels.

The 1886 election saw national crisis interacting with the power of personality on the local level, thus personalising, or at least 'localising', the drama of the Home Rule debate. The local divisions of the previous year did not dictate in simplistic terms the recomposition of the parties in 1886, yet they provided the context from which the electorate viewed the confusing re-grouping of the local elite in terms of local issues. Parker Smith's platforms found Orangemen sitting next to disestablishers, publicans sharing quiet whispers with temperance supporters, Cart Bill devotees sitting beside their previous opponents on the Town Council and former Liberal parliamentary candidates flanked by the Dames of the Primrose League. It is thus difficult to determine the exact *meaning* of the election result which saw Barbour retain the seat with a slim majority of 566, polling 3,057 votes against Parker Smith's 2,491.

Provost Cochran viewed Barbour's victory as a lesson to the 'Upper Ten', a class in Paisley who had dominated local politics for too long.[66] Yet, clearly, with Thomas Glen Coats still in the Gladstonian ranks, the situation was not that simple. Barbour, however, was in no doubt that the result had proved the continuum of the burgh's radical past:

> In 1832, at the time of the passing of the Reform Bill, Paisley was Radical. Paisley has been Radical ever since, and it is Radical now. (Cheers.) Without being a prophet, I can tell you that Paisley will be Radical in the future – (Cheers.) – and whoever may come to contest this seat again, I would advise him not, so to speak, to have a political platform composed of a little here and a little there; of proportional representation if you like, proportional everything; a kind of 'mixy maxy' thing *that has no proper name*. (Cheers.) ... Paisley people do not understand political acrobats such as that.[67]

Yet, this was not simply a victory for radicalism. Many who had supported a strong line on disestablishment and municipal reforms the previous year were found in the ranks of those following Parker Smith – a man whose establishment credentials were well known.

Such apparent confusion alerts us to the futility of explaining '1886' in terms of party or interest labels. Clearly at this point of conjunctural crisis for the Paisley electorate, both Liberals and Unionists, the key

66 Ibid., 9 Jul. 1886.
67 Ibid., 9 Jul. 1886 [my italics].

determinant was the meanings they invested in the twin motivational forces of 'Radicalism' and 'Union'. Unlike their representation on party platforms, for the voter, support for one did not exclude sympathy and commitment to the other. Both forces existed independently of their organised manifestations. The key feature, therefore, of the election result of 1886 was less that it represented a Liberal victory than that it showed an electorate almost equally divided between *two* new parties – one bereft of many of its members, the other an uneasy union between an older grouping and the haemorrhage of its opponents' membership. '1886' thus represents two critical conjunctural changes – first, the early stages in the recapitulation of Paisley's radical tradition, through which Liberalism, its guarantor since the 1860s, would lose its exclusive rights to its articulation, initially to the right, and ultimately to the emergent independent left; and secondly, the fracturing of the hegemonic political power of local industrial elites who found themselves on opposing sides in the new party structure, speaking 'different languages'.

Liberal Organisation: Threats to the Established Order

The question of identity, the creation of new and the adaptation of old, was a crucial question in the election of 1886. Liberalism had to be re-defined in opposition to its 'bastard' offspring, as well as to a Conservatism, the emphasis of which had changed from Protector of the Faith to Protector of the Empire. Home Rule thus went beyond the re-alignment of policy to a re-definition of Liberal identity. This had critical practical implications for the organisation of all parties at the constituency level.

On 11 November 1886, the new High Street Rooms of the Liberal Club were inaugurated in the presence of the marquis of Ripon. Paisley Liberal Unionists remained members of the Liberal Club for many years after the creation of their own association in April 1887, thus acting as an obstacle in the process of Liberal political realignment at the local level. However, following the Liberal Club's annual general meeting in December 1886, the presidency and key offices were generally held thereafter by prominent Gladstonians whose influence was evident in the choice of speakers and topics at subsequent lectures and demonstrations.

In 1889, however, allegations were heard at the Liberal Club AGM of Liberal Unionist members hindering plans for a Home Rule meeting, a prominent member in their ranks, James Barr, having just been elected a vice-president of the club. Cochran spoke against Unionist office holders:

> He objected to their appointment to office because of their antagonism to the principles held by the Liberals whom they earnestly wrought to defeat ... He held that there could not be a

> more insane procedure than to make Unionists leaders of the Paisley Liberals.[68]

John Millar, president of the club, objected, arguing that 'The differences among Liberals, if dealt with wisely, cautiously and prudently would disappear.'[69] Thereafter, Barr's election was affirmed by a show of hands, those in favour of his appointment outnumbering those against by approximately four to one. Cochran, on his appointment as an honorary president of the club the following year, again voiced his opposition to Liberal Unionists on the executive committee of the club but attracted no support.

Nevertheless, new forces were pushing towards a more definitive statement of local Liberalism, separate from Unionist and indeed Whiggish apathy. Just days after the 1886 poll, the *Paisley Chronicle* called for the combination of Paisley radicals in an association 'free from the domination and withering influences of either 'dissenting Bishops' or purse proud Autocrats'.[70] Two weeks later the same newspaper lamented the death of the recently established Liberal Association and bewailed its inactivity and the 'benevolent neutrality' of the Liberal Club at the recent contest.[71] In conclusion, the *Chronicle* declared:

> We believe that the great cause of the want of the Liberal organisation in Paisley is the unsatisfactory composition of the Liberal Associations which have been formed. As a rule they have not been fair types of the robust Radicalism of Paisley ... The term 'Liberal' is very elastic and may mean anything or nothing at all. There are members of these Associations who are as Conservative in their instincts and opinions as the most thorough going Tory. Far too much attention has been paid of the opinions of the moderate Liberal, and there has been more anxiety to have the Classes of Paisley on our side, than to act up to the aspirations of the democracy.[72]

The *Chronicle* then recommended the creation of a Paisley Radical Association, 'A society which shall be based on democratic and Nationalist principles; and an association which shall represent the progressive Radicalism of Paisley'.[73]

Such calls for radicalism in Paisley form part of a wider Scottish theme in these years, as protests were being made in support of the open

68 Ibid., 28 Dec. 1889.
69 Ibid., 28 Dec. 1889.
70 *Paisley Chronicle*, 10 Jul. 1886.
71 Ibid., 24 Jul. 1886.
72 Ibid., 24 Jul. 1886.
73 Ibid., 24 Jul. 1886. A similar state of affairs had been highlighted in the national Liberal press the year before when *Reynolds' Newspaper* had called for London Radicals to form an association on the Birmingham model, adding: 'The word "Liberal" now means nothing': *Reynolds' Newspaper*, 29 Nov. 1885. See Lawrence, 'Popular radicalism and the socialist revival in Britain', p. 174.

discussion of policy matters in the Scottish Liberal Association [SLA] both by its members and those of the new National Liberal Federation of Scotland, established in 1885.[74] At a meeting of the general council of the SLA in February 1886, concerns had already been voiced regarding the formation of 'Radical Associations and Junior Liberal Associations' in the large towns.[75]

The growth in the Scottish Home Rule movement clearly fed the demands for such associations in Paisley. Barbour had paid lip-service to demands for Scottish Home Rule at the 1886 election; however, as an issue, it attracted the radical elements of the local party far more than the party elite. On 18 October, a branch of the Scottish Home Rule Association was established at a public meeting chaired by Provost Cochran in Paisley. Though J. M. McCallum, Peter Eadie and other prominent Liberals were present, the absence of the thread interest was notable.

The crofting question also roused local radical sentiment in favour of Liberal organisational reform. In 1886, Barbour, who had failed to vote for the amendments to the Crofters' Bill moved by the Crofters' MPs, defended his actions by painting the proposed legislation as 'an unnecessary interference with the rights of property'. He judged there was nothing desirable in laws 'to increase the number of places where there are crofters'. He continued: 'If the crofters could only see it, they could get better land and better sunshine where they would be much happier in mind.'[76] Such rhetoric failed to impress local radicals, whose sympathies towards Irish Home Rule owed as much to the land reform clauses in the bills as their proposals for representative government. 'The Highlander', Scotland's equivalent of the 'noble' yeoman or peasant in the typology of English land reform rhetoric, was a powerful symbol of the anti-landlordism which, owing much to Henry George, activated radicals in the 1880s and beyond. Barbour's apparent 'lukewarm' commitment to the crofters' cause succeeded only in isolating radical sentiment still further from orthodox Liberal platforms.

The calls for reform that were heard for a Radical Association in 1886, however were never acted upon.[77] A long silence separated this enthusiasm and its re-emergence in January 1890 when the *Paisley Daily Express* called for 'a vigorous Liberal Association in town'.[78] The Liberal Association inaugurated in 1885, beyond a report of its AGM in February 1887, had been silent. In that year, of its five vice-presidents, two were Unionists.[79] In 1890, the press was peppered with references to

74 See Kellas, 'Liberal Party in Scotland', esp. pp. 9–10.
75 EUL, Special Collections, SLA Collection, Minutes, vol. II: 1881–1893, Meeting of the General Council, 19 Feb. 1886 (p. 81).
76 *PDE*, 25 Jun. 1886.
77 Ibid., 4 Jul. 1885.
78 Ibid., 27 Jan. 1890.
79 *PRG*, 5 Feb. 1887.

Liberal apathy, yet the *Express* proposal remained just another voice of good intent.[80]

It was not until the following year that Paisley Liberals established a new Liberal Association [PLA], a Women's Liberal Association having been formed the year before. At the founding meeting, Thomas Glen Coats explained how, 'out of deference to the Liberal Unionists' and 'a feeling that it might cause disunion in the Liberal Club', the old Association 'was not pushed on'.[81] Now, 'they must face the inevitable in the knowledge that many of those who left them would never come back'.[82]

In terms of leadership, the new associations failed to represent a new departure. Thomas Glen Coats occupied the position of president in the new association, while the treasurer was John Lochhead of Kerr & Sons, thread manufacturers; the secretary was the lawyer Alfred McNaughton; and the vice-presidents included J. A. Brown of Brown & Polson, Treasurer Wilson, a shawl manufacturer, and Rev. Dr Hutton of Canal Street United Presbyterian Church. The Paisley and District Women's Liberal Association [PWLA], formed in 1890, was similarly dominated by the wives, daughters, mothers and sisters of the Liberal elite. The treasurer of the PWLA was Mrs J. M. McCallum, wife of the soap manufacturer; among its vice-presidents were Mrs Coats of Ferguslie, wife of Thomas Glen, Mrs Wotherspoon of Maxwellton House, wife of the local cornflour manufacturer and Mrs Dunn of Kensington, London, wife of the Paisley-born merchant William Dunn; and chairperson of the acting committee was Mrs Allan Coats.

Paisley's Liberal associations thus remained dominated by the local industrial elite. Though seriously diminished since the Unionist purge, their 'class' character remained very much intact. The year 1886 had clearly failed to create a clean Whig–Radical cleavage in the Liberal ranks in Paisley. Created in the same year as the local Trades Council, the new PLA of 1891 ultimately failed to live up to its promise of regeneration, just when a viable radical alternative to contemporary Liberalism was beginning tentatively to assert itself. In 1891, Rev. Dr Hutton emphasised the gravity of the situation they were facing, remarking, in quasi-Gramscian terms: 'This was one of those historical transition periods, the lines of cleavage seemed strong and the chasm widened. Men had to make up their minds which way to go.'[83]

The platforms of the local branches of the Irish National League of Great Britain [INL] in this regard, posed simultaneously as Liberal defenders and portents of its ultimate doom. Paisley's Irish-born population stood at around 4,994 in 1881, representing just under 9%

80 Ibid., 17 May 1890; *PDE* 28 Jan. 1890; 11 Apr. 1890.
81 *PRG*, 24 Jan. 1891.
82 *PDE*, 20 Jan. 1891.
83 *PRG*, 21 Nov. 1891.

of the total population.[84] In terms of over-all numbers, the Irish population had hardly changed since the 1830s, the post-Famine immigration merely acting to 'counteract the losses through mortality and out-migration' without seriously augmenting its overall size.[85] Collins makes the point that, whilst the rate of movement of Irish families into Dundee 'increased substantially' in the years from 1835 to 1851, in Paisley 'the in-movement of Irish families decreased sharply during the depression years of the early 1840s and scarcely increased at all during the post-1845 period'.[86] The history of the Paisley Irish is thus one of a community of long-standing by the 1880s, whose demography had little to distinguish it from that of other town residents.[87] Though concentrated as a community in 'the Sneddon', apart from the obvious religious differences, the Irish no longer represented that 'something other' which the female-dominated Irish work-force in Dundee represented in the late nineteenth century. That such features of a group's history should have consequences for their later response to political change has gone largely unconsidered in the annals of Scottish politics which tend to draw on an undifferentiated 'Scottish' or 'West of Scotland' stereotype of the Irish community, based largely on the Glasgow experience. Yet, in the context of the Irish 'Buddy', the established nature of the group appears to have had important implications for its reaction to the emergent social agenda in the politics of the late nineteenth century.

In November 1886, William Redmond addressed a meeting of the local A. M. Sullivan branch of the INL. 'Paisley', he noted, 'had been known to the members of the party to which he belonged as a place where there was a good fund of Irish nationality, combined at the same time with a great fund also of sound Scottish Radicalism'.[88] It would have been surprising had the Irish weaving families that migrated to Paisley in the early nineteenth century not co-operated in the radical politics of these years. Indeed, recent research has highlighted the significant role of Irish immigrants in early Scottish radicalism in the Renfrewshire area.[89] It seems likely, therefore, that in terms of an established group identity, leaving to one side the question of Irish Home Rule, the Paisley Irish, as a stable and established community in the burgh, shared many of the radical traits of their Scottish neighbours. Such a shared political identity, it is suggested, ultimately made the

84 McCarthy, *Social Geography of Paisley*, Appendix N (a).

85 Collins, 'Irish Emigration to Dundee and Paisley', p. 199.

86 Ibid., p. 200. Note, however, that although Paisley's Irish population increased by only 1% in the years from 1841 to 1861, the number of Irish in Renfrewshire increased by 13%: McCarthy, *Social Geography of Paisley*, p. 114.

87 Ibid., pp. 202–3.

88 *PDE*, 23 Nov. 1886.

89 M. Mitchell, 'Irish participation in Scottish radicalism', Glasgow Labour History Workshop Seminar, 1994 (unpublished paper).

transition from Liberal to Labour politics far easier for many in the Paisley branches of the Irish National League than in other branches in Scotland, and made them dangerous allies for the Liberals as early as the 1880s.[90] As Ian Wood has made clear, the league in Scotland 'assumed an increasingly important role in the labour and radical politics of west and central Scotland in the late nineteenth and early twentieth centuries'.[91]

By March 1889, Paisley was home to four branches of the INL and a branch of the Young Ireland Society, established in March of that year. Most active among these was the A. M. Sullivan branch, named after the former editor of the *Nation*, and later the Justin McCarthy branch. However, the Robert Emmett branch also proved active, as did the Mrs Davitt branch of the Ladies National League, established in 1887. Co-operation with the local Liberal Party was highlighted by the number of Liberals chairing demonstrations and St Patrick's Day celebrations, which in the years following Gladstone's declaration for Irish Home Rule were held under league rather than chapel auspices. Despite its co-operation in Parnell's call to support Conservative candidates in 1885, following 1886, the local league explicitly called on its members to support Liberals both in parliamentary and municipal elections.[92] Yet, even in the 1880s, the league's radicalism in Paisley was clearly going beyond the conventional Liberal programme.

Much influenced by John Ferguson, Paisley League platforms were among the first in these years, apart from the Co-operative movement, to concentrate on radical collectivist solutions to social ills, and attack landlordism as part of an exploitative *class* system. In August 1886, J. O. McShane, a Johnstone Nationalist, addressed the usual weekly meeting of the A. M. Sullivan branch of the league. 'It is', he said,

> the same privileged class of tyrants who have devastated and plundered the people of Ireland, sent millions of them to the poor-house, the emigrant ship and the grave. It is the same *foul system* that is working its ruinous effects in Scotland and England as well.[93]

The traditional radical focus on the landowning classes is evident, yet, moving beyond this Ferguson broadened the attack to encompass the urban capitalist dimension. At the St Patrick's Day festival in Paisley in 1887 he commented that every observer must see that:

90 Here it is useful to highlight a phenomenon addressed by Knox, who has drawn attention to the fact that, by as early as 1871, the predominance of Paisley-born heads of households employed by local textile companies was under threat and that in a survey of household heads employed in textiles, the number of Irish-born increased from 5.7% to 10.5% between 1871 and 1891. Knox uses such statistics to highlight the background to the fragmentation of the social cohesion at the centre of the paternalistic ideal: Knox, *Hanging by a Thread*, pp. 159–60.

91 Wood, 'Irish immigrants and Scottish radicalism', p. 75.

92 *PDE*, 26 Oct. 1886.

93 Ibid., 24 Aug. 1886 [my italics].

they are upon the eve of some tremendous change in our social system. The system, which is grinding down the labourers into the slums of our large towns and depopulating the country, must come to an end.[94]

The following year – the same year in which Ferguson supported Hardie's independent candidature at the Mid-Lanark by-election – a Paisley league demonstration addressed by Ferguson, concluded with a resolution in favour of a Scottish legislature with full control of Scottish questions. Then, in 1893 Ferguson, speaking at a demonstration in Paisley in aid of the Evicted Tenants Fund, declared: 'Religious dissensions no longer divided them. Popery and Protestantism had now nothing to do with it. They were on the march for bread and butter, for good houses and for healthy families.'[95]

The themes of nationalism, both Scottish and Irish, and an emergent broad-based anti-landlord critique of social ills, rooted in the experience of the Irish tenantry and Scottish crofting population were thus interconnected. They represented, as we saw earlier, a potential twin threat to the Liberal *status quo*, leading as they did to demands for a more thorough-going radicalism within the Liberal Party itself and the initial development of an independent labour voice.[96] Whilst, throughout the 1890s, the INL in Paisley, and more specifically the Justin McCarthy branch, maintained its loyalty to local Liberalism, signs were clearly evident that a social agenda beyond the Home Rule cause was emerging – a theme most explicit in Nationalist relations with local Liberal Progressives who, in 1896, formed the Advanced Radical Association [ARA].

The PLA, formed in 1891, had by the following year established a series of ward committees throughout the burgh to organise the local Liberal vote through lecture programmes and voter registration. By 1893, however, the initial energy shown by the committees in hosting lectures was declining, and little was heard of their work beyond annual reports of their general meetings. Indeed in 1893, the Conservatives were outstripping the Liberals at the local Registration Court, securing 107 lodger and ordinary claims against the Liberals' 84.[97]

94 Ibid., 18 Mar. 1887.

95 Ibid., 24 Nov. 1893.

96 Note the following from Keating and Bleiman, *Labour and Scottish Nationalism*, p. 52: 'support for Home Rule in the early days was an integral part of the character of the Scottish Labour Party, part of its shared background with radicalism'. In this context it is clearly significant that in 1886, the Aberdeen Trades Council, a leading force behind the creation of the Scottish United Trades Councils' Labour Party in 1892, passed a resolution in favour of Home Rule for Scotland and proved influential in the establishment of a local branch of the Scottish Home Rule Association in the area: K. D. Buckley, *Trade Unionism in Aberdeen, 1878–1900* (Aberdeen, 1955), p. 95.

97 *PDE*, 30 Jan. 1893.

During this same period, the Liberal Club, too, was showing signs of decline. On entering its new premises in 1886, the club had boasted a membership of 1,200; by 1891 it had fallen to 1,000, and despite a small increase in 1893, had fallen to 907 in 1895.[98] The cost of membership for many had possibly become prohibitive during this period: in 1889 the cost of annual subscription had been raised from 6s. 6d. to 8s. 6d.[99] At the general meeting in 1891, John Paton, a cabinet-maker and member of the club's general committee, suggested a 'system of advertising' to attract new members.

> Let them get a list of working men in the largest establishments in town and circular these [he suggested], setting forth the advantages of membership. His opinion was that to the great bulk of the tradesmen the club was unknown. They passed and re-passed it, and would not enter, thinking it was too big for them.[100]

Peter Eadie then suggested a reduced membership of 5s. for apprentices, yet nothing seems to have been done to implement either of these suggestions.

The club's lecture programme, until 1893, was largely of an educational character, presentations being held in 1892, for example, on 'Thomas More's *Utopia*', 'France under the Third Republic' and 'Ruskin'. Yet, in 1893, there seems a heightened awareness of social reform in lectures such as that of October on 'A New Radical Programme', presented by the Editor of the *Glasgow Echo*.[101] The following January, the Liberal Club hosted a lecture on 'The Relation of Liberalism to the Labour Movement', during which the speaker encouraged the acceptance by Liberalism of 'the principle of state interference, of state intervention with a view to the greater equalisation of wealth and the improvement of the conditions of Labour'.[102] Clearly, even if in a limited sense, the Liberal elite was reacting to demands for reform.

Many Paisley Liberals were acutely conscious of the seriousness of the Labour threat during these years. In 1892, Alexander Reekie, a member of the Liberal Club, warned that 'the necessities of the hour and the indifference of both the great parties of the state to labour matters made it necessary to create an Independent Labour Party'.[103] Yet, though occasionally ward meetings focused on radical themes, Paisley's existing Liberal organs seemed unprepared, if not altogether unwilling, to claim the 'Labour Question' as their own.

98 Ibid., 17 Dec. 1891; 28 Dec. 1895.
99 Ibid., 28 Dec. 1889.
100 Ibid., 17 Dec. 1891.
101 Ibid., 31 Oct. 1893.
102 Ibid., 24 Jan. 1894.
103 *PRG*, 10 Dec. 1892.

The impulse behind the formation of the ARA was concentrated on such inadequacies in the Liberal establishment to formulate a progressive programme.[104] Established in January 1896 at a meeting of 'those favourable to the formation of an association for the furtherance of advanced Radical principles', the association highlights the existence of a core of Liberal Progressives in Paisley, unprepared to follow blindly the Old Liberalism of the elite. As such, they illustrate a dynamism in late nineteenth-century Scottish Liberalism frequently ignored in theses which choose instead to focus on the inevitability of its decline and the stultifying impact of its apparently overwhelming Gladstonian character. The ARA's founding resolution read thus:

> That whereas the Liberal Association is at present inactive and ineffectual for the propagation of Radical principles, this meeting considers it necessary to form an advanced Radical Association which shall by every legitimate means stir up political interest among the electors and make strenuous efforts to secure adequate representation in Parliament.[105]

The core concerns of the ARA significantly ran parallel to those of the emergent Labour movement in the burgh, and clearly illustrate the potential of Scottish Liberalism, in these years, to react positively to the Labour challenge for working-class representation. James Wallace of Braehead, a local dentist and one of the founding members of the association, made clear that: 'They were not endeavouring to form a split in the Liberal party; but to prevent two or three individuals in an official capacity from regulating the electoral affairs of Paisley at the expense of the industrial classes.'[106] Until April, little else was heard of the new association, beyond a couple of letters from Wallace in the local press. Then, at a meeting in the Tannahill Hall, office-bearers were elected and the objects and programme of the association adopted. The office-bearers were overwhelmingly middle class in composition, though the executive committee was said to be 'large and representative'. Wallace was elected president; Bailie Fisher of Fisher & Co., engineers, and Bailie Souden – a councillor who, in the past had been endorsed by the Trades Council and had chaired one of the first ILP meetings in the

104 Seven years earlier in Dundee similar disaffection had led to protests against Firth as Liberal MP for the town. 'On the 13th May [1889] the Radical Association passed resolutions expressing unqualified condemnation of the neglect of Mr Firth MP of the vital interests of radicalism since he entered Parliament for the city, and requested him to resign his seat at once in order that the city might obtain a real and not a shoddy representative': D. Lowe, *Souvenirs of Scottish Labour* (Glasgow, 1919), p. 32. Such developments echo national concerns. At this level, Liberal Progressives were articulating radical social policies through the Rainbow Circle and the *Progressive Review* (est. 1896): Belchem, *Popular Radicalism in Nineteenth-Century Britain*, p. 143.

105 *PRG*, 25 Jan. 1896.

106 *PDE*, 25 Jan. 1896.

town – became vice-presidents; Hugh Beveridge, a builder, became the treasurer; and Joseph Black Jr, a local journalist, was elected secretary.

The objects of the association were to be two-fold, recalling Paisley's radical past: 'To maintain and enforce the thorough representation of the burgh on Radical principles' and 'government of the people, for the people, by the people'.[107] The programme adopted included the payment of MPs; one man, one vote and a second ballot; payment of election expenses from the rates; universal suffrage for adults of both sexes attaining the age of twenty-one with three months residence for registration; the increase in the age of half-timers to fourteen years; the election of Prime Minister and Cabinet by the party returned to power; 'Home Rule All Round'; the abolition of the House of Lords and all hereditary titles; the disestablishment and disendowment of the Church of Scotland; free state secular education up to and including the universities; old age pensions; the municipalisation of the drink traffic; triennial parliaments; the end of 'perpetual pensions'; the abolition of all property qualifications for public office; the taxation of land values, ground rents and mining loyalties; the election of JPs by town and county councils; and the prohibition of canvassing at elections.[108]

The following week, a letter under the title 'The Radical Revolt at Paisley' appeared in the *Glasgow Evening News*, providing a commentary on established Paisley Liberalism:

> It is true that Liberalism has been 'cornered' in Paisley by a select few who, if they are rather dull, are impeachable respectable and wealthy ... The fabled old Chartist fire, which is popularly supposed to inspire the 'buddies' at election times is a hoary old chestnut, in which the truth has not abode these last thirty years. The old weaver is dying out, the younger man is a critic of fitba'.[109]

Even at this early stage, the association was said to have 'won considerable sympathy in town', and soon attracted the qualified support of the Irish Nationalists at a meeting of the Justin McCarthy branch of the INL in April.[110]

Over the next few months, propaganda was limited, and largely took the form of highlighting the hostility of William Dunn (the burgh's new Liberal MP) to a thorough-going radical programme, most notably in his sympathies for the reform – rather than the abolition – of the House of Lords and his support of the award of a perpetual pension to the duke of Coburg. In May, however, the association embarked on a serious attempt to attract the support of other Scottish Liberal associations for the composition of a new programme of reform, asking them to discuss

107 Ibid., 4 Apr. 1896.
108 Ibid., 4 Apr. 1896.
109 Reprinted, *PRG*, 11 Apr. 1896.
110 Ibid., *PDE*, 14 Apr. 1896.

such a measure at a meeting to be held in Glasgow in October.[111] In promoting such an endeavour, the ARA in Paisley anticipated a prominent national theme of the succeeding year, during which the National Liberal Club issued a circular to all local party branches requesting their opinion on the direction of party policy.[112] However, nothing seems to have come of ARA plans for an October meeting, and although a similar plan was re-launched in December, Paisley's proposition even then attracted a muted response.

In February 1897, the secretary of the SLA received a letter from the Glasgow Blackfriars Liberal Association in the course of which the association detailed a communication it had received in December from the Paisley ARA which read:

> The Executive of the Paisley Advanced Radical Association are desirous of knowing if your Association would join with them in addressing a circular to the various Liberal and Radical Associations of Scotland, suggesting the holding of a conference at an early date for the purpose of considering and recommending a line of policy to the leaders of the Liberal Party. The unsatisfactory state of the Party at the present moment is we believe due largely to the fact that the leaders are not agreed upon a programme; each advocating his own particular policy, and our association feel strongly that there is urgent need for the immediate placing of an authorised programme before the constituencies if the party is to escape a repetition of last election, crushing defeat.[113]

Blackfriars opposed the Paisley association's propaganda methods, pointing out that:

> the method of convening such a conference as you desire has hitherto been through the Scottish Liberal Association and we feel that it would be unwise for any association to take such action as you suggest until they had at least an opportunity of dealing with the matter in the usual way.[114]

However, Blackfriars subsequently forwarded a resolution to the SLA in the manner outlined, requesting the executive to convene a national conference for the purpose of considering 'the present position of the Liberal party and formulating a programme'.[115] Such a conference was never held.[116]

111 Ibid., 9 May 1896.
112 *PRG*, 9 Oct. 1897.
113 EUL, SLA Collection, Minutes, vol. IV: 1893–1898, Western Committee Meeting, 3 Feb. 1897 (pp. 284–5).
114 Ibid., p. 285.
115 Ibid., p. 284.
116 Note also that the ARA had recorded a favourable response to their suggestion from Hutchesontown Liberal Association: *PDE*, 7 Sep. 1897.

In response to the National Liberal Club circular of September 1897, however, the ARA suggested the creation of a Liberal programme, including payment of members of parliament, the 'Free Breakfast Table', taxation of land values and mining royalties, manhood suffrage and the second ballot, the abolition of the House of Lords and 'Home Rule all Round', with Ireland having a prior claim.[117] Having received a copy of the ARA's recommendations, Dunn replied:

> I am quite at one with you that it is desirable that the Liberal Party should take energetic and definite action, and decide on a programme, when there is a prospect of a general election. I have ... promised to support many of the questions you mention.[118]

The ARA considered this response inadequate.

Clearly, the ARA succeeds in establishing the existence, *at a grass roots level*, of an enthusiasm for progressive reform, unreflected in Liberalism's national Scottish bodies. Due to the lack of a sufficient number of local studies in Scotland, the protestations of the SLA have tended to be taken as largely representative of the 'national will' and thus a radical undercurrent has been somewhat ignored. Hutchison's statement that 'Liberals ... made few bids to court the working-class vote in Scotland by any display of commitment to the demands made by Labour' clearly mistakenly extrapolates, from SLA policy, the attitude of Liberals 'on the ground'.[119] Alternatively, *despite* the apparent radicalism which both Kellas and Brown identify in the SLA at this time, by way of contrast to its southern neighbour, for some Scottish Liberals it was clearly not going far enough.[120]

In 1894, the joint committee appointed by the Western Committee of the SLA and the Glasgow Liberal Council to consider Liberal – ILP relations concluded that:

> The programme of the 'Independent Labour Party' is purely socialistic, their leaders declare unqualified opposition to the Liberal Party and do all they can to break it up. The Committee therefore do not see that there is any basis upon which united action can be taken.[121]

Even though the question of relations with the ILP would be raised by the SLA later in 1894 and again in 1896, non-co-operation with 'the Socialist Party' proved the dominant attitude of the executive.[122]

117 *PDE*, 7 Sep. 1897.

118 Ibid., 23 Sep. 1897.

119 Hutchison, *Political History of Scotland*, p. 180.

120 Kellas, 'Liberal Party in Scotland', p. 13; S. Brown, '"Echoes of Midlothian": Scottish Liberalism and the South African War, 1899–1902', *SHR*, lxxi (1992), pp. 161–2.

121 EUL, SLA Collection, Minutes, vol. IV: 1893–1898, Meeting of the Joint Committee of the Western Committee of the Scottish Liberal Association and the Glasgow Liberal Council, 11 May 1894 (pp. 92–3).

122 Ibid., Minutes vol. IV: 1893–1898, Executive Council Meeting, 14 Jun. 1894 (p. 120); Western Committee Meeting, 2 Dec. 1896, pp. 275–6.

In 1896, however, the Paisley ARA, a body which by 1897 had affiliated to the SLA, put forward a proposal for an Advanced Radical Party, in which would be merged the Paisley radicals, the local INL, the ILP and 'the Socialists'.[123] At a meeting of the local INL, Wallace recommended that these associations 'arrange themselves as a solid body against the designs of the official Liberal and the influence of wealth', adopt a candidate who would be judged against Dunn in a local plebiscite in which, he felt sure, 'the minority' would be forced to acquiesce'.[124] McGlame, the president of the Justin McCarthy branch of the INL, thereafter promised to 'do all in his power to forward the amalgamation of the radicals, the Irish Nationalists, the ILP and the Socialists'.[125]

Whilst nothing came of the planned alliance, the proposal represents the possibility acknowledged by some Liberals of harnessing the energy of the new Labour movement for Liberal interests. No references have been found of the local ILP ever discussing the proposal, though limited municipal co-operation between the ARA and the ILP in 1897 is proof of a degree of Liberal sympathy with the ILP at a grass roots level which is largely absent in the records of the national party hierarchy.

Though similar to the Stalwart grouping in Glasgow formed around John Ferguson which, in 1896 as the Workers Municipal Elections Committee, drew up a nine-point programme of reforms they wished to see implemented in local government, the proposed Paisley alliance differed in three important aspects.[126] It was to be established as a *parliamentary* electoral body; it included Liberals; and it excluded the Co-operative movement and the trades unions. John M. Robertson, the late 'Radical' candidate for Northampton, reflected on the new grouping later in September 1896, when he addressed the Paisley ARA:

> The mere existence ... of the Advanced Radical Association in Paisley as elsewhere through these three kingdoms, was evidence of new political life, and it might be the beginning of a new political era ... It was a fallacy to assume that the Liberal party was always one and the same thing ... the Liberal party was being reconstituted.[127]

Liberalism, according to Robertson, was 'in a stage of transition, or new life'.[128]

Due to the lack of official national pronouncements on co-operation and the absence of a Lib-Lab pact in Scotland during the Edwardian years, the 'Lib-Lab' theme in English politics of the late nineteenth

123 *PDE*, 8 Sep. 1896.
124 Ibid., 8 Sep. 1896.
125 Ibid., 8 Sep. 1896.
126 See J. J. Smyth, 'The ILP in Glasgow, 1888–1906: the struggle for identity', in McKinlay and Morris, *ILP on Clydeside*, pp. 20–55.
127 *PRG*, 3 Oct. 1896.
128 *PDE*, 30 Sep. 1896.

century has been considered to have few Scottish parallels. That being the case, the argument that Scotland managed the birth of Labourism from Old Liberalism without much evidence of transitional 'labour pains', has largely passed historical notice or been accepted as a reassuring characteristic of Scottish 'exceptionalism' for those who seek to legitimate a historical agenda of Scottish 'separateness'. Just as New Liberalism has been considered a phenomenon 'distant' from the Scottish experience, so Lib-Labism has largely been considered an unfortunate phase for a few, between the darkness of Gladstonianism and the true light of a Labour class consciousness. Rather, it is a crucial and largely forgotten stage in the conjunctural crises which elemented the organic 'change' to Labour in Scotland and, for Paisley, the re-definition of its radical past. The ARA represents, as does the 'battle' for the dominance of the Trades Council in these years, parallel movements in the general metamor-phosis of the identity of the Paisley radical consciousness.

The PLA, however, failed to share the enthusiasm of its radical associates, clearly illustrating a comparable conservatism at the 'top' of the local party structure to that of the national Scottish party. In 1897, the recently knighted Sir Thomas Glen Coats commented that '[he] did not think they needed to be in too great a hurry to formulate a definite political programme for the Liberal Party', and reflected that the Newcastle Programme was 'too big'.[129] The ARA's first annual report declared that 'the older Association [had] done absolutely nothing [that] year in the way of Liberal propaganda' and the speeches delivered under Liberal Club auspices had been delivered by 'men who displayed little or no sympathy with the more advanced Liberalism ... professional exponents of the officialism, as contrasted with the popular aspirations of the party'.[130]

Meanwhile, at an ARA meeting in October 1897 activists were encouraged to 'permeate the Liberal Party with new ideals, new ambitions, new determinations'.[131] Calls were heard for Labour and Liberalism to combine to reform the political machinery, 'to get the main points that the Chartists worked for sixty years ago' in order then to institute new social measures.[132] However, the only lasting legacy of the ARA in this regard was its success in placing the taxation of land values at the top of the local agenda. Following a lecture from John Paul, author of *The Single Tax*, in December 1897, attended by numerous councillors and sponsored by the ARA, the local Town Council passed a resolution in favour of the rating of land (apart from improvements) for local purposes.[133]

129 *PRG*, 9 Oct. 1897.
130 *PDE*, 1 Feb. 1897.
131 *PRG*, 9 Oct. 1897.
132 Ibid., 9 Oct. 1897.
133 *PDE*, 16 Mar. 1898.

Coinciding with growing demands for direct labour representation in municipal politics, the politicisation of organised labour following the Engineers' Lock-out of 1897 and growing frustration with the dominance of the industrial elite in Paisley, the 'death' of the ARA in September 1898 marked a critical stage in the appropriation by Labour of the radical agenda which, by this time, had failed to find support in established Liberal organs.

At Sir William Dunn's annual meeting of his constituents in 1898, it was the locked-out engineers under the leadership of Councillor Brown, a former president of the local ILP, who led the protest against Dunn by moving the amendment that Dunn was 'neither a fit nor proper person to represent the burgh in Parliament'.[134] Brown continued:

> He had put the amendment ... because he believed that the interests of Sir William Dunn, and the class to which he was related, were diametrically opposed, and never could be reconciled, to the interests of wage earners.[135]

The *Gazette* reported that whilst the chairman failed to acknowledge it, on a show of hands, the amendment was carried.

The following month, the second annual report of the ARA announced the executive's disapproval of Sir William Dunn as Paisley's Liberal representative. 'The time has now arrived', it declared, 'to adopt a candidate who will, by his voice as well as by his vote, give expression to the democratic sentiments of the constituency.'[136] Sir William's opposition to the abolition of the house of lords was apparently 'sufficient' in the eyes of the ARA to 'disqualify him as a Radical candidate'.[137] The ARA's opposition was thus framed in the rhetoric of 'democracy' and the representative principle. The absence of the 'class' argument used by Brown the previous month is notable and highlights the emergence of an exclusively 'Labour' interpretation of the radical agenda, one which even the most progressive Paisley Liberals would not harness. It is surely no coincidence that in this year, three Labour representatives were elected to the Town Council.

Thereafter, as the radical agenda became increasingly dominated by demands for direct labour representation, nothing is heard of the ARA beyond a brief 'obituary' in the *Gazette* in September. James Wallace himself, however, seemed to personify this early stage of labour development, when, having been presented with a gold-mounted riding whip by the Paisley District ASE for his assistance during the lock-out, he noted: 'whatever shibboleth the professional politician comes under,

134 *PRG*, 15 Jan. 1898.
135 Ibid., 15 Jan. 1898.
136 *PRG*, 5 Feb. 1898.
137 Ibid., 5 Feb. 1898.

whether Liberal or Tory, recognise him not, but get *one of your own order* to represent your views and aspirations'.[138]

The unity of interests which encompassed the shared ideology, essential for the continuity of the Liberal hegemony, was thus clearly under threat in the final years of the nineteenth century. The processes which engendered this change illustrated the stages in the development of a new social consciousness, the creation of which became imperative as an ideology of class drew strength from apparent abuses of local power and the existence of unrepresentative elites, and as the established order proved reluctant to adapt. Liberal organisational impotence clearly reflected deeper problems of ideology.

Organising Unionism

In 1885, the Paisley Conservative Association [PCA], established in 1878, was 'remodelled, so that it might be more influential and representative'.[139] In the past, the members of the association had simply elected a general committee of fifteen and the office-bearers. Under the new system, the general committee, in addition to these fifteen representatives, was to be composed of the secretaries of each ward committee; the directors of the Beaconsfield Club and other delegates, making up fifteen representatives in total from the ward committees and twelve from the Beaconsfield Club. The industrial elite, however, still retained the pre-eminent positions in the association. Archibald Craig of Gateside, proprietor of A. F. Craig & Co., engineers, held the post of president; William Bow of Bow, McLachlan & Co., engineers, occupied the post of vice-president alongside Alexander Fullerton (Millenpark) of Fullerton, Hodgart & Barclay, proprietors of the Vulcan Foundry and Engine Works, George Hamilton (Blacklands) of Adam Hamilton & Sons (bleachers, dyers and finishers), and Daniel MacKenzie of MacKenzie Bros, starch and cornflour manufacturers. Yet the new structure was a *potentially* inclusive one, and by 1890 a notable number of small employers, craftsmen and the new breed of clerical worker and accountant were evident in representative positions in the association.[140]

In 1886 the PCA affiliated to the National Union of Conservative Associations for Scotland [NUCAS], following that body's amalgamation with the National Constitutional Association the year before. In March, echoing the concerns of the Paisley branch the previous year, the NUCAS Central Council recorded its opinion that 'further steps should be taken without delay to place the organisation on a directly popular and elective basis'.[141] In this sense, the Conservative Association reforms

138 *PDE*, 20 Feb. 1899 [my italics].
139 Ibid., 27 Apr. 1885.
140 *Paisley Directory* (1890–1891).
141 NLS, SCUA, Acc. 10424/60, NUCAS, Central Council Minutes: 1882–1889, 17 Mar. 1886 (p. 92).

in Paisley in the 1880s may be seen as part of the wider Conservative organisational developments of the time which saw the number of affiliated associations in the NUCAS rise from 83 in 1883 to 245 by the end of the century.[142]

Conservative relations with the local Liberal Unionists after 1886 were to dominate and indeed determine the history of Conservative fortunes in Paisley until the end of the century. Although in June 1886 the NUCAS Central Council resolved that 'all Conservatives [should] ... record their votes for the Unionist candidate whether Conservative or Liberal and ... do their utmost to secure his return', this directive proved unpopular among many Paisley Conservatives.[143] The PCA annual report in February 1887 recorded that whilst acting in accordance with the leadership recommendations in supporting Parker Smith at the recent election, this arrangement had proved 'unsatisfactory to very many members'.[144]

In terms of elite domination, the newly formed Paisley Liberal and Radical Unionist Association [PLRUA] of April 1887 very much resembled its Liberal 'parent'. Its first president was Provost John Clark of Largs, its first chairman, Archibald Coats, and its vice-presidents included Stewart Clark, the former MP and current member of the Executive Committee of the WSLUA; James Clark, Liberal candidate nominee in 1885; Peter Coats Jr; Hugh H. Smiley of Kerr & Sons, thread manufacturers; John Polson; John Logan of Logan & Gardner, shawl manufacturers; John P. Kerr of the Underwood power loom mills; and ex-Provost MacKean, the starch manufacturer.[145] Yet, as its title would suggest, the new association styled itself very much in the manner of a new Liberalism.[146] At its inauguration, ex-Provost Clark emphasised that 'They were now as they formerly were – Liberals.'[147]

In the first two years of its existence, the PLRUA appeared on good terms with its Conservative colleagues, its local influence receiving a boost in January 1889 with the creation of a local branch of the West of Scotland Women's Liberal Unionist Association. Conservatives and Liberal Unionists co-operated in a number of demonstrations, the Rev. Dr Brown of St James's United Presbyterian Parish encouraging the PLRUA at its first AGM to be 'ready at all times to co-operate heartily

142 Urwin, 'Development of the Conservative Party Organisation', p. 97.

143 NLS, SCUA, Acc. 10424/60, NUCAS Central Council Minutes: 1882–1889, 16 Jun. 1886 (p. 99).

144 *PRG*, 26 Feb. 1887.

145 Ibid., 16 Apr. 1887.

146 Note that, apart from the Ayr Association, the PLRUA was the only West of Scotland Branch to stress its Radical roots in its title.

147 *PRG*, 16 Apr. 1887. In this the Paisley Liberal Unionists very much followed the determination of the Constitution of the West of Scotland Association which stated in Object '2' that 'The membership shall consist of Liberals and Radicals': NLS, SCUA, Acc. 10424/19, WSLUA Minutes: 1886–1894, 'Constitution and Rules', October 1886.

with their friends of the Conservative Party'.[148] Yet by 1889 disunity was evident.

In April of that year, Paisley Liberal Unionists made tentative plans to encourage Archibald Coats to stand as the local Unionist candidate at the next parliamentary election, no Unionist candidate having been before the Paisley electorate for three years. Archibald Coats, however, refused to stand and many local Conservatives, feeling that, having supported a Liberal Unionist in 1886, it was now their turn to propose the next Unionist candidate, determined to adopt Major McKerrell, who was said to be 'extremely popular with all classes in Paisley'.[149] At a meeting of the Conservative General Committee at the end of the month, this stance was endorsed by the local Conservative leadership and 'loud complaints were made as to the dilatory tactics of the Liberal Unionist Executive'.[150]

Such complaints mirror the concerns of the NUCAS at this time, which had highlighted in 1889 'the difficulty there was in proceeding with organisation and the selection of candidates in consequence of the attitude of the Liberal Unionists'.[151] Indeed Charles B. Renshaw, the future MP for West Renfrewshire, pointed out two months later that 'a feature in every report' from the west 'was the want of Liberal Unionist organisation', a factor which he recommended should be 'pressed urgently upon the Liberal Unionist Whips'.[152] The outcome of a subsequent meeting with the Liberal Unionists was later considered 'unsatisfactory'.[153]

Throughout 1890, letters appeared in the local Paisley press asking 'Where is the candidate?', some authors echoing Conservative beliefs that the Liberal Unionists were to blame for the apparent inactivity:

> The impression that is now getting abroad is that, having failed to secure a candidate, certain members of the party, rather than support a Conservative Unionist, persist in keeping the matter in a state of suspended animation and, in fact, would sacrifice the chance of securing the seat rather than see it contested by a Conservative.[154]

Having reached 'stalemate', the Liberal Unionists resolved in August to consult the national leadership regarding the choice of candidate. In April 1890, however, the Conservatives were still holding out for their own choice of candidate. Nevertheless, the following month they agreed

148 *PRG*, 5 Nov. 1887.
149 Ibid., 27 Apr. 1889.
150 *PDE*, 23 Apr. 1890.
151 NLS, SCUA, Acc. 10424/61, NUCAS Minutes: 1888–1893, General Council Meeting, 20 Feb. 1889 (p. 44).
152 Ibid., General Council Meeting, 17 Apr. 1889 (p. 54).
153 Ibid., ref. to Joint Meeting with Liberal Unionist Association, 8 May 1889.
154 *PDE*, 18 Jan. 1890, letter from 'Forward'.

to place the whole matter in the hands of the national leadership in London. A panel made up of Lord Hartington, Joseph Chamberlain, Lord Salisbury and A. J. Balfour was to decide between the nominee of the Liberal Unionists – R. W. McLeod Fullarton, a London barrister – and Major McKerrell, the nominee of the Conservatives.[155] The panel came to their decision in June and the following December, a crowded Unionist demonstration, comprising both Liberal Unionists and Conservatives adopted Major McKerrell as their candidate, on the motion of ex-Provost Clark, a Liberal Unionist. McKerrell concluded at this meeting that they 'were determined to sink all petty party differences'.[156]

Thereafter, throughout the rest of the 1890s, it was the Conservatives of Paisley who dominated Unionist politics in the burgh and provided the initiative behind new organisational and propaganda schemes; their strength was reflected in their power to determine the choice of candidate in both the 1892 and 1895 elections. Whilst in 1893, Archibald Coats, a Liberal Unionist, had provided the finance for a house-to-house canvass to gauge Unionist support in the burgh, by 1899, the Liberal Unionists appeared so apathetic as to show little commitment to the holding of an annual meeting.[157]

By way of contrast, at the Conservative Association's AGM of April 1893, plans were put in place for the creation of a reading room for working-class Unionists, and by June of that year subscriptions were being raised to finance the project.[158] Although devoid of a reading room until February 1895, the East End Unionist Association Rooms were opened in October 1894, and within weeks, 180 members had been recruited. Throughout 1895, the East End Association proved active, meeting fortnightly and organising a regular winter lecture programme, and by 1896 could boast a membership of 320. In June 1895, a Central Unionist Association was established with rooms in Old Sneddon Street, again the result of the motivation of the local Conservatives, and designed 'chiefly for the convenience of working men'.[159] Before the official opening, the Central Association had attracted over 200 members.[160] Both associations proved a key focus of organisation for the Unionists, making up, to some extent, for the apathy of the PLRUA.

Such organisational enthusiasm is clearly in marked contrast to the Liberal experience of these years when Liberal Club membership was marked by progressive decline. As social centres as well as political

155 *PRG*, 12 Apr. 1890; 10 May 1890.
156 Ibid., 27 Dec. 1890.
157 NLS, SCUA, Acc. 10424/19, WSLUA Minutes: 1886–1894, 29 Dec. 1893, 12 Jan. 1894; WSLUA Minutes: 1894–1900, Report Submitted to Business Committee, 21 Apr. 1899 (pp. 283–4).
158 *PDE*, 22 Apr. 1893; 24 Jun. 1893.
159 Ibid., 13 Jun. 1895.
160 *PRG*, 6 May 1899.

bodies, the new Unionist associations may have attracted some members with their relatively low subscriptions who may not have been political activists or indeed sympathisers. Yet, the explicit and determined organisational focus on the burgh's working classes reveals a critical awareness in the Unionist ranks, in contrast to the apparent inaction of the Liberal elite, of the power of the new democracy and the potency of the 'Labour Question'.

Unionist organisation in the burgh, however, went beyond the official party bodies, extending into the cultural and associational life of the town via organs such as the Primrose League, the Beaconsfield Club, the Orange Lodges and, for a time, the Fair Trade League. Such bodies were more than associated interest groups or the coat-tails of the party bodies. They were rather both context and components of a wider Unionist philosophy. Through such bodies, new 'recruits' were instructed in a broader appreciation of Empire and the religious dimension of the political struggle. As a consequence, politics attained cultural expression, and party policy was absorbed as a social as well as a formal ideological expression of identity.

Paisley boasted the first branch of the Primrose League in Scotland, Habitation No. 232, which in 1886 had around 375 members. In that same year a second 'all female' branch was established in Paisley, the Abercorn Habitation, No. 666, which by April had attracted 800 members.[161] This 'flowering' of the Primrose League on the banks of the Cart was perceived as part of a local Conservative resurgence in the 1880s. Charles Bine Renshaw went so far as to describe Paisley in 1887 as 'the centre of the rising successes of the Conservative party in Scotland'.[162] Yet it is doubtful to what extent the progress of the Primrose League in Paisley can be attributed to a 'plebeian' commitment to the philosophy of 'Tory Democracy' which Jon Lawrence has identified in many areas in England during this period.[163] Although in 1893 the Grand Council of the Primrose League in Scotland proved relatively enthusiastic in organising open meetings for the discussion of labour questions in the major towns, the following year the same body refused to recommend a resolution to put social reform to the front of the Conservative Party programme. [164] Furthermore, though Martin Pugh has located a 'significant working-class membership' gathered in the Paisley habitations, their influence was slight, their voice muted and their views far from progressive.[165]

161 Ibid., 24 Apr. 1886.
162 *PDE*, 29 Jun. 1887.
163 Lawrence, 'Class and gender', p. 632.
164 NLS, SCUA, Acc. 10424/1, Primrose League (Scotland) General Council Minutes: 1885–1904, 2 Mar. 1893 (p. 76); 21 Dec. 1894 (p. 93).
165 M. Pugh, *The Tories and the People, 1880–1935* (Oxford, 1985), p. 133.

The Beaconsfield Club followed this 'traditional' line. Established in 1880, by 1885 it had a membership of 421.[166] Its directors were mainly middle-class employers and financial and legal agents, its president being for many years William Abercrombie Jr of Sutherland Abercrombie, soap manufacturers. Its reports appeared in the local press, yet seldom did they attract more than a cursory acknowledgement beyond confirming the club's continued existence well into the twentieth century, or reflect any serious political consciousness beyond the hosting of various lectures and the occasional inter-party billiard tournament. Yet, though lacking serious political 'clout', it is notable that its membership paralleled the growth in Unionist support evident in the East End and Central Associations, rising consistently, if not dramatically, throughout the 1890s on average, by about fifty new members each year.[167]

The Fair Trade League, established in Paisley in 1885, though vanishing from the political stage in the late 1880s, reflected a reforming current at that point unrepresented in the Conservative and Unionist Associations. On 14 April 1885, a meeting was held to gauge the extent of support for tariff reform in the burgh; on 11 June the Paisley branch was established. Its chairman was William Rollings, a well-known local trade unionist, and its secretary was Charles Jago Gregg, a publishing and advertising clerk for the *Glasgow Herald* and well-known local Orangeman and Conservative, replaced in 1886 by another Orangeman, A. B. Maxwell, an employee of the Ferguslie Fire Clay Works.[168] The league attracted many middle-class sympathisers, a meeting in November being notable for the attendance of William Bow of Bow & McLachlan, engineers, the league's future honorary president; George L. Houston of Johnstone Castle; Henry Wallace, the chemical manufacturer; John Craig, a local builder; and A. C. Ingram of the Caledonia Oil Works.[169] During 1885 the league distributed around 30,000 pamphlets on the fiscal question in the local area and in the first annual report it was announced that the views of the league 'have now the support of our most influential townsmen'.[170] Though it alleged its supporters were not confined to Conservatives alone, Conservative bias was apparent in both its leadership and rhetoric.[171]

Most notable, in the sense that it goes some way to reinstating Lawrence's theory regarding working-class support for Conservatism in this period, are the league's working-class supporters, which included J. Wilkinson, secretary of the local Engineers' Society. Rollings's appeal to such men was explicit:

166 *PDE*, 30 Dec. 1885.
167 *PRG*, 9 Feb. 1895; *PDE*, 7 Dec. 1896.
168 *PDE*, 3 Jun. 1885; 16 Nov. 1886.
169 *PRG*, 6 Nov. 1885.
170 *PDE*, 20 Feb. 1886.
171 Ibid., 20 Feb. 1886.

> The working men had to fight and fight hard for every extra shilling they received. He was bound to say that if something was not done to give the British workman a fair chance with foreign competition, in another ten years we would be much worse off than we were forty years ago, and it was for the working class to say how much longer they would willingly submit to its baneful influence.[172]

William McAllister, an ironmoulder and former member of Glasgow Trades Council, spoke to a meeting of the league in February 1886 said to have been 'representative of the working classes', highlighting the paradox of 'protectionist' trade unionists supporting the Liberal free trade ethos.[173] Elaborating a critique of the 'foreigner' in classic Tory style, the league underlined the existence and indeed the popularity of a 'popular' Conservatism in Paisley independent of formal party bounds and clearly sympathetic to the ethos of 'Tory Democracy'. Yet as trade improved and the political scene became dominated by Home Rule politics, references to the league become scarce and though its office-bearers are listed in the *Paisley Directory* as late as 1891, future directories fail to record the league's existence.

Perhaps foremost among the 'secondary' Conservative organs to elaborate a truly populist Unionism in these years were the Orange lodges. McFarland has already shown the importance of the Orange movement in the foundation of the Paisley Conservative Association in 1878, when six Orangemen were elected to the new association's management committee.[174] Even after this time, however, they remained a powerful force in dictating the character of Paisley Conservatism.[175]

In 1886 the threat of Irish Home Rule threw into relief the continued influence of Orangeism in the Paisley Conservative ranks.[176] At the thirtieth annual Orange and Protestant soirée that December, Sir Archibald Campbell MP, addressed an 800-strong crowd, referring to Gladstone as 'the henchman of Mr Parnell', and the following year, William Abercrombie, president of the Beaconsfield Club, joined Lord Frederick Spencer Hamilton in addressing the same body, attacking Gladstonian co-operation with the Irish Nationalists.[177] Orange Lodge meetings resounded to Unionist rhetoric and engaged openly with current political themes of the day, with representatives regularly

172 *PDE*, 3 Jun. 1885.
173 Ibid., 22 Feb. 1886.
174 E. W. McFarland, *Protestants First: Orangeism in Nineteenth-Century Scotland* (Edinburgh, 1990), p. 163.
175 This conclusion coincides with McFarland's appraisal that it is not until 1900 that it becomes possible to trace 'some faltering in Orange involvement with Conservatives': ibid., p. 193.
176 In 1885, the local Orange lodges had proved important supporters of Major McKerrell at the general election: *PDE*, 12 Dec. 1885.
177 *PDE*, 6 Nov. 1886.

attending Conservative meetings on the lodges' behalf. [178] Indeed, in 1890 the Paisley lodges formalised their political activities by establishing an electoral committee, one year *before* a directive from the Grand Council encouraged districts to embark on such organisation.

As the Unionist wrangle over their choice of candidate dragged on in 1890, the Orangemen of Paisley district held a special meeting during which 'the action and inaction of the Executive of the Conservative Association [came] in for hearty condemnation'.[179] Thereupon it was decided to embark upon a scheme for better political organisation of the movement. It was agreed

> That the secretaries of the various lodges in the district be instructed to prepare a return of all the voters on their respective lodge rolls, together with the names and addresses of all electors among the friends and followers of their several lodges, and send same to the district secretary within three months of this date.[180]

The electoral committee was composed of a general committee on which all members of the order were represented and an executive, made up of the district office-bearers and various lodge masters of the area. Within weeks of establishment, it was active at the local registration court, supporting Unionist voter claims, and had attracted the attention of the *Belfast Weekly News,* which highlighted the new committee's potential in stimulating the other Unionist organisations in the town.[181] In February 1891, Charles J. Gregg, lodge district secretary and former Fair Trade League office-bearer, defended Orangeism's involvement in politics: 'It is impossible to separate Orangeism from politics without shattering the whole fabric of the Institution. Why, the fundamental principle of Orangeism is a distinct alliance of religion and politics.'[182] Four months later such sentiments were echoed by the Scottish Grand Master, Colonel Saunderson, who impressed upon a national meeting of Orange delegates the 'necessity of the society in all districts taking a more active part and identifying themselves as such, more closely with politics'. He stressed, 'the society would only command respect and consideration in Scotland when it became a powerful political agency'.[183] Thereafter, the meeting resolved to form political committees in every district in Scotland, with a central council meeting regularly in Glasgow.[184] The Orange movement thus remained a potent political force both nationally and locally throughout the late Victorian period, more so than is perhaps implied in McFarland's description of the

178 See *PDE*, 18 Feb. 1889.
179 *PDE*, 24 Apr. 1890.
180 Ibid., 24 Apr. 1890.
181 As cited: *PDE*, 20 Oct. 1890.
182 Ibid., 2 Feb. 1891.
183 Ibid., 19 Jun. 1891.
184 Ibid., 19 Jun. 1891.

institution during these years as a 'special "interest group" among the broader Unionist forces'.[185] Indeed, continued political involvement was encouraged on Paisley Orange platforms throughout the 1890s, when the high profile of Orange influence in the Unionist party was emphasised by a motion in support of the Unionist government at the annual Grand Orange Lodge demons-tration in Clydebank in July 1897, moved by Bro. Alexander MacFarlane of the Paisley District – the secretary of the western office of the NUCAS.[186]

Paisley Conservatism and the Unionism of the post-1886 years thus articulated itself through various socio-political vehicles: in formal terms, possessing more social organs for the dissemination of its ideology than its Liberal opponent. Whilst the official party bodies were still dominated by the industrial elite, the evidence of the Central and East End Unionist Associations, the early support for the Fair Trade League and the continued influence of the Orange lodges, demonstrated, as in Glasgow, 'a large working-class element' behind the Conservative cause.[187] Indeed, in 1891, Paisley's Chartist veteran, Robert Cochran, commented on the 'lamentable' sight of 'working men joining the Tory ranks'.[188]

Though Hutchison has questioned the degree to which such support may be explained in terms of the attraction of Tory Democracy, stressing instead the traditional appeal of foreign policy and ecclesiastical issues for the Glasgow working classes, the Paisley experience alerts us to an emergent and popular commitment to social reform within Unionist bodies in these years.[189] During the 1885 election Dr Fraser (a future ardent Liberal Unionist) remarked that, on consideration of McKerrell's electoral address

> [He] had never read so Liberal a Tory address ... His professions are most excellent – in fact, if he were to stand alone and not represent a party, why we might all here support him – or very nearly at any rate. (Applause.)[190]

During the election, McKerrell declared himself in favour of 'taxing luxuries to obtain the necessary revenue for free education', voiced sympathy for temperance reforms and continually stressed the Conservative record on social reform.[191] Though Parker Smith proved more sympathetic to Hartington-style Unionism than the radical Chamberlainite alternative, many Paisley Conservatives whose youth was

185 E. W. McFarland, 'The Loyal Orange Institution in Scotland, 1799–1900' (Glasgow University, Ph.D. thesis, 1986), p. 385. McFarland clearly misrepresents formal and independent statements of Orange commitment to Unionism in this period as proof of the lack of a former 'automatic' participation in Conservative politics. Rather, formal declarations reflect more the culmination of informal alliances than their disintegration.

186 *PDE*, 12 Jul. 1897.

187 Hutchison, 'Glasgow working-class politics', p. 124.

188 *PRG*, 4 Apr. 1891.

189 Hutchison, 'Glasgow working-class politics', p. 125.

190 *PDE*, 13 Nov. 1885.

191 *PRG*, 10 Oct. 1885.

frequently the focus of comment, proved sympathetic to growing calls for reform. One wrote as 'Young Paisley' in 1890 in sympathy with the idealism (if not the ideology) of Edward Bellamy's *Looking Backward* and another, 'Truth Before Party', defended the Conservatives' record on reform in a long debate conducted through the letters pages of the local press later that year.[192] Indeed, the year before, the Primrose League in Paisley repudiated claims that the recent Local Government Bill of the Unionist Government proved that 'the Tories had stolen the Radical clothes whilst the Radicals were bathing'.[193]

In the 1890s, the appeal to the working man and to social issues became more explicit, achieving organisational expression in the two new Unionist Associations in the burgh and rhetorical expression in the general elections of 1892 and 1895. Indeed, it was in 1892 that the National Constitutional Labour League in London offered the services of a Labour candidate in the Unionist interest for nomination in Paisley to stand against Dunn.[194] Emphasis was consistently being placed on the labour and social legislation of current and previous Conservative administrations, and appeals for the introduction of pensions and other social reform measures became the common currency of Unionist lectures, even to the extent of an attempt to secure the temperance vote in 1895 by the adoption of the policy of a plebiscite on the municipalisation of the drink traffic.[195]

Evidence therefore exists which suggests greater support in Scotland for the ethos of Tory Democracy than commentators such as Hutchison have acknowledged. Indeed, together with Orangeism, Freemasonry, qualified Protectionism, the early roots of working-class Imperialism and Evangelical Protestantism, Tory Democracy was clearly an important impulse in the motivations of working-class Conservatives and Unionists in Scotland, not to mention a potential 'pull' factor for many Liberal Unionists whose reforming zeal remained even after their exodus from the Liberal ranks.

Working-class Conservatism and Unionist interventionism, however, ought not to be separated from the greater themes of a growing 'labour consciousness' among the working classes in this period. In July 1894, Charles J. Gregg, who later that year moved a motion in favour of a legislated 'Eight Hour Day' at the Paisley Parliamentary Debating Society, announced to a demonstration of the Orange Lodges of Renfrewshire, that 'he was a Conservative because he was a working man, and because he was a working man, he recognised that his interests were best served by a Tory Government'.[196] As Alan J. Lee has made clear:

192 *PDE*, 4 Mar. 1890; 22 Nov. 1890; 24 Nov. 1890. Note comments regarding the youth of the Conservative support: *PDE*, 28 Nov. 1888.
193 *PDE*, 20 Apr. 1889.
194 *PDE*, 2 Jun. 1892.
195 *PRG*, 2 Mar. 1895.
196 *PDE*, 13 Jul. 1894.

> such men and women ... were no eccentric fringe ... their ideology was not just an interesting paradox. They were rather an integral part of the development of working class ideology during a period when the stresses of a maturing economy and the strains of an emergent formal democracy were having their greatest effect.[197]

With this in mind, the evolution of the Labour interest in Paisley must be seen as merely one manifestation among many of working-class concern with changes in the socio-political and economic environment.

Labour and Local Government

Bill Lancaster's model of fragmented labour politics is one which is critical to any understanding of the emergence of the independent labour voice in Britain in the late nineteenth century:

> Up to 1906 labour and socialist politics were essentially local. Where distinct, independent, working class institutions occur they tended to be the product of specific struggles within individual communities. Therefore to understand the emergence of independent labour as a political force it is necessary to study the movement's origins in individual localities. Once this exercise has been undertaken the historian will perhaps not be too startled to find that the early labour party did not present a crystallisation of the movement nationally but rather an attempt to form a gel out of stubborn ingredients, the most obdurate one being an intense sense of parochialism amongst the rank and file.[198]

Paisley thus represented one part in the labour jigsaw, the overall history of which emerged from the manner in which the different pieces fitted together, rather than in the final 'picture' which transpired at the end of this process.

Although evidence exists of a trades' organisation in Paisley during the 1870s, the most influential antecedent, in ideological terms, of the political labour movement which would emerge as a potent force in the 1890s proved to be the local Co-operative movement, whose platforms shared parallel concerns regarding the division of wealth and the social 'system' with the radicals of the Irish League, local land reformers and the progressives in the local Liberal party.[199] Although the co-operative

197 Lee, 'Conservatism, traditionalism and the British working class', p. 98.

198 W. Lancaster, *Radicalism, Co-operation and Socialism: Leicester Working-Class Politics, 1860–1906* (Leicester, 1987), p. xviii.

199 William Gallacher Library, STUC, William McQuilkin Collection, W. McQuilkin, Draft Document: 'Paisley and the Trade Union Movement' (1930), p. 17; *NBDM*, 20 Mar. 1873; 27 Mar. 1873. Whilst William McQuilkin states that 'The Paisley Trades Council was formed in 1874', references in the *North British Daily Mail* (*NBDM*) in 1873 indicate a relatively active trades association of sorts which, in March, considered the possibility of putting forward candidates for the School Board elections.

commonwealth was not as yet perceived as 'coterminous' with its socialist counterpart, the ideology of co-operation, 'looking forward to the communal ownership of the instruments of production' and back to the self-governing ethos of the old artisan workshops, established a critical 'point of contact' between local Liberalism and the socialist vision.[200]

Paisley boasted four Co-operative societies in the 1880s: the Paisley Equitable Society, established in 1858, the oldest such society in Renfrewshire; the Paisley Manufacturing Society, established in 1862 by a group of handloom weavers, and Scotland's oldest manufacturing Co-operative society; the Paisley Provident Society, established in 1860; and the Underwood Coal Society, established in 1872.[201] The Provident Society, claiming in 1905 to supply the 'necessaries' of five-sixths of the town's thread mill workers, clearly highlighted the potential of the Co-operative store to 'dissolve the link between the working class neighbourhood and the retailer'.[202] (It is surely no coincidence that it was Co-operative activists who became the first working-class representatives in Paisley's local government, taking over from the established shop-keeping interest.) Furthermore, the social life of the societies, most evident in the Women's Guild and the Education Committee, by creating 'a social environment beyond work' for its many members, and asserting the organisation's influence as 'a lively presence in neighbourhood life', proved important in challenging the cultural and social hegemony of the industrial elite.[203]

However, Paisley's Co-operative societies, whilst advocating somewhat radical social measures, remained strong supporters of the Liberal Party throughout the 1880s and beyond. Provost Cochran proved a staunch ally of local co-operation during these years, although increasingly the message from Co-operative platforms hinted strongly of a growing independence from established politics. In January 1887, Henry Rowley of the London Labour Association, and regular speaker at Provident Society lectures, addressed Paisley Co-operators thus:

> He asked whether it was desirable that there should be always capitalists as apart from the labourer. Whether there should be masters and men; or whether there should not be brethren labouring for each other's good, with a common purpose and a common object?[204]

200 Lancaster, *Radicalism, Co-operation and Socialism*, p. xxi.

201 Paisley Co-operative Manufacturing Society Ltd, *Jubilee Souvenir of the PCMS Ltd, 1862–1912* (Paisley, 1912)

202 *Handbook to the 37th Annual Co-operative Congress, Paisley, Renfrewshire* (SCWS, Glasgow, 1905), p. 218; Savage, *Dynamics of Working-Class Politics*, p. 129.

203 Joyce, *Work, Society and Politics*, p. 116; Savage, *Dynamics of Working-Class Politics*, p. 129. See also D. Rowat, *Jubilee of the Paisley Provident Co-operative Society Limited, 1860–1910* (Paisley, 1910).

204 *PRG*, 15 Jan. 1887.

That November, however, he differentiated between Co-operative goals and those of the socialists: 'Socialism meant compulsory combination; Co-operation meant voluntary association.'[205]

With the assistance of the Greenock Trades Council, Paisley's Trades Council was revived in February 1891, the previous body having collapsed 'through want of energy and enthusiasm on the part of the members', according to James Giffen, a plumber, and the Trades Council's new president.[206] Dominated by the skilled unions, with James S. Munro as vice-president and Robert McAuley as secretary, both representatives of the Amalgamated Society of Engineers [ASE], and William Meiklejohn of the Powerloom Carpet Weavers Association as treasurer, the Trades Council was to prove the vehicle through which Paisley trade unionism became a political as well as an industrial force during the 1890s.

Until 1894, Trades Councillors participated in local government as a campaigning interest group rather than contenders for office. During the Cart crisis of October 1891, when the Cart Trust was forced to appeal to the town council for additional borrowing powers, secured on increased rates, James Giffen appeared on the 'improvers' platform, insisting that the increased shipping which would arrive in Paisley as a result of the reforms would lead to the development of new industries. He noted:

> A great many gentlemen were coming forward now talking about taxation, and pretending to pity the poor ratepayers. He told the audience this – it was for their own self-interest that these men came forward; they did not care a penny for the ratepayers in general.[207]

Yet such rhetoric did not represent a serious threat to the established elite. That April, Giffen had appeared on Thomas Glen Coats's nomination 'ticket' for the School Board election and the following February the Trades Council supported local Liberals in the Parochial Board elections. As in Aberdeen in the late 1880s, the Paisley Trades Council pursued a policy of 'backing any candidate, already nominated, who promised to support a particular aspect of Trades Council policy'.[208] In September 1892, however, attempts were made to formalise this approach when a Trades Council committee was formed to compose a list of questions to be sent to municipal candidates to elucidate their views on key labour questions.[209] Such a procedure was once again followed in 1893, all replies being written and returned to the Trades Council for consideration.[210]

205 *PDE*, 9 Nov. 1887.
206 Ibid., 6 Feb. 1891; 12 Feb. 1891.
207 *PRG*, 31 Oct. 1891.
208 Buckley, *Trade Unionism in Aberdeen*, p. 127.
209 *PDE*, 14 Sep. 1892. See below, Appendix 5.
210 *PRG*, 30 Sep. 1893. See below, Appendix 5.

However, it was during this year that initial attempts were made to nominate working men for public boards. At a Trades Council meeting in July, the newly appointed president, William Brown – the blacksmiths' delegate and president of the local branch of the Scottish Labour Party [SLP] which had been established in October 1892 – reflected on the desirability of 'having working men representatives on the various municipal boards'.[211] Brown pointed out that 'every class except the working class is represented on these boards, and that as a consequence when questions affecting the interests of labour came before them, they received scant consideration'.[212] Following the meeting, the matter was remitted to a sub-committee to look out for suitable candidates. Though by the end of the month the sub-committee had formulated a programme of reforms approved by the council, no candidates were nominated. The annual general meeting of 1894 reflected: 'suitable men with sufficient time at their disposal could not be got'.[213]

Although material success had not been achieved, the evolving ideas behind *working-class* representation were clearly undermining the philosophy of common interests which had sustained elite domination in local government to this point. The idea that there existed 'special' interests relevant to one section of the community threatened the idea of local politics as the expression of a unified body and replaced it with a theory of exploitation.

The annual report of February 1894 went on to suggest a levy of ½d. per week on the 3,000 trade unionists which the Trades Council claimed to represent would be sufficient to support three working men representatives. However, opposition to this proposal was notable at a meeting later that month, and, though adopted, gained the active support of only the blacksmiths' and the carpet weavers' unions.[214] The following month, however, a solution to the financial worries of the council seemed in sight when, at a meeting of Co-operators and Trades Council delegates, it was agreed to form a committee 'to take joint action in matters affecting the interests of both organisations'.[215]

In April that year, John Alexander, a jacquard machine maker, and Robert Tweedale, a shoemaker and director of the Equitable Co-operative Society, became the first 'labour' candidates to stand for local office under the joint auspices of the Trades Council and the Co-operative movement in Paisley when they contested the School Board Elections.[216] Alongside them, heralding future division, was Patrick Barr,

211 *PDE*, 5 Jul. 1893.
212 *PRG*, 8 Jul. 1893.
213 Ibid., 17 Feb. 1894.
214 *PDE*, 28 Feb. 1894.
215 *PRG*, 24 Mar. 1894.
216 Of the £10 incurred in election expenses by the two 'official' candidates, the Trades Council share amounted to only £2, the rest being made up by the Co-operative Societies.

an embroiderer and previous member of the Parochial Board, who, having been 'thrown over' by the joint committee, was standing as an 'independent labour candidate' in which regard he had attracted the support of many prominent local trade unionists. All three candidates stood on a platform of free books and greater opportunities for working-class children, especially with regard to grammar school entrance. In the end, however, only Tweedale proved successful, being elected to the board with a vote of 4,315.[217]

By September, however, the 'honeymoon period' in Trades Council–Co-operative relations was over. That month, a Labour Representation Committee was established by the Co-operative societies in which, it had been planned, the Trades Council was to have three out of the fifteen members. A Trades Council Meeting on the 25th agreed by a majority of one, however, not to co-operate in this endeavour, on the grounds that its proposed representation was not proportional to its membership.[218] The committee, nevertheless, went ahead, and on 9 October proposed to finance a Trades Council nominee regardless, encouraging the council to reconsider its decision. The Trades Council, however, refused such finance, arguing that the Co-operative movement would thus have power to select a candidate in its own interest who might not necessarily reflect the council stance on important issues.[219]

A fortnight later, William Brown, the former president of the Trades Council (he had been replaced by Wallace, the mason's delegate in May) and president of the local ILP branch, which had developed out of the SLP in 1894, became the first ILP candidate for local office for the fourth ward in the Town Council elections. At the regular Trades Council meeting that week a deputation from the ILP appealed for the council's support in Brown's candidature.[220] The council agreed, co-operating in the formation of a joint election committee and circulating subscription sheets among the members of its affiliated societies to defray Brown's expenses.

Though Brown lost the election to Paisley's new provost, Archibald MacKenzie, the starch manufacturer, polling 472 votes to MacKenzie's 988, his candidature represents a significant point of progress in the politicisation of the Trades Council, moving as it did closer to a political body explicitly hostile to Liberalism and the established order and into a more lukewarm relationship with the local Co-operative movement.[221]

In February 1895, the Co-operative activists held an exclusive meeting to decide on their candidates for the forthcoming Parish Council elections.[222] Among the chosen nominees were William Brown and

217 Alexander polled 2,964 votes and Barr, 1,747.
218 *PRG*, 29 Sep. 1894.
219 *PDE*, 10 Oct. 1894.
220 *PRG*, 27 Oct. 1894.
221 *PDE*, 21 Nov. 1894; 27 Nov. 1894.
222 *PDE*, 22 Feb. 1895.

Andrew Hammond, treasurer of the Trades Council and secretary of the local ILP. Yet in addition the list also included active Co-operators such as William B. Flockhart, a committed Unionist and future president of the Provident Co-operative Society who, in 1897 as a foreman at Thomas Reid & Sons, would lead strike-breakers against the ASE. At the regular Trades Council meeting, Brown asked the delegates whether he ought to stand under Co-operative auspices. 'For his own part', he commented, 'he strongly objected to several of the Co-operative nominees, as there were amongst them at least one who had done everything in his power to thwart the efforts of the trade unionists to improve the conditions of the workers'.[223] Such sentiments were echoed by James Munro of the ASE, president of the Trades Council between 1892 and May 1893, and others, yet Brown and Hammond were ultimately left with a free hand.

A joint meeting of Co-operators and trade unionists was held in March, in the course of which a new list of candidates was drawn up excluding Flockhart, amongst others. The following month, nine candidates, including Brown and Hammond, stood for election under the joint auspices of the Trades Council and Co-operative movement.[224] Of those only two were successful, the Co-operators, John Holms and Robert Henderson in the first ward. Between them, however, Brown and Hammond, both in the fourth ward, polled 729 votes – around eighty more votes than the candidate who topped the poll in that ward.

Coinciding with these elections, the Town Council itself was in crisis, as a result of its decision, made in late 1894 without consulting the electorate, to add eight new councillors to the existing five ward system rather than creating new wards. This attracted the condemnation of what seemed to be the majority of the population. Despite appeals to Provost MacKenzie to convene a public meeting to discuss the situation, the council voted at a meeting in January by eight votes to seven to confirm its earlier decision to make no alteration to the number of wards.

At a Trades Council meeting in January, William Brown moved a resolution, subsequently adopted, 'That the Trades Council protest against the action of the Town Council in not taking the opinion of the rate-payers regarding the re-arrangement of the Wards.'[225] The following week, Brown in action again, as president of the ILP, echoing the cries of past Paisley reformers, 'made an earnest appeal to all *democrats* to resist every attempt to introduce either one man rule or clique rule, that would try to override *the popular voice*, or seek to

223 Ibid., 27 Feb. 1895.

224 David T. Hutchison, a plasterer, also attracted support from labour organs, most notably, the Paisley Labourers Union and John Holms, the successful Co-operative candidate. He was unsuccessful in the election and attracted only 258 votes: *PDE*, 30 Mar. 1895.

225 *PDE*, 16 Jan. 1895.

establish their own ideas in opposition to *the mandate of the citizens*'.[226] Meanwhile, a petition against the council's actions was being distributed throughout the burgh, attracting 800 names by the end of the month.[227]

In February, a council meeting once again confirmed its decision, by the slimmest of margins, to persist with the five ward system, ex-Provost Clark suggesting an increase in ward numbers would result in greater expense at election time. [228] In February, the Scottish Secretary ordered a court of inquiry into the Paisley situation, and in March the court met under Sheriff Cheyne to consider the application of Paisley Town Council for an increase in its membership. Its findings were that membership was to be increased only in conjunction with an increase in the number of wards to eight.

Just as the court of inquiry was meeting, protests were being heard for working-class representation on the Infirmary Board, and on 9 March a committee was established, representing twenty-four public works, to petition the Infirmary directors.[229] The following month, after the conclusion of the Parish Council elections, a deputation made up of William Brown, as a representative of the workers employed by Clark & Co.; John Millar of Fullerton, Hodgart & Barclay, and an ILP member; James Gibb of W. McGhee & Sons; John Holms of the Co-operative Coal Society and recently elected parish councillor; John McIntyre of the Glenfield Works; and John Munro of the Manufacturing Co-operative Society made their appeal to the Infirmary directors. That July, the directors conceded to the demands. Although working-class members were not guaranteed, their names were to stand alongside others on voting sheets at elections for the board.

Thus the Parish Council elections took place at a time of heightened awareness regarding the representative deficit in Paisley's public boards. At a meeting in March, Hammond complained: 'They had long enough been represented by shopkeepers and retired gentlemen, who had plenty of time, and wanted a little honour and glory.'[230] Labour's entry into local government was thus motivated by a traditional *Liberal* concern with representative democracy and the inter-relationship of taxation and representation. The radical legacy was clearly evident, and echoed the concerns of a past radical age rather than anticipating the vision of a socialist millennium. 'Labour' was already contending for the radical mantle.

In October 1895, under the joint auspices of the Trades Council and the ILP, William Brown was elected as town councillor for the fifth ward, coming top of the poll with a vote of 439, defeating James

226 Ibid., 21 Jan. 1895 [my italics].

227 Ibid., 22 Jan. 1895.

228 Ibid., 1 Feb. 1895.

229 At this time, e.g., the Victoria Infirmary in Glasgow had four working men on its Board and Kilmarnock's Infirmary had five: *PDE*, 13 Jun. 1895.

230 *PDE*, 22 Mar. 1895.

Winning, an accountant and local temperance activist; Bernard McGhee, grocer and INL activist; Alexander MacFarlane, organising secretary of the Western Division of the NUCAS; and William Baird, a local saddler.[231] Brown's programme supported the direct employment of municipal labour at trade-union rates, an eight-hour day with full liberty of combination and a minimum wage of 21s. for all adult council employees, the erection of artisans dwellings by the council to be let at cost, the abolition of all insanitary dwellings, and the taxation of land values.[232]

Following such success, in 1896 the Trades Council, ILP and Co-operative Societies collaborated in the campaign to elect Andrew Hammond, William Greig, of the Amalgamated Society of Joiners and Shipbuilders and the current Trades Council president, and the ILP-er John Hamilton of the Tailors Union to town council office in the first, third and seventh wards respectively. Such co-operation seemed to herald a new era of class consciousness, Hamilton defending his position as a purely 'working-class' candidate, and emasculating claims of sectionalism by openly agreeing to allegations that his mandate would come less from the 'community' than a section of it.[233] The *Gazette* challenged the candidatures as faddism on the part of local trade unionists, and attacked the introduction of explicitly political issues into local contests as a move towards the introduction of clique and 'party' in municipal elections.[234] However, all three candidates, whose programmes echoed many of Brown's concerns the previous year, were defeated, securing around 25% of the votes cast.

Internal tensions within the 'Triple Alliance' of Trades Council, Co-operators and ILP soon rose to the surface.[235] The contradictory position of the Co-operative movement, as simultaneously employer and working-class representative, proved disruptive of the evolving labour consensus when in 1897 a strike by weavers at the Colinslee factory of the Co-operative Manufacturing Society, highlighted the movement's divided interests.

One hundred female weavers at the Colinslee works went on strike on 27 February, claiming that the poor quality of the yarn in the webs they were working meant that they could not keep up their previous production rate and were thus losing pay. Following a deputation from the workers, the Co-operative directors promised an investigation into

231 Note that D. T. Hutchison was also elected to the Town Council for the fifth ward this year, securing 395 votes.
232 *PRG*, 2 Nov. 1895.
233 Ibid., 24 Oct. 1896.
234 Ibid., 24 Oct. 1896.
235 LSE, ILP Archive, ILP 1/1, NAC Minutes 1893–1896, Monthly Report from Tom Mann, Organising Secretary, 29 Mar. 1894: Note that the Glasgow ILP had collaborated in a similar fashion with the Trades Council and local Co-operators at the School Board elections of 1894.

the allegations if the 'girls' returned to work. This they did, on 1 March, but not being satisfied with the directors' reply to a second deputation, struck work again. On 3 March, the factory manager, who had informed the directors of the women's complaints on 18 February, demanded a decision from the directors, whereupon, this not being forthcoming, he resigned. Thereafter, a notice was posted in the works declaring that those workers who had not returned to work by 10 am on the 4th 'would be considered as having resigned their situation'.[236]

On 9 March William Greig, the president of the Trades Council, stressed the plight of the Colinslee strikers and the treatment they had received from the directors at a council meeting, emphasising that their wages had decreased by half since the introduction of the new yarn. The council promised to do everything in its power to prevent the victimisation of the workers and Councillor Brown reflected that 'the treatment meted out to the girls was not one whit worse nor better than that they were accustomed to receive from private employers'.[237]

In the end the majority of workers returned to work by the 10th and six women were 'dismissed'. On 19 April, however, a letter in the *Express* revealed that the dispute was far from over. Signed 'The Colinslee Workers', it detailed the contents of a recent circular sent by the Paisley Co-operative Manufacturing Society to its customers and shareholders. The circular apparently stated that the directors, after having received 'reports from experts on the yarn complained of, and having interviewed the managers and male workers in the factory and warehouse', found that 'the girls had broken faith with the directors, that they had no just cause for their action in ceasing work, that they were precipitate in their action, and their position was ultimately untenable'.[238] The letter from the 'girls' had been drafted by Thomas Loudon, the Trades Council secretary, and appeared in the *North British Daily Mail* and the *Glasgow Weekly Mail*. Its consequences were dramatic.

Rejecting pleas for arbitration, and arguing that the letter had been

> concocted and invented ... for the purpose of seriously injuring the business of the society in the eyes of its numerous shareholders and customers, making it appear that the factory was improperly conducted ... that the products of the factory were imperfect for the market, and that the treatment of the employees of the factory was unjust

the Manufacturing Society took the six sacked workers to court to sue them for damages.[239]

On 15 May, the Trades Council called a special meeting to arrange support for the workers at which, amongst others, Robert Tweedale of

236 *PDE*, 4 Mar. 1897; 9 Mar. 1897.
237 Ibid., 10 Mar. 1897.
238 Ibid., 19 Apr. 1897.
239 Ibid., 19 May 1897; 21 May 1897.

the Equitable Society offered to act as guarantor for the workers' legal expenses. Though the action was called in the Small Debts Court on 20 May, the case was not heard until the 31st. Meanwhile, the action of the Co-operative directors was being openly criticised by local labour activists. Brown maintained that the directors had acted all along 'much worse than the modern 'capitalist' or 'employer of labour' and identified a 'plutocratic element' in the local movement.[240]

Sheriff Cowan, however, ultimately found on behalf of the Co-operative Society, concluding that the workers had been treated fairly and had received excellent wages and conditions from their employers.[241] That night, the Tailor's Society, who had themselves gone on strike against the Co-operative Manufacturing Society in 1891, proposed that 'The Trades Council as a body refuse any further invitations from the Renfrewshire Co-operative Conference Association, to be present at their meetings, and further refuse conjoint action with them.'[242] However, on the motion of Harry Baird, of the Amalgamated Society of Carpenters and Joiners and ILP president from 1896, it was agreed not to pass the resolution. Instead, a motion was passed declaring the Manufacturing Society to be unrepresentative of the other Co-operative bodies.

Yet the Colinslee dispute had encouraged the growth of an existing suspicion of the Co-operative movement, one which would continue until 1924. Though gaining support in their campaign against the Traders Defence Association and through their assistance, later that year, to ASE strikers, the Co-operative movement after 1897 proved a focus of discord within the labour ranks – a force which both impeded the growth of an explicitly socialist labour critique of local ills and delayed the 'strange death' of Liberalism in the burgh.

That October, without Co-operative support, Harry Baird was nominated under the joint auspices of the Trades Council and the ILP as a labour candidate in the Town Council elections for the eighth ward. Again, the *Gazette* decried the candidature as sectional representation. Again, Baird's programme was a virtual mirror image of Brown's in 1895, but, again, the labour candidate was defeated.[243]

Labour's fortunes, however, were to change in 1898, when, following the engineering lock-out, demands for direct labour representation on public boards attracted new support, encouraged by the politicisation of the recent dispute and a growing awareness, following an outbreak of enteric fever in the burgh, of the need for municipal intervention in the sphere of public health and housing for the working classes.

240 Ibid., 31 May 1897.
241 Ibid., 2 Jun. 1897.
242 See ibid., 17 Jun. 1891; 2 Jun. 1897.
243 Harry Baird polled 197 votes against Councillor Leitch's 349 to lose the seat: *PRG*, 30 Oct. 1897.

From the beginning of the engineering dispute in Paisley it became clear that the outcome of the strike would have a profound impact on how trade unionists in the burgh would in future view the demands of 'authority'. At the close of the first day of industrial action Hugh Glover, the Trades Council representative and former president of the 2nd branch of the local ASE, reported to the Trades Council that men in one shop had stopped work only to find five constables standing at the gate of the works. Glover continued: 'The action of the authorities in sending these men there was ... altogether uncalled for, and reflected on the character of the men who were as peaceable and law-abiding *as any other class in the community*.'[244] The dispute, in graphic and immediate terms, illustrated to both the engineers and the general Paisley work-force the 'them and us' philosophy which was at the root of demands for direct working-class representation. The lock-out of 1897–8 made an impact on the entire district, the thousands who gathered for demonstrations far out-numbering the estimated 700 organised unionists involved directly in the dispute.[245] Indeed, in the final report of the lock-out committee, unionists acknowledged that 'Paisley people had been very loyal indeed.'[246]

Throughout the dispute, through lectures, demonstrations and fund-raising events, the ILP successfully politicised the industrial action by emphasising its national scope and the 'class' motives of the federated employers. Speaking in Paisley at the height of the lock-out, Keir Hardie commented that the 'unrighteous battle' being fought by the Employers' Federation was supported by the agencies of 'the State' and that 'the Socialist movement in Great Britain had received an immense impetus' from the Engineers' dispute.[247]

Yet, more importantly in local terms, the dispute proved a focal point upon which sectional impulses gave way to united expressions of traditional protest directed against the non-union blackleg and the anti-union boss – individuals rather than abstract class groupings. Likewise, the 'heroes' were lauded. James Blackie, an engineer imprisoned for thirty days for intimidation, was greeted at the railway station on his return to Paisley by a crowd of hundreds and a number of musical bands which then processed him through the town, revisiting the scene of the intimidation before returning to the Cross and then to a presentation ceremony where Blackie was given gold cuff-links by the spoolers of the Ferguslie Mills, who themselves had recently been on strike.[248]

Echoing the tactics of the meal mobs of the eighteenth century, protesting crowds followed blacklegs home.

244 *PDE*, 14 Jul. 1897 [my italics].

245 J. Brown, *From Radicalism to Socialism: Paisely Engineers, 1890–1920*, Pamphlet 71, History Group of the Communist Party (n.d.), p. 8.

246 PAEU, ASE (Paisley: Third Branch) Minute Book, 28 Feb. 1898.

247 *PRG*, 16 Oct. 1897.

248 *PDE*, 1 Dec. 1897.

> In one of the foremost brakes was a non-unionist engineer belonging to Paisley and he was immediately 'spotted', and the crowd followed him along Moss Street and High Street to his home in Storie Street, hooting and jeering at intervals. Several hundred men took part in the demonstration, and all along High Street it was watched by many curious eyes from shops and houses. In front of the man's dwelling place in Storie Street the crowd halted, and after some more cheering and hooting were about to disperse when another non-unionist employed in the same works passed down the street. He was at once noticed and the crowd transferred their unwelcome attentions to him, following him, hooting and booing, to his house in Stow Place.[249]

Popular protest was thus very much local in character and remained, to a certain extent, driven by personality as much as principle. Harry Baird, speaking at a 10,000-strong demonstration in October recalled the local protests of the past:

> In trying to form these trade unions their forefathers had suffered much persecution and imprisonment, and the workers of Paisley by their presence that day demonstrated that they had the courage and intention to maintain these rights.[250]

At this same meeting effigies representing 'opponents of the men's cause' were carried on poles, then set ablaze:

> One of the figures was apparently meant as a parody on a well-known employer; another represented a local non-unionist; another was labelled 'A Jubilee Foreman' and the fourth 'Colonel Liar' ... the flames devoured the helpless figures, cheer after cheer was raised.[251]

Local and national concerns thus co-existed and determined a style and language of protest which, whilst focused on the present, owed a great deal to the past.

During the period from April 1897 to April 1898 the Trades Council drew strength from the publicity surrounding the lock-out and recorded a two-fold increase in its membership.[252] Whilst the politicising impact of the lock-out had not sufficiently established itself by the time of the 1897 Town Council elections to aid in Harry Baird's campaign, its impact was clear in the 1898 contest during which strength was drawn from a new determination which evolved in the Trades Council following the dismissal of Councillor Brown from his employment with Clark & Co. due to his involvement in the lock-out.

249 Ibid., 28 Aug. 1897.
250 Ibid., 18 Oct. 1897.
251 Ibid., 23 Oct. 1897.
252 Ibid., 23 Apr. 1898.

In October 1898, the ASE (Second Branch) voluntarily increased its members' contributions to the Trades Council from 2d. to 6d. and declared their unanimous support for those trade unionists contesting for local office.[253] The Third Branch, meanwhile, had sent its first delegates to the Trades Council that September and in October agreed to levy its members in support of direct labour representation and approved the creation of a standing committee for municipal representation.[254] The following year, the Third Branch voted nine to four in favour of the promotion of direct Labour representation in parliament.[255] Having been addressed by Councillor Brown, the Paisley branch of the Operative Bricklayers Association agreed in September 1898 to give its full support to working-class candidates at the municipal elections.[256] Though for many unions this enthusiasm did not last long – the United Plumbers, whilst appearing at a labour representation conference in 1898, dismissed working-class municipal representation as 'a sham business' in 1900 – it was enough to secure sufficient support for the election of three Labour town councillors in October 1898.[257]

The 1898 campaign coincided with a heightened awareness of Paisley's poor record in public health. By the 1870s, Paisley had earned the reputation of 'the dirtiest and most unhealthy town in Scotland' and was regularly appearing at the top of the death-rate tables of the eight principal Scottish towns even in the 1890s.[258] In 1898 the focus of concern was on the water supply. Mary McCarthy has commented on the 'tardy' attitude of Paisley towards improving its drainage system in the late nineteenth century, stressing that it was not until 1923 that a sewage disposal plant was established for the area at Laighpark.[259] In 1898 the result of such 'tardiness' was an outbreak of enteric fever, concentrated in the New Town area in the east where overcrowding was high and long-standing due to the depopulation of other areas as a consequence of street widening in the earlier decades of the century. Around fifty people died of the fever in this year, though notifications of the disease exceeded three hundred.[260]

In September the Town Council suppressed a medical report which indicated the water supply as the probable cause of the fever in the East End for fear that it would 'create alarm'. Yet by the end of the month a report presented by Dr Donald, the Medical Officer for the burgh, to the Council's Public Health Committee concluded that 'substantial evidence'

253 PAEU, 651.77 Ren – 10, ASE (Paisley: Second Branch) Minute Book, 3 Oct. 1898.

254 PAEU, ASE (Paisley: Third Branch) Minute Book, 12 Jul. 1898, 10 Oct. 1898, 7 Nov. 1898.

255 Ibid., 24 Apr. 1899.

256 PCL, 651.77 Ren–10, Operative Bricklayers Association, Minute Book 1895–1902, 8 Sep. 1898.

257 ML, Social Sciences Department, Trade Union Archives, Paisley District Lodge of United Plumbers of Great Britain and Ireland, Minutes, vol. I: 1888–1900, 21 May 1900.

258 McCarthy, *Social Geography of Paisley*, p. 12.

259 Ibid., p. 130.

260 Ibid., p. 121.

had been brought forward which indicated that valves in 'terminal end pipes' in the East End were failing to operate, thus causing contamination of the water supply from sewerage outlets.[261] The cause of the fever and the actions of town councillors became a test case at the elections the following month.

Bailie Smith was typical of local Liberal and Unionist councillors when he declared 'he had no belief whatever in the theory of Dr Donald'; ex-Bailie Goudie likewise announced that 'he didn't agree for a moment with Dr Donald's water theory'; ex-Treasurer Paton declared that the public were being too hard on the Public Health Committee and considered the water 'pure', and Bailie Souden concluded that there could be many reasons for the fever outbreak.[262] Their views appeared to be confirmed when, on 11 October, Glasgow's water engineer concluded that the drainage system had not caused the fever.[263] However, three days later, the results of a laboratory test of water samples from the area concluded that the bacilli which had caused the fever had appeared as the result of the poor drainage system.[264] A meeting of council called to consider the report agreed that its findings would not be submitted for publication. Even after the report, however, Liberal and Unionist councillors appeared on platforms to defend the purity of the water supply, blaming the outbreak on infected workers in a local dairy.[265] By contrast, Councillor Brown and the Labour candidates who stood for office supported Dr Donald's report and encouraged immediate action. They attacked the 'shuffling' of the council and highlighted their unresponsive attitude to an epidemic which had hit a predominantly working-class area as an example of the 'classes' ignoring the plight of the 'masses'. Harry Baird, standing for office in the Second Ward, declared:

> if elected to Council, he was going there to represent an interest, to represent a section of the community, a section that had never hitherto been represented to any extent, and a section that had most need of representation – *the working class*. [266]

Yet the 'working class' was once again defined in *local* terms. At a campaign meeting on 25 October, John Kent, standing for the seventh Ward, illustrated this locally and historically determined analysis when he declared that

> He was proud to be a citizen of Paisley, as his father and grandfather had been, for the town had an ancient, honourable and inspiring

261 *PRG*, 1 Oct. 1898.
262 Ibid., 15 Oct. 1898.
263 Ibid., 15 Oct. 1898.
264 Ibid., 15 Oct. 1898.
265 Ibid., 22 Oct. 1898.
266 Ibid., 29 Oct. 1898 [my italics].

> history ... In 1842 ... owing to the collapse of handloom weaving, there were 12,000 of the inhabitants receiving relief, and Thomas Carlyle, in a letter to Dr Chalmers, had given a graphic word-portrait of the 'pallid Paisley weaver'. He could understand the Corn Law Rhymer giving vent to the invocation:
>
> When wilt thou save the people?
> O God of mercy, when?
> The people, Lord, the people;
> Not crowns or thrones, but men.
> Flowers of thy heart, O Lord, are they;
> Let them not pass like weeds away
> Their heritage a sunless day
> God save the people.
>
> But the people must, socially and municipally, work out their own salvation ... The improvements in the social condition of the working classes had been largely due to movements emanating from themselves – such as the trade union and co-operative movement – and it would be so in the future. Only they must awake to their duties and responsibilities, and take their share in the management of public affairs.[267]

Labour failed to break its local bounds in Paisley in 1898; its goals, motives, rhetoric and ideology were limited by local concerns and the substance of a local history of protest. This, however, proved both its limitation and its strength. The Socialist message, to have meaning, was interpreted through a chain of local associations, conventions and traditions. ILP activism during the lock-out had not established a new world view but resurrected an older idiom which, as yet, had not become broad enough to encompass the national scope and millennial outlook of Socialism.

It is important to note that the men who were nominated as Labour candidates in 1898 did not rely on ILP or Co-operative support, but were supported by a newly established Workers Municipal Election Committee, instituted by the Trades Council and composed of trade unionists. Whilst William Greig lost to ex-Bailie John Andrews in the fourth ward, the election of Harry Baird in the first, Councillor Brown in the fifth and John Kent in the seventh wards represented the height of Labour's success in the pre-1900 period. More importantly, however, the success signifies a movement away from the *ad hoc*, informal alliances with the Co-operative movement and the ILP of the 1880s and early 1890s to a more formal and trade-union dominated local Labour organisation.

[267] *PDE*, 26 Oct. 1898.

Baird's defeat in 1897 had highlighted divisions in the Labour movement when the Co-operators refused to be involved in a united body of trade unionists and ILPers. Despite Co-operative assistance to the locked-out engineers, it was concluded by a Trades Council sponsored Committee in February 1898 that future organisation in support of direct Labour representation should concentrate on the views of trade unionists themselves. The committee noted: 'In former years they had co-operated with other working class organisations with the object of attaining the end they had in view, but it was the opinion of the committee that they should now strike out for themselves.'[268] Whilst some Trades Council members objected to treating the question of direct working-class representation as a 'purely trade union one', the recommendations of the committee were approved and delegates sent to various local union branches to discuss the question of representation on local boards. Following the elections, however, it was decided to appeal to other working-class organisations in the town and in January 1899 it was agreed to establish the committee as a standing body including Co-operative representatives, under the title of the Paisley Workers' Municipal Elections Committee [PWMEC].[269]

The PWMEC nominated two candidates for Town Council office in 1899 – William Greig and John Arthur – and voiced support for ex-Bailie A. R. Pollock, a former member of the ARA. Though Pollock was successful, Greig and Arthur were both defeated, leading to cries for better organisation among the working-class organisations in the town.[270]

Municipal involvement in the 1890s reflected the fragmented character of Labour organisation in the burgh, and emphasised the nature of the divisions and animosities which bedevilled Labour's challenge until 1924, the most lasting of which proved to be that between the new Labour Party and the Co-operative movement. Yet, in the 1890s, Trades Council and ILP relations likewise did not attract universal approval.

'Working-Class' Politics

The Trades Council, whilst being represented by James Giffen on the executive of the Scottish United Trades Council Labour Party [SUTCLP] in the early 1890s, had always contained an element opposed to overt political association and a majority whose sympathies were overwhelmingly Liberal in character.

During the 1891 parliamentary by-election, the council declared its support for the Liberal candidate, William Dunn, despite a Scottish Labour Party [SLP] resolution to the effect that 'the adoption of such a

268 Ibid., 23 Feb. 1898.
269 Ibid., 13 Jan. 1899.
270 Ibid., 8 Nov. 1899.

man as Mr Dunn by the Liberal Party is an insult to the democratic working men of Paisley', and confessed its ignorance of the Paisley men, Brown and Henderson, who had supported this resolution at a meeting of the SLP Executive.[271]

Thereafter, the Trades Council enjoyed a relatively amicable relationship with Dunn throughout the early 1890s. Following his election, Dunn regularly sent the Trades Council copies of bills entering the Commons which dealt with labour issues, and in May 1892 wrote to the council: 'There is no body of men for whom I have a greater respect than the Trades Council, and I hope that the next Parliament will contain more representatives of the working man than the present one does.'[272] That year Dunn voted in favour of the Eight Hours Bill and in this same letter voiced his support for the Small Holdings Bill and the taxation of ground rents. Though occasional criticism was noted, most especially from William Brown, Dunn managed to contain the demands of the Trades Council until the late 1890s. In 1893 he wrote that 'The labour question appears to me the most important and pressing of our day. It affects the whole Empire, and all its relationships, – monetary, commercial, industrial and social.'[273]

In the 1890s, the Trades Council's relationship with the emerging independent Labour political movement was ambiguous and qualified. Support for Dunn co-existed with explicit support of the SUTCLP and, after 1893, support for the ILP. The period was thus one in which emerging paradoxes and apparent divergences were seeking resolution – problematics made yet more complex by the post-1886 identity crisis in the Liberal party. In this, the Paisley Trades Council's experience resembled that of many other councils and working-class communities. In Rochdale, during the period 1890–5, Coneys has identified the first attempts to undermine the town's Gladstonian Liberalism, but has highlighted the Trades Council's reluctance to challenge the two party system.[274] In Aberdeen, Buckley has drawn attention to a growing awareness among many trade unionists that 'the changes they envisaged could not be encompassed within the Liberal Party', co-existing with pragmatic co-operation with the Liberals when the occasion demanded it.[275] In West Yorkshire, Laybourn and Reynolds, moreover, have stressed the longevity of Old Liberalism, which maintained its influence until 1918, despite the ILP's capture of many trades councils in the early 1890s.[276]

Trades Council support for the SUTCLP in Paisley was qualified from the beginning and grew to outright opposition as Chisholm Robertson

271 *PRG*, 30 May 1891; *PDE*, 3 Jun. 1891.
272 *PDE*, 25 May 1892.
273 Ibid., 14 Dec. 1893.
274 Coneys, 'Labour Movement and the Liberal Party in Rochdale', p. 17.
275 Buckley, *Trade Unionism in Aberdeen*, pp. 127–8, 143.
276 Laybourn and Reynolds, *Liberalism and the Rise of Labour*, pp. 4–6, 203–4.

moved the party into an antagonistic position towards Keir Hardie. In August 1892, the Trades Council had opposed the SLP's affiliation to the SUTCLP, severely criticising SLP candidates who had stood against Liberals, thus 'letting in' Conservatives. By October, however, the SUTCLP itself came under similar criticism when Trades Council members declared SUTCLP opposition to Liberal candidatures 'detrimental to the true interests of labour' and raised the phantom of 'Tory Gold' finance.[277] However, whilst some Paisley trade unionists had evidently become attracted to the programme of the Scottish National Labour League, which was promoting co-operation with the Liberal Party as the surest way of achieving labour goals at this time, the Trades Council, following assurances from Chisholm Robertson, decided at the next fortnightly meeting to continue to be represented on the executive of the SUTCLP. Four months later, following the motion of Andrew Hammond (at this time an SLP member) that the SUTCLP had failed to justify its existence, James Munro, the current Trades Council president, and Wallace, the masons' delegate and future president, defended Trades Council affiliation to the party as it represented the only party whose membership was exclusive to trade unionists. The meeting, however, went with Hammond, agreeing not to send a representative to the party's Aberdeen conference.

Throughout 1893 and thereafter, SLP, then ILP, influence in the Trades Council grew significantly, especially during Brown's presidency from May 1893 to May 1894, when labour representation in local government became a key concern.[278] Indeed, at the fifth annual conference of the SLP in January 1894, representatives attended from the Paisley Trades Council and the local branches of the Associated Shipwrights Union and the Amalgamated Society of Wood Turners, in addition to local SLP delegates.[279] Yet such influence did not meet with unreserved approval from all the affiliated trade unions.

In September 1894, William Brown proposed that the Trades Council support a Labour Day demonstration. William Greig, the Joiners and Shipwrights' delegate, opposed the proposal, saying that such a suggestion would 'meet with scant support from the trades unionists of the town, as it emanated from a small and insignificant party with whom they had little sympathy.'[280] Supporting Greig, James McPhee, the representative of the Power Loom Carpet trade, 'referred in disparaging terms to the Independent Labour Party, who, he believed ... were chiefly responsible for Mr Brown's motion.'[281] When put to a vote at the following meeting, only the Bakers' Union and the Carpet Weavers

277 *PDE*, 26 Oct. 1892.

278 In Nov. 1893, the Trades Council sent three delegates to the Fifth Annual Conference of the SLP in Glasgow.

279 Lowe, *Souvenirs of Scottish Labour*, p. 128.

280 *PDE*, 12 Sep. 1894.

281 Ibid., 12 Sep. 1894.

opposed Brown's proposal. McPhee thereafter resigned and his union refused to appoint another delegate.

There then followed an acrimonious debate between McPhee and the Trades Council in the columns of the *Express*. In a letter of 26 November, McPhee suggested that the Trades Council had backed out of their agreement with the Co-operators that October, only to 'make room for Brown and his friends [the ILP]' and went on to claim that 'with a few exceptions, the Trades Council is composed of gentlemen belonging to the ILP'.[282] The following day Thomas Loudon, Trades Council secretary, replied to the allegations, maintaining that out of twenty-two delegates, only six were connected with the ILP.[283] Then Brown, referring to McPhee, claimed that 'He had made a mistake when he became a member of the Trades Council by thinking that he would be able to pulverise the Socialists in the interests of Liberalism.'[284] McPhee, however, maintained his position, observing that the six or eight ILPers who attended meetings normally peopled by only ten to fourteen persons had the power to 'carry anything brought before the meeting'.[285]

Opposition carried on into 1895. Prominent ILPers on the Trades Council attacked the Trades Union Congress's [TUC's] decision not to allow Trades Council membership of its Parliamentary Committee. But the ILP's stance was not shared by everyone. Fierce criticism came this time from the Engineers. Smith, one of the ASE delegates, noted at a council meeting in March that his union had approved of the Trades Councils' removal from the TUC sub-committee on the grounds that Congress would thus be prevented from being influenced by 'persons outwith Trades Unions'.[286] A letter in the *Express* the following day, from a Boilermakers' representative – a union which had removed its delegates from both the TUC and local Trades Council – applauded the engineers' position and asked, if others followed suit: 'what will be left to give the colour of importance to the socialist clique that is riding the Trades Council to death?'[287]

By the late 1890s, however, the ILP had established its presence in Paisley, having grown out of its first premises – a shop on New Street – and further from its Liberal roots. In 1895 the party appealed to J. Shaw Maxwell to stand for Paisley at the election that year in the ILP interest. Though he declined their invitation, he maintained:

> I am strongly convinced that Paisley is one of the Scottish seats which should be immediately attacked by our party ... Although the

282 *PDE*, 27 Nov. 1894.
283 Ibid., 28 Nov. 1894.
284 Ibid., 29 Nov. 1894.
285 Ibid., 29 Nov. 1894.
286 Ibid., 13 Mar. 1895.
287 Ibid., 14 Mar. 1895.

numerical strength of the [ILP] in Paisley may not justify the hope that we can at once capture the seat ... it is gratifying to know that the fate of both Liberal and Conservative Governments is in the constituencies rapidly coming within our grasp.[288]

Though no branch minutes remain from which we may gauge the level of ILP membership in Paisley, we may deduce from Paisley's position as one of only three Scottish constituencies being considered tentatively in 1898 as a seat to be contested at the next election, that the ILP's National Advisory Council certainly credited its local influence.[289]

Beyond organisation and inter-associational relations, however, in ideological terms, the significance of Labour politics before 1900 lies in its attempted reformulation of Paisley's radical tradition, appropriating Liberal myths rather than destroying them.

In January 1893, ex-Provost Cochran chaired Keir Hardie's first political meeting in Paisley. Having stressed the 'commercial class' dominance of the Liberal Party, Hardie reflected on Paisley's industrial past and the traditions of the Paisley weaver:

> He rejoiced to come to a town like this, with its glorious traditions and memories of the past; he liked to come amongst the weavers and sons of weavers, to the men who, while plying their shuttles, had had time to read and study. But all that was passed, and when they compared the life of that kind of man with the man who was the slave of the factory whistle ... they saw how much the working classes had gone back in independence as compared to the good old days of seventy five years ago.[290]

It was the weavers themselves, rather than the party they had come to support, who, according to J. Bruce Glasier, speaking in Paisley the year before, had driven the protests for reform:

> The Liberal party deserved no credit for what had been done by men *who called themselves Liberals* and Whigs one hundred years ago ... The Liberal ideas of the people had come to them independent of the Liberal party, having been introduced by agitators, and the Liberal party had been forced to adopt them ... there was not much difference between the Liberal and the Tory parties, as the Liberal party resisted reforms and the Tory party just resisted them a little longer.[291]

288 *PRG*, 29 Jun. 1895.

289 In addition to Paisley, Glasgow (Camlachie) and Glasgow (St Rollox) were considered 'tentative fixtures'. The only Scottish constituency to be considered 'deemed' was Dundee: LSE, ILP Archive, ILP 1/3, NAC Minutes, 1897–1899; Parliamentary Committee Report, 22 Jul. 1898.

290 *PDE*, 28 Jan. 1893.

291 *PRG*, 3 Dec. 1892 [my italics].

Glasier thus questioned, not just the ancestry of contemporary Liberalism, but the changing definition of the word 'Liberal' itself. For the Labour left, the 'name' was no longer enough – it sought its substance, and in this way challenged its Gladstonian prophets by appealing to a history they had apparently abandoned. Yet Liberalism showed a strong resilience to Labour's challenge in these years. Though losing ground in local government to the emergent Labour voice, the local Liberal elite was never threatened by more than three Labour representatives in the Town Council and the ARA revealed a Liberalism which still had the power to possess the past whilst capturing the demands of the future.

The Liberal Continuum : The Elections of 1891, 1892 and 1895

O Paisley! never let thy sons
Their Liberal sires disgrace;
As an MP for thee, O let
No Tory show his face!
Thy sons make heroes of the free
Them properly array;
Upon the mighty battlefield
Place round their brows the bay.

One hour of Patrick Brewster grant!
The slogan to upraise;
The Radicals to triumph lead
And Tory ranks abase.
One hour of Patrick Brewster give!
With Paisley's Grand Old Man,
To fill the Radicals with fire
In their prevailing van.[292]

The 'lyric' above, written during the 1891 Paisley by-election necessitated by the death of William Barbour in May, alerts us to the persistent association of Paisley's radical history with the Liberal Party, even in this period of challenge from both 'left' and 'right'. Local personalities (Patrick Brewster), metaphorically linked with national figures ('the Grand Old Man'), became potent symbols of the radical continuum seen to endorse the party's new local champion. Commitment to the cause was perceived as a duty, an act of loyalty to a heroic 'familial' ancestry elemented by the fathers ('sires') of the current generation ('sons'). Imagery of liberation and servitude, of justice and tyranny, are dramatically juxtaposed, echoing the rhetoric of an older Liberalism. Constructed in poetic form, the structure of the piece itself

[292] *PDE*, 25 May 1891, extracts from 'Radical Lyric' by Donald Cameron.

recalls the age of the 'weaver poets'. Thus, a locally and historically determined radical tradition is evoked to endorse Paisley's identity as a Liberal constituency.

Having acknowledged the tensions evident in Paisley politics throughout the late Victorian period, the parliamentary elections of 1891, 1892 and 1895 clarify the manner in which, electorally at least, the Liberal party retained hold of Paisley. It is clear that both because and in spite of the growing strength of local Unionism and the increasing dominance of social questions in political debate, Liberalism proved an *adequate* creed for the majority of Paisley voters. Looking at each election in turn, our focus will be on the persistence of the Liberal hegemony and its continued articulation of the rhetoric of radicalism.

At a crowded meeting of the Liberal Association in May 1891, William Dunn was unanimously adopted as the Liberal champion to stand against Major McKerrel.[293] William Dunn, born in Paisley in 1833, was by 1891 a successful merchant, having made his money through trade in the South African colonies and the Orange Free State as an employee, then as sole proprietor, of Messrs MacKie, Dunn & Co. of Port Elizabeth. Having returned to London in 1860, he stood as the Liberal candidate for West Renfrewshire in 1866, losing to Sir Archibald Campbell by 533 votes. To a certain extent, the fight of 1891 resembled that of Barbour's first victory in 1885 when personalities had fractured the Liberal cause until the eve of the election. Yet, by 1891, local animosities based on personalities were part of a national process where Liberalism sought redefinition in the light of the Unionist challenge.

Dunn's programme was a solid articulation of moderate Scottish Liberalism, calling for reform of the voting registration procedure, Home Rule for Ireland, taxation of ground rents, McLaggan's Local Veto Bill and disestablishment of the Church of Scotland. Though challenged over his involvement in the liquor traffic to the African colonies, he apparently sustained the support of the temperance lobby and secured the official Irish vote (estimated at around 660 votes) despite his qualified support for Home Rule only 'as it was consistent with the integrity of this great Empire'.[294] Against this, McKerrell, whilst stressing the need for social reform and confessing a degree of sympathy with calls for reform of land taxation, voiced his opposition to One Man One Vote, Home Rule, disestablishment and state interference in labour relations. On the day of the election, Dunn polled 4,145 votes to McKerrel's 2,807 – a majority of 1,338 for the Liberal Party. On the surface, therefore, 1891 seems to reflect the simple tale of the persistence of the Liberal hold on Paisley. Yet two phenomena alert us to the challenge from left and right – the proposed candidature of Dillon

293 On the death of William Barbour in 1891, Thomas Glen Coats was requested to stand as Liberal candidate for Paisley, yet he declined due to the demands of his business.
294 *PDE*, 23 May 1891.

Lewis and the political rhetoric of a fractured Liberal creed evident on political platforms and in the political poetry which dramatised the election.

On 19 May, the election address of Edward Dillon Lewis, a London barrister, appeared in the Paisley press. Claiming to have been invited to stand in the Liberal interest in the burgh, following Thomas Glen Coats's rejection of the Liberal nomination, he called for shorter parliaments, the end of the hereditary principle, disestablishment of the state church, the end of coercion in Ireland, local self-government for all the British provinces, the taxation of the land as a substitute for rating, and housing reform for workmen's dwellings.[295] Eleven years before, Dillon Lewis had stood in the Labour interest for Middlesborough, coming third with 1,171 votes in an election which the Liberals won.

In Paisley, it remained far from clear who, if anyone, had requested Dillon Lewis to head north. Thomas Glen Coats received a letter of introduction for Dillon Lewis signed by James Grahame, a Liberal Unionist, of the National Securities Insurance Corporation in London, which expressed Grahame's pleasure in introducing Dillon Lewis at the same time as affirming his pledge to fight against Dillon Lewis 'in every possible way'.[296] Meanwhile, it was announced by the Press Association that Dillon Lewis had had talks with Labour representatives in London before arriving in Paisley.[297] Amidst such confusion and apparent lack of local support, he proposed to go to the poll as an 'Independent Radical and Labour' candidate.[298]

Six days after the publication of his election address, however, Dillon Lewis retired from the contest at his first and last Paisley meeting, announcing that he had received several letters from prominent Liberals – among them Edward Marjoribanks, the Scottish Liberal Whip – encouraging him to step down.[299]

In a decade when Michael Maltman Barry – infamous carrier of the 'Tory Gold' to two Social Democratic Federation [SDF] candidates at the 1885 general election – was emerging as a strong influence on H. H. Champion in Aberdeen and, indeed, in the same year as Barry stood in the Conservative interest in Banffshire, it is not surprising that allegations were rife that Dillon Lewis had been a Tory 'dupe' sent to divide the Liberal vote in Paisley.[300] Though no evidence has emerged to substantiate such claims, Dillon Lewis's proposed candidature certainly caused alarm in Liberal circles, who evidently feared that his radical programme would attract some of their more progressive voters. Indeed, at a meeting of the SLP in Glasgow, it was reported that Dillon

295 Ibid., 19 May 1891.
296 Ibid., 20 May 1891.
297 Ibid., 22 May 1891.
298 Ibid., 22 May 1891.
299 *PRG*, 30 May 1891.
300 See J. T. Ward, 'Tory Socialist: a preliminary note on Michael Maltman Barry (1842–1909)', *Journal of Scottish Labour History* (1970).

Lewis had offered to stand in the Labour interest, and Paisley delegates, estimating that had he gone to the poll he would have attracted between 1,500 and 2,000 votes, encouraged Hardie, George Mitchell and George Carson to co-operate with the Scottish Home Rule Association [SHRA] to bring forward an 'advanced candidate in room of Dillon Lewis'.[301] Whilst the Trades Council remained loyal to Dunn, the candidature fiasco of Dillon Lewis and the SLP's subsequent condemnation of Dunn's candidature in Paisley reflect the initial hesitating steps of the labour movement into parliamentary politics in Paisley and a questioning of party Liberalism by its advanced wing.

By far the majority of Liberal energies were devoted to counteracting the Unionist challenge. With Home Rule kept tactically in the background, the battle-ground was the field of local politics and the ambiguous position of the Liberal Unionists within a local rhetoric composed of stark alternatives – Radical/Tory; the People/the Aristocracy – and a locally defined typology in which recognisable personalities still mattered.

Illustrating the interface between localism and national political imperatives, an unknown poet, exploiting the popular 'Tullochgorum', explicitly adapted the older political themes of the reel to current dilemmas:

Come, gie's a sang, the Major cried –
Amen! the Unionists replied –
Ye needna langer try tae hide
    Your turn'ed Toryorum;
Whig an' Tory now agree,
    Whig an' Tory, sic a story!
Whig an' Tory now agree
    An' every hall a Forum.

    Whig an' Tory now agree
    Blaw your bags wi' mirth an' glee –
    I maun dance wi' Provost C.
    The reel o' Tullochgorum.[302]

On the political platforms, the same concern with the language of the fight was evident. At a Unionist campaign meeting on 25 May a written question was presented to McKerrell asking: 'Kindly state whether you are standing as a Conservative or a Unionist?'

McKerrell – What is the difference? (Laughter.)
A Voice – There's a big difference.
Another voice – I'll answer the question: the ane's an open Tory, an' the ither's a cloaked Tory. (Laughter.)[303]

301 *PRG*, 30 May 1891. The SHRA had been disappointed with Dunn's response to questions regarding Scottish Home Rule, but finally supported his candidature.
302 *PDE*, 30 May 1891.
303 Ibid., 26 May 1891.

It was against such apparent inconsistency and allusions to deceit that Paisley's radical tradition was placed: something which the Liberals presented as simple, straightforward, understandable and most importantly, the historical (and hence) 'natural' expression of Paisley politics as opposed to the invented and therefore artificial tenets of the new Unionism. Dunn, by stressing his local origins – 'he was always proud to say that he was a Paisley man and lad' – depicted himself as the personification of the tradition – 'a Liberal of the old type of Paisley' – whose views could resonate with identifiable or remembered local antecedents.[304] On a Liberal platform during the election, Robert Wallace, the Liberal candidate for West Edinburgh in 1886, declared:

> he refused to believe that the unbroken tradition of the past was going to be broken through now – (Cheers.) – and that this burgh which politically at least had never been defiled by Tory membership was going at last to alter that character and soil its garment politically.[305]

'Paisley' thus had an identity at once independent of its citizens, both past and present, yet constituted by them in the sense that their *actions* and *experiences* elemented a larger collective memory which determined the perspective from which politics attained *meaning*. The identity of the 'community', set apart from the self-interest of its individual members, was thus perceived as possessing a power of influence over the electorate whose adherence to its traditions defined the local 'code' through which apparent deviance could be explained. Unionism and local Unionists were thus perceived as 'dis-loyal', as this extract from a letter from 'Radical' makes clear: 'Be not deluded with such nonsense as the "integrity of the Empire". Look after the "integrity" of Paisley. In Mr Dunn we have a candidate whose opinions will sustain the political traditions of Paisley.'[306]

Whether or not such rhetoric was effective in 'saving' recently 'lapsed' Unionists from a greater commitment to the new Unionist ethos is debatable.[307] Its influence was rather of a defensive nature, its power of persuasion being focused on Liberals whose faith had, perhaps, been shaken since 1886, though they remained in the Liberal fold. It was, in this sense, a sermon preached to the converted: a call for stability rather than 'progress'.

Yet, as we have seen, the emergence of such rhetoric on Liberal platforms coincided with divisions in the Unionist alliance in Paisley,

304 Ibid., 20 May 1891.
305 Ibid., 22 May 1891.
306 Ibid., 26 May 1891.
307 Note that MacKenzie, a local Unionist, appeared on Dunn's first election platform of the contest, highlighting the qualified nature of the Unionist alliance when, after 1886, the Irish question was frequently allowed to drop as the major focus of electoral campaigning and parliamentary debate.

leaving one to suspect that even after defection to the 'Right', the potency of the radical tradition qualified the support of many Liberal Unionists for their new political colleagues for some time after 1886. Indeed, after the poll in 1891, McKerrell recommended that only Chamberlain could win Paisley for the Unionists and concluded: 'Their defeat might be in some small measure due to the fact that there was still a certain amount of latent want of common zeal between the two sections of the ... Unionist party.'[308]

The following year, facing the prospect of a general election, the reluctance of the local Liberal Unionists to contest Paisley against Dunn was notable.[309] On 14 June, the lawyer Christopher N. Johnston was adopted at a meeting held under the auspices of the PCA as the Unionist candidate in the coming general election, yet commentators considered the Liberal Unionists 'apathetic' and indeed 'hostile' to his candidature.[310]

Johnston's candidature, however, represents a critical point in the differentiation of the Liberal and Unionist identities when, calling on the legacy of John Bright and the radicalism of Joseph Chamberlain, Paisley Unionists challenged the exclusive rights of the Liberal Party to the radical inheritance.[311] As Bailie Eadie commented during the campaign, 'they could scarcely tell a Tory nowadays from a Liberal. They went masquerading about the town and everywhere else with Liberal clothing on.'[312]

As Fforde has made clear, the decade following the Reform Act of 1884 witnessed an 'advance of social reform legislation' and the 'materialisation of political discussion'.[313] In such a context, Fforde views the apparent interventionist tendencies of some Conservatives in this period as 'pragmatism' and 'principled opportunism' rather than evidence of a genuine commitment to collectivist solutions to social ills.[314] Churchill, Chamberlain and Rollit are considered 'prominent proponents of tactical reform [who] were distinguished from their colleagues by the methods they advocated not the goals they sought'.[315] Thus, according to Fforde, the adoption of 'moderate left-wing policies constituted one of the chief devices by which the Conservative party sought to meet the challenge of the radicalising Left'.[316] And he warns us

308 *PDE*, 2 Jun. 1891.
309 Ibid., 15 Jun. 1892.
310 Ibid., 16 Jun. 1892.
311 Note that C. N. Johnston was born at Sands in Perthshire in 1857 and was thereafter educated at St Andrews, Edinburgh and Heidelberg. He was called to the Scottish bar in 1880 and had acted as private secretary to Lord Ernest Hamilton when he contested Paisley in 1884. For some time, he had been joint editor of the *Campaign Guide and Election Hand-book for Unionist Speakers*.
312 *PDE*, 30 Jun. 1892.
313 M. Fforde, *Conservatism and Collectivism, 1886–1914* (Edinburgh, 1990), p. 18.
314 Ibid., pp. 69–70.
315 Ibid., p. 74.
316 Ibid., p. 75.

that 'to take their professions of interventionism seriously is to mistake the deliberate image for the calculating reality – face value should not be overvalued'.[317]

Yet, is such scepticism valid when one looks closer at the Scottish perspective or indeed the position in Paisley? Fforde's thesis concentrates largely on an English cultural context and focuses on the Conservative Party with little attention paid to the evolution of the Unionist alliance beyond a fleeting reference to the 'secession of the Liberal Unionists' in 1886.[318] In Scotland, the processes involved in the creation of a *Unionist* identity – separate from both its Liberal and Conservative antecedents – necessitated and encompassed growing demands for social reform. These, if the case of Paisley is representative, emanated from the branches rather than the diktats of the political hierarchy. In Paisley such demands resonated with a traditional radical sensibility which had been carried over into Unionism by 'former' Liberals and the need to detach local identity from its expression in Liberal party politics.[319]

In 1890, Lord Wolmer addressed the WSLUA, arguing that 'There [were] more, infinitely more, Liberal Unionists among the working class in any given constituency than any gentleman here has any idea of.'[320] And he continued that organisational reforms would be futile without 'the sympathy and the support of the working man. A party not based on the following of the working men, a party not strong in their sympathies with the working men, is a house built on sand to be swept away in the first political storm. (Hear, hear.)'[321] He claimed for the Unionists the title of the 'working man's party' and proceeded to stress the social reforms of the current Unionist administration.

Following the expansion of the electorate in the 1880s, such an appeal to the working class was evidently a prudent measure – declarations of sympathy and support cost nothing until they were forced into legislation. Yet, Fforde's contention that Conservative interventionism as a pragmatic method rather than a goal did not alter the essential identity of the party is misguided. The very fact that interventionist reform was

317 Ibid., p. 161.

318 Ibid., p. 70.

319 With reference to the evolution of tariff reform as a critical component of interventionist Conservatism, this view has recently been contested by: E. H. H. Green, *The Crisis of Conservatism: The Politics, Economics and Ideology of the British Conservative Party, 1880–1914* (London, 1995). Here Green emphasises that: 'The thesis that tariff reform was, in essence, a Liberal Unionist policy is initially compelling, but does not bear close inspection': p. 6. Peter Cain, however, in response to Green, has countered that 'it is impossible to understand the roots of Edwardian radical conservatism without according Joseph Chamberlain a larger and more destabilizing role than Green assigns him': P. Cain, 'The Conservative Party and "Radical Conservatism", 1880–1914: incubus or necessity?', *TCBH*, vii (1996), p. 375.

320 NLS, SCUA, Acc. 10424/19, WSLUA Minutes: 1886–1894 (Press Cutting), 16 Apr. 1890, p. 118.

321 Ibid., p. 119.

seen and accepted by many as the only way forward highlights a critical change in the identity of the right, and throws into relief the fact that politicians could not always shape the circumstances within which they operated and were frequently shaped by them. Motive and method cannot be as simplistically differentiated as Fforde would have us believe.

Social reform represented a point of contact in Liberal Unionist and Conservative policies in Scotland during the 1890s, an area of potential unity apart from the Union upon which the two groups could negotiate a wider programme relevant to a growing electorate increasingly driven by 'interest' or 'materialist' politics. In October 1893, Hon. Hugh F. Elliott, addressed the WSLUA, encouraging social legislation 'in the interest of the masses'. He continued: 'Social and labour questions were those which must in future be dealt with and looked fairly in the face ... It was not as Unionists he called on them to look at them but as Liberals and as Radicals.'[322] The year before, the Executive Committee of the WSLUA passed a resolution in favour of 'an advanced Liberal programme [which] should be adopted and promulgated by the party'. Meanwhile, since 1887 the NUCAS had been active in promoting a Conservative reform agenda, beginning in that year a series of pamphlets focused on social reform – 'Artisans Dwellings', 'Masters and Workmen', 'Public Health', 'Legislation affecting Land', 'Factories and Workshops', and so on.[323] Though no united programme was created, the high profile of social issues on Unionist platforms in the 1890s shows a growing sympathy with statist solutions to 'the Social Question' which, while attractive as a way of securing the working-class vote, were also critical to the processes through which Unionism sought to distinguish itself from the pre-1886 party system and establish unity in its ranks.

The author of pamphlet No. 4 in the *Real Conservative Reforms* series, 'Masters and Workmen', was Christopher N. Johnston, the Unionist candidate for Paisley in 1892. His election address, encouraging support for the 'progressive policy of the present Government', clarifies the character of Unionist social reform in this period. He declared:

> I am in favour of the simplification of the Transfer of Land, Greater facilities for the Acquirement of Land for Public purposes and Dwelling Houses, the Abolition of Primogeniture and Entail, Popular Control of the Drink Traffic, State Aid to Insurance against Old Age, Amendment of the Law of Employer's Liability, Reform of the Poor Laws and of Parochial Administration, the Extension of the Factory Acts, with Special provisions against Sweating, and the Prohibition of Pauper Immigration from Abroad ...

322 NLS, SCUA, Acc. 10424/19, WSLUA Minutes: 1886–1894, General Council Meeting, 12 Oct. 1893 (p. 288).

323 NLS, SCUA, Acc. 10424, NUCAS Central Council Minutes: 1882–1889, 16 Nov. 1887.

> As combination for lawful ends by lawful means has secured to the working classes industrial freedom, so I look to co-operation gradually to secure for them in the future a larger share of the wealth which their industry has helped to create ...[324]

Whilst Johnston lost the election to Dunn, his candidature reflected a clear interventionist element on the right which would assert itself again during the 1895 contest when Alexander Moffatt contested the seat for the Unionists.[325]

Moffatt's address mirrored many of the concerns of Johnston three years earlier, with the addition of the reform of the House of Lords, land and house purchase measures for Scotland similar to those awarded to Ireland, the extension of employers' liability to all accidents in industrial employment, the granting of powers of compulsory purchase to municipal authorities for dwelling houses or other purposes of general utility and the establishment of Conciliation Boards for the prevention of strikes. Such proposals attracted much attention; William Galbraith – a prominent member of the ARA – attacked Moffatt's suggested municipal reforms as 'pure Socialism', more fitting for an ILPer.[326] And William Greig, the president of the Trades Council, drew attention to the similarities of Moffatt's social programme with that of his Liberal opponent.[327] Whilst, like Johnston before him, Moffatt lost to Dunn, this time by 3,062 votes to 4,404 – a Liberal majority of 1,342 – Moffatt had polled more votes for Unionism (or Conservatism) than any other candidate in Paisley's electoral history.

Despite local Unionist organisational successes, their increasing focus on social questions, and the emergent Labour voice, Paisley remained a solid Liberal constituency throughout the 1890s. The franchise factor must surely have had an impact on Liberalism's continued electoral success. Even after the 1884 reforms only 63.3% of the adult male population of the United Kingdom qualified for the franchise, a figure which, if plural voters are subtracted, declines to about 59%.[328] Until 1918 the popular will expressed itself through the intricacies of the 1884 qualification and notoriously inefficient registration systems: systems which, 'conceived in the last days of Whiggery and born of compromise', the Liberals became adept at 'playing'.[329] Yet, whilst drawing strength from the inadequacies of the 1884–5 Franchise Act and the weakness of both its old and new opponents, the Liberal Party maintained its position primarily by containing successfully, in both organisation and ideology, the paradoxes of its radical inheritance.

324 *PDE*, 27 Jun. 1892.
325 See below, Appendix 4.
326 *PRG*, 6 Jul. 1895.
327 *PDE*, 11 Jul. 1895.
328 Blewett, 'Franchise factor in the United Kingdom', p. 31.
329 Ibid., pp. 56, 29.

Patrick Joyce has made clear the processes which destroyed the 'politics of culture' that bolstered Liberal electoral dominance in the north of England and heralded the dominance of 'class' in the late Victorian period, stressing that

> The transition from cultural to class politics involved a change of consciousness because the old politics had rested on social foundations in which the lives of successive generations had been rooted. Change came when these foundations were shaken.[330]

As social and industrial change did not affect all regions simultaneously, the transition towards class politics was a fragmented one, in which local imperatives determined its character and chronology. As P. F. Clarke has noted, 'national movements of opinion were mediated through local influences which could modify their effect in a striking fashion'.[331]

In Paisley, the language of class had, before 1900, succeeded in capturing only a minority of the Paisley population, and an even smaller percentage of the electorate. Yet, we can detect in 1898, in the last breaths of Liberal Radicalism in Paisley, as the ARA's agenda was absorbed by the forces of organised labour, the incapacity of the established Liberal organs to articulate a new radicalism, increasingly elaborated in class terms. 'Luckily' for Paisley Liberals, the South African War diverted attention from domestic politics – the traditional forum for the elaboration of class-based political analysis – to the realm of Empire where the local dominance of Liberal Imperialism thwarted Unionist claims as the 'national' party and adorned a flagging Liberal elite with the cloak of patriotism.

Yet the Liberal electoral campaigns of the 1890s in Paisley reflect a surprising self-confidence in a party preparing, according to Dangerfield, to meet its 'Strange Death'. Rather, the evident assurance reflects the continued strength of the Liberal Party in the early 1890s, its power in registering the popular will and its ability to contain the demands for direct Labour representation via 'appeals to past services and expressions of sympathy'.[332]

Four years before instituting the ARA, James Wallace appeared on Dunn's platform during the 1892 election and announced:

> The reason of their meeting to devise ways and means to assist Mr Dunn was not because he was a Liberal, not because he was a townsman, not because he had been cradled, as it were, in the nursery of Radicalism, but it was because Mr Dunn represented,

330 Joyce, *Work, Society and Politics*, p. 32.
331 Clarke, 'Electoral sociology of modern Britain', p. 54.
332 J. Brown, 'Attercliffe, 1894: how one local Liberal party failed to meet the challenge of Labour', *JBS*, xiv (1975), p. 52.

> and he hoped he would do his very best to do justice to, the great working population. (Cheers.)[333]

Dunn's address to the Paisley electorate of this year noted that

> During the short time I have been in Parliament, I have voted in favour of Disestablishment in Scotland and in Wales, One Man One Vote, and the extension of the Franchise to Women. I voted also for an Eight Hours Day for Miners, for Payment of Members of parliament and for an Amendment of the Law of Conspiracy in so far as it unjustly affects Trade Combinations.[334]

Labour issues dominated Liberal platforms in both 1892 and 1895, with Dunn recording in 1892 that

> The labour question was a most important one, and on its proper solution depended, to a great extent, the happiness and the welfare of the industrial population of the country. (Cheers.) In the future discussion of labour problems and in framing legislation upon them it was very important that more of the labour leaders should be in the House of Commons ... The Liberals were anxious to increase the number of labour members.[335]

Whilst Coneys has noted Liberal indifference to working-class representation in Rochdale during these years, and concluded that 'the continual refusal of Liberals to consider working-class demands proved to be the crucial reason why the ILP was able to successfully develop in Rochdale', this scenario has to be qualified in the case of Paisley.[336] The ARA represented what proved to be local Liberalism's final chance to accommodate and thus de-activate the Labour threat. As such it proves the existence of a progressive element in Paisley Liberalism, anxious to adapt to the demands of a new age. Its lack of success highlights the continued strength of the established industrial elite in the local political structure and marks the point when the shared ideology, essential to the perpetuation of the Liberal hegemony, fractured under the pressure of competing alternatives to, and interpretations of, radicalism. Yet the Paisley Liberal establishment, rhetorically at least, voiced a sympathy with the cause of working-class representation and it seems that before 1900, this, along with Dunn's moderate Liberalism, was *enough* for the majority of Paisley citizens.

In Joyce Brown's critical account of the Attercliffe Liberal Party of 1894, she notes the local Liberal Party's 'failure to comprehend the political potential of the growing class consciousness among the workers

333 *PDE*, 18 Jun. 1892.
334 Ibid., 27 Jun. 1892.
335 Ibid., 2 Jul. 1892.
336 Coneys, 'Labour Movement and the Liberal Party in Rochdale', p. 101.

... [and their] inability to cope with the rapidly expanding demand for direct Labour representation'.[337] Reading backwards, with the gift of hindsight, an anachronistic *potential* in Labour's challenge in the 1890s diverts our attention from the continued success of the Liberal Party in *containing* the challenge from the 'left'. After all, in 1894, the Liberals retained the Attercliffe constituency and in Paisley, whilst the ARA grew from frustration with apparent Liberal inaction regarding Labour matters, it is important to note that it operated *within* the Liberal body politic, seeking reform from within its ranks.

Throughout the 1890s, 'old Liberals and new Socialists', shared a 'set of common intellectual reference points' not yet clearly differentiated as the property of one 'cause' or the other.[338] In certain instances 'currents' of this shared radicalism proved 'more intellectually coherent and remained more politically appropriate' to the problems faced by labour activists, and indeed the electorate, for longer than is generally recognised.[339] Socialism and indeed Labourism, in this context, remained 'rebels' from Liberalism without an apparent or indeed pressing cause. In Gramscian terminology, the forces of opposition, seeking to demonstrate that the necessary and sufficient conditions already existed to make possible, and hence imperative, the accomplishment of certain historical tasks, had failed in the pre-1900 period to demonstrate the necessity of their reforms.[340] No *new* ideological, philosophical or political polemics had been concretely established and, importantly, the disposition of social forces remained unchanged.[341]

However, in Paisley, Liberal successes reflected victories for a familiar radical tradition; thus the Liberal continuum of the late-Victorian period was qualified by its continued guardianship of a 'set' of contradictory impulses and methods born of another era.[342] In the 1890s Labour had clearly not seriously challenged Liberal dominance, yet the failure of the ARA by 1898 to absorb, in the Liberal interest, a growing sense of community based increasingly on 'class' rather than deference, marked the increasing impotence of the hegemonic elite to reflect a supposed shared identity.

337 Brown, 'Attercliffe, 1894', p. 52.

338 Biagini and Reid, 'Preface', *Currents of Radicalism*, p. 17.

339 Ibid., pp. 17–18.

340 As Belchem has noted, 'given the adaptability and continuing popularity of Liberalism, there seemed neither space nor need for an independent Labour Party': Belchem, *Popular Radicalism in Nineteenth-Century Britain*, p. 147.

341 Note Lowe's commentary on James Macdonald's candidature in Dundee in 1892: 'The harvest was not ripe and the reapers were not many': Lowe, *Souvenirs of Scottish Labour*, p. 86.

342 Note the comment in the ARA's first Annual Report: 'The question of whether the action of the association would coincide with that of the Liberal Association in the event of an election was not a question to cause disquietude seeing that their one concern would be to *guide themselves by Radical principles* and the wishes of the majority of Liberal electors in town': *PRG*, 30 Jan. 1897 [my italics].

At the close of the 1892 contest the *Express* warned:

All political partisans of whatever colour, will have to give considerably more attention in the future than they have done in the past to labour questions and the voice of labouring men ... Quite evidently ... there is a party within the ranks of labour which is determined to make its influence felt at all hazards.[343]

343 *PDE*, 8 Jul. 1892.

CHAPTER FOUR

'Mild Liberalism and the Divine Rights of Capital': Paisley Politics, 1900–1914

Women and Factory Politics

As the economic locus of the potent strands of dependency and authority which guaranteed cohesion at the centre of the hegemonic relationship, the thread mills of the Coats combine in Paisley provided the context within which power was exercised at the point of production. They thus posed simultaneously as the ultimate symbolic guarantors and potential destroyers of the hegemonic power-base. Stable work-place relations and accepted internal hierarchies of authority were critical to the continuity of the influence of the elite in the local community. In this regard, as the mediating group between work-place authority and the local community, the overwhelmingly female work-force of the mills occupied a fundamental position in the processes through which power sought legitimation. Indeed, it may be suggested of Paisley, alongside Patrick Joyce's Lancashire, that the female textile operatives proved 'an important force making for the *status quo*'.[1]

Recent scholarship in women's and feminist history has, however, located a sub-text within the history of paternalism in the evolution of a patriarchal culture in which gender operated as a determining feature in definitions of 'skill' and work-place control.[2] Taking such considerations on board, it becomes clear that the apparent simplicity of Joyce's phrase must be challenged. In addition to their economic role, it is evident that

1 Joyce, 'Factory politics of Lancashire', p. 529.

2 For the Scottish perspective, see Gordon, *Women and the Labour Movement in Scotland*. The English experience is considered in D. Busfield, 'Skill and the sexual division of labour in the West Riding textile industry, 1850–1914'; and M. Savage, 'Women and work in the Lancashire cotton industry, 1890–1939', both in J. A. Jowitt and A. McIvor (eds.), *Employers and Labour in the English Textile Industries, 1850–1939* (London, 1988), pp. 153–170, 203–23; J. Lown, 'Not so much a factory, more a form of patriarchy: gender and class during industrialisation', in E. Garmarnikow, D. H. J. Morgan, J. Purvis, and D. E. Taylorson (eds.), *Gender, Class and Work* (London, 1983), pp. 28–45; J. Lambertz, 'Sexual harassment in the nineteenth-century English cotton industry', *History Workshop*, xix (1985), pp. 29–61; E. Higgs, 'Women, occupations and work in the nineteenth-century censuses', *History Workshop*, xxiii (1987), pp. 59–80; N. G. Osterud, 'Gender divisions and the organization of work in the Leicester hosiery industry', in A. V. John (ed.) *Unequal Opportunities: Women's Employment in England, 1800–1918* (Oxford, 1986), pp. 45–70; and S. O. Rose, '"Gender at work": sex, class and industrial capitalism', *History Workshop*, xxi (1986), pp. 113–31.

the experiences of Paisley's female operatives illustrate a 'gender dimension' in the history of Paisley's 'factory politics' which served to intensify paternalist control in the mills and perpetuate a concept of 'family' within the wider community which defined and restricted the political role of women.

As Judy Lown has noted, patriarchal authority 'constituted a structure and set of principles which were embodied in varying institutional and customary forms [and as such must] be analysed as part of the material arrangements of the society and subject to historical change in the same way as other material forms'.[3] It is to these processes of change that this chapter will appeal as determining factors which dictated the recapitulation of women's role *alongside* and *interacting with* the social and political readjustment already evidenced in the emergence of a 'class society'. In this way it will become clear that the initial faltering steps in the 'awakening' of 'class' consciousness among the women workers of Paisley in the period from 1900 to 1914 illustrated the limitations of the popular ideology of the radical tradition which was at the centre of hegemonic political power, and the persistence of the imagery of patriarchy which underpinned the 'separate spheres' of gender relations in the work-place and beyond.

As we have seen, a new equilibrium established itself in the labour market in Paisley in the mid-nineteenth century, as women replaced men as the major employees of the textile industry, and male employment became increasingly located in the engineering trades and industries developing in Renfrewshire and Clydeside. Due to the relative abundance of alternative male employment, this transition seems to have occurred without much hostility from the male workers – their new employments tending, on the whole, to be 'skilled' and higher paid in comparison to mill work.[4] Those adult males who remained in the mills tended to occupy supervisory jobs as foremen and overlookers or occupied the skilled posts in the engineering shops which evolved as a consequence of the increased mechanisation in the spinning and finishing flats. As a result, women's employment was largely restricted to jobs termed 'unskilled' and promotion opportunities were, at best, limited.

The evolution of patriarchal control in the mills was thus facilitated by a clearly segregated labour market in the wider community within which concepts of appropriate 'men's' and 'women's' work frequently coincided with popular constructs of 'skilled' and 'unskilled' employment and were reinforced by the specific labour requirements of the

[3] Lown, 'Not so much a factory', p. 31.

[4] Whilst this aspect of the changing industrial character of the Paisley work-force requires further research, it is clear that similar transitions happened elsewhere. See T. Koditschek, 'The gendering of the British working class', *Gender and History*, ix (1997), p. 345.

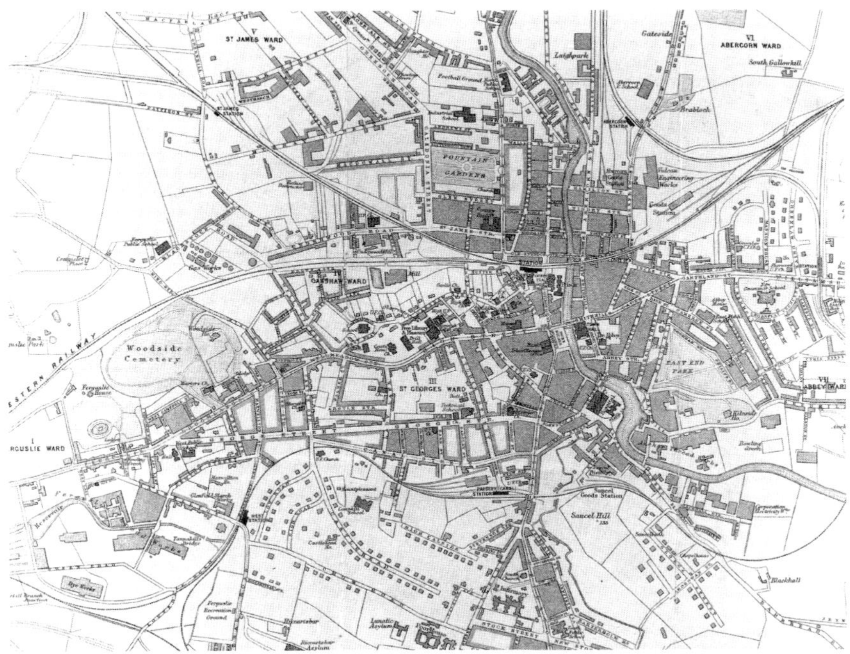

1. Paisley in the 1890s. (*Reproduced with permission from Renfrewshire Council (Paisley Museum).*)

2. Anchor Mill, Paisley. (*Reproduced with permission from Renfrewshire Council (Paisley Museum).*)

3. Peter Coats presents a grateful Paisley with a museum and library. Coats' gift was announced in 1867 and the building was tranferred to the Town Council in 1870. (*Reproduced with permission from Renfrewshire Council (Paisley Museum).*)

4. George A. Clark and other members of the Clark family funded the new town hall which was handed over to the Corporation in January 1882. (*Reproduced with permission from Renfrewshire Council (Paisley Museum).*)

5. Even outwith the workplace, the factory could frame employees' experience and recreation. This picture shows the Anchor Boy Scouts (est. 1915).

6. Bowling Club Fête Day (1916).

7. Thread works outing (1913).

8. Girls' hockey teams were established for Ferguslie (1912) and Anchor (1923) workers. The Anchor Recreation Club pictured here was opened in 1923. (*This and the three preceding illustrations are reproduced with permission from Renfrewshire Council (Paisley Museum).*)

9. Weaving looms, Paisley Co–operative Manufacturing Society, Colinslee (c.1880s) : scene of industrial action in 1897. (*Reproduced with permission from Renfrewshire Council (Paisley Museum).*)

10. Neilston strike (1910). (*Reproduced with permission from Renfrewshire Council (Paisley Museum).*)

11. The 'The Church Question' was a major issue at the 1885 general election. (*Reproduced with permission from Renfrewshire Council* (*Paisley Museum*).)

12. Unionism's dashing suitor eventually proved unable to win Miss Paisley's hand. (*Reproduced with permission from Renfrewshire Council* (*Paisley Museum*).)

13. Celebrating victory during the Boer War. (*Reproduced with permission from Renfrewshire Council (Paisley Museum).*)

14. Turning heads: the Prince of Wales' visit to Paisley in 1921. (*Reproduced with permission from Renfrewshire Council (Paisley Museum).*)

15. Street oratory, County Square, Paisley (c.1900). (*Reproduced with permission from Renfrewshire Council (Paisley Museum).*)

16. Sma' Shot Day Parade, Gauze Street (1890s). (*Reproduced with permission from Renfrewshire Council (Paisley Museum).*)

17-18. Paisley women, seen here in two studio portraits, worked in a variety of contexts, such as thread-mills and munitions factories, during World War One. (*Reproduced with permission from Renfrewshire Council (Paisley Museum).*)

19. A young Willie Gallacher. (*Reproduced with permission from Renfrewshire Council (Paisley Museum).*)

mill-owners.[5] The local economy thus determined, and was determined by, male dominance over the definition of 'skill' as a mask behind which gender divisions, rather than those merely of occupational suitability, necessarily operated.

Critical in this regard were the male overlookers, described by Melling as 'pivotal figures in many of the staple industries', standing as they did between the demands of capital and the sympathies of labour.[6] It is unclear whether these individuals performed the same recruiting role in Paisley as did their counterparts in many of the Lancashire mills, but their role in the perpetuation of patriarchal power relations within the mills and deferential politics in the local community was fundamental. In 1907 *Forward* devoted an entire article to the 'Paisley Mill Foreman', sketching his recruitment following the presentation of birth certificate, testimonials and proof of religious denomination and church attendance, through the probationary period and compulsory evening classes to his eventual accession to supervisory power over the girls who 'ofttimes ... [look upon him] as their common enemy ... a bully'.[7] Indeed, Coats's archives record the experience of one female worker who complained, through a letter written by her father, of the 'petty tyranny and persecution she had to put up with at the hands of her foreman'.[8]

Even outwith the mill itself, the influence of the foreman's paternalist masters thrived. *Forward* commented further:

> It is common knowledge and not regarded in any phenomenal light that [in] the whole army of Coats' foremen, sub-managers and managers, none has been known to identify himself with any more advanced form of thought than that which pertains to mild Liberalism and the divine rights of Capital ... He may not hold any political opinions, but he is permitted to denounce Socialism and Socialists and to vote either Liberal or Tory, according to the guidance of the boss who controls his destiny.[9]

Patriarchy and the demands of paternalist politics were thus married in the figure of the fore*man* or overlooker, the physical manifestation of the sexual hierarchy in the mill and the parallel father/husband figure whose role reconstituted family authority within the mill gates. Here, the relatively low age of the female employees on entering the thread works and the high proportions of half-timers possibly had the effect of enhancing this transference of concepts of male authority between home

5 Knox, *Hanging by a Thread*, p. 85.

6 J. Melling, '"Non-Commissioned Officers": British employers and their supervisory workers, 1880–1920', *SH*, v (1980), p. 191.

7 *Forward*, 5 Oct. 1907.

8 UGABRC, JPC Collection, 199/1/2/1, Letter Book: 1905–1911, Thomas Wedworth (11 West Street) to John Walmsley (J. & P. Coats) regarding the plight of his daughter, Annie, 18 Feb. 1907.

9 *Forward*, 5 Oct. 1907.

and work.[10] Furthermore, in comparison to the cotton towns of the north of England and indeed the jute mills of Dundee, female operatives in the Paisley mills – as was shown earlier – were generally single, leaving work on marriage seldom to return.[11] In this way, it may be argued that gender roles which stipulated the governing duty of woman as wife and mother imposed tighter restrictions on Paisley's female population than those of other textile communities and thus acted as a more stubborn obstacle to the evolution of class-based definitions of economic exploitation. The work-place experience was only temporary and, even during this relatively short period, proved an extension of the female's subordinate position within the home.

In the 1900s, however, important features of work-place discipline and the production process changed in a manner which encouraged conflict, undermined the reciprocity which guided paternalist relationships, and challenged the stabilising qualities of patriarchal organisation. Here, undoubtedly, the influence of the trade-union movement is critical, yet the impulse behind conflict was rooted in the work-place experience and the articulation of inherently non-institutional forms of female protest.

One indicator that fundamental change was occurring in the female operatives' experience of work may be abstracted from length of service records of female employees. Here, the underlying trends are threefold. First, during the initial decades of the twentieth century there was a substantial decline in the average length of service for full-time female operatives.[12] Of those female workers taken on full time in 1895 whose date of departure is recorded, the average length of service was 16.5 years, with some workers 'serving' the company nearly forty years. In contrast, of those workers taken on in 1900, only 15.43% recorded service of sixteen years and over. For workers hired in 1905, this figure had fallen to 3.31%, and of those hired in 1910, only 19.57% recorded service of fourteen years plus.[13] Secondly, there was a dramatic increase in workers leaving Coats within the first year of employment. Of those workers hired in 1900, none was recorded as leaving within the first four years of employment. By 1905, however, 31.06% of those hired that year had left by the end of the year.[14] Finally, though no records illustrate it in systematic form, there was a substantial increase in the hiring of labour on a short-term basis after 1900.

10 PM, JPC Collection, 1/5/41, Index of Female Employees.

11 Here, it may be stressed that Knox's interpretation of Coats' employment registers for 1902 misinterprets the number of women leaving to be married. Knox focuses on a proportion of 6% *stated in the register* as leaving employment to be married but fails to acknowledge the likelihood that many catalogued as 'left' did so to marry without revealing their future intentions: See Knox, *Hanging by a Thread*, p. 160.

12 See ibid., p. 83.

13 PM, JPC Collection, 1/5/41, Index of Female Employees.

14 Ibid.

When one considers the necessity of a low labour turnover in the process of identification between employee and employer, the implications of such trends for the perpetuation of the paternalist hegemony become clear. Patrick Joyce has highlighted the importance of the long-term attachment to the factory which proved a chief source of 'community cohesion' and 'a considerable force for continuity and stability' in the Lancashire mill towns.[15] After 1900, the instability resulting from the increased labour turnover in Paisley proved significant in undermining loyalty to the textile firms, a trend which was exaggerated during the 1914–18 war as the attractions of the high paid munitions industry encouraged a temporary haemorrhage of Coats's workers from the mills.

Yet, it is in the character of female involvement in strike action and trade unionism that one can most clearly identify the tensions involved in initial attempts to organise female protest on class lines.

Anticipating a planned ILP lecture by Katherine St John Conway in 1893, Paisley Trades Council initiated steps to form a women's union in the town, the first meeting of which took place on 3 May under the chairmanship of 'Clear-heid' Cochran, who reflected on the failure of previous attempts at organisation several years before. Fifty female members were recruited to the Paisley Women's Federal Union at this meeting, their number increasing to 120 by the end of the month. In November, the union affiliated to the Women's Protection and Provident League, yet by March the following year the Trades Council complained that local women were not taking organisation seriously, treating the union as a 'joke', a 'burlesque'.[16] The local press falls silent on the Federal Union thereafter and the question of female organisation does not feature highly in Trades Council business until 1897 and the aftermath of the Colinslee dispute, when the council planned an organisational meeting for 'after the Fair'. That winter, however, the ASE lockout dominated Trades Council business and no fresh attempt was made to organise women workers until the 1900s when the motive force behind organisation was generated by the women themselves.

The years from 1900 to 1908 mark a period of notable conflict over wages and conditions between the female operatives and management of the Paisley mills. In addition to strikes, internal complaints procedures reflect the disruption of industrial stability and the dislocation of the bonds of deference and patriarchy. Complaints from guide cutters in 1908 regarding promotion were met with the following words from the manager:

> we were not prepared to be dictated to, as to what was to be done ... we could see no cause for the attitude they had taken up, and if

15 Joyce, *Work, Society and Politics*, p. 119.
16 *PRG*, 10 Mar. 1894.

they could better themselves elsewhere they are quite at liberty to do so; but we cautioned them to consider well before taking such a step, because if they left the employment on such a grievance, there would be little likelihood of their ever being re-engaged.[17]

The delicate balance between compromise and control had clearly shifted towards greater authoritarianism on the part of the mill management as reciprocity seemed to give way to threats of retribution. This is only partly explained in terms of the managerial revolution which occurred in the structure of the mills following their moves towards amalgamation and limited company status. Yet what had caused such a transition in industrial relations?

When the Paisley thread industry doubled its capacity in the period from 1867 to 1890, the voice of conflict from the operatives was relatively still. Yet, the era of stagnation, noted by Robertson from the 1890s, coincided with an era of enhanced protest.[18] Paradoxically, the roots of protest lay in continued innovation in the production process rather than in technological backwardness – the conventional scapegoat for British industrial decline during this period. Strikes were concentrated among the unskilled trades of the finishing departments of the mills and more specifically among the copwinders, conewinders and hankwinders, whose jobs, paid at piece rates, were becoming increasingly mechanised. Yet the rhetoric of the strikers and their style of protest reflected broader concerns in which the male figures of the foreman, sub-manager and manager figured prominently in a developing demonology.

In 1900, the grievances of the six hundred copwinders who struck work at the Ferguslie mills were listed as follows:

1. That owing to the introduction of a patent into their machines their work was now heavier and their wages smaller, the difference being stated to be as much as 5s., 6s. and even 7s. in the fortnight.

2. That the baskets of yarn were too heavy to be carried by them to certain of the flats, and that either hoists should be provided or that parcels should be made lighter ...

3. That favouritism was being shown by certain foremen in the distribution of work among the girls.[19]

The male foreman, as the key representative of management in the work-place and a crucial intermediary in the communication and

[17] PM, JPC Collection, 1/5/45, Wages Complaints Book, Managers Report 66, 15 Apr. 1908 (p. 29).

[18] A. J. Robertson, 'The decline of the Scottish cotton industry', *Business History*, xii (1970), p. 121.

[19] *PRG*, 3 Mar. 1900.

implementation of new work practices, proved an important figure in determining the articulation of sexual grievances alongside those of work-place control. The two became inseparable. Industrial capitalism, as Sonya Rose has made clear, 'took shape in and was shaped by an already gendered world'.[20] Thus change, when it occurred, sought its place in a gendered labour hierarchy and industrial disputes reflected processes through which 'class' and 'gender' were being reinterpreted *simultaneously*.[21]

The Labour press was of importance in depicting the struggle of the Paisley mill girls as a gender struggle, though significantly it did so by reworking the dominant doctrines of 'separate spheres'. In 1906, the new *Paisley Observer* focused on the role of the male hierarchy of the mills: 'Under the managers there are sub-managers and under the sub-managers foremen – and all imbued with the same spirit, drive!, drive!, drive!'.[22] Reflecting on the 'tyrannical rule of the foreman', the *Observer* went on to describe his 'hounding' of the exhausted female workers.[23] In 1907, *Forward* stressed the obstacle of the foreman in attempts at female unionisation in the mills, where the women were met 'with more opposition from these allies of the exploiter than from the exploiters themselves'.[24] During a strike of that year *Forward* again addressed the role of Coats's male employees when it asked

> What was the attitude of the male workers at the mill in regard to this dispute? One of abject servility. There was not one man's voice raised on behalf of the rights of their fellow workers. The fight ... was maintained by women and boys. To such a humiliating degree can the spirit of man be broken in Paisley![25]

Women 'going it alone' were clearly throwing into stark relief the *unmasculine* cowardice of the Paisley male as well as his lack of class consciousness, and the inappropriate exploitation of the mill girls by their male overlookers whose actions usurped the traditional protective role of the male. Indeed, the consequences of such dangerous nonconformity had implications for the future morals of the women themselves, as the *Observer* made clear in an article of 1906, tracing the fall from virtue of one dismissed striker who, 'once ... a merry spirited lass and the only support of her mother', had become 'of bad character'. It warned that 'hunger is at all times stronger than virtue'.[26] The stark

20 Rose, 'Gender at Work', p. 114.

21 Lown, 'Not so much a factory', p. 32. See also Koditschek, 'Gendering of the British working class', pp. 333–63; and A. M. Scott, 'Industrialization, gender segregation and stratification theory', in R. Crompton and M. Mann (eds.), *Gender and Stratification* (Cambridge, 1986), pp. 154–83.

22 *Paisley Observer*, 30 Mar. 1906.

23 Ibid., 30 Mar. 1906.

24 *Forward*, 15 Jun. 1907.

25 Ibid., 5 Oct. 1907.

26 *Paisley Observer*, 6 Apr. 1906.

sexual segregation in the labour market thus facilitated a situation whereby economic conflicts with authority became test cases of gender roles.

The strikes of the 1900s, however, were clearly differentiated from others of the period as 'women's' strikes in which male operatives (except for unskilled boys and apprentices) took little part. Sympathetic strike action taken by women in departments unaffected by the cause of dispute further encourage this identification of industrial and gender issues. In 1904, striking hankwinders of the polishing department of Clarks's Seedhill Mill were joined first by whitewinders, ballers and spoolers and then other departments, until by the fifth day of strike action, one thousand girls had struck work.[27] The following year, the Seedhill hankwinders struck work again in response to falling wage rates. Less than a week later 2,000 workers were out on strike.[28] Such displays of solidarity among non-unionised workers highlight the potential for non-institutionalised protest among the female operatives. As Eleanor Gordon has highlighted, non-union and unorganised are far from synonymous terms.[29] In both the above disputes the company directors were forced to abandon piece rates, at least for a limited period, and in the case of 1905, compensated some workers for loss of earnings.

Throughout the 1900s, the style of the women's protests was defined and judged according to conventions of gender. In 1900, the *Gazette* concluded that the copwinders on strike that year being 'unorganised' were 'thus unfitted for the conduct of a dispute with their employers through agents, *after the manner of men*'.[30] During the 1904 dispute it printed the following poem:

BRIDGET BURKE
Went to work
  N.M.T. to wind,
But the wage – well, the wage –
  Wasn't to her mind,
So she struck,
Looked like pluck,
  Very, very sad too,
Thursday came – in again –
  Couldn't help it, had to.[31]

The women strikers were frequently depicted as having little knowledge or appreciation of the matters in dispute. 'It must be said', wrote the

27 *PRG*, 14 May 1904.
28 Ibid., 18 Mar. 1905.
29 Gordon, *Women and the Labour Movement in Scotland*, p. 131.
30 *PRG*, 10 Mar. 1900 [my italics].
31 Ibid., 14 May 1904.

Gazette in 1905, 'that it is not every girl that could tell what they were striking for'.[32] A style of protest which failed to find accommodation in the conventions of trade unionism was thus described as a serio-comic interlude in the otherwise male-dominated world of labour relations.

Such attitudes were mirrored in the local press coverage of the carnival-style atmosphere of the strikes. Consider the following from the *Express* in 1905:

> Yesterday ... the town ... [was] made aware ... that the strike had really assumed greater proportions. The demonstration was confined to a humorous one, and a band of young folks with tin cans and other primitive instruments, along with an alleged effigy was observed in one thoroughfare. At another part, a herring was pressed into the service, and the crowd played battledore and shuttlecock among themselves with this.[33]

Pipers, marches, peasemeal throwing, hooting and shouting, stabbings with hatpins, the 'mobbing' of the town's trams and the occasional appropriation of a candy barrow are described as the characteristic 'ornamentation' of the strikes of the 1900s. Such burlesque has been noted by Gordon in other women's strikes during this period, and highlighted as a source of irritation to male unionists who encouraged 'order' and calm.[34] Independent, spontaneous action posed as the clear antithesis of the respectability fostered by the craft unions, yet as such it is of the utmost importance as a defining feature of female protest.

Clearly, the mobilisation of thousands of non-union female labour required the prior existence of informal internal support networks within the mills which, in turn, emphasise the communitarian – as opposed to formal associational – bonds between the workers. Jan Lambertz has emphasised how 'familial protection systems ... complement[ed] ... collective resistance to unacceptable working conditions' in the English cotton mills, yet is clear from the community-based character of protest among the Paisley thread workers that beyond this, the locality proved a significant forum for and influence upon militant action among women.[35] They took their protests to the streets rather than the board-room.

However, whilst a realisation of a common grievance frequently translated into distinctively 'female' expressions of unity; such protests – framed by patriarchal conventions – resulted paradoxically in the reaffirmation of women's distinct and subordinate position within the work-force and community.[36] The critical strike weapon was the

32 Ibid., 18 Mar. 1905.

33 *PDE*, 15 Mar. 1905.

34 Gordon, *Women and the Labour Movement in Scotland*, pp. 132–3, 179.

35 Lambertz, 'Sexual harassment', p. 46.

36 Steinberg has recently highlighted how E. P. Thompson addressed aspects of this ironic dilemma in class formation in *The Poverty of Theory*: Steinberg, 'Culturally

usurpation of gender norms and their appropriation in the interests of the female workers against both their male bosses and obstructive male colleagues. Such patterns of protest posed ironically as exemplars of female potential in the elaboration of a class-based ideology of industrial exploitation and confirmation of women's separate and isolated position within the general labour movement. Industrial militancy thus exploited and reinforced defensive, conventional concepts of gender roles.

Whilst limited attempts had been made by the Trades Council in 1900 and 1904 to absorb the enthusiasm generated by strike action in the interests of unionisation, it was not until 1906, encouraged by the propaganda of the *Paisley Observer*, that the council made a concerted effort to organise the 'Paisley mill girls'.

Printed between 1905 and 1907, the weekly *Paisley Observer* (becoming the *Scottish Observer* in April 1906) focused attention on the conditions of the Paisley mill workers in a series of articles, the first of which coincided with the general election campaign of 1906. Demanding the speedy organisation of the 'mill girls', the *Observer* articles represented a determined attempt to undermine the paternal 'charade' of the Coats combine and elaborate a wider class message based on the experiences of the female workers. The Coats family, it noted,

> are moved with the sufferings of a heroine in a sentimental novel or a tale of slum-life in a book; but they overlook the number of suffering heroines who are slaving daily, from morn till night, in an atmosphere worse than tropical – slaving that they might have enough to eat and be clothed respectably – while at the same time they are like bees in a hive who strive and toil to make a comb, which the enterprising bee-keeper comes and lifts in due season and eats himself.[37]

In March 1906, the Trades Council agreed to renew attempts at organisation 'in view of the evidently increasing discontent among local women workers with their labour conditions'.[38] Yet despite recent disputes in the spooling department at Ferguslie and among the copwinders of the Anchor Mills, the organisation meeting held the following month attracted a meagre audience.[39] Just over a week later, however, the tide seemed to be turning, following a communication of 3 May from the directors of J. & P. Coats, which announced that plans for the erection of a new mill and extension to the spinning mill at Ferguslie would not go ahead. The *Gazette* reported:

> We are informed that the persistent attempts to make mischief between the company and their workers are the cause of the

speaking', p. 205.

37 *Paisley Observer*, 23 Mar. 1906.

38 *PRG*, 31 Mar. 1906.

39 *Scottish Observer*, 27 Apr. 1906.

> Directors considering it for the best interest of the Company to abandon the idea of any increase in Paisley.[40]

The following week, a deputation from the Town Council who waited upon the directors was further led to understand that the company 'did not care to take the risk of the outcome of dissensions steadily sowed among their workers by Socialist agitators'.[41]

Two days later, an 'overflowing' meeting was held under the auspices of the Trades Council, during which a branch of the Women Worker's Union was established. Taking the platform, Mary MacArthur framed the case for organisation in opposition to the paternalism of the thread syndicate:

> They were told of all the good things the Coats and Clarks had done for Paisley. What had Paisley done for them? (Applause.) She considered that Paisley had done a great deal more for Clark, Coats and Company than they had done or could possibly do for Paisley. (Applause.) ... The thread combine was not in the industry for philanthropic purposes ...[42]

Yet her appeal was couched in the rhetoric of women's role as mothers. MacArthur continued:

> She wanted them to realise that the question of Trades Unionism made for true manhood, the dignity of women, and the future of little children. It would mean brighter, better and happier lives for everyone. If not for their own sakes, then for the children's sakes she urged them to join this movement.[43]

Still, therefore, the intrinsic two-in-one-ness of the gender and class agendas was asserted, but in a manner which posed little threat to wider societal sexual norms. As Koditschek has made clear,

> rhetorical tropes were not suspended in some pure discursive vacuum, but were inextricably connected to concrete social practices, social structures, and struggles which loaded the dice in favor of (and against) certain cultural or ideological outcomes, insuring that certain visions and rhetorical constructions would rise to dominance and become hegemonic, while others became attenuated, foreshortened and foreclosed.[44]

All the speakers at the meeting denied that recent attempts at unionisation had resulted in Coats's decision to abandon their plans for expansion, and cast the workers and unionists in the role of convenient

40 *PRG*, 5 May 1906.
41 Ibid., 12 May 1906.
42 *Scottish Observer*, 11 May 1906.
43 Ibid., 11 May 1906.
44 Koditschek, 'Gendering of the British working class', p. 353.

scape-goats. At the close of the meeting two hundred women had been enrolled as union members.

Yet support was far from unanimous. The day after the meeting, Mary MacArthur was forced off a lecture platform outside Clarks' Seedhill Mill and later attributed the hostility to the 'pressure brought on the girls by their parents and by local tradesmen'.[45] The spoolers at the Ferguslie works thereafter issued a statement condemning the union and confirming their 'confidence that the directors of the firm will continue to deal justly with them'.[46] Later that week, a letter appeared in the *Gazette*, from 'A Mill Worker', encouraging girls who had a complaint not to join the union but to go to the 'masters' 'with that confidence a little child approaches its parents'.[47] Clearly patriarchal authority asserted a powerful counter pressure on the claims for unionisation.

Whilst the abandonment of the new mill was later explained as a consequence of the restrictive labour surplus in the Paisley area, Coats's show of industrial 'muscle' made a deep impression on many workers.[48] Thereafter, their apparent *volte face* in June, when, in a letter to the Town Clerk, the company declared itself 'in no way opposed to the workers forming themselves into a union for the protection and promotion of their interests', convinced no-one.[49]

Billed as 'Labour's Reply to the Coats's Thread Combine', the ILP held a demonstration on 29 June in an attempt to politicise the recent attempts at organisation in the mills. To thunderous applause in the crowded hall, Keir Hardie, taking the platform, proposed the creation of an 'industrial commonwealth based on the socialisation or common ownership of land and capital', as the only alternative to the current slavery of the work-force.[50] Yet the audience was dominated by males and the area *set aside* for female workers was practically empty. In immediate terms, the conflict had failed to engender an active political appreciation of the industrial struggle among the female work-force.

The following year, a strike of female operatives in the Anchor Mills in sympathy with the plight of striking boys in the turning shop brought about the temporary closure of both the Anchor and Ferguslie works, and heralded a return to spontaneous industrial activity in the mills and a revival of the communitarian character of protest. Ten days before the strike began, however, a *Forward* journalist commented that the membership of the union established the year before was 'anything but large' and that the 'interest manifested in it by the mill girls [did] not

45 *PDE*, 18 May 1906.
46 *PRG*, 12 May 1906.
47 Ibid., 12 May 1906.
48 Ibid., 19 May 1906.
49 Ibid., 16 Jun. 1906.
50 *Scottish Observer*, 6 Jul. 1906.

justify [him] saying anything very flattering as to its influence'.[51] During the dispute which saw 12,000 workers thrown idle, no attempt was made to unionise the workers, and when they returned to work they did so under conditions which stipulated a two-week period of notice before they could embark on strike action in the future. In 1908 sixty conewinders at the Anchor works were dismissed when, in April, they struck work without notice.

The increased authoritarian stance of Coats's management eliminated the potential for industrial action of the nature which, to date, had proved the most popular response to grievances – the spontaneous strike. That such an approach proved successful may be evidenced in the fact that no major disputes were recorded in the Paisley mills during the period of 'classic' industrial militancy, between 1910 and 1914. The Neilston strike of 1910 elicited little response from the Paisley work-force, despite direct appeals from the strikers themselves who marched into Paisley on 18 June carrying a banner bearing the words: 'NEILSTON EXPECTS THE PAISLEY GIRLS TO JOIN THE UNION'.[52] The following month, a meeting organised by the National Federation of Women Workers in Paisley attracted such a small audience that it had to be abandoned.[53]

The strictly segregated female labour market in Paisley made gender concerns at once obstacles to, and critical components of, a developing class analysis of society for women workers.[54] Furthermore, the power of patriarchal norms in both the work-place and beyond as part not only of the language of industrial paternalism, but also of the trade-union movement and the family, determined restricted parameters of action. Such norms could on occasion be appropriated in the interests of the women workers but only at a cost – the further re-affirmation of their 'separateness' in the labour movement. The predominantly non-unionised character of the female thread operatives on the eve of the Great War was thus determined not merely by the failure of contemporary union strategy, but by the power of distinctive local imperatives which consolidated a social vision of 'woman' as ultimately defined by her domestic role.

The implications of such disunity between the sexes for the success of the political Labour movement are complex, though its 'exclusive' radical heritage and consequent failure to create an inclusive agenda

51 *Forward*, 14 Sep. 1907.

52 *PDE*, 20 Jun. 1910.

53 Ibid., 12 Jul. 1910.

54 Chamberlain fails to appreciate the importance of the sexually segregated labour market of towns such as Paisley when he writes: 'the increasing tendency towards the modern pattern with giant factories employing much greater numbers of workers, created exceptionally favourable conditions under which more articulate working men could promulgate the ideas of (trade) unionism and later, support for a Labour Party': C. Chamberlain, 'The growth in support for the Labour Party in Britain', *BJS*, xxiv (1973), p. 484.

should not go un-noted. Joan Wallach Scott has stressed the dual processes of inclusion and exclusion in the definition of 'class' politics in nineteenth-century Britain and the consequent elaboration of a Chartist construct of 'class' which, by isolating property as the means of access into the social contract, automatically excluded women.[55] The consequences of this definition Scott considers of long-lasting significance in the evolution of the British Labour movement:

> no matter how much later struggles stressed the need for a reorganisation of the economy ... the invocation of universal human rights was carried on within the masculine construction of property and rationalist politics. One result of this was to push alternative conceptions of class ... to the periphery. Another effect was to render sexual difference itself invisible ... Women then had two possible representations. They were either a specific example of the general experience of class and then it was unnecessary to single them out for separate treatment ... Or, women were a troubling exception.[56]

Evidence of this duality is clearly apparent in the foregoing consideration of women's involvement in trade unionism in Paisley. Yet more significantly, in the light of such an appreciation, the ambiguity of women's position within the Paisley labour movement – the identity of which relied substantially on the legacy of its Chartist past – becomes more readily explicable. The simultaneity in the evolution of class and gender, viewed in this light, has clear implications for any analysis of political change. As Sally Alexander has made clear:

> Whatever their intentions, the Chartists by deleting women, the factory reformers by submitting to the principle of the protection of women and every working-class custom, insofar as it refused an equal status to women within the class, placed women in a different relationship to the state than men.[57]

The consequences of this legacy were evident in Labour's response to the strikes of the 1900s. At once invisible and yet all too evident, women's experience failed to find accommodation in the class rhetoric of the Labour movement which consequently proved powerless to politicise, in any meaningful manner, the conflicts of these years and mobilise the women workers of Paisley to any appreciable degree. Yet,

55 J. W. Scott, 'On language, gender and working-class history', in L. R. Berlanstein (ed.), *The Industrial Revolution and Work in Nineteenth-Century Europe* (London, 1992), p. 169. See also Koditschek, 'Gendering of the British working class', p. 344.

56 Ibid., pp. 172–3.

57 S. Alexander, 'Women, class and sexual differences in the 1830s and 1840s: some reflections on the writing of a feminist history', *History Workshop*, xvii (1984), p. 146. Note: In 1906, Mary MacArthur encouraged the women of Paisley to 'come into the Socialist movement, in which they would find an opportunity to help their fellow *men*' – a clear illustration of the confused gendered legacy of Labour's radical past: *Scottish Observer*, 6 Jul. 1906 [my italics].

far from considering such a 'missed opportunity' for Labour – women, after all, before 1918 possessed little electoral 'capital' – it is important to acknowledge Labour's gendered consciousness as an intrinsic feature of its evolution – a process conditioned by wider societal sexual mores against which relatively few working women in this period chose to take a public stand. In this sense the patriarchal code as a bulwark of paternalist organisation stood, on the eve of the Great War, as a meaningful, and thus largely unchallenged feature of a still potent local Liberal political consensus which stood in opposition to the evolution of a class-based political agenda.

Locality and Class: The Evolution of a 'Labour' Identity

Established in 1899, the Paisley Socialist Sunday School, under the presidency of James Love of the Patternmakers Society and former Trades Council president (1897–8), had secured a membership of around eighty children by 1902. Eight years after founding the school, Tom Anderson returned to Causeyside Street and commemorated the visit in an article in *Forward*:[58]

> Paisley School, in point of number and efficiency is in the front rank. The school was opened by singing 'Hark, the Battle Cry is Ringing'. The junior roll was next called by a young girl. The senior roll by a handsome lass. Then the next hymn, 'An Offering to the Shrine of Power our Hands will never Bring'. The president then asked for texts, and no fewer than twenty-one texts were forthcoming ... Then we had the monthly texts, written on the blackboard in this style. Text:
>
> Our Field –
> The World.
>
> Our Cause –
> Humanity.
>
> The Unity of Labour is
> The Hope of the World.
>
> That brought us to our third hymn, 'Have you Heard the Golden City' ... the speaker for the day was Comrade McPhee, a member of the school. His subject was Robert Tannahill.
> 'Robert Tannahill ... was a man of the common people ... an idealist and great lover of Nature ... He laughed at pomp ... He was against militarism and Landlordism. Had Robert been with us today he would have been an advanced Socialist.'[59]

58 *Forward*, 2 Feb. 1907.
59 Ibid., 2 Feb. 1907.

Anderson then rose to address the audience:

> My story was a short one entitled 'A FAIRY STORY', and concluded thus:- And the fairy said to the people, these people display their wealth to debase you. And a big man in the crowd, on hearing these words, threw a stone ... and struck the fairy ... and killed her. The story is founded on a report of a fashionable wedding which was celebrated last week in Paisley between Miss May Coats and Percy Illingworth MP.[60]

Illustrating the manner in which the universalism of socialism acquired a distinctively local dimension, Anderson's account of this Sunday school meeting identifies, by way of allegory, two key features of the Paisley Labour movement in the period from 1900 to 1914 – its growing commitment to national and explicitly *political* solutions, to social and industrial grievances, and its concurrent continued embeddedness in a peculiarly local heritage, the contemporary expression of which sought potency in a locally generated vision of class. The apparent contradictory nature of these dual principles was seldom criticised – the reformist strategies of the new Labour movement generally succeeded in holding them in equilibrium by focusing attention on practical issues rather than utopian missions. It is with these considerations in mind, therefore, that this chapter traces the evolution of Labour in Paisley from its industrial roots to its emergence as an established local political party.

As a policy bridging local and statist concerns, municipalisation proved a conjunctural stage in Labour's evolution of a distinctive political programme in Paisley. Michael Savage, in differentiating local capacities for certain 'types' of struggle – mutualist, economistic, statist – has stressed that

> The different types of struggle are not simply the product of tactical and strategic thought, but are brought about primarily by elements of local social relations which allow one form of struggle to take place rather than another.[61]

Whilst such a formulation runs the risk of facilitating unprofitable *post hoc* arguments, it is useful in contextualising the evolution of policy in terms of developing social structures. Seen in this light, Labour's growing concern with municipalisation may safely be analysed against the backdrop of declining hegemonic power structures in the locality, the intrusion of state agencies in the recruitment and protection of labour, and the growing politicisation of unskilled labour, more commonly moved by economistic concerns.[62]

60 Ibid., 2 Feb. 1907.
61 Savage, *Dynamics of Working-Class Politics*, pp. 40–1.
62 Ibid., p. 49.

With the ghost of the Cart fiasco still colouring local attitudes to municipal endeavour, the question of Paisley's local tramway service dominated local politics between 1900 and 1901. In January 1900, the town councils of Paisley, Johnstone and Renfrew rejected a privately sponsored tramways bill, introduced by the Irish entrepreneur William Martin Murphy. A month later, following protests in favour of Murphy's scheme, Paisley Council acquiesced, on condition that they would be free to negotiate more favourable terms for the locality. Johnstone and Renfrew, however, remained firmly opposed. In March, therefore, on the casting vote of Provost MacKenzie, Paisley Council agreed to petition for powers to run the tramways themselves. A week later, however, the examiner approved Murphy's Glasgow District Tramways Bill, on the grounds that Paisley had initially approved the scheme, and Paisley thereafter was forced to negotiate terms with Murphy. In April, when no mutual agreement emerged over the time period determining Murphy's control of the service, however, the Town Council decided to petition against the bill. Again, following public protests, the Council gave in at the end of the month and agreed to approve Murphy's scheme on condition that he allow Glasgow Corporation to run trams to Paisley Cross.

Having passed both readings in the House of Commons, however, the Tramways Bill was rejected at the committee stage in July, as committee members proved unconvinced of the degree of local support for the scheme and suspicious of new terms which had appeared 'on the table' but were not incorporated in the bill itself. A re-committal proved unsuccessful and Murphy declared his intention to reintroduce the bill should he secure sufficient local support. The following month, Murphy outlined his new bill to a supportive meeting of local rate-payers. Unable to reach a resolution, the Town Council put the question of the tramways to a referendum.

Here it is important to interrupt the narrative to stress the wording of the alternatives presented in the referendum. The question was put to the ratepayers in the following form:

1. Are you in favour of the Corporation promoting a Tramways Bill?
2. Are you in favour of a private company promoting a Tramways Bill?[63]

Paisley ratepayers were thus faced with an ideological as opposed to a pragmatic practical choice between given alternatives. The question was not whether they supported Murphy's scheme as it stood that October, but whether they favoured, in principle, a municipal alternative.

[63] *PDE*, 30 Oct. 1900.

The referendum, which attracted only 40% of the local electorate, recorded a majority of 3,616 votes to 2,022 in favour of a private scheme.[64]

In January 1901, Murphy submitted a Draft Provisional Order of his proposed, newly titled, Paisley District Tramways Bill. At the end of the month, however, the Town Council rejected the order by sixteen votes to six, and in February the examiner declared that due to the withholding of local support for Murphy's measure, the order had failed to comply with standing orders.[65] The following month, Paisley Town Council negotiated a deal with Glasgow Corporation for the administration of a tramways service to the eastern boundary of the burgh, yet, only a matter of days later, it was announced that Lord Morley and the Commons Committee, acknowledging Paisley's previous support for Murphy and the County Council's sympathy with his proposal, had dispensed with the standing orders and allowed Murphy's order to pass.[66]

In May, an inquiry, led by the earl of Camperdown, the earl of Glasgow, Sir John Kinloch MP and Charles Guy Pym MP, into both Murphy's and the council's proposals was held in Glasgow. On 9 May, they concluded in favour of Murphy's scheme on condition that Paisley Corporation would be free to take over the service at the end of twenty-five years, and in August the bill was given royal assent.[67]

The 'Tramways Question' threw into relief new power groupings in Paisley, determined by their relation to the movement in favour of government intervention in society and the economy – both local and national. In this manner, the controversy at once distilled broader national questions regarding the role of government and drew from local experience the power of the state in controlling local conditions and self-determination.

The spontaneous support for Murphy's scheme in 1900, most especially from the residents of outlying areas, reflected less a commitment to free enterprise than their determination for an improved service. The unprofitability of the Paisley Tramways Company was a constant feature of concern throughout the late nineteenth century. Indeed, in the half-yearly reports ending December 1900 and June 1901, total receipts failed to meet expenditure.[68] Yet, following a protest meeting of ratepayers organised in April 1900 by ex-Provost Clark and Charles J. Gregg – two leading local Unionists – support for Murphy's bill grew to acquire an explicitly political dimension. At a meeting held on the 27th of that month, organised by the new self-styled 'Ratepayers'

64 Ibid., 5 Nov. 1900.

65 Ibid., 29 Jan. 1901.

66 Ibid., 15 Mar. 1901.

67 Ibid., 9 May 1901; Paisley Tramways Order Confirmation Act, 1911 [ch. cxxviii; 18 Aug. 1911].

68 Ibid., 26 Mar. 1901.

Committee', J. T. Hellyer, a local inland revenue officer, declared that the Town Council was 'divided into two sections – one clamouring for municipalisation pure and simple, the other for a town's bill, not to use themselves, but that they might put it up for auction to the highest bidder'.[69] The question was now no longer simply that of improved services but had rather become a test case for local municipal policy.

Opposing the Ratepayers' Committee, the Paisley Workers Elections Committee [PWEC], which had grown out of the PWMEC, proved disunited, its weak opposition highlighting broader national themes of a Labour party in its initial stages of organisation. In April 1900, the PWMEC sent the following resolution to Paisley's Town Clerk:

> That this meeting (representing trade and Co-operative societies with an aggregate membership of 9,000) is of opinion that no scheme which does not provide for the municipal ownership and control of the tramways will be satisfactory to the working classes of Paisley.[70]

Following this declaration, however, the Underwood Co-operative Coal Society withdrew their support for the PWMEC, declaring that 'that body had failed in the objects for which it was formed, and had attended to other matters for which it had no mandate from the Society'.[71] A week later, the Equitable Co-operative Society followed suit. [72] In this manner, the local Labour movement stood bereft of Co-operative support in mid-1900, the Provident Society having already refused to participate in the PWMEC in January.

During a critical period in the politicisation of the local party, the Paisley Workers' Parliamentary Elections Committee [PWPEC] and the PWMEC were amalgamated in September 1900. Yet the earlier secession of the Co-operative Societies from the PWMEC over the 'Tramways Question' prepared the ground for future opposition from its ranks in the new body regarding the efficacy of political involvement. In this way, the 'Tramways Question' had long-lasting implications for local Labour Party organisation and strength.

Whilst fears engendered by the Cart experience and suspicions regarding Glasgow's encroachment into Paisley burgh conditioned many responses to the question of municipalisation, it is clear that the debate threw into relief the 'choices' which would dominate a new era of British politics in which the role of government was central. Local issues were acquiring a national dimension.

More so than any other, the 'Housing Question' drew on the energies aroused by the debate over the tramways, and widened the discussion on

69 Ibid., 28 Apr. 1900.
70 Ibid., 16 Apr. 1900.
71 Ibid., 21 Apr. 1900.
72 Ibid., 27 Apr. 1900.

municipalisation to include the question of municipal provision of working-class rented accommodation and central government finance. In comparison to other towns in Scotland of comparable size, Paisley's housing provision was poor and levels of overcrowding in some instances exceeded those of Glasgow (see Appendix 6.) From evidence presented by William Kelso, Paisley's sanitary inspector, the Royal Commission of 1918 concluded that much of 'the overcrowding in Paisley ... has come largely from the action of the local Authority in condemning and closing old houses. The new houses [are] ... too expensive for the class of people dispossessed, who belong to the poorest class of the population.'[73] Indeed many who had not suffered eviction, Kelso maintained, resided in one-room houses as larger properties proved too expensive to rent. A survey of the occupations of the householders of overcrowded residential properties in 1913 highlights this fact – the majority of the male householders being listed as 'labourers'.[74] Twenty-two years earlier, Kelso's conclusion had been much the same, when he wrote in the annual report for 1896 that 'It is perhaps one of the most difficult social and sanitary problems of the day to provide adequate house accommodation for the labouring class at a rent within the reach of their income.'[75]

Whilst housing had always been a key concern of Paisley activists, the publication of the local Housing Sub-Committee's report of December 1900 served to establish its presence as a critical component of progressive politics. Chaired by the Labour Councillor, Harry Baird, the committee echoed many of Kelso's complaints and recommended that,

First:- The Housing of the Working Classes Act (1890) be adopted.

Second:- That a Standing Committee be appointed to be known as 'THE HOUSING COMMITTEE'; this Committee to carry out such schemes as the Council may from time to time approve.

Third:- In order to make an immediate and serious start, this Committee should take necessary steps to provide and equip satisfactory lodging house accommodation that will suffice for present as well as probable requirements for the immediate future.

Fourth:- That a scheme should be instituted to erect in different parts of the town houses to suit those who have already been displaced by alterations and improvements, above detailed, as well as, prospectively, houses for those who will be displaced by contemplated street improvements. The Committee do not think it right to demolish until the compulsory vacancies have been

73 *PP*, 1917–18, Cd 8731, XIV: *Report of the Royal Commission on the Housing of the Industrial Population of Scotland, Rural and Urban*.

74 W. W. Kelso, *Sanitation in Paisley: A Record of Progress, 1488–1920* (Paisley, 1922), p. 334.

75 Ibid., p. 181.

filled up by new and appropriate dwellings and lodging-house accommodation.[76]

The final sentence of the report, as given above, assumes a social responsibility of local government in addition to that of its facilitating role as town planner, and posits a duty on the council, held previously to be that of private enterprise. As such it represents a significant move in the direction of interventionism. Yet, whilst in February 1901 the committee's recommendations were adopted at a special council meeting, little was done to implement them.

Following repeated Trades Council vacillation on the housing question throughout 1900 and 1901, in March 1902 the Trades Council hosted a public meeting at which the Paisley Tenants' Protection Association [PTPA] was established. Over the next ten years the PTPA grew in numerical strength and local influence, gaining, in John Stewart, its first Town Councillor in 1902, assisting in the formation of the Glasgow Tenants' Protection Association in 1904 and reaching a peak in membership of 664 in 1909.[77] The association, under the direction of Alex Fyfe, elected first president of the Scottish Tenants' Association in 1912, took a leading role nationally, campaigning against the missive system and rent increases and, by pamphleting numerous local authorities and interested parties, did much to raise the profile of Sir Alexander Cross's house letting legislation.[78]

In the local context, the PTPA proved a key organ for *community*-based protest, most especially in 1912 when trade unions, the Co-operative societies and various political groups campaigned against increased rents, payments in advance and the collection of rates by factors. Yet, whilst initially appearing as a Labour body, highlighting the ignorance of Sir William Dunn MP in 1902 ('having been so long from Paisley I am not acquainted with the customs existing between landlords and tenants there'[79]), the PTPA became a broad-church affair, with identifiable local Unionists and Liberals appearing on its platforms and on its list of office-bearers by the mid-1900s. As such it became a forum for progressive social inquiry, attracting the support of Paisley's new MP, John McCallum, in 1907. The association stressed practical solutions to material problems which affected the entire working-class community. Its emphasis on interventionist government action was styled as a *defence* of working-class interests rather than as a programme for wider social change. Yet, the oppositional stance it adopted against the interests of private enterprise and its appeals for government-sponsored reform highlight a growing acceptance in the community at large, of centralised

76 *PRG*, 13 Oct. 1900.
77 *PDE*, 15 Jan. 1909.
78 Sir Alexander Cross, Liberal Unionist MP, Glasgow (Camlachie), 1892–1910 (Jan.).
79 *PDE*, 10 Apr. 1902.

statist solutions to social problems. In its seventh annual report, the association's opinion in this regard was explicit : 'permissive legislation would only lead to endless confusion and strife ... it must be made statutory'.[80]

The PTPA, whilst non-aligned politically, nevertheless contributed to the rich associational life of the emergent left in local Paisley politics. As such, it may be considered as a component of an associational 'network' in Paisley along parallel lines to those identified by Joan Smith and Alan McKinlay in Glasgow which have been considered crucial to the early development of socialism in that city.[81] Yet, whilst hindsight may facilitate such conclusions, it is clear that the PTPA owed more to antilandlordism than the drive of sectional socialism and, as an organisation of varied members, blurred distinctions between socialism and the progressivism of the established parties. Labour's support from such groups in these years was conditional rather than absolute and as such their positive legacy for the movement must be qualified.

In 1911 conflict arose over increased rents implemented by the Paisley and District House Factors Association and protest was co-ordinated by the Trades and Labour Council [TLC], the PTPA and the Co-operative societies. A suggestion to invite ILP co-operation was rejected.[82] When, in 1912, the ILP was invited to send platform delegates to an indignation meeting over continued housing problems, invitations were also circulated to trade-union branches, the British Socialist Party, the UIL and the Orange lodges.[83] In this manner, community 'networking' with regard to social reform did not necessarily channel activism exclusively in the interests of the Labour party. It is still to be proven, given Scottish Liberalism's continued success at the polls on an increasingly socially orientated manifesto in these years, that 'instead of the development of "progressivism", Labour and Socialist policies became an increasingly independent and established strand among working-class thought' in Scotland.[84]

Municipalisation as a bridge between the pragmatism of local reform and the idealism of a national socialism, did not prove a straightforward route to power for Labour in Paisley. Rather, the tramways controversy and the emergence of the housing agenda highlighted the multitude of competing progressive voices which were proposing an interventionist style of government in the light of new social imperatives in these years, and illustrated the disunity of a Labour movement whose reliance on its Liberal inheritance, whilst acting as its major source of power and focus

80 Ibid., 15 Jan. 1909.

81 Smith, 'Taking the leadership of the Labour movement; McKinlay, 'Labour and locality', pp. 48–59.

82 PCL, Archival Collections, ARC 316–31, TLC Minutes, 7 Feb. 1911.

83 Ibid., 7 Mar. 1912.

84 Joan Smith makes this case for Glasgow: Smith, 'Taking the leadership of the Labour movement', p. 65.

of identity, simultaneously inhibited the creation of a distinctively *new* political alternative.

Organising Labour

Labour's performance in local government elections throughout the Edwardian period in Paisley was spasmodic, with periods of concerted effort interspersed with periods of inactivity. In 1900, the PWEC put up only one candidate for municipal office, the tailor John Hamilton, who lost his fight in the second ward, having secured only 200 votes. No Labour candidates were nominated for the School Board elections that year and in 1901 ex-Bailie William Brown re-entered local politics, only to be defeated, his new occupation as a publican having lost him much of the 'respectable' working-class vote. No Labour candidates contested the elections of either 1902 or 1903, and, whilst William Greig secured the seventh ward for Labour in 1904, enthusiasm for his candidature came mainly from the Amalgamated Society of Carpenters and Joiners of which he was the local secretary. William Brown, standing in the third ward, was again defeated. In 1905, the Trades Council, having left the search for possible candidates until early October, was unsuccessful in securing any candidates, and whilst in 1906 Labour entered the race for municipal honours early, both its official candidates – Brown in the third Ward and Archibald McPhee, a 'traveller', in the fifth – were defeated. That April, however, Labour secured two seats on the School Board and the following October secured a further two seats on the Town Council with Brown in the first Ward and Harry Baird in the second. Yet at this election William Gallacher and Archibald McPhee, nominated initially by the local SDF but standing under Trades Council auspices, were soundly defeated. The year 1908 brought the death of ex-Bailie Brown and no new Labour contests for Town Council representation, and whilst Archibald McPhee stood independently in 1909, he lost in the fifth Ward, securing only 305 votes. In the School Board elections of that year only ex-Bailie Kent proved successful for Labour.

Beyond this, in the period from 1910 to 1914, an era associated with aroused working-class protest, Labour's fortunes changed little. Harry Baird was re-elected to the Town Council, as was Robert Russell, where they were joined by Alex Hair in 1913; John Kent was re-elected to the School Board in 1911, and John Henderson secured a voice for Labour on the Parish Council in 1910. In terms of effective local political influence, clearly little had changed since the 1890s.

Poor organisation and disunity among Labour's component groups can only partly explain this apparent lack of progress. The politics of personality were clearly still powerful in these years and the fear of increased rates which attended all proposals for municipal reform should not be ignored. It is apparent that the local Liberal hegemony remained on the ascendant. Service and efficiency remained the by-words of local campaigning rather than the rhetoric of a new 'Commonweal'. Statist solutions may have been emerging but were not yet the determinants of municipal electoral behaviour.

The problems faced by the national Scottish Labour movement, first as the Scottish Workers' Parliamentary Elections Committee [SWPEC] and thereafter as the Scottish Workers' Representation Committee [SWRC], had both their parallel and root cause in the disunity and organisational confusion at the constituency level. Whilst it has been convention to stress the weakness of the Scottish Labour movement in these years in comparison with its English neighbour, little has been done to trace this weakness to its source. The financial problems of the SWRC were, at root, problems of support and, as such, problems of organisation on the ground.

The PWPEC, established in February 1900, having taken over the municipal electoral responsibilities of the PWMEC in September, restyled itself the Paisley Workers' Elections Committee [PWEC], with responsibilities for both local and national political involvement.[85] Soon after, however, the Equitable and Provident Co-operative Societies seceded from the new body, declaring their reluctance towards active involvement in the interests of political representation.[86] Whilst the Paisley Co-operative Societies remained regular contributors to national SWPEC and SWRC funds, their rejection of local involvement in a body initially dominated by Co-operative representatives – the first president of the PWPEC was a representative of the Provident Co-operative Society and the first chairman of the PWEC was Arthur Baird of the Equitable Co-operative Society – proved a devastating blow to the PWEC.[87] The minutes of the PWEC in 1901 are dominated by criticisms of poor attendance at meetings and in 1902, the Trades Council, worried by the Committee's inaction, felt compelled to request a policy statement in anticipation of the next general election.[88]

Hereafter, the minute book of the committee falls silent, becoming a record of Trades Council meetings rather than those of the PWEC – a fitting memorial to a committee that had little to show for its activities at this point, beyond a £6 financial deficit.[89] In January 1903, the Trades Council, having received no answer to their request of the previous year,

85 PCL, Archival Collections, ARC 292 Ren–1, Paisley Parliamentary Elections Committee Minutes, 1 Sep. 1900.

86 Ibid., 13 Oct. 1900; 13 Dec. 1900.

87 Annual SWRC Conference Reports indicate annual contributions ranging from £1 to £6 6s. forthcoming from the 3 Paisley Co-operative Societies, the Provident Society proving the highest and most regular contributor, and the Equitable contributions ceasing after 1900: NLS, PDL 30/4 (1–16), SWPEC Annual Conference Reports: 1901–1906.

88 PCL, Archival Collections, ARC 292 Ren–1, Paisley Parliamentary Elections Committee Minutes, 30 Aug. 1901, 8 Jul. 1902.

89 Ibid., 16 Sep. 1902.

rejected a proposal to canvass delegates regarding support for Labour parliamentary representation in the burgh, in favour of a further plea to the PWEC, but yet again no response was forthcoming. In March, the Trades Council appealed to the SWRC for support, and in May began plans for a general meeting of trades unions and the ILP to gauge the degree of local parliamentary interest. Going it alone, the Trades Council affiliated to the SWRC in July 1904 and two months later took over the duties of the PWEC, which disbanded in August.

Whilst Robert Smillie announced to the fifth annual conference of the SWRC in January 1905 that the Paisley ILP had invited him to stand for the burgh in the Labour interest, it was not until April 1905 that the Trades Council organised a meeting of local trade unions and the ILP to discuss the promotion of a Labour candidature at the next general election.[90] Only one trade union recorded its disapproval of parliamentary intervention, yet when asked about financial support, the majority of delegates present refused to pledge their associations to any contributory scheme.[91] At this point two representatives from the Lanarkshire Miners' Union announced that, in line with the political programme of the Miners' Federation of Great Britain, their union was willing to finance the candidature of a Labour challenger for parliamentary office in Paisley. Thereupon a committee was appointed to approach trade unions in the burgh whose national lists of candidates had not yet been allocated constituencies, and to draw up a list of possible candidates whose names would come before a second meeting of trade unionists and ILP delegates. A month later, Robert Smillie defeated John Laidler and William T. Newlove, both of the Operative Bricklayers Society, to become Paisley's first Labour parliamentary candidate.[92]

Although Smillie lost the general election of January 1906, a local Labour Representation Committee which had been set up during the election, and had proved an effective organ of propaganda, was made a standing committee in February, responsible, like the PWEC before it, for all political organisation in the burgh.[93] Yet, one week later, in response to a circular to all trade unions to reappoint their delegates, only one reply (from the Scottish Carters' Association) was received. Between 1906 and 1910, the local Representation Committee, whilst meeting on a regular basis, failed to mobilise enthusiasm for either local or national electoral affairs – a situation most graphically illustrated by Labour's poor performance at local elections in this period. In 1907, the committee's chairman, John Hamilton,

90 *PDE*, 30 Jan. 1905.
91 *PRG*, 29 Apr. 1905.
92 Ibid., 3 Jun. 1905.
93 Ibid., 10 Feb. 1906.

> deplored the want of interest amongst the workers, and suggested that an effort should be made to reach the indifferent and try to make them understand that unless they took some interest in their economic conditions, their fate would be from bad to worse.[94]

Following the Osborne Judgement, however, the question of parliamentary representation gained a higher profile. At a 'huge' demonstration in October 1910, organised by the local Representation Committee, a resolution was approved, declaring 'political action' to be 'a recognised function of the Trades Union Movement', and in a rousing speech, Keir Hardie drew on Paisley's radical past to assert the 'rights' of Labour:

> Paisley had won for itself a splendid record in the days when the working class was fighting for its own enfranchisement, and the sons of the men who fought for the vote were now going to fight for the right to use it in the way they thought best. (Cheers.)[95]

National events, by impinging on local traditions, re-formed the question of Labour representation as a reworking of a recognised dialectic of 'rights' and 'exploitation'. Hereafter doubts regarding trade unionism's political role seldom emerged.

Three months later, negotiations began to amalgamate the Trades Council and the local Labour Representation Committee and in August 1911 the Paisley Trades and Labour Council [TLC] was established and soon became affiliated to the national Labour Party.

The organisational problems faced by the Paisley Labour movement throughout the Edwardian period in many respects mirror those of the national Scottish movement – financial difficulties, changing and competing membership frameworks, and the political vacillation of the Co-operative societies.

The National Executive of the Labour Party had been calling for a more centralised British party since 1903, with a common fund, constitution and list of candidates.[96] Yet despite an agreement in 1906 detailing the parameters of SWRC and Labour Party influence and allowing for the affiliation of the SWRC to the Labour Party, the eighth Annual Conference of the Labour Party at Hull confirmed the Labour Party's desire for the interests of Scotland and England to be 'looked after from the same headquarters'.[97] That May, the Labour Party began affiliating

94 *Forward*, 29 Jun. 1907.

95 *PDE*, 4 Oct. 1910.

96 Andersonian Library, British Labour Party, National Executive Committee Minutes, 17 Dec. 1903.

97 NLS, PDL 23, *Report of the Seventh Annual Conference of the Labour Representation Committee (1907)*; *Report of the Eighth Annual Conference of the Labour Representation Committee (1908)*.

Scottish societies and the dissolution of the SWRC followed some months later.[98]

Even after the consolidation of the Labour Party in Scotland, however, organisation still proved problematic. In a report on the Scottish Conference in Edinburgh of 1911 it was noted that:

> The Political organisation of Scotland is not quite so good as it might be ... The steady and persistent work of local Labour Parties is not so marked in Scotland as in England. For this to some extent there is an inclination to blame the Central Executive, but we do not think our Scottish friends quite appreciate how much this form of excellence depends upon local workers.[99]

The amalgamation of industrial and political concerns in the body of the Trades and Labour Council in Paisley in 1911 went some way to improving Labour Party organisation in the burgh. Indeed in February 1912, Robert Russell of the ASE and president of the TLC announced an 'elaborate organising scheme by which the electors of the town would be kept in closer touch with the Council and be kept fully posted up on questions of local and national politics by means of a monthly distribution of literature.' He explained:

> The services of the younger men in the Trade Union Movement are to be requisitioned for this purpose. The Trade Union Committee are to visit the branches in town periodically with the same end in view, and the Press Committee are to back up these efforts by contributions to the press.[100]

It is unknown to what extent this scheme was put into action; however, it is clear that as a body the TLC on the eve of war, whilst unsuccessful in local electioneering, evolved as a sound basis for future organisation, representing around forty trade unions and 4,000 organised workers in 1912.[101]

The Labour party, however, still remained only one vehicle of a Labour political consciousness in these years and in this sense, judged alone, reflects neither the strength nor the complexity of working-class organisation on the eve of war. The Co-operative movement, the SDF (and later the Social Democratic Party and British Socialist Party) and the ILP highlight a Labour movement within which a 'Labour identity' was still in the process of formation.

98 NLS, NE 506a.14, *Report of the Ninth Annual Conference of the Labour Representation Committee (1909).*

99 NLS, British Labour Party, National Executive Committee Minutes, 15 Aug. 1911.

100 *PDE*, 16 Feb. 1912.

101 TLC, 13 Nov. 1912.

Co-operative Politics

Representing the dual interests of employer and employee, the Co-operative movement in Paisley occupied a frequently contradictory position in the town's Labour history during the Edwardian period. In practical terms this manifested itself in frequent disputes with local unions whose interference in the internal labour relations of the societies was condemned, and with the wider Labour movement after 1911 when the local Co-operative societies sought the status of Approved Societies under the National Insurance Act.[102] However, of more lasting significance was the stance adopted by the Co-operative movement towards political involvement in these pre-war years.

In national terms, it has been convention to stress the stronger commitment of the Scottish Co-operative movement to independent political action in comparison with its southern neighbour.[103] An unqualified acceptance of such a generality, however, ignores the debates over political action which animated the Scottish Co-operative movement throughout the Edwardian period – debates critical to the character of the Scottish Labour movement as a whole and central to the processes through which a separate Labour identity was refined.

In October 1903, the Paisley Eastern Unionist Association applauded the Provident Co-operative Society's decision to adopt a neutral political stance.[104] Whilst continuing to contribute financially to local Labour electoral expenses, endorsing certain TLC municipal candidates and indeed contributing regularly to national Labour party funds, the Provident Society, alongside the Equitable, Underwood and Manufacturing Societies, adopted a lower profile in local Labour politics after 1900. The formation of the SWRC and LRC as independent national parties at once clarified political boundaries and necessitated a sectional declaration on policy which threw local and national Co-operative bodies into confusion and highlighted the self-evident fact that Co-operative membership was independent of political affiliation.

Whilst the 1897 Co-operative Congress in Perth had voted overwhelmingly for William Maxwell's resolution in favour of Co-operative MPs in parliament, the response to the central board's circular calling for subscriptions was disappointing. Less than £80 was raised from twenty-eight societies and whilst twenty-four more pledged support, forty-seven large societies declared against the scheme and refused to

102 TLC, 27 Mar. 1912: In 1912, the Trades and Labour Council condemned Co-operative attempts to become Approved Societies.

103 Cole emphasised: 'The feeling in favour of independent political action was on the whole strongest in Scotland and in the South of England, or rather London': G. D. H. Cole, *A Century of Co-operation* (Manchester, 1944), p. 312. Note also Henry Murphy (SCWS president) at the First Annual Conference of the SWPEC: 'Co-operators across the border are not as frightened as their English brethren of a new departure': LSE, ILP Archive, ILP 1/4, NAC Minutes, 30 Jan. 1901.

104 *PRG*, 3 Oct. 1903.

put the matter before their members, and thirty additional societies declared their opposition.[105] In 1900 the annual conference voted 905 to 409 against direct parliamentary representation.[106] Hereafter the key question would be affiliation to the new Labour party.

In January 1904 the Renfrewshire Co-operative Conference Association debated the question of tariff reform, and, by an overwhelming majority, re-affirmed their commitment to free trade. Throughout the debate, the Paisley delegates were to the fore: Robert Tweedale of the Equitable Society seconding the motion in favour of free trade, W. B. Flockhart and Mr Kerr of the Provident Society moving and seconding the amendment in favour of fiscal reform, and C. J. Gregg, the prominent local Unionist, moving a resolution for political neutrality, seconded by a further Paisley Co-operator, Thomas Rigg.[107] Most notably, however, John Maclean, representing Pollokshaws, moved:

> that the only way of escape from the wage slavery to which the working class has at present to submit is by the formation of a Labour Party, whose object shall be the socialisation of the means of production and distribution and whose immediate programme shall contain the nationalisation of railways, mines and lands.[108]

This amendment received only sixteen votes.

The debate highlights the variety of views encompassed within the Paisley Co-operative movement in these years and clearly illustrates the need to qualify assumptions regarding Scottish Co-operative militancy.

In June 1905, the Co-operative Congress was held in Paisley. One month before, a committee, dominated by W. B. Flockhart and C. J. Gregg, was established to organise local Co-operators opposed to the introduction of politics into the movement.[109] The Paisley Congress was dominated by the question of affiliation to the Labour party, and the new committee organised a meeting on the eve of the affiliation debate to muster support against political involvement. Whilst Congress voted by 654 votes to 271 in favour of taking 'a larger share in the legislation and administrative government of the country', the motion that such a goal would 'be best accomplished by co-operators allying themselves with the Labour Representation Committee' was defeated by almost 700 votes.[110]

In 1906, the response of the local societies towards the call for greater political awareness was again muted, and at the congress of that year the

105 T. F. Carberry, 'An Examination and Evaluation of the Co-operative Party of the Co-operative Union Ltd' (London University, Ph.D. thesis, 1966), p. 8.

106 Ibid., p. 9.

107 *PDE*, 25 Jan. 1904. Returning to the Provident Society a few days later, C. J. Gregg moved a motion disapproving of political questions entering the affairs of the society. The motion was defeated. *PDE*, 29 Jan. 1904.

108 Ibid., 25 Jan. 1904.

109 Ibid., 19 May 1905.

110 Carberry, 'Examination and Evaluation of the Co-operative Party', p. 13.

resolution adopted in Paisley was overturned. Thereafter no national directives were passed regarding political involvement until 1912, when it was agreed that the Co-operative movement should participate in a joint consultative committee with the TUC and the Labour Party. In 1913, however, the Aberdeen Congress carried a motion opposed to association with the Labour party.

Whilst the Paisley experience highlights that even after 1906 co-operation continued between co-operative societies and the Labour Party, their commitment was qualified and restricted mainly to local municipal politics and even then was a pale reflection of the joint action characteristic of the late nineteenth century. There is little in the experience of Paisley to confirm Pollard's thesis that after 1905 the Co-operative movement 'came to assume without question that ... not only the trade unions but also the Labour party were "natural allies"'.[111] Whilst not denying the continued support of many Co-operators for the Labour Party, their failure to take the majority of the movement with them must stand as the ultimate test of Co-operative sympathies. In this regard, the Scottish experience, as evidenced in Paisley, was little different to that of many English constituencies. Again, pragmatic communitarian concerns, rather than an unqualified commitment to the Labour party, facilitated the growth of a social consciousness which, whilst progressive, was not necessarily committed to either class politics or a socialist(ic) interpretation of society's ills.

Loose Threads: Paisley Socialism

In Lennox Kerr's *Woman of Glenshiels*, Donald Maxwell, Mary's first suitor, is a socialist. Discussing Donald with her fellow workers, Mary is told that

> Working men could not afford to be Socialists. Socialists threatened the very structure of life. It was a disease worse than cancer or consumption. Donald must be cured ...
> 'We ken maist men have their weaknesses, but they have to settle doon some time ... It disna matter whether its drink or socialism.'
> Socialism, then, was the devil entering a working man. Witchcraft had gone and Socialism had come.[112]

In the Edwardian period, socialists, as much as the aristocratic Tory, were critical figures of the Liberal demonology against which Liberal virtues were defined and through which political perversions were isolated and caricatured. In this regard the Paisley socialists whom Willie Gallacher joined around 1905 illustrate an unintegrated strand in the

[111] S. Pollard, 'The foundation of the Co-operative Party', in A. Briggs and J. Saville (eds.), *Essays in Labour History, 1886–1923* (London, 1971), p. 191.

[112] Kerr, *Woman of Glenshiels*, pp. 110–11.

radical thread of Paisley politics, unaccommodated in the radical rhetoric of liberal constitutionalism. Having joined the ILP in 1905, Gallacher came to the conclusion that 'while there was a strong sentimental desire for something better animating the leaders of the ILP, there was a complete lack of Marxist theory to guide and direct their practical work'.[113]

Gallacher left the ILP after a few months, and joined the Paisley branch of the SDF, a body which, at that time, boasted less than ten members and met irregularly after hours in a shoe-repairer's shop.[114] Hereafter, the SDF's fortunes improved. Premises were secured for meetings and open air lectures were held in the Jail Square. In February 1907 *Forward* announced that the SDF branch was being revived and within a couple of months the branch had affiliated to the local Labour Representation Committee.[115] However, that November, despite the committee's support for the SDF candidates at the recent Town Council elections, the SDF disaffiliated from the Labour ranks and in December withdrew from the Renfrewshire Socialist Federation.[116] Whilst no reason is given for such dissension, it is clear that many SDF members were growing tired of Labour compromises. In August an SDF speaker at the Jail Square had 'caused a bit of a sensation' by encouraging socialists to fight 'the namby-pamby Labour Humbugs' as well as the 'orthodox' political parties.[117]

In September 1907 John Maclean began a series of economics classes in Camphill School in Paisley and despite Gallacher's temporary removal to America in 1909, the Social Democratic Party, or SDP (the SDF had changed its name at the end of 1907), managed to establish itself as a voice in the community. Matching its lecture campaign, which featured 'names' such as Victor Grayson and Tom Mann, with a cultural programme which included cricket matches in the summer on the Gleniffer Braes, the SDP developed a social as well as a political profile in the burgh. In March 1911, however, *Forward* complained that 'The Socialists in Paisley have been for too long disunited. They have spent much valuable time and effort squabbling about abstract theories instead of combining to effect practical improvements in the burgh.'[118]

That July, despite objections from the local ASE branches that the SDP 'had no sympathy whatever with Trade Unionism', the SDP joined

113 W. Gallacher, *Last Memoirs* (London, 1966), p. 36.

114 Ibid., pp. 36–7. Note: no references have been found to a local branch of the SDF before 1907 either in the local press or in Trades Council or trades union minutes although James J. Smyth refers to the existence of Paisley branches of both the SDF and the Socialist League in the 1880s: Smyth, 'Labour and Socialism in Glasgow', p. 31.

115 *Forward*, 16 Feb. 1907, 4 May 1907.

116 Ibid., 30 Nov. 1907. (Whilst Gallacher's memoirs record that he stood for Council office in 1909, securing 187 votes, rather, he stood for the seventh Ward in 1907 and gained 177 votes.)

117 Ibid., 3 Aug. 1907.

118 Ibid., 18 Mar. 1911.

the newly formed Paisley TLC.[119] Within months, however, the socialists withdrew, their removal in this instance being occasioned by the council's affiliation to the Labour party.[120]

More dissension was to follow. Later that year, the local SDP, following the lead of John Maclean and Victor Grayson, emerged as the British Socialist Party [BSP], and in 1912 Gallacher stood again for the seventh ward under their auspices. Following negotiation with Gallacher, the TLC proposed to recommend his election to the working-class electorate of Paisley, yet within a week their proposal was rebuffed by the BSP.[121] In a communication to the TLC the local BSP stated that:

> as Mr Russell [the TLC president] was an avowed meliorist and the Trades and Labour Council, an organisation without a definite policy, they could not submit their candidate for approval of the Council. The fight, it continued, so far as the BSP is concerned is Socialism against all comers.[122]

The TLC voted to let the matter drop, but in the elections that October Robert Russell stood against Gallacher in the seventh Ward, securing the seat for Labour and pushing Gallacher into third place with only ninety-nine votes. A BSP offer to co-operate with the TLC in a demonstration against militarism the following month was rejected, the council suggesting that, in the light of recent events, they would prefer to 'go it alone'.[123] Only the immediate threat of war drew Gallacher and the BSP back into the Paisley TLC in July 1914. [124]

For most of the Edwardian era, therefore, the SDP/BSP in Paisley adopted a stance of non-co-operation with, or hostility to, the Labour organisations of the burgh – one more source of disunity in a fragmented labour body politic. They asserted an independence which relegated them to the fringes of the emergent Labour movement and asserted an oppositional heritage and outlook which determined their 'separate' post-war vision. As such, their history is one at once running parallel to, and divergent from, that of the Labour Party – a loose strand in the radical thread which, in the pre-war period, illustrated the ideological dependency of Labour on its Liberal roots.

The ILP: Cultural Expressions of a Labour Identity

> When the new ILPer accepted the 'Right Hand of Fellowship' she, or much more commonly, he, accepted entry to a social fraternity as much as [a] political party. Quite apart from the choirs, rambling

119 TLC, 13 Jul. 1911; 2 Aug. 1911.
120 Ibid., 8 Nov. 1911.
121 Ibid., 11 Sep. 1912.
122 Ibid., 18 Sep. 1912.
123 Ibid., 20 Nov. 1912.
124 Ibid., 15 Jul. 1914.

> clubs, and debating societies, ordinary branch life was dominated by an individual and collective search for personal improvement firmly rooted in artisanal culture.[125]

From an early stage, the Paisley ILP established itself as a new source of working-class cultural identity. Through its orchestra and choir, its literary and speaking classes, sales of work, Sunday literature stall and weekly Hippodrome lectures, it established an associational framework separate from, and in opposition to, those engineered by factory paternalism or embedded in an ideology of deference.[126]

It is clear, however, that such associational vibrancy failed to be translated into increased party or electoral strength. In Scotland as a whole, Hutchison has shown how the increase in the number of ILP branches, from 98 in 1906 to 130 in 1913, is 'a misleading index of the vitality of the ILP', many branches being based on 'slender support'.[127] In 1908, Scotland had 14.8% of the total branches but only 10.6% of the national membership, and in 1913–14 this amounted to only 2,720 members.[128]

Whilst no figures are available for the Paisley branch, sufficient evidence exists to point to the fact that it fitted the Scottish trend. In 1907, a *Forward* correspondent, following a poorly attended ILP lecture in Paisley, asked, 'where are the boasted 300 members of the ILP of a Sunday night?'[129] Three years later, another Paisley correspondent reflected that despite apparently successful propaganda, a 'comparative small number of members' was being added to the branch as a result.[130]

Membership problems, furthermore, were exacerbated by apathy.[131] In 1900, a National Advisory Council proposal to contest Paisley at the next general election was met with indifference from the local ILP members, and despite Smillie's candidature in 1906, partly initiated by the local ILP, by 1914 Paisley does not appear on the list of constituencies either endorsed or provisionally approved to be contested at the anticipated general election.[132]

Locally, the ILP's relationship with other Labour bodies after 1900, like that of the Co-operative societies, was in stark contrast to their pre-1900 endeavours to work *through* the Trades Council. In 1912, the Paisley TLC complained of the prolonged absence of the ILP delegate,

125 McKinlay, 'Labour and locality', p. 50.

126 In the late nineteenth century, Joyce has clearly highlighted how 'the club movement did something to take the factory out of direct party politics': Joyce, 'Factory politics of Lancashire', p. 545.

127 Hutchison, *Political History of Scotland*, pp. 246–7.

128 Ibid., p. 246.

129 *Forward*, 9 Feb. 1907.

130 Ibid., 26 Mar. 1910.

131 Again, this 'fits' Hutchison's evaluation of the pre-war ILP in Scotland. See Hutchison, *Political History of Scotland*, p. 248.

132 LSE, ILP Archive, ILP 1/4 and 1/7, NAC Minutes, 8 Jan. 1900; 1 Mar. 1900; 28 May 1900; 14 Jul. 1914.

Mr Henderson, from their meetings and, as we have seen, the ILP 'took a back seat' in the housing agitation of the pre-war years.[133] Problems were compounded in 1913 when Henderson, a parish councillor, was repudiated by the TLC for appearing drunk on a Labour platform during the municipal campaign of that year and 'bringing the movement into disrepute'.[134] Whilst the ILP and the TLC still 'shared' many common members – most notably Robert Russell, ILP literature secretary and TLC president from 1911; James Macdonald, chairman of the ILP, vice-president of the TLC in 1912 and School Board member from 1914; George Robertson, plumber and ILP nominee for the Parish Council in 1913, and James Love of the Patternmakers' Society, ILP secretary and former Trades Council president – the ILP *as an organisation* in itself failed to translate apparent local enthusiasm for reform into membership, finance or electoral power.

In 1907, *Forward*'s 'Paisley Notes', composed by J. S. Mason, a future Trades Council president and a member of the Paisley ILP, commented that, whilst the 'brilliant Saturday night Socials of the ILP are still crowded ... the Sunday night lectures are welcomed by an audience dispersed through the hall on the one person per form system.'[135] Clearly cultural vibrancy failed to engender political commitment.

This apparent paradox is one which is only partly explained by the ever present problems of finance and organisation within the ILP. Rather, the current historiography of these years is partly responsible for its creation. Smith's claim that 'In Glasgow the ILP represented evolutionary municipal socialism, never simply a shallow electoralism' results in an argument which, by judging the ILP's performance according to vague criteria of social networking and looking disdainfully on electoral work as a less fitting test of strength, distorts the reality of a party which remained very much a minority interest for the Scottish working class.[136]

Smith and McKinlay, by employing ill-defined terms such as 'ethical socialism', 'evolutionary municipal socialism' and 'popular socialism', posit an exclusivity in the ILP's ideology in these years, explicitly 'different' to that of the established political parties, which succeeded in establishing the ILP as an alternative to the *status quo*. Yet, simultaneously, McKinlay stresses that the ILP in Glasgow exemplified a 'tolerance of diversity which blurred the boundaries between its ethical socialism and, on the one hand, progressive liberalism and, on the other, Marxism'.[137] McKinlay fails to qualify that on occasion such tolerance,

133 TLC, 24 Jan. 1912.

134 Ibid., 15 Oct. 1913; 5 Nov. 1913. (Henderson, having appeared drunk at several Parish Council meetings thereafter was again repudiated by the TLC in 1914 and asked to resign his seat: TLC, 18 Mar. 1914.)

135 *Forward*, 16 Mar. 1907.

136 Smith, 'Taking the leadership of the Labour movement', p. 61.

137 McKinlay, 'Labour and locality', p. 50.

which he views as a 'strength', a 'quality', of the early ILP, did not always operate, either partly or indeed exclusively, in its favour. The efficacy of 'broad-based coalitions' and 'over-lapping self-governing communities' must ultimately be tested against such quantifiable data as membership figures and electoral performance. When this is done, it is clear that the politics of the community did not by necessity always work to the ILP's advantage.[138]

As Smith rightly suggests, 'in this period the ILP was busy defining itself against Liberalism and also against right wing Catholicism', yet she fails to appreciate the extent to which this process was only partly accomplished by 1914.[139] 'Ethical socialism' was itself a product of the Liberal heritage and thus an ideology which, as statist social policy became common currency in the electoral addresses of the established parties, became harder to claim as Labour's own.

Once again, the radical legacy proved a critical determinant of Labour's fortunes, at once awarding it with a recognisable rhetoric and political lineage and restricting its evolution beyond the recapitulation of familiar injustices.[140] The Paisley Labour movement on the eve of the Great War thus remained caught in the contradictions of its past without sufficient ideological resources to compete with a Liberal party which, until 1914, proved sufficiently capable of adjustment to the imperatives of the new century.[141]

1900: Empire and Elections

> Shortly after four o'clock two uniformed bands passed down High Street, followed by thousands, largely mill girls, augmented by the school children. Down Moss Street, round the Sneddon, and into the Square they all marched. There were hurried effigies borne by the crowd with the explanatory word 'Kruger' tacked in front ... There were banners ... rosettes, ribbons, and noise.[142]

The sights and sounds of the Paisley scene described here, following the relief of Ladysmith during the Boer War, were repeated two months later when Mafeking was taken by the Imperial forces. Yet, whilst the war prompted the burgh to displays of patriotism, the 'Khaki' election of that year was marked by local apathy and the failure of the Unionists to

138 Ibid., p. 51.

139 Smith, 'Taking the leadership of the Labour movement', p. 70.

140 In 1910, Tom Johnston's Forward Publishing Company produced a volume of the 'Chartist and Socialist Sermons' of the Rev. Patrick Brewster of Paisley Abbey, claiming that in a new era 'only *Forward* ... [stood] for the same cause as Patrick Brewster': T. Johnston (ed.), *Rev. Patrick Brewster: His Chartist and Socialist Sermons* (Glasgow, 1910).

141 Hutchison, *Political History of Scotland*, p. 238.

142 *PRG*, 3 Mar. 1900.

channel imperial enthusiasm into electoral results.[143] As Hugh Cunningham has made clear: 'What is striking is the extent to which working-class people imposed their *own* interpretations on patriotic institutions and occasions.'[144] In Paisley, the burning of an effigy, a traditional form of radical protest, was employed to assert an interpretation of victory quite at odds with Unionist propaganda, making the Liberal electoral victory in Paisley, secured against such a jingoistic back-drop, more explicable. Paisley Liberals, in contrast to their Unionist opponents, asserted an imperialism more easily accommodated within local political traditions. As in the years of the Napoleonic Wars, patriotism became 'a political prize much fought over ... and while in the circumstances of war ... it became more associated with loyalty to government, it never lost its accompanying rhetoric of liberty.'[145] At the Liberal Association General Meeting in 1900, Robert MacFee, president of the Liberal Club, commented:

> The hoisting of the British flag at Bloemfontain and Pretoria would mean equality to the white races. It meant the abolition of slavery, protection of the native races, an open door to the trade of all countries, freedom to all missionary enterprises, and settled government and law and order; these were surely worth having ... This war had made Liberals Imperialists.[146]

Sir William Dunn, having resigned his position as honorary consul general of the Orange Free State in Britain in October 1899, following the ultimatum to the British government, proved a consistent Liberal Imperialist throughout the war years and an outspoken supporter of Lord Rosebery, whom he considered 'the general best able to lead the Liberal ranks to victory'.[147] In 1900, therefore, Dunn's victory in Paisley against the Unionist, Captain Campbell Swinton of Berwickshire, stood as evidence of Liberal Imperialist potential in an election which saw the Liberals lose their majority of Scottish seats for the first time since the Reform Act of 1832 and the Unionists record a gain of seven seats in Scotland.[148]

Dunn, by exploiting the enthusiasm for empire created by the war, proved adept at translating such patriotism along identifiably Liberal lines, combining the imperial message with an interventionist domestic social programme. Echoing Rosebery's concerns in his rectorial address to Glasgow University in November 1900, Dunn's election campaign was

143 Cunningham suggests that this was a pattern which was repeated throughout the country: H. Cunningham, 'The language of patriotism: from radical opposition to Tory jingoism, 1750–1914', *History Workshop*, xii (1981), p. 25.

144 Ibid., p. 25 [my italics].

145 Ibid., p. 15.

146 *PDE*, 2 Mar. 1900.

147 *PRG*, 9 Jun. 1900.

148 Brown, 'Echoes of Midlothian', pp. 170–1.

dominated by appeals to social reform in the interests of national efficiency. In a speech in October, Dunn reaffirmed his commitment to

> the provision of decent dwellings for the working classes at moderate rents; compensation to all workers for all accidents; old age pensions as soon as a practical scheme can be devised; Poor Law reform; eight hours day for miners; shorter hours in shops; further amendment of the Factory Acts; taxation of land values; local veto and Sunday closing; licensing reform and the reduction of licenses ... development of secondary and technical education.[149]

In comparison, Captain George S. Campbell Swinton, a former officer of the 71st Highland Light Infantry, the Unionist candidate, adopted as recently as September, attempted to steal the Liberal's Imperial 'thunder'. His election address sought to cast doubts on the Liberals' commitment to empire and to army reform, and in later speeches he sought to 'tear' from Dunn 'that Imperialist coat of many colours which seemed to fit him so badly'.[150] In terms of domestic policy, however, Swinton presented a catalogue of Liberal inadequacies and radical failures without offering any detailed Unionist alternative.

Whilst Dunn, a Liberal Imperialist, secured the seat with a healthy majority of 1,058, the election itself signified little change in Paisley's political identity.[151] Though the *Gazette* sought in vain to distinguish between the Liberal Imperialism of Sir William Dunn and the Toryism of Captain Campbell Swinton – 'it is khaki now instead of either red or blue' – Dunn's victory represented less a victory for the Rosebery school than a reaffirmation of a long-standing political loyalty in the face of Tory opposition.[152] Evenly matched in their evident commitment to the empire in a period of national crisis, Dunn's local connections, his continued support from the Irish community (despite his opposition to the institution of a Catholic University in Ireland), and his consistent avowal of the old radical shibboleths, 'Peace, Retrenchment, and Reform', secured the seat in an election, according to the *Gazette*, 'unworthy to be treated seriously'.[153]

Dunn's campaign, however, is significant in highlighting the evident adaptability of pre-1914 Liberalism to the challenges of both left and right. The Liberal Imperialists' message attracted notable support from prominent industrialists and businessmen in the west of Scotland, most notably Sir Charles Tennant, Joseph Maclay, Sir James Bell, Robert Lorimer and Sir Thomas Glen Coats – the very class from which Liberalism had suffered the most significant haemorrhage of support

149 *PDE*, 2 Oct. 1900.
150 Ibid., 2 Oct. 1900.
151 See below, Appendix 4.
152 *PRG*, 22 Sep. 1900, 6 Oct. 1900.
153 *PDE*, 3 Oct. 1900; *PRG*, 6 Oct. 1900.

after 1886.[154] Nationally, Rosebery and the Liberal League may have spawned a leadership crisis in Scotland and eventually become the victims of the growing unpopularity of the war in 1901 and the threat of Chamberlain's tariff reform campaign.[155] However, the evocation of a Liberal imperial mission *during the war itself* prevented an even more pronounced swing against the Liberals in the 1900 election.

The acceptance of the labels of 'Radical' and 'Imperialist' as definitions of two oppositional strands within the Liberal Party in Scotland in the period from 1900 to 1905 confuses the machinations characteristic of all leadership struggles with wider ideological differences which were frequently more apparent than real, and thus overlooks the shared concerns of both groups with social reform. In this context, the growing commitment to social issues within the Scottish Liberal ranks, identified by Hutchison, seems less surprising, emerging as it did from a wide, if ill-defined, consensus, rather than from conflict.[156]

Liberalism in Paisley, 1900–1910

At a meeting of the Western Committee of the Scottish Liberal Association in 1908, the secretary explained that

> a very large number of meetings were being held in various constituencies in the West of Scotland by the Tariff Reformers and by the Socialists, and at most of these meetings a great deal of literature was being distributed and Associations were now asking for assistance from headquarters to meet these attacks.[157]

Until 1910, Liberal policy in Scotland more frequently represented responses to the stimuli of distinctive right and left programmes, than the elaboration of a self-motivated agenda of reform. While from 1903 to 1906 the major oppositional threat came from Chamberlain's tariff reform scheme, thereafter the social agenda which proved integral to the fiscal debate began to assert greater power. Now, however, the arguments were articulated in different terms, as the Labour party began to consolidate its organisation north of the border.

Chamberlain's announcement of his fiscal reform programme in 1903 injected vigour into the Paisley Liberal movement, the organisation of which remained unchanged from its late nineteenth-century format

154 Hutchison, *Political History of Scotland*, p. 228.

155 Brown, 'Echoes of Midlothian', p. 171.

156 'It seems likely', writes Hutchison, 'that most of the rank and file Liberals were not reluctant followers of the new social radical policies enacted by the Liberal movement, implying that the adjustment to twentieth-century politics had been achieved before 1914 without breaking up the party': Hutchison, *Political History of Scotland*, p. 238.

157 EUL, SLA Collection, Minutes, vol. IX: 1908–1925, Western Committee Meeting, 11 Nov. 1908 (pp. 11–12).

throughout the Edwardian period. In February 1904, the Liberal Association's annual report recorded that:

> The past year had in a marked way been one of Liberal revival, and evidence had been given of Liberal principles having a vitality and strength which had surprised the opponents of progress, and given new heart and courage to those who, during long years had patiently toiled and hoped that better times yet awaited the party.[158]

Between 1903 and 1906 Liberal lectures and meetings were dominated by the fiscal question and the reassertion of the continued power of free trade. In October 1903, an overflow meeting had to be held to accommodate the crowds who gathered to hear Herbert Asquith denounce Chamberlain's tariff proposals and at meetings held by Lloyd George, Lord Crewe and Haldane over the next three years, audiences reaffirmed their commitment to free trade by attending in their thousands.

Styling their protests in line with the rhetoric of the Anti-Corn Law League of the previous century and raising the spectre of increased food prices, the Liberal activists of these years proved that free trade remained a meaningful and popular policy for the majority of the Paisley electorate. Indeed, in December 1903 even the ILP held a meeting to discuss the 'Tariff Question', attracting support from the Trades Council, the UIL and the Co-operative societies. Here, Dr Clark, the former MP for Caithness, was met with cheers when he declared: 'All tariffs, whether for Protection or for revenue, were equally evil. They were all alike cruel, crafty contrivances to make the rich richer and the poor poorer.'[159]

Such may stand as evidence of the continued attractiveness of Liberalism in Paisley in these years. Liberalism, rather than Labour, secured the greatest political dividend from the re-emergence of the free trade question at the front of the political agenda.[160] Despite evident similarities, in comparison to Labour, 'the Liberals had a more attractive and distinctive economic appeal'.[161]

Inherent in the tariff reform debate itself, however, was the popular acknowledgement of the urgency of social change. Thus, whilst after 1906, tariff reform nationally became less of an issue, the heightened awareness of social problems which it had facilitated fed into growing concerns regarding the rise of independent Labour politics.

158 *PRG*, 6 Feb. 1904.

159 Ibid., 12 Dec. 1903.

160 According to Trentmann, free-trade addressed voters as consumers and thus went some way to undermining Labour's identification of the electorate in relation to the means of production and their class: F. Trentmann, 'The strange death of free trade: the erosion of "liberal consensus" in Great Britain, *c.*1903–1932', in Biagini, *Citizenship and Community*, p. 222.

161 Tanner, *Political Change and the Labour Party*, p. 422.

In 1909 Willie Gallacher of the SDF moved an amendment to the usual motion in support of Paisley's MP, John M. McCallum, at the annual constituency meeting which demanded that: 'in future they cease to give their support to Mr McCallum and that they consider the advisability of putting forward a workers' representative instead of a master'.[162] Whilst seconded, the amendment was defeated by an overwhelming majority in favour of McCallum. Taking the stand, McCallum stressed that 'he was not there as a Labour representative, but to represent the whole community'.[163]

In Paisley, Liberalism proved capable of accommodating the most pressing demands of labour whilst reasserting a popular vision of community, rather than class-based politics, which remained personal and locally defined. Before 1914 the housing question, as we have seen, was still to be appropriated as a 'Labour issue', but rather proved a key feature of Liberal local policy, assuring the continued support of many working-class groups for Liberalism. McCallum met Labour protests over the Osborne Judgement with explicit support for the continued political involvement of trade unions and, as a prominent temperance activist and supporter of New Liberal measures, proved adept at playing the 'labour card'.

Yet, in terms of grass-roots Liberal Party membership, worrying signs were emerging of the distinct failure of the local associations to mobilise greater support. From its peak of over 1,000 members in the late 1880s, the Paisley Liberal Club boasted only 864 members in 1908, a figure which declined annually throughout the immediate pre-war years.[164] The construction of a new billiards room in 1902 failed to attract new members, and increasingly complaints were heard at Liberal meetings that the young males of the town were more interested in football than politics.[165] Whilst the Paisley Women's Liberal Association continued to be active, supporting its own candidates in School Board elections and encouraging a greater commitment from the local associations for women's suffrage, Paisley had no branch of the Young Scots (established in 1900), considered by Hutchison as a critical feature of Liberalism's influence in these years.[166] In this regard, Hutchison's national perspective of a vital Liberal movement in Scotland fails to reflect Paisley's poor organisation on the eve of war. In comparison, Labour's vibrant associational life held portents of Liberalism's post-war eclipse as the cultural guarantor of Paisley's local political identity.

162 *PRG*, 23 Jan. 1909.
163 Ibid., 23 Jan. 1909.
164 *PDE*, 8.12 1908.
165 Ibid., 20 Feb. 1904.
166 Hutchison, *Political History of Scotland*, pp. 232–3.

Radicalism, Tariff Reform and the Evolution of Popular Unionism, 1900–1910

Drawing upon 'the vocabulary of Manchester Liberalism while updating it in the fashionable guise of efficiency', tariff reform was the ultimate expression of the radical roots of Paisley Unionism during the Edwardian period.[167] Misinterpreted as the mere 'principled opportunism' of a party seeking a populist response to 'the challenge of collectivism and democratisation',[168] its true significance is to be found less in its 'electoral genesis', as an apparent attempt to 'cut the ground from under the Labour Party', than in its reassertion of a radical heritage from which the Liberal Unionists had strayed after 1886.[169]

Whilst acknowledging that 'tariff reformers were not entirely friendless north of the Tweed', Hutchison has emphasised that few prominent Scottish industrialists committed themselves to tariff reform.[170] In this context, therefore, the presence of Archibald Coats and W. H. Coats at the founding meeting of the Glasgow and West of Scotland Branch of the Tariff Reform League and the latter's subsequent appointment to its Executive Committee, is surprising and alerts us to the local imperatives which determined the complex character of tariff reform in Scotland.[171] Rather than destroying 'Toryism's greatest strength, its local community-based character', the tariff reform campaign in Paisley merely threw into relief the tensions which had always existed within the local movement.[172] It also illustrated competing interpretations of the Unionist vision in an era challenged by wider definitions of state responsibility, and re-affirmed the roots of popular Unionism in the burgh's radical past.

In November 1902, John Moffat of Ardrossan, having previously contested Elgin Burghs against Asher, the late Solicitor-General, was adopted as the Unionist candidate for Paisley, a town with which he was personally connected through his aunt, Mrs Arthur of Barshaw, a Liberal, who in 1873 headed the poll as Paisley's first female member of the School Board.[173] Described as 'a young politician of promise' by the WSLUA in 1903, Moffat revealed a keen but controversial interest in social reform from an early stage in his candidature when, at the seventeenth AGM of the WSLUA in January 1903, he spoke at length on

167 F. Coetzee, *For Party or Country: Nationalism and the Dilemmas of Popular Conservatism in Edwardian England* (New York, 1990), p. 69.
168 Fforde, *Conservatism and Collectivism*, p. 88.
169 E. H. H. Green, 'Radical Conservatism: the electoral genesis of tariff reform', *HJ*, xxviii (1985), p. 686. Green establishes his position when he writes, 'Chamberlain's launching of the tariff reform campaign is thus explicable in electoral terms as an attempt to compensate for the Conservatives' apparent loss of support.' (pp. 687–8).
170 Hutchison, *Political History of Scotland*, p. 219.
171 GCA, Parker Smith Collection, TD1/46, Cuttings (various).
172 Lawrence, 'Class and gender', p. 650.
173 *Bailie*, 25 Jun. 1873.

the 'disadvantages the tenants of small houses experienced' in Scotland.[174]

Hereafter, Moffat's candidature was to be marked by controversy. While the business committee of the WSLUA maintained an 'open mind' on the fiscal question throughout 1903, supporting Balfour's Sheffield programme that October, Moffat pushed for a more determined stance, calling for 'a further resolution of approval of Mr Chamberlain's policy' at the general meeting of December 1903 and requesting a special conference on fiscal policy at an executive committee meeting a week later.[175] The nineteenth annual report of the WSLUA recorded in 1904 that: 'As regards the fiscal question, we welcome within our ranks Liberal Unionists of all shades of opinion, who are prepared to support the Unionist Government', yet Moffat, whilst voting for the resolution, declared that: 'he would have had much greater pleasure in supporting some resolution of a decidedly whole-hogger tendency'.[176]

Unsuccessful in his attempts to push the WSLUA towards a commitment to Chamberlain's tariff reform vision, Moffat turned his attention on Paisley where his influence was critical to the pre-war development of Unionism in the burgh. Both in terms of organisation and ideology, Moffat's influence on the local party was to remain long after he himself had gone.

In co-operation with his 'agent' Ernest Druce, a self styled 'writer' and 'scholar' and old university friend from Northamptonshire, Moffat reformed the local Liberal Unionist Association in order to attract greater working-class support. Throughout Moffat's time as the Unionist candidate, meetings and demonstrations were more regular, ward committee membership increased substantially and a committee of management was established within the association to co-ordinate propaganda and encourage local activism. In 1904, Druce boasted of a membership of 1,000 and claimed that: 'the Liberal Unionist Association is a highly efficient political organisation, and ... the power and influence which were at one time in the hands of the cliques ... have been transferred from them to it'.[177]

Yet, Moffat's crucial influence was as a proponent of a popular Unionism which was explicit in its appeal to the working class and articulated in a rhetoric which confirmed its radical inheritance. 'The country is sick to death of the old hypocrisies!' declared Moffat in April 1904 at a Unionist demonstration 'very representative of the working classes', and the following year, in an address to a crowded meeting in the town hall, he reflected:

174 NLS, SCUA, Acc. 10424/21, WSLUA Minutes: 1900–1910, Annual General Meeting, 21 Jan. 1903.

175 Ibid., Business Committee Meeting 10 Jun. 1903; Business Committee Meeting 30 Oct. 1903; Annual General Meeting 3 Dec. 1903; Executive Committee Meeting 9 Dec. 1903.

176 Ibid., Annual General Meeting 23 Nov. 1904.

177 *PDE*, 27 Dec. 1904.

> In all directions it was the aim of the capitalist to take advantage of the undefended condition of the labourer, to force him to work the longest hours for the least pay, to keep a check on him as regarded education ... with a view to preventing him from raising himself to a position of independence, to turn him as much as possible into a tool or a machine, and, finally, to take from him the right of combination and the power to resist the extortionate demands of his employer. He said it with sorrow and regret ... he said it ... to urge them to see that no efforts are spared to induce Parliament to pass remedial measures, if that be possible ... before the rights of the working classes have been forever lost and swallowed up in the encroaching tide of militarism, capitalism and the other 'isms' which are threatening them. (Applause.) It was his wish to urge them to look to their weapons and their cause before other decisions similar to the Taff Vale decision had quite reduced them to the level of old-time serfs, who had no legal rights of combination and picketing.[178]

From the floor, a voice declared, 'You talk like a Radical.'

The language is that of the independent artisan, of 'rights', and of the exploitation of privilege and the exaltation of a community of interests which echoed the inter-class unity of Paisley's earlier Chartists. Indeed, Moffat's assertion of the contemporary challenge to 'the undoubted rights and privileges of the working classes – privileges which they, in common with all free men, had possessed from time immemorial', consciously recalls the language of an earlier radicalism.[179]

From the beginning, the tariff reform campaign in Paisley focused on local manifestations of the industrial consequences of foreign tariffs, most especially Coats's continued expansion in America and the increasing competition of foreign thread producers, and raised the ghost of the shawl trade tragedy. Likewise, Moffat's doctrine of working-class exploitation sought local exemplars and found them in the industrial elite which, since 1886, had dominated local Liberal Unionism.

Rumours of a 'split' in Paisley's Unionist ranks circulated from December 1903, and coincided with Moffat's protests against WSLUA fiscal policy.[180] Local disaffection with Moffat focused on his domination of the local party of which he had been appointed president in March 1904, and over which, it was considered, Ernest Druce, as secretary, held too much influence. Matters came to a head in December 1904 when Moffat addressed a demonstration in Paisley attacking his opponents within the local party as 'nominal Unionists', denounced the Conservative

178 Ibid., 17 Mar. 1904; *PRG*, 30 Dec. 1905.

179 Ibid., 30 Dec. 1905. See also M. W. Steinberg, '"The Great End of All Government ...": working people's construction of citizenship claims in early nineteenth-century England and the matter of class', *IRSH*, xl, Supplement 3 (1995), pp. 19–50.

180 *PRG*, 19 Dec. 1903.

Campaign Guide and declared 'the only real living power in British politics' to be Mr Chamberlain.[181] The following week, the Eastern Unionist Association demanded an explanation of his allegations but Moffat refused to reply, asserting he was not compelled to explain himself to that body.[182] A week later the duke of Abercorn, an honorary president of the local Beaconsfield Club, withdrew his support for Moffat.[183] Moffat replied that such action was typical of the measures which were being adopted by 'several plutocrats whose hostility towards ... [him was] the result of [his] well-known sympathy with the working classes'.[184]

The controversy continued, the letters columns of the local press becoming dominated by the issue until January 1905, when several prominent members of the Liberal Unionist Association resigned. On 12 January, sixteen vice-presidents of the Liberal Unionist Association resigned office, among them Archibald, Peter, Daniel, and James Coats; James and Stewart Clark, William Arrol, J. A. D. MacKean and John Fullerton – referred to by Moffat as 'paltry intriguers'.[185] A few days later, Lord Kelvin, an honorary president of the association, joined their ranks.

At the end of January, Chamberlain wrote to Archibald Coats disassociating himself from Moffat's political stance, which was becoming increasingly critical of Balfour and the Conservative party. In February, both the Eastern Unionist Association and the Conservative Association withdrew their support for Moffat, who had written earlier that month in the *Daily Record* that Balfour[186]

> is unfitted to his present position because, though possessed of great talent, and a courteous, philosophical disposition, he is without a spark of genius and completely fails to understand or appreciate the needs and the thoughts of the working classes.[187]

Moffat's onslaught continued, and at a Unionist demonstration in Paisley in May he referred to the Government as 'Mr Balfour's Cabinet of Nonentities' which stood for 'all that is truly and in the worst sense reactionary in political tradition'.[188] Later that month he followed this up with a series of letters in various daily newspapers detailing 'How to Get Rid of the Prime Minister'.[189] By June, his position as the Unionist candidate had become untenable and on the 15th he resigned. 'Gradually', he wrote in a communication to the press,

181 *PDE*, 7 Dec. 1904.
182 Ibid., 17 Dec. 1904, 20 Dec. 1904.
183 Ibid., 27 Dec. 1904.
184 Ibid., 28 Dec. 1904.
185 Ibid., 12 Jan. 1905.
186 *PRG*, 28 Jan. 1905.
187 As quoted in *PDE*, 6 Feb. 1905.
188 *PDE*, 3 May 1905.
189 *PRG*, 20 May 1905.

> it has dawned on my mind that a Unionist candidate is one who is expected to defend and maintain existing abuses, and all that makes for social inequality, and not to offer criticism or to express a wish that these evils be remedied.[190]

Thereafter Moffat denounced tariff reform as a policy to 'enslave ... the masses' and declared that 'if in future I take any part in politics it will be as a Liberal, and not as a Conservative or Unionist'.[191]

Whilst the press reflected on Moffat's candidature and conversion to Liberalism as a joke and a fiasco ('Moffat Madness'), Moffat's explicit attempt at the 're-identification of Unionist interests with those of the working classes' is of crucial importance to our understanding of Edwardian Unionism.[192] Moffat's reassertion of the radical roots of Liberal Unionism reflected the ambiguous character of the Unionist-Conservative alliance in these years and the incomplete process of political realignment which had been necessitated by the Home Rule legislation of 1886. The Paisley experience thus contradicts Green's recent identification of tariff reform as a 'genuinely Conservative' policy and his assertion that Liberal Unionist/Conservative differences were blurring long before 1912.[193] Fluidity rather than rigid dogmatism characterised popular interpretations of party differences in these years, and highlighted the inadequacies of the political labels which had evolved through the attempted institutionalisation of older genuinely plebeian traditions. Moffat's evident popular appeal illustrated how Paisley's radical heritage could be utilised to work against its more conventional interpretation when the defensive and collaborationist elements of the radical creed were brought to bear on contemporary issues. After 1886 the radical tradition was no longer the exclusive property of the Liberals, but a depository of concepts, principles, rhetoric and conventions common to all political contenders.

The Paisley Unionist organisations in 1906 returned to their previous quietude under the dominance of the elite which had abandoned Moffat, leaving his wider vision to be absorbed by the local Tariff Reform League, established in the burgh after his departure. Over the next four years the league's active propaganda throughout Renfrewshire threw into relief the inaction of the established Unionist bodies and provided an important focus for radical working-class Unionists.

The traditional Unionist organisations, however, were far from dormant. A Paisley branch of the Women's Liberal Unionist Association was established in December 1905, and by 1909 was forced to look for larger premises due to its increased membership. The Primrose League, whilst showing evidence of decline in the immediate pre-war years,

190 Ibid., 17 Jun. 1905; *PDE*, 16 Jun. 1905.

191 *PDE*, 16 Jun. 1905.

192 *PRG*, 20 May 1905 (quote from a letter from Moffat to the press dated 18 May 1905).

193 Green, *Crisis of Conservatism*, pp. 6, 314–15.

maintained a membership of over 300 throughout the period and the Beaconsfield Club, though adopting a lower profile than in previous years, remained active, expanding and improving its premises in 1908. Yet the main transformation was in the organisation of the political associations themselves.

In 1906 a letter appeared in the *Express* highlighting that the 'Paisley Conservative Association has to all intents and purposes been defunct – a mere farce – apathy and indifference having marked its would-be existence.'[194] Since 1900 the local press had recorded only two meetings of the Conservative Association, the political lead having been taken by the Liberal Unionists since the defeat in the khaki election. In December 1906, however, under the chairmanship of Charles Jago Gregg and with the encouragement of the NUCAS, which was attempting to encourage a reform of the national electoral machinery following the 'electoral rebuff' of that year, plans were drawn up for the reformation of the local association.[195] In April 1907 an organisation committee of twenty members (including Liberal Unionists) was established to consider the best way forward.[196]

In 1908, however, the organisational focus changed when, in October, the Conservative Association and Liberal Unionist Association merged to form the Paisley Unionist Association, four years before the national bodies united as the Scottish Unionist Association.[197] Yet, whilst negotiations regarding the merger had been going on since January, it is clear that the creation of the new joint association did not herald the resolution of the ambiguities inherent in the 'Unionist identity'. In a speech at the founding demonstration, the new Unionist parliamentary candidate announced that:

> the ideals of the old Conservative party and the Liberal Unionist party were practically the same, for did they not realise that the Unionist party of today largely embraced the Liberal principles of many years ago prior to the great mistakes that the Liberals made in 1885? Did they not realise that the Liberal Unionists were simply what they might call the more progressive members of the great Unionist party?[198]

Over the next few months four district committees were established, in the north, south, east and west of the town, and in 1909 an organising secretary was appointed for the burgh. In this regard, Paisley's experience was in keeping with the national trend towards greater Conservative organisational efficiency identified by Hutchison, who has

194 *PDE*, 11 Oct. 1906.
195 Ibid., 5 Dec. 1906. For the wider national picture, see Hutchison, *Political History of Scotland*, p. 221.
196 *PRG*, 6 Apr. 1907.
197 Ibid., 17 Oct. 1908.
198 Ibid., 17 Oct. 1908.

reflected that at this time: 'The re-energising of constituency organisation was generally impressive in its speed and thoroughness.'[199]

Yet, whilst by 1909 local Unionists identified 'a recrudescence of political thought in the community, which was tending towards the Unionist side', and repeated lecturers focused on the working classes as Unionism's new constituency, the crucial focus of working-class interest up to 1910 was the Tariff Reform League.[200]

Between 1905 and 1910 the number of Tariff Reform League branches in Scotland increased from fourteen to 182 and proved active agencies of Unionist reform.[201] In Paisley, beginning with a membership of just thirty in 1906, numbers rose to 162 within a year, and by 1908 exceeded 200.[202] Moreover, between 1906 and 1909, the Paisley members were instrumental in the establishment of league branches in Johnstone, Greenock, Renfrew, Barrhead, Neilston and Elderslie, and assisted in the registration of sympathetic Unionist voters. Throughout the summer and winter, lecture campaigns were held, and in July 1909 a crowd of around 1,000 attended a demonstration in Dunn Square to commemorate Chamberlain's birthday.

Foremost among the leadership of the Paisley League were W. B. Flockhart and C. J. Gregg, who in 1905 had led the fight against the introduction of politics into the Co-operative movement at the annual Congress of that year. Their presence as the first president and secretary respectively of the Paisley League illustrates the extent of working-class interest in tariff reform in Paisley during these years and its accommodation within broader conventional labour bodies.

Successive league lectures focused on working-class welfare, speakers reflected a strong bias towards labour issues and, in illustrating their policies, lecturers employed Paisley's history to assert the movement's connection with an older working-class legacy.[203] In 1909, an article in the *Gazette* reflected on Paisley's weaving past:

> One of our staple makes was a honeycomb woollen wrap shawl; we made it season after season, and sold it at 6 shillings and nine pence. In one year a syndicate of Elberfeld makers through their London agency, who supplied the capital, flooded our markets with the same shawl selling it at 6s. 3d. and continued to do so till opposition on our part ceased. Then, as a matter of course, the prices were gradually raised to 7s. and three pence. Thus, in one short season, was the making of this staple article extinguished and the labour of 500 Paisley handloom weavers with their accessory adjuncts of spinners, dyers, warpers etc., conveyed over to Germany,

199 Hutchison, *Political History of Scotland*, p. 222.
200 *PDE*, 23 Feb. 1909.
201 Hutchison, *Political History of Scotland*, p. 220.
202 *PDE*, 28 Feb. 1907; 25 Feb. 1908.
203 For the national perspective, see Howe, 'Towards the "hungry forties"', p. 199.

> where today to supply our own and colonial markets with this self same shawl 1,000 operatives are at work ... had we been able to retain the making of this shawl in our own hands ... how many of those old men ... it would have saved from the Poorhouse, and dying there as too many of them did.[204]

Tariff reform was thus styled as a defensive measure in the interests of the preservation of a distinctive local culture, more normally associated with the Liberal ethos of the independent 'respectable' working class.[205] The ultimate failure of the movement therefore, was less the simple consequence of the longevity of the attractive power of free trade and 'Old Liberalism', than the expression of the victory of one radical interpretation of the contemporary social agenda over another and the continued sympathy of the working classes toward the taxation of land, rather than food, as the most egalitarian source of revenue for welfare reforms.[206] Liberalism won by default.

Three Strands of the Radical Thread: The General Elections of 1906 and 1910

> Utopias, or abstract rationalism, have the same importance as old conceptions of the world which developed historically by the accumulation of successive experience. What matters is the criticism to which such an ideological complex is subjected by the first representative of the new historical phase. This criticism makes possible a process of differentiation and change in the relative weight that the elements of the old ideologies used to possess. What was previously secondary and subordinate, or even incidental, is now taken to be primary – becomes the nucleus of a new ideological and theoretical complex.[207]

Paisley's radical tradition was not the exclusive property of the emergent Labour Party during the Edwardian period. Rather, the party's attempted re-interpretation and appropriation of it forms part of a general process through which political identities were realigned. Repeated reflections from all sides that Labour in this period was securing as many votes from Unionists as from Liberals highlight the consequences of this forgotten shared legacy.[208] The evolution of

204 *PRG*, 13 Feb. 1909.

205 See Trentmann, 'Strange death of free trade', pp. 219–50. Whilst Trentmann's definition of Liberal 'community' consciousness is national in scale, the analysis he presents is entirely appropriate for localities like Paisley, where major sources of industrial wealth were seen to be dependent on free trade.

206 D. J. Dutton, 'The Unionist Party and social policy, 1906–1914', *HJ*, xxiv (1981), pp. 871–84. Here Dutton highlights that many Unionists recognised 'the folly of running food taxes against land taxes'.

207 Gramsci, *Selections from the Prison Notebooks*, p. 195.

208 See, e.g. (a) Tom Mann's comment in an interview with the *Weekly Dispatch* in 1894 that 'wherever the ILP have a firm hold, as in Lancashire and Yorkshire, one third of

popular Unionism emerges thus from the same continuum which transmuted radicalism into its Labour guise.

Using the general elections of 1906 and 1910 as 'windows' on this process, it becomes immediately apparent that this cross-party re-evaluation of Paisley's past reflected an emerging material crisis in the hegemonic power of the local industrial elite brought to the fore, as we have seen, by economic changes in the workplace and the attempted fracturing of community politics into those of class. Liberalism represented a 'nexus of classes' whose competing interests would ultimately determine its inability to adopt the rhetoric of class politics.[209] Yet until 1914, containment and control rather than conflict determined the character of the silent revolution in Paisley radicalism.[210]

In January 1906, George H. Coats announced to a crowded meeting in the Clark Town Hall that 'the real Radical Party, in the old genuine and splendid sense of the word, was not the party of the Liberals, but the party of the Unionists'.[211] At the subsequent election, three candidates sought 'the weaver vote': for the Liberals, John M. McCallum, Dunn's successor, a local soap manufacturer; for the Unionists, J. A. D. MacKean, a director of a local starch works; and for Labour, Robert Smillie, the miners' leader. Each stressed a different strand of the radical thread: McCallum drew on the legacy of the Anti Corn Law League, placing free trade to the fore in his campaign; the Unionists drew on the anti-clerical tradition and the constitutional roots of democracy; whilst Smillie stressed a new class interpretation of a familiar dialectic of economic exploitation and 'justice'. Yet, though McCallum's victory highlighted Paisley's continued commitment to the party of Gladstone, his opponents' campaigns indicated the growing popularity of political alternatives.[212] The *Gazette* remarked at the height of the campaign that of the 'brilliant colours and striking drawings [posted on the hoardings] to arrest the attention ... all, or nearly all ... seem to advertise the Unionist and Labour candidates' claims for support'.[213]

Among other notable attempts at prising victory from the Liberals was the institution by the Unionists of a working-class propaganda machine: 'The First Division of the Light Brigade'. Throughout the election

our men have been Tories, one third Liberals and one third political non-descripts.': LSE, ILP Archive, ILP 1/1, NAC Minutes: 1893–1896, loose leaf, *c.*Mar. 1894; also (b) Report of the Western Division of the SLA which reads 'It was apparent from the figures that a considerable proportion of the Labour Party's vote was drawn from the Unionist Party as well as from the Liberal Party ...': EUL, SLA Collection, Minutes, vol. VII: 1899–1908, Western Organising Committee Meeting, 8 May 1907 (p. 509).

209 Gramsci, *Selections from the Prison Notebooks*, p. 156.

210 See S. Den Otter, '"Thinking in communities": late nineteenth-century Liberals, idealists and the retrieval of community', in E. H. H. Green (ed.), *An Age of Transition: British Politics, 1880–1914* (Edinburgh, 1997), p. 84.

211 *PRG*, 6 Jan. 1906.

212 See below, Appendix 4.

213 *PRG*, 13 Jan. 1906.

campaign, the brigade, led by prominent working-class Unionists, conducted open air meetings and delivered 'shirt sleeve' orations on 'Current Politics from the Tory Working Man's Standpoint'.[214] Whilst such organisations were evident in various English elections in the period, the Paisley division represents the first and perhaps only Scottish example of such Unionist 'Stormtroops'. In Paisley, their lectures attracted large audiences throughout the campaign and were instrumental in framing the tariff question along lines sympathetic to labour interests.

All three parties focused their campaigns on a narrow range of issues which became dominated by expressions of sympathy, if few concrete promises of assistance, to the working-class electorate. Temperance remained a crucial focus of interest,[215] yet former Liberal shibboleths – Home Rule, disestablishment, land reform – featured low down on the list of current political concerns.[216] Ultimately, the domination of tariff reform in the campaign debates created a political capital in free trade which Labour proved incapable of prising from the Liberal Party, and the Unionists, despite innovative electioneering, failed to convince a sufficient proportion of the organised Labour vote of tariff reform's radical credentials.[217]

To view Smillie's achievement of around 2,500 votes in this election as a portent of future Labour strength in the burgh is to rest historiography on the basis of hindsight and hypothesis rather than fact. Instead, in the context of 1906, and against the background of the continued disunity of the local Labour ranks, Smillie's performance, rather than heralding the emergence of a new challenger, confirmed Liberalism's continued hold on Paisley. Smillie himself admitted that while 'their hopes went up as they went along ... it had been proved to them that the time was hardly yet'.[218] Economic power, social structures, local industrial prosperity and the articulation of a familiar ideology, whilst clearly under attack from various sources, remained strong enough to maintain the Liberal hegemony in 1906.

1908, however, heralded a change in the economic prosperity of the burgh. In April the *Gazette* reported:

214 *PRG*, 5 Jan. 1906.

215 Smillie's association with a Public House Trust lost him a large proportion of the temperance vote, including that of the SDF's Willie Gallacher.

216 For a detailed analysis of the declining importance of disestablishment in Scottish politics, see Machin, 'Disestablishment and democracy', pp. 120–47.

217 Ramsay MacDonald highlighted that '(Chamberlain) attempted to found a *prima facie* argument that Trade Unionists ought to be Protectionists on the superficial resemblance between the two movements. But even when the Trade Unionist could not argue the difference, he *felt* the difference and remained unconvinced': J. R. MacDonald, 'Mr Chamberlain as a social reformer', in Rt. Hon. Viscount Milner *et al.*, *Life of Joseph Chamberlain* (London, *c.*1914), p. 191 [my italics].

218 *PRG*, 20 Jan. 1906.

> Dull trade is very general in town at present, and short time notices have been posted up in many of the works. Veteran tradesmen say they have never known so much trade depression, and the truth of their statement is verified by the fact that many who have been a life-time employed in one firm have just been put on the idle list. One workman who has had to go has been 50 years in a shipbuilding yard in town, while others can claim 25 or 30 years' service.[219]

Joan Smith has identified the slump of 1908 as 'the real turning point for the growth of the Labour movement in Glasgow', pointing to the mobilisation of 35,000 marchers in June and a 7,000-strong demonstration at Glasgow Green in September as evidence of the awakening of a distinctively 'Labour' consciousness among the city's workers.[220] Yet Paisley's experience illustrates the limits of such 'hunger politics' in the development of the Scottish Labour movement. Here, despite an estimated 4,000 unemployed in October 1908, only sixteen trades turned out for a 'disappointing' 'Right to Work' demonstration in July.[221] The following year, with the trade depression still posing a local problem, the Trades Council rejected a proposal to organise a demonstration in the interests of the 'out of work', noting that 'previous attempts in this direction had failed mainly through the indifference of the unemployed themselves who would not turn out'.[222]

Whilst the slump of 1908, therefore, did not lead *directly* to the mobilisation of a stronger local Labour movement, its impact on local politics was profound. Alongside the increase in short-term employment of women at the thread mills, the depression of 1908 encouraged a feeling of occupational instability among the engineers in the town which militated against their close identification with Liberalism and challenged the deferential relationship at the heart of the Liberal hegemony by illustrating that, in a changing world market, local industry and industrialists could provide no guarantee of continued prosperity.

Furthermore, the response of the local Distress Committee to rising unemployment in the town did nothing to foster confidence in the local political elite. From 1905 to 1908 the inaction of the committee was repeatedly criticised by the Trades Council and the ILP, and attracted rebuke from the secretary of the Local Government Board.[223] In

219 Ibid., 25 Apr. 1908.
220 Smith, 'Taking the leadership of the Labour movement', p. 65.
221 *PRG*, 17 Oct. 1908, 1 Aug. 1908.
222 *PDE*, 28 Jul. 1909.
223 PCL, 362.5, o/s PC4868, Letters to the Distress Committee on Unemployment, 1906–1908: Letter to F. Martin (Town Clerk) from Hugh Lorimer (Secretary Paisley Labour Representation Committee) 8 Nov. 1906; Letter to F. Martin (Town Clerk) from George Watson (Secretary Paisley ILP) 12 Nov. 1906; Letter to F. Martin (Town Clerk) from Thomas Loudon (Secretary Trades Council) 19 Dec. 1906; Letter to F. Martin (Town Clerk) from Secretary of the Local Government Board 29 Jan. 1907.

comparison to the activities of parallel committees in Aberdeen and Dundee, the Paisley members seemed at best reluctant to intervene in the local labour market, preferring instead to leave matters to the Association for Improving the Condition of the Poor.[224] As late as May 1907, the terms of the 1905 Unemployed Workmen Act had not been employed in the burgh and repeated calls from other Scottish committees to campaign in favour of greater powers in dealing with local unemployment received a lukewarm response.[225] When, in January 1908, the Trades Council had calculated that 1,500 men were unemployed in the town, the committee had registered only eighty-seven males and five females.[226]

Ultimately, however, it was the Unionists, rather than Labour, who in Paisley exploited the depression to its greatest political potential. Captain Duncan Campbell, the Unionists' new prospective candidate for Paisley, was adopted by the local party in September 1908 and immediately styled Unionist propaganda as the defence of working-class interests. In May 1909 he began a series of 'short talks with workers' at the gates of several large concerns in the towns, using the recent slump as an illustration of the inadequacies of free trade and the threat of cheap foreign labour.[227] Meanwhile the Labour ranks were divided on political involvement, leaving the election of January 1910 in the hands of the two established parties.

During the election campaign, the level and impact of Unionist organisation and propaganda was striking, with Campbell holding 103 meetings in thirty-two days at the end of 1909. Developing the tactics of the 'Light Brigade' in 1906, Campbell presented to the electorate a popular Unionism, or 'Imperial Labourism', in which 'the foreigner' replaced 'capital' as the foremost economic threat to labour's security:

> many of our old businesses were going to the wall, and unemployment was the great evil of our time. Why? because the foreigner was not taxed, and because our own industries were taxed by our own government.[228]

Tariff reform was portrayed as an adjunct to, and a natural progression from, defensive craft sectionalism. In these terms, voting Unionist was framed, not in terms of a self-denying deference, but as a material realisation of physical need, current exploitation and future protection – terms through which Campbell claimed his 'right' to the radical tradition. The Liberals, rather than the Unionists, he claimed, had

224 PCL, 361 Ren–1, ARC 252, *Reports of the Distress Committee, 1905–1914*, Committee Minutes, 11 Jan. 1907; 24 May 1907; 31 Jan. 1908.
225 Ibid., 16 Dec. 1907.
226 Ibid., 31 Jan. 1908.
227 *PDE*, 11 May 1909.
228 *PRG*, 25 Dec. 1909.

deviated from its call. At a meeting in January Campbell was supported in this view by Sir Robert Finlay, the late Attorney-General:

> Paisley had been intensely conservative in its Liberalism. (Laughter.) He thought that in Paisley, as elsewhere in Scotland, people had commenced to enquire whether what was masquerading under the name Liberalism was really the genuine article. The packet was the same, the label was the same, but somehow or other the goods had changed.[229]

The reference to labelling echoed a further focus of Campbell's attack on McCallum – his local image and industrial credibility – two features critical to the perpetuation of Liberal claims on local loyalties. Campbell highlighted the wording on McCallum's 'A1 Soap Powder' boxes:

> **A1** SOAP POWDER MAINTAINS THE WELL-KNOWN SUPREMACY OF THE BRITISH-MADE ARTICLE. YOU ARE RESPECTFULLY INVITED TO TEST ITS SUPERIORITY AND, IF SATISFIED, TO REFUSE THE GOODS WITH WHICH FOREIGN LABOUR HAS FLOODED THE MARKETS OF THIS COUNTRY AND SO THIN THE RANKS OF THE GREAT ARMY OF THE BRITISH UNEMPLOYED.[230]

McCallum was taken to task for his apparent hypocrisy in defending free trade whilst selling his goods and defending his workers with a 'Protection' slogan. Campbell thus highlighted a contradiction at the heart of local industrial paternalism.

In reply to a questionnaire issued by the Trades Council, Campbell went a step further than McCallum in his claims on the labour vote when he announced that he 'recognised the principle of the right to work' – a response which, thereafter, was approved by *Forward* in an article which depicted McCallum as a 'notorious reactionary'.[231] Whilst his opinion in this regard did not endear him to some local Unionists, who considered it 'the very height of Socialism', his response reflects the extent to which Campbell stretched the conventional parameters of party politics.

Whilst winning the election with a majority of 2,922 the Liberal Party's counter-attacks appear slight and far from convincing against such strong opposition.[232] McCallum's campaign, guided by claims to the moral high ground of principle, avoided Campbell's material economic challenge, but instead offered vague promises and appeals to radical constitutional rhetoric. In response to a letter from Campbell, McCallum considered the fiscal question thus: 'Your position and mine have been

229 Ibid., 15 Jan. 1910.
230 Ibid., 13 Jan. 1910.
231 *PDE*, 10 Jan. 1910; *Forward*, 14 Jan. 1910.
232 See below, Appendix 4.

clearly defined. You believe in *artificial law* in connection with commerce; I believe in *natural law*.'[233]

The key dynamic of the January election – the question of the house of lords – spawned further claims to old radical principles:

> The question of the hour was – Were we to make the laws in our way, or were we to be governed by 600 immovable Peers? This was no common election: it was a Bannockburn. (Loud applause.)[234]

As in 1906, when the apparent threat to free trade occasioned a national Liberal landslide, in 1910, the Liberals maintained their majority in Paisley, thanks again to a familiar appeal, this time against aristocratic injustices. McCallum framed his victory in terms of a long-established social morality: 'These were principles which they would readily bleed and die for rather than give them up, and they were determined ... to maintain their traditions.'[235] Unionist vitality thus met Liberal traditionalism and was ultimately found wanting. The power of the past was emphasised by the president of the Beaconsfield Club when he declared: 'there was many a man present who would have voted for Captain Campbell, but who was still chained to his old traditional vote'.[236]

The 'traditional vote' was tested again less than ten months later, when a second general election was called for December. Not wanting to court defeat a second time, and voicing sympathy with McCallum, many Unionists were unconvinced about contesting the burgh again.[237] On 26 November, however, A. R. Jephcott was unanimously adopted as Unionist candidate for the burgh. 'Paisley has now a "working man" Unionist candidate, who goes to the poll on Monday', declared the *Gazette*.[238]

Jephcott, a native of Birmingham, was a well-known trade unionist and councillor in his home town. A member of the ASE, he became president of the Birmingham District Committee and was president of the Trades Council between 1889 and 1891. In 1895 he was elected to Birmingham City Council as the representative for the largest ward in the town, having been appointed to the School Board the previous year.[239] His history was thus the 'classic' route to power of the traditional Labour activist, but Jephcott undermined conventional stereotypes in his commitment to Unionism.

Jephcott's programme was a mixture of trade-union pragmatism and imperial rhetoric within which echoes of Moffat and Campbell could be

233 *PRG*, 1 Jan. 1910 [my italics].
234 Ibid., 25 Dec. 1909 (Speech made by Provost Eadie).
235 Ibid., 22 Jan. 1910.
236 Ibid., 22 Jan. 1910.
237 See letters column: *PDE*, 18 Nov. 1910.
238 *PRG*, 3 Dec. 1910.
239 Ibid., 3 Dec. 1910. Additional details regarding Jephcott's personal history were supplied by Prof. W. H. Fraser to whom my thanks are extended.

heard. He claimed to support tariff reform 'from the standpoint of [the] defence of [the] employment of the people' and declared that 'he was a tariff reformer because he was a trade unionist' implying a natural inevitability of one, following on from the acceptance of the other.[240] Most importantly, however, he continued the tradition of reaffirming Unionism's radical inheritance. This may be best illustrated by the seven points addressed to the 'Electors of Paisley' in Jephcott's campaign literature (see Appendix 7). The capitalisation and bold-face lettering isolate the essential distinctions between the two parties and policies, which, standing juxtaposed, are given meaning through contrast and comparison with their apparent 'opposite'. Principles normally associated with the Liberal tradition of government are appropriated by the Unionists and their candidate, 'billed' in this literature as 'THE WORKING MAN UNIONIST CANDIDATE'.

Clearly popular Unionism reflected more than the cunning calculation of party bosses exploiting an appeal to the working class for electoral benefit, and must be analysed at the constituency level to appreciate fully the complexity and variety of interpretations which national policies could adopt when expressed at the grass-roots level. As Patrick Joyce has made clear, '"labourism" was quite compatible with a range of political ideologies and parties, including those that had little to do with class'.[241]

The December election, however, confirmed the persistence of Liberal power in the burgh, with McCallum securing victory with a majority of 2,689.[242] Again, the statement from the Beaconsfield Club president confirmed the importance of tradition: 'he was of opinion that if the majority of the working people had got rid of their *inherited politics*, they would have supported their fellow workman, Mr Jephcott'.[243] Liberalism's message, however, evidently still appeared a pertinent one for the majority of the Paisley electorate in 1910.

It was in the blending of 'New Liberal' concerns with 'Old Liberal' sympathies – most notably the campaign for Scottish Home Rule, the re-emergence of the Land Campaign after John Sinclair's Small Holdings legislation of 1906 and the 1909 Budget – that the crucial determinants of continued Liberal success in Paisley may be found.[244] In this regard, Paisley's experience was very much in line with the general Scottish 'picture'.[245] It was precisely because Scottish Liberalism maintained a

240 *PRG*, 3 Dec. 1910.

241 Joyce, *Visions of the People*, p. 333.

242 See below, Appendix 4.

243 *PRG*, 10 Dec. 1910 [my italics].

244 A Paisley branch of the Scottish Patriotic Association was established in 1908 and Home Rule was a clear focus of McCallum's campaign of December 1910. See *PRG*, 3 Dec. 1910.

245 Nicholls has recently suggested that 'there was never any evolutionary progress from *laissez faire* to state intervention. Both strategies have been present throughout the history of the liberal capitalist state, and the prominence of either at any particular

foot in each century, permitting Old and New Liberalism to 'coexist peacefully in one party', that it was successful in attracting Labourists, New Liberals and reluctant Progressives, thus 'driving the appeal of Labour into retreat' and 'stealing the thunder' of the Unionists.[246] By stressing the collective as well as the individualistic elements of the Liberal heritage, Liberalism thus proved adept at gauging the extent to which tradition could be tested whilst preserving its meaning and electoral potential.[247]

1910–1914: Conflict and Covenant

A recent essay has considered the years from 1910 to 1914 as representing

> a major challenge to the unilateral control which many employers had exercised over their labour force ... a mighty push by labour against what has been called 'the frontier of control' between management and workers ... [an era in which] alternative socialist, industrial unionist and syndicalist ideologies were gaining support.[248]

This partial resurrection of the Dangerfield 'Crisis' theory demands closer investigation in the context of Paisley, where its assumptions regarding the extent and political impact of local strike activity prove unfounded. Surveying the Board of Trade's annual returns of strikes and lock-outs, only one 'principal' dispute is recorded in these years – a strike by Paisley carters in March 1911 in which only 300 workers took a direct role.[249] Even although more detailed research of the local press 'throws up' further examples of strike activity in the Paisley area, there is no evidence that any disputes were initiated or influenced explicitly by syndicalist doctrine, the majority being occasioned by wage demands.

In 1912, however, a strike by the male dyers of the Ferguslie mills over a recent pay award elicited the following response from Coats's directors in the form of a notice posted throughout the mills:

moment has to be understood by reference to the specific historical context.': D. Nicholls, 'The New Liberalism – after Chartism?', *SH*, xxi (1996), p. 341.

246 Hutchison, *Political History of Scotland*, p. 241. Note further that in May 1911 the Paisley Trades Council passed a resolution recording their approval of the National Insurance legislation of the Liberal government: *PDE*, 17 May 1911.

247 The extent to which collectivism was 'alien' to classical Liberal doctrine in the nineteenth century has recently come under discussion. See E. H. H. Green, 'An Age of Transition: an introductory essay', in Green, *Age of Transition*, pp. 3–4; E. F. Biagini, 'Liberalism and direct democracy: John Stuart Mill and the model of ancient Athens', in Biagini, *Citizenship and Community*, pp. 21–44; and M. C. Finn, *After Chartism: Class and Nation in English Radical Politics, 1848–1874* (Cambridge, 1993).

248 Glasgow Labour History Workshop, 'Roots of Red Clydeside: the labour unrest in West Scotland, 1910–1914', in A. J. McIvor and R. Duncan (eds.), *Militant Workers: Labour and Class Conflict on the Clyde, 1900–1950* (Edinburgh, 1992), p. 81.

249 Strikes and Lock-Outs: *Board of Trade Report (1910–13)*: *PP*, 1911, XLI, Cd 58550; 1912–13, XLVII, Cd 6472; 1914, XLVIII, Cd 7089; 1914–16, XXXVI, Cd 7658.

> It is perfectly well known to our workers that in the past no distinction of any kind has been made between those who belong to a Union and those who do not, but when a small number strike at the instigation of a Trade Union Secretary in Bradford, involving the risk of a general stoppage of work, we are compelled in the interests of the business and of our workers to do our best to prevent a recurrence of such a strike, which may deprive many thousands of their means of livelihood over a long period. It has therefore been decided to discontinue employing dyers who belong to this Union, which has brought the men out on strike because we granted an advance to the majority but declined to give it to those doing less skilled work.[250]

The union ban was thus announced in terms which appealed to acknowledged obligations on each party as participants in a deferential relationship. The company framed its case as a defence of the livelihood of the local community, of which it appeared as guarantor, against the infringement of 'outsiders' who had disrupted the harmony of local labour-capital relationships despite the company's defence of skill differentials within the local labour hierarchy.

Whilst the National Society of Dyers and Finishers [NSDF] disputed Coats's interpretation of events and its general secretary, Arthur Shaw, headed north to negotiate with the company, no further industrial action was taken, and a letter from the NSDF secretary to the Trades and Labour Council recorded in August that the company's policies 'were having the effect desired'.[251]

The incident illustrates the continued control Coats managed to exert over industrial relations throughout the period and its maintenance of arbitration structures free from the interference of union delegations. Yet the dyers' incident further highlights the changing nature of Coats's industrial paternalism during these years, when the strength of reciprocity at the heart of the paternal relationship was clearly giving way to greater direct and uncompromising control, stripped of the hegemonic illusion of its legitimacy. Arthur Shaw considered Coats's actions to be 'autocratic', and the local NSDF delegate to the Trades and Labour Council reflected on the 'vindictive spirit of the firm'.[252] Whilst some 'rewards' were given to men who left the union, the 'stick' was far more apparent than the 'carrot'.[253]

Therefore, only in the most qualified sense may the roots of 'Red Clydeside' be traced back to a pre-war state of industrial crisis in the west of Scotland. Containment and control, rather than conflict, marked a Paisley work-force still very much influenced by an ideology of

250 *PRG*, 27 Jul. 1912.
251 TLC, 21 Aug. 1912.
252 Ibid., 19 Jun. 1912; 26 Jun. 1912.
253 Ibid., 21 Aug. 1912.

respectability and pragmatic reformism, framed by the parameters of achievable short-term goals. At a meeting of the Trades and Labour Council of March 1912, dominated by discussion of the coal strike of that year, the president, Robert Russell of the ASE, declared that 'the present dispute gave ample illustration of the growing futility of strikes' and recommended that 'a better and more powerful weapon ... [was] the proper use of the ballot'.[254]

Whilst the Unionist Social Reform Committee (est. 1911) and the developing strands of New Liberalism were establishing the pre-eminence of the 'Social Question' on the national domestic agenda, such concerns in the immediate pre-war years, were ultimately overtaken by the re-emergence of the Irish question and the gathering momentum of Lloyd George's Land Campaign.[255] After a thirty-year incremental process of realignment in party politics, on the eve of war, these issues succeeded in defining in more concrete terms, the differences of the major parties, by re-emphasising the causes of division in 1886 – the land and constitutional claims of Gladstone's proposed Irish legislation. In both these issues the appeal to the past was evident, with the Ulster Covenant drawing direct power from the rhetoric of the seventeenth-century Protestant reformers and the land campaigners, following a long tradition of anti-landlordism. Yet old battles were made to give way to new when in the summer of 1914, war disrupted the radical continuum and heralded the emergence of a new political community.

254 TLC, 27 Mar. 1912.

255 For further information regarding the role of the Unionist Social Reform Committee, see: J. Ridley, 'The Unionist Social Reform Committee: wets before the deluge', *HJ*, xxx (1987), pp. 391–413; Fforde, *Conservatism and Collectivism*, esp. chap. 3.

CHAPTER FIVE

'There are No New Liberals Being Born': Paisley Politics, 1914–1924

The War Years: 1914–1918

In a memo to Asquith of 1921, Robert Cecil reflected on the political consequences of the Great War: 'there is a more or less conscious impression that the war was a proof that there was something wrong in the old political organisation of society'.[1] From a perspective three years after the armistice, Cecil's observation, refined by the gift of hindsight, has a deterministic quality which distorts the war experience by its appeal to an uncomplicated line of reason. Rather, the political consequences of the war were neither as direct nor as immediately perceivable as Cecil would have us believe. Through a close analysis of how war affected the Paisley locality, it becomes clear that the war both clarified and clouded popular perceptions of the state, the social order and local industrial structures.[2] The *meaning* of such discourses as emerged translated only slowly into political change and even then relied to a great extent on a pre-war political vocabulary.

Whilst war-time Cabinet intrigue and parliamentary controversies would later become significant factors in post-mortems on the Liberal corpse, on a local level, political change emerged from a vortex of social, economic and cultural changes which reformed the loci of working-class identity – the home, the work-place and the local community. Bernard Waites has emphasised the effect of war in 'clarifying connections between class position and social privilege and disadvantage', arguing that through war they became 'more transparent'.[3] Yet too great a concentration on the evolution of 'class' masks the variety of the experiences which together created class identity. With this in mind it is first necessary to explore the different experiences of working-class men and women in Paisley during the period from 1914 to 1918.

The wage disputes and records of unofficial strikes which pepper the minute books of Paisley trade unions and engineering employers' archives are testament to the character of war-time struggles within the male-dominated workplace. These restructured the basis of negotiation

1 BLO, MS Asquith II.34, fo. 7, Robert Cecil to H. H. Asquith (Jun.–Aug.) 1921.
2 This view is echoed by Turner in *British Politics and the Great War*, pp. 2, 395.
3 B. Waites, *A Class Society at War: England, 1914–1918* (Leamington Spa, 1987), p. 16.

between employer and employed and destabilised the hierarchy of 'skill' which had determined institutional forms of working-class political expression. Dilution, deskilling and the narrowing of wage differentials between skilled and supervisory, and semi- and unskilled labour intensified pressures already present in the pre-war workplace.

In February 1915, the local branch of the Amalgamated Toolmakers recorded its opposition to the introduction of women workers on shell-turning lathes at Arrol Johnstone's who, by May of that year, were replacing skilled turners at such operations.[4] The following year the TLC voiced concern at the large number of Lancashire women being employed at Babcock & Wilcox, and later that year launched a protest against the employment of reformatory boys from the Kibble Institute at Beardmore's and Campbell & Calderwood's. [5] In May 1916, the United Machine Workers' Association sought legal advice regarding the case of a skilled machinist who had been moved to a lower-paid manual job on the shop-floor at Babcock & Wilcox.[6] Furthermore, just as the skill differential was under threat, so too was the wage differential which confirmed the value of the skilled workers' hierarchy.[7] In 1918, the foremen of Fullerton, Hodgart & Barclay, which, for the duration of the war, manufactured torpedo shell casings as a controlled establishment under the terms of the Munitions of War Act of 1915, appealed to the company's directors that 'they were not satisfied with the bonus they were receiving, their contention being that the men under their charge were earning higher wages than they were receiving as foremen'.[8] Such concern was mirrored the previous year by the directors of A. F. Craig & Co., the local foundry works, who reflected on the need to bring foremen's wages into line, following wage increases for other grades.[9] Such are but a few examples of the concerns which, as the war proceeded, re-formed the parameters of craft control and relations within the work-place.[10] As the context within which the wider themes of industrial militancy took shape, the defensive roots of protest were marked and had profound implications for the way in which future political concerns took shape.

4 GCA, TD1137, Amalgamated Toolmakers (Paisley Branch), Minute Book 1914–1915, 2 Feb. 1915; 25 May 1915.

5 *PDE*, 17 Mar. 1916; TLC 13 Sep. 1916; 7 Feb. 1917.

6 GCA, TD1137/1–6, United Machine Workers Association (Paisley Branch), Minute Book: 1907–1918, 22 May 1916.

7 Rex Pope has estimated that there was a 14% narrowing of the wage differential between skilled and unskilled workers in the engineering industry during the war: R. Pope, *War and Society in Britain, 1899–1948* (Harlow, 1991), p. 24.

8 UGABRC, UGD 120/1/1/6, Fullerton Hodgart & Barclay Collection, Minute Book: 1913–1919, 15 Jul. 1918 (p. 182).

9 UGABRC, UGD 173/1/1, A. F. Craig & Co. Collection, Minute Book: 1895–1921, 3 Dec. 1917 (p. 315).

10 See also Brown, *From Radicalism to Socialism*, pp. 14–15.

That the war-time experience of Paisley's working women was going to differ from that of their male counterparts was evident within weeks of the declaration of war. In October, a TLC survey of local unemployment highlighted the fact that a 'large number of girls were unemployed', and, whilst a survey of affiliated unions in December 1914 uncovered less than 200 unemployed members, the report emphasised that this figure was deceptive, with many more workers on short time, and concluded that 'the depression in trade was being mostly felt by women workers'.[11] Yet conditions were soon to change.

As Scott and Cunnison made clear in 1924, 'one of the chief sources of labour for dilution purposes in the engineering trades' was the cotton industry.[12] In Paisley – an area where the sexual equilibrium of the local labour market was composed upon lines of segregated productive enterprise – the entry of women into the metal trades threatened not just male craft consciousness, but the wider character of the 'unskilled' labour market. From a figure of 3,758 in 1911, the number of women employed in the metal trades in the Clyde district rose to around 18,500 in 1916.[13] For Paisley, this shift had obvious consequences for the thread interest. Attracted by the higher wages being offered in the rapidly expanding munitions factories, Coats attempted to secure their female work-force by offering war bonuses and allowances which were increased at regular intervals.[14] The extent to which such increases proved sufficient to maintain the work-force, however, is unclear. A survey of the full-time female workers taken on in one mill in 1910 indicates that 19.56% left the firm's employ during the war years.[15]

War-time experience of a different industry challenged the determining influence of the Coats combine over the female perspective of work. In Paisley this was dramatically illustrated by the location of the National Filling Factory at Georgetown, near the village of Houston. Operations began here in September 1915 and employed around 15,000 workers, of which an estimated 13,500 were women.[16] The *Express* described it as 'a little world and compact unit in itself', with 'its own Post Office, its shop, its public hall ... its missionary, its nurse, its Masonic Lodge, its book club, its monthly journal, its dramatic society, its choir and orchestra [and] its flower plots and vegetable allotments'.[17] Yet the legacy of 'Georgetown' must be qualified by the acknowledgement that the majority of its workers came from Glasgow, transported

11 *PDE*, 14 Dec. 1914.

12 W. R. Scott and J. Cunnison, *The Industries of the Clyde Valley During the War* (Oxford, 1924), pp. 126–7.

13 Ibid., pp. 96–7.

14 Pope estimates that whereas wages on a whole were 55% above 1914 levels by 1917, in cotton they had only increased by 14%: Pope, *War and Society in Britain*, p. 25. See also *PDE*, 10 Nov. 1916; 8 Nov. 1917.

15 PM, JPC Collection, 1/5/41, Index of Female Employees.

16 *PDE*, 30 Jan. 1918.

17 Ibid., 30 Jan. 1918.

daily to work on twelve specially commissioned trains. This was a mobile population within which the interactive bonds of work-place, locality and community were never formed. Whilst a work-place identity clearly existed, it was contained within the compound and proved transitory, as the existence of the factory was ultimately determined by the pursuit of the war. As such, Coats's dominance within Paisley burgh in its broadest sense, as the originary source of the area's industrial identity, was never seriously threatened.

By far the most serious threat born of the war to the hegemony, so long nurtured by Coats's industrial strength, was the formation of a local branch of the General Textile Workers Union in 1917, the wider unionisation of women and the unskilled in other industries and, most importantly, the politicisation of the 'craft' unions.[18] Yet, in order to be a meaningful challenge to the existent hegemony, both the source *and* the expression of economic power – the work-place *and* the community – had to form dual concerns for the emerging labour ranks. The creation of strong working-class institutions through which alternative industrial visions could be formed is a critical feature of the war years and it is to these we will now turn to explore the manner in which discontent sought expression.

As with the industrial crises of the immediate pre-war years, so industrial unionism and syndicalist impulses have long been considered the ideological roots of the Clyde Workers Committee [CWC] and the trade-union militancy in the Clyde district, following the passage of the Munitions Act of 1915 and the establishment of the Dilution Commission in 1916. Scott and Cunnison drew parallels with the motivations behind Connolly's Socialist Labour Party and the legacy of De Leonite syndicalism, and more recently Knox has emphasised the influence of the International Workers of the World on William Gallacher, chairman of the CWC.[19] Taken as confirmation of the revolutionary potential of the 'Red Clyde' years, the reliance on this supposed ideological legacy has invested the CWC with a philosophical heritage it is ill-equipped to sustain, and has spawned academic debates which misguidedly judge the revolutionary potential of the shop-stewards' movement against inappropriate international criteria and the absolutes of class war rhetoric. The experience of the Paisley TLC during the war years, however, alerts us to a further philosophical influence of these years – guild socialism – which successfully recasts the moderates of the movement – those who were ultimately to shape the

[18] Ibid., 6 Oct. 1917; TLC, 21 Jun. 1916: Here it is noted that 90% of the women employed at Fairfield's had joined the Workers' Union. This mirrors a national trend which saw the WU's female membership increase from 4,000 in 1914 to 80,000 in 1918: Pope, *War and Society in Britain*, p. 23.

[19] Scott and Cunnison, *Industries of the Clyde Valley*, p. 139; W. W. Knox, *Scottish Labour Leaders, 1918–1939: A Biographical Dictionary* (Edinburgh, 1984), p. 114.

labour politics of the west of Scotland – as the radical reformers they were, rather than the revolutionaries they never posed to be.

In December 1916, John Paton, an ASE member from Cardonald, resigned as secretary of the Paisley TLC. Then, as editor and leader of the active Glasgow branch of the National Guilds League [NGL] – composed largely of moderate shop stewards – he began publication of the *Guildsman*, which later, as the *Guild Socialist*, became the official organ of the NGL.[20] Paton's influence on the Paisley TLC was profound. In May 1917, he addressed the council on 'Trade Unionism and Idealism', and two months later the council voted by twenty votes to three to become affiliated to the NGL.[21]

Whilst, like many of their fellow Glasgow unionists, the Paisley Labour movement showed almost unqualified support for the shop-stewards' movement – petitioning for the release of the deportees, sending money to the Clyde Workers Fund, holding receptions for Gallacher on his release from prison in February 1917 and welcoming his return to the TLC as the BSP delegate in June – the influence of the NGL on the Paisley movement seems to require explanation. Further consideration, however, reveals a 'logic' in the commitment to league philosophy which at once clarifies the position of industrial unionism as part of the continuum of labour development rather than an awkward dividing line between pre-war labourism and post-war socialism, and undermines the contention that the ideals of 'industrial democracy' threw the ILP into 'ideological confusion' and pragmatic, opportunistic compromises with the shop-stewards' leadership.[22]

Aside from the *Worker*, one of the few ideological 'blue-prints' of the wider aims of the shop-steward's movement to emerge from the war years was a pamphlet entitled *Towards Industrial Democracy: A Memorandum on Workshop Control,* jointly composed by John Paton and William Gallacher and published by the Paisley TLC. The pamphlet outlines the steps leading to the workers' control of industry, but while syndicalist rhetoric is apparent, the concerns of guild socialism are also to the fore. Scott and Cunnison remarked on the CWC's rejection of syndicalism's 'intuitionalism', the belief in 'the inspiration of the moment' as the guide to revolutionary strategy, and the Clydesiders' qualified belief in the general strike only as a means to a greater end.[23] Paton and Gallacher's pamphlet is testament to such scepticism and to guild socialism's influence on the movement towards industrial democracy. As such, it highlights the paradoxes of Paisley's role in the 'Red Clyde' story

20 TLC, 20 Dec. 1916; S. T. Glass, *The Responsible Society: The Ideas of the English Guild Socialists* (Reading, 1983), pp. 39, 51.

21 TLC, 4 Jul. 1917.

22 See McKinlay, 'Doubtful wisdom and uncertain promise', pp. 129–30.

23 Scott and Cunnison, *Industries of the Clyde Valley*, p. 150.

whilst suggesting a solution – as yet untested – to the problematics which the war years pose to the history of the radical continuum in Scotland.

Guildsmen 'visualised a peaceful and gradual transfer of power from the employers to the unions by a method of "encroaching control"'.[24] The influence of this gradualism is evident in *Towards Industrial Democracy*, where the organisation of 'a system of Workshop Committees' is emphasised, its structure encompassing workshop, departmental and district committees and resting on the 'solidarity' of the workers, rather than the destructive power of the general strike which is never mentioned. The emphasis on production as the key to power corresponds to critical influences on the NGL: the producers' co-operative movement and Owenite philosophy. Moreover, the moral denunciation of 'wage slavery' in the pamphlet's opening paragraphs highlights the influence of the guild's position on the functional status the worker had acquired since the imposition of large-scale industrialisation had undermined his control over production – echoes of Carlyle and Ruskin.[25]

In terms of Paisley's experience, guild socialism paradoxically proved the bridge between the industrial unionism of the war years and moves towards parliamentary representation. Whilst many authors have referred to the coalescence of industrial and political concerns during the war, few – beyond pointing vaguely to the community as the locus of operations – have 'unpacked' how this could have worked in ideological and practical terms. Guild socialism's identification of machine production as the root cause of social malaise through its replacement of craftsmanship with 'mechanical drudgery [providing] no scope to the imagination and individuality of the worker', proved critical in the adoption of industrial unionism by the 'orthodox' unions in Paisley.[26] In contrast with Glasgow's experience, established skilled unions could absorb the workshop philosophy without fearing a dislocation in the skill hierarchy. Guild socialism, furthermore, proposed to work through the unions themselves. Whilst a local Shop Stewards' Committee was established in Paisley in 1917, a branch of the Socialist Labour Party was not established until October 1918, and the TLC – explicitly committed to industrial unionism from April 1917 at the latest – remained the dominant influence in the trade-union movement throughout the war years.

Guild philosophy, whilst establishing a useful language of compromise, re-formed modern debates in the familiar guise of radical concerns rather than the 'socialist' dialectic. The concerns of the industrial history classes established under joint TLC/ILP auspices in 1917 resonated with the league's preoccupation with the history and

24 Glass, *Responsible Society*, p. 5.
25 Ibid., pp. 6–7.
26 Ibid., p. 18.

worth of craftsmanship as the key to understanding man's economic enslavement and achieved additional power as a reaffirmation of the value and relevance of Paisley's own tradition of independent craftsmanship. Yet it was the league's theory of class collaboration – *all* men were workers – which most explicitly compromised the emergent confrontationist socialist message being drawn from the experience of war, and reasserted a politics of 'community' and 'self improvement' which would be exploited by the local Liberals in the early 1920s. According to the league, 'socialism, properly understood, was in the interests of *all* classes'.[27]

A brief survey of local trade-union records confirms that industrial unionism and electoral labour politics were seen as neither mutually exclusive nor antagonistic concerns in Paisley, and indeed that they grew together, mutually reinforcing a new awareness of the economic roots of power.[28] As we shall see later, compromise and a growing unity among the political and industrial 'arms' of labour, rather than the ideological dislocation of the left, proved to be the dominant features of the 'Red Clyde' years. Philosophical incompatibility would only translate into organisational fragmentation in the 1920s.[29]

Beyond the factory gates, the community proved to be the immediate locus of protest where the wider philosophical concerns of the workshops gave way to the pragmatic politics of survival. In this regard the role of women was critical yet ambiguous. In Paisley, working-class women entered the labour cause along one major route – the War Emergency Committee – co-operating only in the most qualified sense in the housing agitation and rent strikes more commonly associated with the war-time protests of women in the Clyde district.

Having protested against the lack of working-class representation on the local Citizens Committee, in September 1914 the TLC called a meeting of local trade unions, Co-operative societies and friendly societies from which emerged the War Emergency Committee [WEC]. The committee was established as an advisory facility through which necessitous families would be directed to appropriate funds and authorities for financial assistance during the war, yet the committee's team of fourteen 'Lady Visitors' soon uncovered cases for which practical assistance was necessary. Through its ward committee structure and ladies committee, the WEC established a fund and in 1916 registered itself under the War Charities Act. Contributions came from all the major public works in the area (excluding the thread mills) and

27 Ibid., p. 27 [my italics].

28 Holford's work on Edinburgh suggests that shared membership of both quasi-syndicalist and political movements ensured that the labour movement 'did not split clearly between these two definitions ... [Rather] developments and possibilities were perceived simultaneously in terms of both understandings of "politics"': Holford, *Reshaping Labour*, pp. 161–2.

29 See Holford for the parallel experience in Edinburgh: ibid., p. 205.

fund-raising events contributed to a total income during the war years of £5,232 17s. 8½d. By the close of its operations in 1919, the ladies of the WEC had visited 8,648 cases and out of 1,948 applications for financial assistance, 1,762 had been settled, the total given out in cash grants amounting to over £4,000, with an £1,000 being expended on foodstuffs and clothing.[30]

Whilst the key leadership positions were occupied by men – mainly prominent trade unionists and Co-operative representatives – most of the 'hands on' activity was co-ordinated by the women members, the majority of whom were members of the Co-operative Women's Guilds of the town. The official history of the WEC concludes: 'To those ladies who worked so hard and faithfully during the whole 4½ years we owe a debt we can never repay.'[31]

Through the WEC, the Paisley Labour movement asserted its identity as an effective and active force in the community at large. However, unlike the Preston Labour Party, which exploited its 'record of efficient war administration' in its post-war municipal campaigns, the political impact of the Paisley WEC lay largely in its symbolic quality as a practical expression of labour unity.[32]

The 'rent question' was taken up by the TLC in October 1915, following letters in the local press expressing disgust at 10–20% increases in the rents demanded by local landlords.[33] Encouraged by the support of local engineering unions and a group of activists employed on war work at Fullerton, Hodgart & Barclay's, a 'crowded' protest meeting was held at which a resolution was passed calling on the government 'to take the necessary action to prevent property owners increasing rents and taking undue advantage of war conditions' and promising to 'take strong and energetic steps to combat the ... unwarrantable and unjustifiable action of the landlords and property owners of Paisley'.[34] Less than a week later, a demonstration was held in the town hall which, with the presence of Mrs Barbour, convenor of the Govan branch of the Glasgow Women's Housing Association, and Councillors Kerr and Patrick Dollan of Glasgow, seemed to confirm Paisley's place as part of a unified Clydeside movement.[35] Yet, the role of women in the Paisley rent agitation illustrates an important difference in the Paisley movement. Whilst at the town hall meeting, Mrs Barbour declared that 'this rent

30 E. W. Davis and A. Flockhart, *Paisley War Emergency Committee, 1914–1919: Its History, Objects and Achievements* (Paisley, 1920), p. 4.

31 Dowis and Flockhart, *Paisley War Emergency Committee*, p. 5.

32 Savage, *Dynamics of Working-Class Politics*, p. 164.

33 *PDE*, 5 Oct. 1915; 14 Oct. 1915. Note: in terms of the level of rent rises, the Paisley figures are comparable to those of Govan and Fairfield – the centre of the rent strike movement in Glasgow – where rent rises in 1914–15 were found to range between 11.67% and 23.08%: McLean, *Legend of Red Clydeside*, pp. 21–2.

34 The resolution was largely a copy of that passed by the workers at Fullerton, Hodgart & Barclay. See *PDE*, 16 Oct. 1915; 18 Oct. 1915.

35 *PDE*, 22 Oct. 1915.

question was a woman's fight, and by women it was going to be won', there is little evidence to prove that in Paisley, women showed the activism of their Glasgow 'sisters'.[36] At the beginning of November, a meeting was held to organise the Paisley women in a manner comparable to that of the rent strike committees of Glasgow, Partick and Govan; yet, despite the presence of Mrs Barbour and Helen Crawfurd, little enthusiasm seems to have been engendered.[37] Throughout the winter of 1915 it was the male-dominated TLC, the Tenants' Protection Association and the unions which dominated the rent strike movement – a movement which, by December 1915, had failed to encourage a greater awareness of the broader housing issues associated with the rent question.[38]

In this manner, the rent strike movement in Paisley is more meaningful as an illustrative example of the growing politicisation of the unions than the epitome of female-led Labour community politics. The absence of a unifying 'women's question' during the war in Paisley, it may be suggested, left an ambiguous legacy for Labour which would prove influential in the immediate post-war elections when the women's vote proved a key concern of the major parties.

In general terms, however, growth, unity and successful propaganda were the key characteristics of Labour's war-time experience in Paisley. Energised by the vitality of workshop politics, the socialist associations attracted support and acceptance to an extent never realised in the pre-war climate. Christopher Harvie's identification of 1917 and 1918 as the key years of ILP expansion in Scotland during the war seems to be mirrored in Paisley, where organisers reported 'record' collections at meetings at this time and reported on 'more new members still coming in'.[39] Yet beyond mere numerical support there was a clear qualitative shift in the character of, and relationships within, the socialist ranks during the war years.

In July 1914 William Gallacher and John Campbell re-entered the TLC as BSP delegates, and four months later Gallacher addressed an ILP meeting:

> For many years it had to be admitted the effectiveness of the Socialist and Labour movements had been sadly impaired by internal dissensions and unnecessary criticisms of one another. There were signs, however, and they had hopes, that when this European War was over a new and more powerful working class movement would be prepared to carry on the never-ending war of the workers for justice.[40]

36 Ibid., 22 Oct. 1915.
37 Ibid., 3 Nov. 1915.
38 Ibid., 24 Dec. 1915.
39 Harvie, 'Before the breakthrough', p. 24; *Forward*, 3 Mar. 1917; 15 Dec. 1917. See also Holford, *Reshaping Labour*, p. 159.
40 *PDE*, 17 Nov. 1914.

In the winter months of 1917, and again in 1918, propaganda meetings were held on a regular basis under joint ILP/BSP auspices, attracting large crowds, and ILP and BSP members shared platforms at the Paisley May Day procession in 1918. The speeches focused on the dilemmas thrown up by the war and the challenge of reconstruction: they provided the only political commentary on the international crisis on Paisley platforms, the Liberal and Unionist Associations having abandoned political organisation on the outbreak of war. Yet such unity, whilst a fitting compliment to the welfare and housing struggles in the community, was illusory, being determined by the pressures of war, and eventually fragmented under post-war conditions and the re-establishment of old political infrastructures.[41]

The lasting legacy of this ephemeral war-time unity which proved the greatest influence on the direction of Paisley's post-war Labour community, however, was the politicisation of the Co-operative movement and its entry into parliamentary politics as the Co-operative party.

As Kinloch and Butt have made clear, the war 'gave the co-operative movement a chance to reaffirm its role as a consumer democracy'.[42] In Scotland membership of the Scottish Co-operative Wholesale Society rose from 467,270 in 1914 to 590,710 in 1918, and by 1921 Co-operative membership encompassed 13.6% of the Scottish population, in comparison with 9.5% in the UK as a whole.[43] As a formidable consumer force, the Co-operative movement's entry into politics in 1918, following the famous Swansea Congress of the previous year, has been a source of controversy ever since – the crux of much debate resting on the relative importance of the war-time experience as a motivational determinant behind political action. Pollard has argued that 'there was a long and logical tradition of political involvement and a steady and natural growth of the demand for direct representation of the Co-operative movement as a working-class organisation',[44] and considers the creation of the Co-operative party as part of the general move towards Labour and the left during the war years. However, Tony Adams has argued instead that:

> Pollard exaggerates the growth of the pre-war support for Labour amongst co-operators in an attempt to create a picture of steady evolution towards the modern perception of an integrated labour movement composed of trade unions, the Labour party and the co-operative movement.[45]

41 McKinlay, 'Doubtful wisdom and uncertain promise', pp. 130–1.

42 J. Kinloch and J. Butt, *History of the Scottish Co-operative Wholesale Society Ltd* (Glasgow, 1981), p. 269.

43 Ibid., p. 269.; I. A. Himeimy, 'The Development and Organisation of the Scottish Co-operative Movement' (Edinburgh University, Ph.D. thesis, 1955), pp. 33–4.

44 Pollard, 'Foundation of the Co-operative Party', p. 189.

45 T. Adams, 'The formation of the Co-operative Party re-considered', *IRSH*, xxxi (1987), p. 48.

Adams reasserts the importance of the practical experiences of Co-operators during the war:

> The war repeatedly brought co-operation into direct conflict with a State drawn into increasing levels of economic intervention, a State, moreover, heavily influenced in its decision making by private traders and business men.[46]

The exclusion of co-operators from the Ministry of Food's local committees, the application of Excess Profits Duty on the societies' trading surpluses, food shortages, local rationing and the government's apparent disregard for Co-operative grievances and lobbying are highlighted by Adams as critical determinants behind the Co-operative movement's political involvement.[47] 'There appears', he concludes, 'to be a clear short-term rationale to co-operative political activity without reference to "ideological conversion".'[48] Adams goes on to reinforce his argument by emphasising the fact that the key period of growth for political co-operation came after 1917 when shortages were most acute, and he includes the disarray of the Liberal ranks in government and a growth in support for the co-operative left as additional influences on the Co-operative movement's entry into politics.[49]

In the light of Paisley's experience, Adams's analysis proves the most convincing. Repeated references to the Co-operators' reluctance to take the political road emphasises that, rather than a conversion to socialism, the Co-operative Party represented for many 'a simple extension of ... pressure group politics'.[50] As we have seen in previous chapters, Co-operative involvement in labour politics had always been qualified by the movement's ultimate commitment to its business role, and the Paisley societies embraced a membership of quite diverse political affiliations. This did not change after 1918, and the local Co-operative party branch maintained a passionate stance in defence of its independence from Labour domination throughout the early 1920s.

46 Ibid., p. 55. Elements of this perspective are shared by Paddy Maguire who emphasises the narrow interests of the Co-operative movement in entering politics and the importance of the war-time experience in encouraging moves to independent party status: P. Maguire, 'Co-operation and crisis: government, co-operation, and politics, 1917–1922', in S. Yeo (ed.), *New Views of Co-operation* (London, 1988), pp. 187–206. In this same volume, however, Neil Killingback stresses that whilst the war encouraged a certain rationale for Co-operative entry into politics, the 1920s and '30s provided ample challenges to Co-operation which ensured its continued political involvement: N. Killingback, 'Limits to mutuality: economic and political attacks on co-operation during the 1920s and 1930s', pp. 207–28.

47 Adams, 'Formation of the Co-operative Party reconsidered', pp. 54–6.

48 Ibid., p. 57.

49 Carberry and Cole also point to Liberal disunity as an important factor behind Co-operative political involvement. See Carberry, 'Examination and Evaluation of the Co-operative Party', p. 36; and Cole, *Century of Co-operation*, pp. 316–17.

50 B. Smith and G. Ostergaard, *Constitutional Relations Between the Labour and Co-operative Parties: An Historical Review* (London, 1960), p. 4.

The character and timing of the Paisley Co-operators' entry into politics confirms Adams's contention that government food and taxation policies were critical to Co-operative politics. Having refused to affiliate to the TLC in 1916 on the basis that it was connected to the Labour Party, the Paisley Co-operative Societies, following the lead of the newly established Scottish Co-operative and Labour Council, appealed to the TLC in November 1917 to participate in a protest demonstration against the composition of the local Food Control Committee, established that August and dominated by local shopkeepers, among them William Galbraith.[51] Later that month, the TLC refused to send members to the Town Council's new Food Economy Committee, judging it a 'useless' endeavour which ignored the fact that the real problems were 'scarcity and costliness'.[52] The next month a committee was formed by the TLC to organise propaganda for a food protest demonstration to be held in co-operation with the Co-operative societies and the socialist parties, and in January 1918 a joint Food Vigilance Committee was established with representatives from the TLC, the ILP, the BSP, the Co-operative Women's Guilds and the Co-operative societies.[53]

It is within this context of pragmatic, practical protest against local manifestations of alleged government mismanagement that the closer alliance of the Paisley Co-operative societies and the TLC – the major arm of the Labour body politic – should be considered. Moreover, the anti-profiteering rhetoric which marked the war years also gave added short-term momentum to this new political grouping which could appeal to the electorate as consumers as well as producers.[54] Only when viewed in this manner does the discord of later years become readily explicable and the ambiguous role of the Co-operative party in Labour's rise to power assert its true significance. For the entire Labour movement, the war asserted its own strange logic, and trends and new partnerships established in the years of crisis frequently produced contradictory influences following the dawn of peace.

That the entente with the Co-operative societies would prove a mixed blessing for the Paisley Labour party was evident from the beginning. In 1916, the TLC had first hand experience of Co-operative intransigence when, following years of conflict between the Amalgamated Union of Co-operative Employees and the Shop Assistants' union, it voted by an overwhelming twenty votes to four in favour of the Co-operative Employees' expulsion from the Council – a decision which reaffirmed the STUC's expulsion order earlier that year. Yet throughout the discussions on parliamentary representation held in the winter of 1917,

51 Scottish Co-operative and Labour Council was established in October 1917: see Hutchison, *Political History of Scotland*, pp. 288–9; TLC, 9 Aug. 1916; *PDE*, 9 Nov. 1917.

52 *PDE*, 30 Nov. 1917.

53 TLC, 12 Dec. 1917; 26 Dec. 1917; 16 Jan. 1918.

54 See Holford, *Reshaping Labour*, pp. 103–4, 107.

Co-operative involvement seemed to signal a new era of Labour unity and vitality in Paisley. At a meeting held in November which included representatives of the ILP, BSP, TLC, and the Provident and Equitable Co-operative Societies, it was agreed by fifty votes to two that a Labour candidate would contest the next parliamentary election in Paisley.[55] The following month, a further meeting, this time including representatives of the Paisley Co-operative Women's Guilds, voted more specifically in favour of a 'Labour and Co-operative Candidate'.[56]

Such unanimity, however, was soon shattered when at a meeting of the TLC in March 1918, addressed by Ben Shaw, the secretary of the Scottish Co-operative and Labour Council, it was announced that 'the National Labour Party would not officially recognise a candidate put forward by the co-operators unless their organisation became affiliated to the Labour Party'.[57] At a conference convened by the TLC in April a resolution was passed with only one dissentient voice to the effect that Paisley – despite the Co-operative Defence Committee's proposed candidature of William Gallacher of the SCWS – should be contested by 'a Labour candidate ... under the constitution of the National Labour party' and selected by the Executive Committee of the TLC.[58] In July, John Neil addressed a meeting of trade unionists as Paisley's prospective Labour candidate.[59]

A month later David Wilson, secretary of the local Co-operative Defence Committee [CDC] or Co-operative party, wrote to the local press detailing the intransigent attitude of the TLC, warning that 'unity is not to be had if the only thing the Labour party locally has to say to the Co-operators is "Clear Out"'.[60] Only days later, John Neil withdrew, and, following discussion with the CDC, the TLC endorsed the new Co-operative nominee, John M. Biggar, as Paisley's Labour candidate.[61]

Thus war, whilst a factor tending towards the realisation of a shared body of interests among working-class groups, also encouraged the creation of partnerships which neither followed 'naturally' from the pre-war party structure nor inevitably proved readily adaptable to the post-war world. Furthermore, just as the impact of war did not always

55 *PDE*, 23 Nov. 1917.

56 Ibid., 21 Dec. 1917.

57 Ibid., 2 Mar. 1918.

58 Ibid., 9 Apr. 1918.

59 Ibid., 22 Jul. 1918. John Neil's candidature seems to have originated with the local branch of the ILP and was endorsed by the Parliamentary Committee of the Scottish Divisional Council of the party in May 1918 at the latest and appears as a nomination 'sanctioned or pending' in a confidential memo of the ILP National Advisory Council: LSE, ILP Archive, ILP 3/10, NAC Minutes, fo. 15, Report from Head Office (Francis Johnson), 23 May 1918 (p. 26); fo. 41, Private and Confidential Memo.

60 *PDE*, 6 Aug. 1918.

61 Ibid., 9 Aug. 1918; 4 Oct. 1918. Biggar had already secured the endorsement of the local ILP: *PDE*, 13 Sep. 1918.

operate in Labour's favour in the 1920s, neither did it determine the end of the Liberal world view.

1918: The 'Coupon' Election

At five minutes past eleven on the eleventh of November 1918, Paisley's High Church bell rang out, confirming the declaration of the armistice. The *Gazette* reported:

> There was a speedy 'demobilisation' of the workers, and the centre of the town – the Cross especially – soon became thronged with crowds ... The children and the mill girls were, perhaps, the most demonstrative section of the population. Released early in the day from school, the children paraded the streets in bands, cheering and waving flags, and the apprentices were also in very exuberant spirits. The inevitable happened at the Cross, when the embryo journeymen set fire to the Kaiser's effigy, and there was the smell of burning all afternoon in this neighbourhood.[62]

The scene recalls the jubilation of the Boer War celebrations of 1900, and just as ambiguity surrounded the status of the Liberal candidate and the probability of a Unionist challenge during the khaki election of that year, so too in the 'Coupon' election of 1918, the 'identity' of the Liberal candidate proved critical in determining the character of the campaign.

At a meeting of the Liberal Association on 20 November, Sir John McCallum announced to the audience that he was 'going to vote as a Liberal for the Coalition Government – (Applause.) – should [they] put [him] in by a majority; in all probability voting nine times out of ten with the party in power'.[63] Noting, however, that many local Liberals had approached him to stand as a Coalition candidate, he appealed for 'a couple of days to think over the matter'.[64] During the ensuing week, meetings between local Liberal and Unionist office bearers produced no solution. Whilst at a campaign meeting on the 27th, McCallum was adopted 'as Coalition candidate for the burgh', two days later local Unionists adopted John Taylor, a journeyman furniture-maker from Glasgow, as the official Coalition candidate, his status having earlier been confirmed by his receipt of the 'Coupon'.[65]

Taylor arrived in Paisley as one of twenty-eight candidates nominated by the National Democratic Party [NDP] which had emerged from the British Workers' League in June, styled as *the* patriotic working-class

62 *PRG*, 16 Nov. 1918.
63 *PDE*, 21 Nov. 1918.
64 *PRG*, 23 Nov. 1918.
65 *PDE*, 27 Nov. 1918; 28 Nov. 1918; *PRG*, 30 Nov. 1918. See also *British Citizen and Empire Worker*, 7 Dec. 1918: Here it is stated that Taylor had been the Scottish editor of *Furniture Record* for seven years and as art critic of *The Studio* had lectured widely in Scotland on 'Art and War'.

coalition party.[66] In Paisley, McCallum had been 'black-listed' following the Maurice debate and Younger, having refused to allocate him a 'Coupon', compromised on Taylor, as the Coalition had promised twenty 'Coupons' to the NDP.[67] Thus, two 'Coalition' candidates entered the race, one claiming to be the 'genuine' Coalition candidate, the other holding the official 'ticket'. Questions of 'identity' would dominate the campaign thereafter.

At each public meeting, McCallum, focusing on his war-time record, appealed to the electorate as the true representative of the principles for which the Coalition stood and on 12 December cast Taylor in the role of the impostor: '... trebly labelled ... his coat was of many colours. His voice was the voice of Jacob, but the hands were the hands of Esau.'[68] Rather, McCallum considered his candidature more in accordance with the official line of the Coalition, referring in the same speech to Bonar Law's words in Glasgow on 25 November, when he had said 'it was unfair to ask a pledge from candidates to support measures still to be framed'. McCallum continued: 'Yet Mr Taylor was prepared blindly to support measures which have not seen the light of day, and thus do more than even his leader asked.'[69] For Taylor's part, he repeatedly referred to McCallum's claims of Coalition status as 'bogus' and maintained that McCallum 'would go back to parliament as an Asquith Liberal', thus undermining the power of the Coalition.[70]

Party identities as well as the character and size of the electorate had been re-formed by the experience of war-time politics, and in the 1918 election each party endeavoured to re-define that unity of purpose articulated through the war effort in the context of peace. In doing so they made the first hesitant and tentative steps towards differentiation. As in 1900, the recent war would dominate the 1918 election, bereft of any other determining issue. Yet, reflections on the recent conflict and the prospect of reconstruction, which on first glance appear mere words of patriotism or revenge, clearly had domestic implications in terms of how the candidates viewed the future of the Coalition and the character of the new nation state. All three candidates appealed for the unity of the nation as the 'British race' the 'community' or the 'workers'. The election thus represented a choice between three 'visions of the people'.

The women's vote, the 'Irish vote' and the working-class vote proved the dominant concerns of election commentators and the candidates themselves – the first posing as an unknown, the second as a familiar

66 R. Douglas, 'The National Democratic Party and the British Workers' League', *HJ*, xv (1972), pp. 539–40.

67 Ibid., p. 541. Turner has emphasised that 'the forces of the NDP were concentrated in areas where Labour expansion was feared': Turner, *British Politics and the Great War*, p. 411.

68 *PDE*, 13 Dec. 1918.

69 Ibid., 13 Dec. 1918.

70 Ibid., 11 Dec. 1918.

concern recast in an unknown light following the events of 1916 and the third, the ultimate electoral prize.

In December, the 'Easy Chair' columnist of the *Gazette* declared that the 'candidates are particularly solicitous regarding the women's vote at this election, for it is the great unknown quantity in more ways than one'.[71] Under the Representation of the People Act, the Paisley electorate for parliamentary purposes had grown from 13,587 (in 1914–15) to 38,507 of which, it was estimated, 16,000 were new women voters.[72] Each candidate held special meetings for women, and whilst only Biggar declared openly in favour of granting the suffrage to women on the same terms as men, both McCallum and Taylor stressed their long commitment to the women's franchise. The focus of all three campaigns was 'women in the home' – women as mothers, women as consumers, women as war widows or dependants of battle-scarred campaigners, women as moral guides. All three committed themselves to the raising of the school leaving age to fifteen years as a means of ensuring the health and well-being of the children of the country, promised increased allowances for war widows, declared their support for the Temperance (Scotland) Act and voiced sympathy regarding food shortages. There was little in this regard, therefore, to choose between Paisley's three 'suitors'. Undifferentiated and vague, the sympathetic protestations of the candidates of 1918 alone could not, in and of themselves, have swayed many women to either change their vote or harden their resolve against the other candidates' policies on other matters. In addition, the ambiguous legacy of the war years had failed to isolate a uniquely 'female' issue or movement in Paisley upon which the candidates could be judged. The amorphous 'women's vote' thus proves useless as a meaningful analytic tool in 1918. It is necessary therefore, to consider further determinants on the electorate's actions.

On 8 December, the standing committee of the local Justin McCarthy branch of the UIL recommended that the Irish in the town should vote for Sir John McCallum, and confident estimates gave McCallum, one of only fifteen Liberal candidates endorsed by the UIL in Scotland, 90% of the Irish vote. However, after the meeting broke up, a group of twenty 'dissidents' calling themselves 'the Irish Catholics of Paisley' gathered outside the committee rooms, stating confidently 'that the bulk of the Irish vote would go to Mr Biggar'.[73] Letters in the local press alleged the local UIL branch to be no longer representative of the majority of the Irish electors, yet the UIL maintained its support for McCallum. J. O'D. Derrick, UIL organiser for Scotland, emphasised that 'every vote for Biggar is a wasted one ... Sir John McCallum voted for self-government for Ireland ... and he has an unblemished character so far

71 *PRG*, 14 Dec. 1918.
72 Ibid., 12 Oct. 1918.
73 *PDE*, 11 Dec. 1918.

as extending to Ireland the right to manage her own affairs is concerned'.[74] Sir John's refusal to agree to conscription in Ireland and his defence of the Nationalists' war record may well have secured him a sizeable proportion of the Irish vote, yet it is clear that the Irish electorate could no longer be relied upon *en bloc* by the Liberals. In this regard, Paisley follows a national trend identified by Gordon Brown, who states that in 1918 the UIL 'list' proved ineffective 'not least because there was dissatisfaction locally at the award of the Irish coupon'.[75] In light of the recent Education (Scotland) Act which had increased the profile of Catholic education as a political issue in Scotland, McCallum's opposition to the establishment of a Catholic university in Ireland and Biggar's proven record as a defender of Catholic educational interests as a School Board representative in Glasgow, may have proved a deciding factor in attracting votes to Labour. This was clearly a potentially significant factor at a time when the Irish Catholic electorate increasingly viewed their exclusive politics in terms of their religious rather than their nationalist identity.[76] As a community divided, therefore, the Irish electorate of Paisley, like the 'women's vote', fails to produce a convincing explanation for the ultimate election result, but rather highlights, in disunity, one important determinant of Liberalism's slim majority.[77]

Whilst we must beware not to ask questions of electoral data which they are ill-equipped to answer, the 'even' split at the polls suggests that in the minds of the electorate the political geography of the immediate post-war environment was far from clear. On the questions of housing, socialism and protective tariffs, the 'working-class' vote was divided against itself.[78] At the beginning of the campaign, a vote of censure was moved against Biggar, as a house factor, by the secretary of the Tenants' Protective Association, proving that Labour would not be able to harness in its entirety the enthusiasm for the housing question engendered by the war. Meanwhile, McCallum voiced support for the extension of the Rent Restriction Act for another year and Taylor, for another two. The 'Red Menace' and the 'Bolshevik threat' loomed large in the rhetoric of the campaign, McCallum and Taylor both calling on speakers with first-hand experience of Soviet Russia to call into question the desirability of

74 Ibid., 14 Dec. 1918.

75 Brown, 'Labour Party and Political Change in Scotland', p. 99.

76 Note the following from the *Glasgow Observer and Catholic Herald*, 7 Dec. 1918: 'Mr J. M. Biggar, the Co-operative candidate for the Paisley constituency is a member of the Glasgow School Board. Mr Biggar was a strong supporter of free books for necessitous Catholic children, but the motion was turned down by the solid phalanx of Presbyterian divines.'

77 See below, Appendix 4.

78 Turner has emphasised that this was a national phenomenon. He writes: 'It is ... much more satisfactory, despite the rhetoric of class used so freely by politicians of all shades during the Coupon election, to look to a different and more fragmented model of electoral change': Turner, *British Politics and the Great War*, p. 435.

the socialist utopia. Whilst Biggar declared himself a socialist whose belief was based on 'Christian ethics ... [and] constitutional methods', it is clear that many working-class voters – including many Co-operators – believed Biggar, a long-standing ILPer, to be hiding more sinister intentions underneath the cloak of Co-operation.[79] After the poll, Labour councillor John Elliot estimated that, of the 13,000 Co-operators in Paisley, a majority had voted for McCallum.[80] The fear of post-war unemployment drove others to support Taylor's protectionist proposals which were supplemented by demands for a six-hour day, 'higher wages, 'Imperial Preference', the protection of vulnerable industries, anti-dumping laws and minimum wage legislation. Furthermore, his connection with the British Worker's League [BWL] attracted many trade unionists who had been appalled by the ILP's pacifism and supported the BWL's defence of extensive state control of industry and an interventionist social policy.[81]

Nationally, the election results amplify this picture of politics in a state of transition. The 1918 poll returned only 36 'Wee Free' or Asquithian Liberals – the party of government in 1914 – and fewer than twenty of these defeated a Coalition opponent.[82] The Asquithian Liberals secured only 13% of the popular vote nationally, compared to the Labour/Co-operative vote of 21.4%, and with only 5% of the vote in Glasgow, had proved incapable of holding on to the industrial constituencies of the previously reliable Celtic fringe.[83] The Coalition Conservatives, having secured 332 seats, became the dominant party in the Commons, whilst the Lloyd George Liberals, securing 127 seats, in the following years were increasingly placed in an untenable position as Coalition partners.[84]

Ultimately, the 1918 election in Paisley reflects less a declaration of support for independent Liberalism and the bucking of the national trend than an expression of confusion on the part of an electorate emerging from the abnormality of war into the as yet unclear conditions of peace.[85]

79 *PDE*, 7 Dec. 1918.
80 *PRG*, 4 Jan. 1919.
81 John Stubbs has highlighted that during the war Conservatives had been 'enthusiasts for the increased activity of the state': J. Stubbs, 'The impact of the Great War on the Conservative Party', in G. Peele and C. Cook (eds.) *The Politics of Reappraisal, 1918–1939* (London, 1975), p. 34. Also, Jarvis's latest study, 'British Conservatism and Class Politics', has shown how, in the inter-war years, the Conservatives appreciated the diversity of views and interests contained in the monolithic 'working-class vote' (pp. 59–84).
82 C. Cook, *A Short History of the Liberal Party* (London, 1976), pp. 74, 76.
83 C. Cook, *The Age of Alignment: Electoral Politics in Britain, 1922–1929* (London, 1975), p. 5; Brown, 'Labour Party and Political Change in Scotland', p. 96.
84 Cook, *Age of Alignment*, p. 5.
85 See Turner, *British Politics and the Great War*, p. 426.

1920: Liberalism's 'Indian Summer'

On 10 January 1920, the death of Sir John McCallum heralded the first contest in an independent Liberal seat since the general election of 1918. Since the rout of the Asquithians in the 'Coupon' election of that year, initial Liberal by-election successes in Leyton West, Hull Central and Central Aberdeenshire & Kincardine had proved a false dawn when, after May 1919, it had become clear that 'the initiative in the constituencies had passed from the Liberals to Labour'.[86] In the interim, whilst Sir Donald McLean reluctantly led the Liberal 'rump' in the Commons (Asquith having lost his East Fife seat in 1918), elements of the political confusion which had marked the Labour campaign in 1918 and illustrated the ambiguous legacy of war-time industrial militancy were resolved, going some way to establishing the characteristic party political concerns of the inter-war years. In Paisley three events marked this process of re-formation on the left: the failure of the Forty Hours strike movement; the TLC's adoption of the Labour Party constitution of 1918 and the consequent disaffiliation of the local BSP; and the creation of a local branch of the Catholic Socialist Society.

By the end of January 1919, it was estimated that 15,000 Paisley workers were taking part in the 'Forty Hours' strike and that most of the local engineering and ship-building works had been thrown idle.[87] Meeting at 'the Cross' in Paisley, the strikers heard speeches in support of their cause and co-ordinated a flying picket force to patrol the engineering works of the surrounding area. Whilst the local press commented on the strikers' 'powerful picketing', little disorder was recorded, and following the George Square outrage in Glasgow, local strike co-ordinators encouraged order in the Paisley ranks.[88] By 4 February, however, commentators were recording diminishing crowds at the Cross and by the tenth, the AEU were encouraging a return to work.

As Harvie has reflected, the Forty Hours strike proved a 'powerful inoculation against direct action' for the Clydeside labour movement.[89] The subsequent collapse of the shop-stewards' movement resolved, in a practical fashion, ideological differences which had been blurred by war, and confirmed for many the parliamentary road as the only route to power. Whilst the crowd of 20,000 which greeted Gallacher in Paisley on his release from jail and the continued sympathies of the ILP left with direct action attest to the long death of industrial militancy, after February 1919 it no longer attracted the support it had done in the war years.[90]

86 Cook, *Age of Alignment*, p. 9.
87 *PRG*, 1 Feb. 1919; *PDE* 31 Jan. 1919.
88 *PDE*, 1 Feb. 1919.
89 Harvie, 'Before the breakthrough', p. 26.
90 Alan McKinlay has stressed the manner in which the ILP left wing continued to

Following a visit in March from Egerton P. Wake, national Labour party organiser, the TLC voted in June by twenty-four votes to four to adopt the Labour Party's new constitution, the famous clause four of which committed the party to socialism.[91] At a council meeting in April, John Gormley, the BSP delegate to the council, had moved an amendment against affiliation to the Labour party, and again in June moved an unsuccessful amendment against the constitution. Four months later, its protests having secured only the support of industrial militants from the AEU, the BSP disaffiliated from the TLC.[92] The way was now clear for the establishment of a more coherent Labour identity in Paisley, based on a new consensus over policy, direction and organisation. In the Paisley of the 1920s, as James Brown has made clear, there was a 're-emergence of radicalism based on the demands for working-class liberty and egalitarianism' against which 'the revolutionary core formed during the war was a small minority ... only able to connect with the mass of workers in specific instances of struggle'.[93]

The leftward move of a proportion of the Irish electorate in Paisley evidenced in the division of 1918 was thrown into relief following the election by the creation of a local branch of the Catholic Socialist Society, providing an organised vehicle for the expression of growing Labour sympathies, twelve years after Wheatley's institution of the association in Glasgow.[94] Under the honorary presidency of the ILP Councillor William Regan of Glasgow, the society held regular meetings throughout 1919, culminating in a debate that December on ILP advocacy of social reform and parliamentary action and 'its repudiation of the Dictatorship of the Proletariat'.[95] Whilst there is no record of the outcome of the debate, the event highlights the gradual movement of the Paisley Irish in line with the general concerns of the local Labour movement.

In the months preceding the by-election of 1920, therefore, the strained friendships of the war gave way to a more coherent Labour philosophy and organisation in Paisley. Whilst continued disputes with the Co-operative Party alert us to the fact that Labour realignment was only partially completed in 1919, the major philosophical ambiguities of the war seemed to have been resolved.

The immediate reaction of the majority of Paisley's prominent Liberals and Unionists following the death of Sir John McCallum was that, at the coming by-election, a Coalition candidate should be run

support 'the flagging unofficial shop floor movement' long after February 1919 and has highlighted the ILP's compromise acceptance of 'direct action' as a complement to parliamentary politics: McKinlay, 'Doubtful wisdom and uncertain promise', pp. 143–7.

91 TLC, 4 Jun. 1919; *PDE*, 6 Jun. 1919.

92 *PDE*, 10 Oct. 1919.

93 Brown, *From Radicalism to Socialism*, p. 16.

94 *Forward*, 3 Mar. 1919.

95 Ibid., 20 Dec. 1919.

against Biggar.[96] Just as such a consensus was establishing itself, however, rumours began to circulate that Asquith would be willing to contest the burgh in the interests of Independent Liberalism. The prospect of such a high-profile candidature thereafter caused serious divisions within the Liberal camp. The *Daily Record* commented:

> There are Liberals who want Mr Asquith and no other. There are those who want any Independent Liberal other than Mr Asquith. There are others who are 'swithering' between Mr Asquith and Coalition ... [and] In the last division of the Liberal forces are those who are determined to stand by the Coalition.[97]

Reinforcing such confusion, the Northcliffe press, in a tactical volte-face, proved enthusiastic for the return of the former premier.[98] Rothermere, having condemned the 'Asquith party' in December 1919 for lacking 'a clear line of policy', harnessed the editorial might of his press empire in January in Asquith's interest, heralding him as 'the great advocate of anti-waste'.[99]

It was against such a background of national interest and local division, that the Paisley Liberal Association met on 21 January to decide on a candidate. Standing against Asquith for the Liberal nomination was J. C. Watson, an Edinburgh advocate, a Paisley native and son of the editor of the *Paisley Daily Express*. Whilst it had been made clear that Watson would have been acceptable to the Unionists, Asquith carried the vote, with a slim majority of eighteen.[100] The following evening, the Unionists adopted J. A. D. MacKean, the burgh treasurer, as their candidate.[101] Whilst there were rumours that the Socialist Labour Party would run another candidate, the Paisley by-election quickly resolved into a three-cornered fight between the Liberals, Labour and the Unionists – a fight of national significance in the history of Liberalism.[102] Indeed, Robert Kelley has argued that 'Paisley provides ... a reference point in the history of Liberal thought in Britain.'[103]

Hailed as a second 'Midlothian', the Paisley electorate returned Asquith with a sizeable majority.[104] As the focus of considerable media

96 *PRG*, 17 Jan. 1920; *PDE*, 13 Jan. 1920.

97 *Daily Record*, 17 Jan. 1920.

98 *PDE*, 17 Jan. 1920.

99 NLS, MS Elibank 8804, fo. 225, Rothermere to Alexander Murray, 22 Dec. 1919; fo. 227, 1 Apr. 1920.

100 *Glasgow Herald*, 22 Jan. 1920; *PRG*, 24 Jan. 1920; *PDE*, 22 Jan. 1920. Note: in a Liberal Association which boasted a membership of around 2,000 later that year, only 168 members voted at the nomination meeting.

101 For coverage of Asquith's defeat in 1918, see Ball, 'Asquith's decline and the General Election of 1918'.

102 The SLP, whilst considering running William Paul, the defeated candidate of the Ince (Lancashire) election, decided not to contest Paisley due to lack of finance.

103 R. Kelley, 'Asquith at Paisley: the content of British Liberalism at the end of its era', *JBS*, iv (1964), p. 133.

104 See below, Appendix 4.

attention throughout Britain, the by-election was interpreted as a judgement on Liberalism itself in the context of the confusion into which party politics had been placed since the development of the Coalition administration.

From an early stage, Asquith sought to refine the nature of political identities that had been confused by war-time imperatives:

> a fashion of the hour is to treat these old party names and associations as superstitions and symbols which have ceased to have any living meaning, and the same critics go about representing that it is the duty of intelligent politicians if not to re-learn, they are agreed at any rate, to renounce their baptismal appellations, and to search the political dictionary for some new and alluring label. So far, they do not seem to have been very successful in the attempt ... we are perfectly contented with our old name and our old creed, and, it would be strange if it were otherwise.[105]

What Asquith considered voguish pedantry was, however, the linguistic manifestation of far more profound evolutionary changes. Simultaneously, the Coalition concept of government was threatening the old divide of 'Whig' and 'Tory', whilst Labour was challenging Liberal claims to the radical inheritance. The by-election of 1920 proves significant in the wider political debate on the decline of the post-war Liberal Party insofar as in the person of Asquith, Old Liberal principles faced two opponents both claiming to represent contemporary issues for which Asquithian Liberalism, as an anachronism, proved no alternative. Yet, whilst account must of course be taken of the allure of a 'big name', it is evident that in voting for Asquith, Paisley electors made a conscious statement in favour of 'pre-war' principles in a post-war world.[106]

The manner in which Liberalism's pre-war and war-time record dominated the most heated exchanges of the campaign would suggest that in the Paisley result we may detect a positive vote in favour of Asquithian Liberalism, rather than a 'hollow' negative against socialism or the increasingly unpopular Coalition. Both of Asquith's opponents proved critical of his 'wait and see' compromises during the war years, MacKean claiming that 'the war would never have come to an end under [Asquith's] guidance'.[107] Yet, perhaps more importantly, Asquith's record

[105] *Glasgow Herald*, 27 Jan. 1920. See also R. Quinault, 'Asquith's Liberalism', *History*, lxxvii (1992), pp. 33–49.

[106] Haldane, in January 1920, commented that 'If he [i.e. Asquith] gets in it will be on account of respect for him personally': NLS, MS 6003, fo. 26, Haldane to his mother, Mary Elizabeth Haldane, 28 Jan. 1920. Ball further emphasises the role which public sympathy with Asquith played in re-enforcing his status as Liberal 'leader' during his year outwith Parliament in 1919: 'his defeat in 1918, by attracting widespread public sympathy, actually went some way to consolidating his hold': Ball, 'Asquith's decline and the General Election of 1918', p. 47.

[107] *PRG*, 31 Jan. 1920.

as pre-war Chancellor and Prime Minister came under attack, and, in much broader terms, both attacked the sixty-eight-year-old elder statesman as being trapped in the past. Biggar reflected: 'Mr Asquith's idea was that the old game of politics should continue. That fact showed how aged Mr Asquith was, and how far behind the times he was, and how far he was out of touch with the workers of the country.'[108] Two days later, MacKean echoed these sentiments: 'Mr Asquith was like a Rip van Winkle who had wakened up without realising that the nation had lived a century since the war, and the outlook had entirely changed.'[109]

Asquith, therefore, was to be judged on his past, tested on old promises and damned for old 'crimes'. In response, he made little attempt to refocus the debate. As Haldane commented, Asquith fought Paisley 'on the old lines'.[110] Asquith's past record proved his major weapon in the contest, as he focused on the pre-war Liberal social and constitutional reforms. Unwavering in his defence of 'Liberal principles', as 'a Liberal who requires no qualifying epithet', Asquith, whilst acknowledging the far-reaching changes which had occurred in society and politics since the war, maintained that such changes 'have not made things false which were true before, nor made things true which were false before'.[111] The 'Paisley Policy' which emerged from Asquith's by-election speeches – and which, as a published volume, came to dominate Liberal policy throughout the 1920s – whilst standing as an attempt at 'redefining Liberalism', added little new to the familiar range of Liberal strategies but rather proved to be an attempt at re-establishing an older political critique.[112]

Dominion self-rule for Ireland; proportional representation; the establishment of a partially nominated second chamber; cuts in public expenditure; the taxation of land values; opposition to nationalisation and the bureaucratic management of industry; the local veto and free trade dominated the concerns of the Liberal platforms. The policies would have been familiar to the pre-war electorate. What was different in 1920 was that together they were being utilised as the defining elements of a party consciously fashioning itself as the 'middle party'.[113]

In the long term, this strategy proved a critical determinant of Liberal fortunes in the inter-war period, as Liberalism sought to define itself against two philosophical polarities – the 'great abstractions' which

108 *PDE*, 27 Jan. 1920.

109 Ibid., 29 Jan. 1920.

110 NLS, MS Haldane 6003, fo. 26, Haldane to his mother, 28 Jan. 1920.

111 *PDE*, 28 Jan. 1920.

112 Kelley, 'Asquith at Paisley', p. 138. Here Kelley puts the case for the 'Paisley Policy' as a re-definition of Liberalism. See H. H. Asquith, *The Paisley Policy* (London, 1920).

113 Note comment of William Galbraith, Paisley Liberal Association Chairman at a campaign meeting of 26 Jan. 1920: 'The time had come when they felt they must have a middle party and in a true democracy the middle party whether in or out of office, would always govern': *Glasgow Herald*, 27 Jan. 1920.

Asquith condemned throughout the Paisley campaign. Ultimately, this approach determined a political perspective which would be defined by changing parameters over which Liberalism would have little control – a reactive policy generated by the concerns of its opponents. As Kelley has made clear, Paisley highlighted that the Liberal Party was without 'a clear and vivid picture of its rival' and was, in this manner, a party which was 'in the way of losing its reason for being'.[114]

Ultimately, the result of 1920 has important historiographical significance in its apparent endorsement of a concept of politics based on 'community', unqualified by the polarities of class interests. Asserting a 'common interest' between capital and labour, Asquith suggested alternatives to Labour's nationalisation and capital levy proposals in economic schemes such as Joint Boards of Management, which emphasised decentralised power and sought to diffuse widely the control of industry.[115] The community as 'a wealth-creating, wealth distributing, wealth-consuming and wealth accumulating machine' was to be considered in its entirety.[116] Asquith's victory address made this clear:

> I have put before you that the guiding principle which ought to govern our policy in the future ... the principle that no class and no interest, small or great, important or powerful, including within its ranks the masses of men and women or those raised by the accident of birth and fortune into a privileged position of specialised monopoly and authority – that no interest and no class is entitled to prevail over the predominant interest of the community as a whole.[117]

Whilst some historians have argued that Liberalism proved *incapable* of playing the 'class' card in a political milieu increasingly dominated by class issues, the 'Paisley Policy' highlights rather that at this stage, the Liberal policy was a conscious and calculated *rejection* of 'class politics'. And in 1920 it 'worked'.

In 1920, the divided Irish and 'women's vote' identified in the 1918 election prove to be a persistent leitmotif. In the by-election, the official UIL endorsement went to Biggar, and league representatives, along with those of the new Catholic Socialist Society, were represented on Labour's election committee. Yet dissent in the Irish ranks was apparent, and the local press was inundated with letters in support of Asquith as Ireland's constant champion and allegations that an alien socialist element had flooded the UIL meeting to secure Biggar's endorsement.[118]

114 Kelley, 'Asquith at Paisley', p. 158.
115 Ibid., pp. 141–3.
116 *PDE*, 30 Jan. 1920.
117 Ibid., 26 Feb. 1920.
118 Ibid., 31 Jan. 1920.

Labour was condemned as having co-operated in a coalition government which had initiated countless 'outrages' against the Irish people and Asquith was lauded as a man who could do more than Biggar in the Commons to put the nationalist cause at the forefront of parliamentary concerns.[119] At a meeting of the Paisley UIL branch at the beginning of February it was resolved – allegedly at the instigation of agents for T. P. O'Connor – in opposition to the earlier vote in favour of Labour, that 'no recommendation as to the disposition of the Irish vote in Paisley should be issued'.[120] However, at a general meeting of Irish electors later that day, this recommendation was 'scorned and scouted without shrift or ceremony'.[121] Whilst it is evident that Labour sympathies were growing within the Irish community, such evident division alerts us to the fact that the representatives of the Irish political community were still far from completely detached from their Liberal tradition.

The presence in Paisley of Asquith's daughter, Lady Violet Bonham Carter, throughout the election proved a critical influence on the Liberal contest for the women's vote. The *Express* commented that Lady Bonham Carter had 'won the sympathy of women voters', adding that: 'Her general unostentatious manner and her racy speeches have secured for her a large following.'[122] Indeed, following Asquith's victory, Annie Maxton, speaking at an ILP meeting at Lochwinnoch, put the responsibility for the Liberal success in Paisley firmly on the shoulders of the women voters.[123]

Again, the focus of all three candidates was on women in the domestic sphere, especially on the responsibilities of motherhood. Speaking at a meeting of women electors in the Central Halls, Sir Donald McLean stressed the importance of politics for women in these terms:

> Politics in the home meant the education of their children, the sanitation of the street, the well-being of the home in the prices of articles they bought, the quality of the clothes they wore, and in the whole future of their children.[124]

Yet it would be misguided to assume a unified focus in the women's vote in support of Liberalism (or indeed against Labour). Asquith's pre-war record dominated letters on women's issues in the press, and Biggar maintained the support of the Co-operative guilds. Moreover, Turner's research on the relationship between the sexual composition of local

119 Ibid., 11 Feb. 1920; 28 Jan. 1920.

120 *Glasgow Observer and Catholic Herald*, 7 Feb. 1920; 28 Feb. 1920.

121 Ibid., 7 Feb. 1920.

122 *PDE*, 4 Feb. 1920.

123 *PRG*, 6 Mar. 1920. The local Women's Liberal Association was also credited with securing a considerable female vote for Asquith in 1920. See P. Thane, 'Women, Liberalism and citizenship, 1918–1930', in Biagini, *Citizenship and Community*, p. 78.

124 *PDE*, 2 Feb. 1920.

constituencies and the anti-Labour vote in these years would suggest that the 'apparently strong relationship between female voters and anti-Labour voting [was] an artifact of the socio-economic composition of constituencies'. [125]

Again, it is essential that we look elsewhere for the determining electoral blocs and socio-economic factors which influenced the 1920 result. In comparison with 1918, when only 57.6% of the electorate voted, in 1920, 77.38% went to the polls. By failing to secure 1/8th of these votes cast, MacKean forfeited his £150 deposit. MacKean put his defeat down to the fact that a great many Unionist voters had deserted their cause for Asquith, 'not because they did not want him [MacKean] but because they wanted to keep out Mr Biggar'.[126] Biggar himself concurred with this view ('Asquith has won by Unionist votes'), and drew from his defeat, a lesson regarding class consciousness:

> Had the workers of Paisley been as class conscious as the other parties ... and had been as alive to their own interests as the other classes were to their interests, there would have been no dubiety as to the result.[127]

Yet tactical voting on the right was only one factor which influenced the final result.

For many on the left of the Liberal Party, 1920 represented a reflective stage in the evolutionary process of political conversion – a point 'where men halt between two opinions'.[128] Indeed, Haldane in February 1920 '[did] not think that the main current of political thought either [was] or [would] be deflected' by the Paisley result.[129] Yet it is only hindsight which colours such a statement with the air of prophecy and imparts a scepticism on our assessment of Asquith's victory as a transitory 'Indian Summer' for Liberalism. The 'postal avalanche' of messages of congratulations which arrived at Cavendish Square in February 1920 attests to the vitality with which the Liberal cause was infused following the Paisley by-election.[130] Whilst fleeting, it was nonetheless real.

125 J. Turner, 'Sex, age and the Labour vote in the 1920s', in P. Denley, S. Fogelvik and C. Harvey (eds.), *History and Computing II* (Manchester, 1989), p. 251. Turner emphasises that 'the proportion of women in a constituency's electorate is not merely a demographic variable, as first appears, but a rather subtle and interesting social indicator': p. 253.

126 *PRG*, 28 Feb. 1920.

127 Ibid., 28 Feb. 1920.

128 *PDE*, 23 Jan. 1920.

129 NLS, MS 6003, fo. 60, Haldane to his mother, 26 Feb. 1920.

130 BLO, MS Asquith, II.33, fo. 211, Thomas Nelson & Sons Publishers, Edinburgh, to Asquith, 25 Feb. 1920.

Labour, 1920–1924: A Unity of Purpose?

Reflecting on Biggar's performance at the Paisley by-election some months before, the Scottish Council of the Labour Party recorded in their annual report of September 1920:

> The contest was treated by the press as a Labour fight; and without doubt, the bulk of the votes polled and the work put in were distinctively Labour. Had the Co-operative movement in Paisley risen to the height of its opportunity, Mr Biggar would have been today Member of Parliament for Paisley.[131]

Blame for Labour's defeat was placed firmly at the door of the Co-operators. In defence of local Labour organs, it was noted that David Wilson, Biggar's election agent, had received the 'full assistance' of the Scottish Labour officials, the election agent of the Scottish Mine Worker's Union, the Scottish woman organiser and the Scottish secretary of the Labour Party.[132]

Paisley was a huge undertaking for the Labour movement. By 14 February it was calculated that Labour had held 120 meetings in Paisley and, having entered the field early – Biggar was holding his first meetings while the Liberals and Unionists were still aiming for a compromise candidate – had managed to book up the largest halls in the town for key nights during the campaign period. In most public works there were 'Biggar Committees', attracting votes for their candidate, and whilst Asquith tried to compete, Labour held by far the greater number of work-gate meetings.[133] The Co-operators established a campaign newspaper, the *Paisley Standard*, priced at 1d. with coverage and gossip of the election fight from the Labour perspective, and Labour platforms were graced with 'big names' in the Labour world – among them J. Ramsay MacDonald, Robert Smillie, Pethwick Lawrence and Neil McLean. Yet beneath such an enthusiastic, united front, division was evident in the Labour ranks.

Disharmony among the Labour and Co-operative parties in Paisley is most properly considered in the context of growing scepticism regarding political involvement in the national Co-operative party. Whilst the 1919 Carlisle Congress had voted in favour of a 'Triple Alliance' of Co-operators, the TUC and the Labour Party, 'with the ultimate object of forming a United Democratic or People's Party', the draft proposals for the alliance, drawn up in 1920, were rejected at the Scarborough Congress of 1921.[134] Since 1919, enthusiasm for Co-operative politics

131 NLS, PDL 30/4 (1–16), Report of the Sixth Annual Conference of the Labour Party (Scottish Council), Section 4, p. 8.

132 Ibid., p. 8.

133 *PRG*, 14 Feb. 1920.

134 Carberry, 'Examination and Evaluation of the Co-operative Party', p. 47. Smith and Ostergaard, like Carberry, consider the Scarborough Conference, 'the Co-operative

had waned. In comparison with the 563 societies which had affiliated to the Co-operative Representation Committee in 1918, the Co-operative Party in 1921 could boast only 550 affiliated societies and 'by no means all of these were giving any real support'.[135] By 1922, fewer than 450 societies were making any payment to party funds and by 1924 this figure had dropped to 393 societies, representing a minority of Co-operators.[136] As a corollary, anti-political factions were establishing a stronger hold in many societies. In Scotland, the appearance of James Campsie's Co-operative Members' Defence Association in Govan in 1921, with the aim of halting the 'capture of the Co-operative movement by the Labour Party', highlighted the lasting power of the anti-Labour lobby within the Scottish movement.[137]

Whilst in the Commons, Labour and Co-operative members collaborated on most issues, with many Co-operative MPs taking the Labour whip, such a relationship 'had no counterpart in the relations between the two parties outside parliament', especially at the constituency level.[138] In Paisley, the question over the choice of the parliamentary candidate for the burgh threw into relief the disharmony in Co-operative–Labour relations.

In May 1919 the central committee of the Co-operative Defence Committee, without consulting the local Labour party (that is the TLC), announced that they would again be contesting Paisley in the Co-operative interest. Four days later, a meeting of the TLC voted overwhelmingly to contest Paisley for Labour and initiated moves to select a candidate.[139] In June, the Scottish Advisory Council of the Labour Party, voicing concern over the apparent deadlock in Paisley, sent Ben Shaw to the burgh to discuss the matter.[140] Despite such attempts at reconciliation, in July the local branch of the Scottish Horse and Motormen's Association [SHMA] nominated Hugh Lyon, general secretary of the SHMA and chairman of the STUC, as a potential Labour candidate for Paisley.[141] In September, however, a deputation was sent to the Co-operative 'camp' from the local Labour party, on the request of the local Co-operative party, to discuss the local situation, and in October, Paisley Labour party voted twelve to five against an ILP

Party's last chance to secure an agreement with the Labour Party based on the principle of full equality': Smith and Ostergaard, *Constitutional Relations Between the Labour and Co-operative Parties*, p. 7.

135 Smith and Ostergaard, *Constitutional Relations Between the Labour and Co-operative Parties*, p. 320.

136 Ibid., p. 320.

137 *PDE*, 9 Mar. 1921. Note, however, that it was also in 1921 that the Glasgow and Suburbs Co-operative Conference Association affiliated to the Labour Party despite the fact that this was against Co-operative Party rules.

138 Cole, *Century of Co-operation*, p. 321.

139 TLC, 4 Jun. 1919; 25 Jun. 1919.

140 Ibid., 2 Jul. 1919.

141 Knox, *Scottish Labour Leaders*, pp. 164–8.

resolution calling for a conference on the parliamentary situation, instead opting to send representatives to a further meeting of the Co-operative party.[142] By November (representatives of the Scottish Labour Party Executive having sat in on subsequent negotiations), compromise was reached when at a joint meeting of the Co-operative party and the local Labour party, Biggar was finally adopted as Paisley's Labour candidate.[143]

Only a few days before Biggar's endorsement, it had been agreed by the slimmest of majorities (thirteen votes to twelve) that the Paisley Labour party would endorse Biggar should Hugh Lyon be the only alternative.[144] The 1919 compromise was thus achieved without the unanimous support of the Paisley Labour party and under significant pressure from the national Labour Party executive, conscious that the Paisley case had critical implications for broader Co-operative–Labour relations nation-wide.

Eight months after the 1920 by-election, Labour–Co-operative disagreement re-emerged. On 27 October, the ILP delegates to the political section of the local Labour party announced their party's intention to oppose the adoption of Biggar as Paisley's Labour candidate.[145] Having discussed the situation throughout the intervening months, however, in December, eight affiliated associations voted in favour of supporting Biggar at the next election, whilst five voted for no action on the matter. Only the ILP voted against support for Biggar.[146] Throughout 1921 and the initial months of 1922, co-operation between the local parties seemed established, with joint propaganda meetings being held and joint election committees being established. Yet such apparent unity was deceptive, and we have to look to municipal politics to gauge the true strength of the Co-operative–Labour entente and the extent of Labour support at the grass roots.

The 1918 Franchise Act, as well as enlarging the parliamentary electorate, also 'approximately doubled the number eligible to vote in municipal elections'.[147] Thereafter, it was 'Labour rather than either of its main opponents that launched the largest challenge for local

142 TLC, 10 Sep. 1919; 8 Oct. 1919.
143 Ibid., 9 Nov. 1919.
144 Ibid., 5 Nov. 1919.
145 Ibid., 27 Oct. 1920. Note: the Trades and Labour Council, having established itself as the local Labour party in 1919, in April 1920 divided for organisational purposes into an Industrial and a Political section. Hereafter the local Labour party will be referred to as the Labour party, whilst the abbreviation TLC will continue to be adopted when citing from Labour party minutes in the interests of continuity.
146 TLC, 8 Dec. 1920.
147 C. Cook, 'Liberals, Labour and local elections', in Peele and Cook, *Politics of Reappraisal*, p. 167.

government elections'.[148] In 1919, Labour made 280 gains in the municipal elections in Scotland and in 1920 followed this up by securing over one third of the seats in the newly constituted Glasgow Council.[149] Thus, in general terms, in the immediate post-war years, Scotland as a whole seems to follow the national trend of successive Labour municipal victories identified by Cook.[150] Yet the experience of the Paisley Labour movement disrupts this picture of incremental growth and highlights the reality of Howard's conclusion that, despite dramatic local successes, Labour was 'structurally unprepared for the role it was now destined to play ... [having] no real basis for expansion, no real basis for confidence'.[151]Despite what he identifies as the 'vibrant optimism of the early 1920s', Howard highlights that 'even in areas of solid Labour support it was often difficult to build up mass support'.[152]

In Paisley, a pattern of disappointment and unfulfilled expectations was set in 1919 when, despite sponsoring and supporting five candidates for the Town Council, only one TLC candidate was successful – Harry Baird in the third ward.[153] Whilst two TLC-supported candidates proved successful in the Parish Council elections, and John Elliot (Co-operative party secretary), was returned to the new Renfrewshire Education Authority that April, Paisley clearly does not rate as one of the 'remarkable victories' identified by Cook in 1919.[154] In 1920, Labour representation on Paisley Town Council fell from four seats to two (Baird and Robert Russell remaining). All four Labour Party candidates in 1920 were defeated, as was a Labour Independent supported by the party in the first ward and the Co-operative party candidate, David Wilson, Biggar's election agent. In the wards contested by Labour and the Co-operative party, an average of only 34.7% of the votes went to the 'workers' candidates'.[155]

The year 1920 also highlighted the fragility of Co-operative–Labour relations in local politics. Having endorsed the Labour candidates in the 1919 contests, the Co-operative party in 1920 sponsored a candidate in the eighth ward against two Labour candidates, asserting its right to contest the seat regardless of Labour action and in the process splitting the 'Labour vote'.[156] The following year, the Labour Party, by a large

148 Ibid., p. 168.

149 Brown, 'Labour Party and Political Change in Scotland', p. 130; Harvie, 'Before the breakthrough', p. 27.

150 Cook, 'Liberals, Labour and local elections', p. 169.

151 C. Howard, 'Expectations born to death: local Labour Party expansion in the 1920s', in J. Winter (ed.) *The Working Class in Modern British History: Essays in Honour of Henry Pelling* (Cambridge, 1983), p. 80.

152 Ibid., pp. 80, 73–4. See also Tanner, 'Elections, statistics, and the rise of the Labour Party', pp. 893–908.

153 Note: no Town Council elections were held for the duration of the war.

154 Cook, 'Liberals, Labour and local elections', p. 169.

155 *PDE*, 26 Oct. 1920.

156 TLC, 24 Oct. 1920; 27 Oct. 1920.

majority, decided not to give the Co-operative party preference in the wards it wanted to contest.[157]

Again in 1921, all the Labour and Co-operative candidates were defeated, attracting only 22.43% of the votes cast in the contested wards, as were two candidates sponsored by the Communist party in a contest in which only 51% of the electorate participated.[158] Pointing to 'the apathy of the workers' as being 'one of the causes for the downfall of Labour', Robert Adam, prominent ILPer and Labour party chairman, encouraged the party to organise.[159] But 1922 brought more losses. As in the previous two municipal elections, all the official Labour candidates were defeated, leaving only Harry Baird, who had been returned unopposed, as the sole Labour representative on the Town Council. Even Robert Russell, an established Labour councillor, went down to defeat. The Co-operative party voted unanimously not to take part in the Town Council elections.[160] In the Education Authority elections that April, despite the establishment of a joint election committee comprising representatives from the Co-operative party, the Labour party, the Catholic Socialist Society and the ILP, again, only John Elliot was successful and then only after the Catholic candidates' surplus votes had been divided among the Labour candidates.[161]

In the municipal elections and by-elections of 1923 and 1924, Labour fared little better. Labour sponsored eight candidates, covering seven wards in 1923, yet all proved unsuccessful, gaining less than 30% of the votes cast.[162] In 1924, whilst gaining one more councillor in the figure of the ILPer John Stewart, following a by-election in the seventh ward, Labour lost a further two municipal by-elections and saw both its candidates at the October elections go down to defeat, having secured 32.6% of the votes cast.[163]

Whilst Labour–Co-operative division was clearly partially responsible for Labour's lack of municipal success during the early '20s, it is not the whole story. The appearance of Unemployed candidates in the Parish Council election of 1922 highlights the important economic dimension of the recession of this period which, whilst raising the profile of economic inequality and social injustice, also encouraged growing concerns regarding efficiency and economy and the perennial question of rates increases. In such a context, the Labour reform programme, encouraging as it did increased expenditure on housing, sanitation, direct labour and the municipalisation of local coal and milk supplies, raised fears of increased taxation. Whilst parliamentary platforms

157 Ibid., 5 Oct. 1921.
158 *PDE*, 26 Oct. 1921.
159 TLC, 2 Nov. 1921.
160 PCL, ARC 271, CP Minutes (Paisley Branch), 14 Sep. 1922.
161 *PDE*, 10 Apr. 1922; CP Minutes, 9 Mar. 1922.
162 *PDE*, 7 Nov. 1923.
163 *PDE*, 9 Apr. 1924.

proposed the capital levy as the milch cow to finance the socialist vision, it was the rate-payer who was expected to finance Labour's municipal dreams.[164]

Beyond such economic determinants, however, the role of the ILP demands consideration. In 1920, Thomas Scollan, the ILP delegate to the political section of the Labour party in Paisley, reported to the party that due to a disagreement between himself and the ILP chairman over the advisability of contesting municipal elections he would, in the near future, be removed as the ILP's representative.[165] Two years later the ILP line was being strictly followed by the party's new delegate, Mr Sinclair (also Labour party vice-chairman), when he moved that 'demands were for Parliamentary candidates and not for local administration'.[166] The animosity between Co-operative and Labour forces – in which the ILP played a large part – engendered by the question of the parliamentary candidature further diverted attention away from municipal politics in 1923 and 1924. In Paisley, therefore, it may be suggested that the emphasis on parliamentary politics proved detrimental to the Labour Party's performance at the municipal level. Co-operative bitterness over Labour activities in the parliamentary sphere 'spilled over' into municipal politics, fragmenting the Labour forces. Likewise, increasing ILP influence in the Labour party encouraged a shift of focus towards the state and away from municipal politics in an endeavour to out-manoeuvre the Co-operators.[167] Throughout the 1920s the municipal basis of power was thus neglected by Labour in Paisley.

Finally, it is important to note that in Glasgow, success in 1920 was achieved by the left only in areas where Labour had enjoyed some success before the war. [168] As Smyth makes clear, 'At the same time, where Labour had previously drawn a blank it continued to do so.'[169] Labour's run of municipal failure in Paisley in the Edwardian period was mirrored by its post-war performance. The failure of the pre-war Labour movement to overturn the established Liberal cultural and political hegemony of the locality thus proved to have serious consequences for the post-war Labour Party. By 1924, Labour's municipal and parliamentary performances appear strangely dislocated – parliamentary achievement finding no parallel in local politics and

164 Chris Cook has highlighted the lasting power of Liberals on local councils throughout the 1920s which acted as an obstacle to Labour growth in this area: Peele and Cook, *Politics of Reappraisal*, p. 166.

165 TLC, 13 Oct. 1920.

166 Ibid., 25 Jun. 1922.

167 Note the following statement from McKinlay: 'The centrality of the housing question to Glasgow socialism and the failure of the 1920 rent strike to protect the legislative advances of 1915 confirmed the ILP's concentration on parliament as the key arena of post-war politics.': McKinlay, 'Doubtful wisdom and uncertain promise', p. 141.

168 Smyth, 'Labour and Socialism in Glasgow, p. 335.

169 Ibid., p. 335.

resting on foundations unsupported by the localism which entrenched the Liberal vision.[170]

Unemployment: 1920–1922

Whilst Harvie has considered the 'mounting unemployment' of the immediate post-war years an important factor in Labour's rise to municipal power in Glasgow, Paisley's experience highlights the unreliability of such an argument based on 'hunger politics'.[171] In December 1920, 1,300 names appeared on the register of unemployed in Paisley.[172] Three months later this figure had trebled.[173] At the height of the coal strike in 1921, 4,133 were recorded as 'wholly unemployed' – the majority of them males – and 11,169 were on 'short time' and claiming benefit at the exchange.[174] The vast majority of the 'short time' claimants were women workers from the mills, whose hours had been cut to around twenty-one per week in April.[175] By the end of May, 16,522 workers were claiming benefit.[176] Whilst conditions improved following the end of the strike in June, in December there remained 4,609 wholly unemployed and 1,276 on short time.[177] Further hardship resulted from a scheme introduced by Coats in 1921 for reducing wages in line with the fall in the cost of living, a move which struck at the supplementary wages of women in families whose chief breadwinners were unemployed.[178] By December 1922, 5,604 were still wholly unemployed and 466 were claiming 'short time' relief.[179]

The engineering works in the area were particularly badly hit by the recession. In September 1921, the directors' minutes of A. F. Craig & Co. record that 'no orders are coming in, and there is very little prospect of any in the near future'.[180] In Fullerton, Hodgart and Barclay's, hours

170 Note also that in Aberdeen, Phipps has also found 'little correlation' between Labour's performance in local and Parliamentary elections: Phipps, 'Aberdeen Trades Council', p. 172.

171 Harvie, 'Before the breakthrough', p. 27.

172 *PDE*, 20 Dec. 1920.

173 Ibid., 11 Mar. 1921.

174 Ibid., 10 May 1921.

175 Ibid., 8 Apr. 1921; 14 Apr. 1921.

176 Ibid., 16 May 1921.

177 Ibid., 30 Dec. 1921.

178 Ibid., 5 Sep. 1921; 31 Jan. 1922, 11 Sep. 1922. See also PM, JPC Collection, 1/5/79, 'Anchor Thread Mill – Scheme for Reducing Wages' (1921). Reductions were to be made according to a seven-stage process based on the cost of living index and related to pre-war wage rates. After the first reduction, subsequent reductions would be made only if a drop of twenty points occurred in the cost of living. Also, Coats' Directors Minutes record a reduction in hours in April 1921 in 'the home mills' so as to 'lighten the stocks on hand' and a reduction of 3/- per week on the wages of female workers at Fergulsie in July 1921: UGABRC, JPC, 199/1/1/4, Minute Book, 7 Apr. 1921 (p. 112); 25 Aug. 1921 (p. 122).

179 *PDE*, 22 Dec. 1922.

180 UGABRC, A. F. Craig & Co. Collection, 173/1/1, Minute Book, 22 Sep. 1921.

were cut in May 1921 due to 'the number of cancellations received' and the engine department was put on a three-day week.[181] Two weeks later, foremen were put to work as machinists in an endeavour to 'cut down costs'.[182] At the directors' annual general meeting, it was recorded that 'prospects for the ensuing year are not bright'.[183] By November, the labourers in the foundry shop were working only one week in every three.[184] The 1922 engineering trades lock-out further exacerbated conditions, with apprentices being relied upon to keep the works running during the initial stages of the conflict until May, when the works were forced temporarily to cease operations.[185] With the end of the lock-out in June, however, conditions got even worse, the works' manager commenting in July that 'he did not see any prospect of securing orders for Marine Castings for a considerable time to come'.[186]

In January 1921, the Town Council and the local Co-operative societies set up relief funds and work was provided for the unemployed by the council on road works, at the refuse destructor and as grave-diggers at Hawkhead cemetery.[187] Yet by September, the council's relief fund had been exhausted.[188] Amendments to the poor law, however, meant that by October, the Parish Council was able to issue relief to the able-bodied unemployed and later that month Government grants were made available for work schemes.[189] Nevertheless, for some such measures seemed too little, too late – many workers having exhausted their right to unemployment benefit after months of idleness.[190]

The local Labour party, however, failed to harness the emerging discontent evident in the demonstrations held by the Unemployed Committee at the Abbey Close in the winter of 1921; instead the initiative was taken up by local Communist activists, led by William Gallacher and John Gormley (formerly of the BSP), who spoke on behalf of the unemployed in deputations to the Town and Parish Councils and, in the case of Gormley, led around twenty men as the Paisley contingent on a hunger march to London in December 1922.[191] Whilst strict denials were made that the Unemployed Committee was a Communist association, such worries caused the Labour party to postpone the affiliation of the committee in 1921, although a representative was sent

181 UGABRC, Fullerton, Hodgart & Barclay Collection, 120/1/1/8, Minute Book, 11 May 1921.
182 Ibid., 30 May 1921.
183 Ibid., 2 Aug. 1921.
184 Ibid., 28 Nov. 1921.
185 Ibid., 13 Mar. 1922; 1 May 1922.
186 Ibid., 17 Jul. 1922.
187 *PDE*, 12 Jan. 1921; 14 Jan. 1921; 28 Jan. 1921.
188 Ibid., 9 Sep. 1921.
189 Ibid., 29 Sep. 1921; 7 Oct. 1921.
190 Ibid., 9 Sep. 1921; 14 Sep. 1921.
191 *PRG*, 10 Sep. 1921; 17 Sep. 1921; *PDE*, 9 Sep. 1921; 13 Sep. 1921; 14 Sep. 1921; 2 Dec. 1922.

as a delegate from the Labour party to the committee.[192] In January 1922, however, a deputation from the Unemployed Committee complained of the Labour party's 'failure to organise the unemployed on a proper basis' and pointed to the apathy of the trade unionists with regard to the unemployment question.[193] The following month, the Unemployed Committee was allowed to affiliate to the local Labour party at no fee.[194] Whilst in the long run this decision proved a dangerous precedent – the Communist party was allowed to affiliate the following year – it is the initial inaction of the local Labour party over the plight of the unemployed which calls for special attention at this stage, proving as it did, critical to their fortunes in the local elections of these years.

In Lennox Kerr's novel, *Woman of Glenshiels*, his depiction of the social impact of the economic recession highlights the political energy Labour failed to absorb in these years. Initially Mary, the central character, is unconcerned at the plight of the unemployed 'labourers and navvies' who were first hit by the economic downturn: 'She clung to her trust in the right of a good man to keep his job ... Labourers and other unskilled men weren't as journeymen who had served five, six or seven years apprenticeship to become indispensable craftsmen.'[195] Yet her husband Dan is soon laid off and travels to Glasgow in search of work:

> As a journeyman he had had the status of a protected, privileged servant of capital. His very clothes were a uniform. Other workers, like labourers and navvies, might have to hawk their labour and to bargain, but no journeyman ... no union-protected journeyman should be forced to go the round of works' gates. It was an offence against his royal dignity.[196]

Before, Mary had been content that whilst 'Dan was Labour ... that wasn't Socialism'.[197] Yet when unemployment strikes the family, fine definitions are gone from Mary's reasoning: 'the real facts were their men didn't work because the yards were empty. They weren't really concerned with reasons, only effects.'[198]

1922 General Election

From the perspective of 1926, Asquith (then Lord Oxford and Asquith), reflected on the period from 1919 to 1922 as 'the darkest days for

192 TLC, 21 Dec. 1921.
193 Ibid., 25 Jan. 1922.
194 Ibid., 1 Feb. 1922.
195 Kerr, *Woman of Glenshiels*, p. 191.
196 Ibid., pp. 194–5.
197 Ibid., p. 189.
198 Ibid., p. 254.

Liberalism which I have ever known'.[199] As Gordon Brown has made clear: 'From Paisley to the break-up of the Coalition the divisions within the party were never far from the surface.'[200] As futile secretive plans were made and unmade for Liberal fusion on a national level under Lord Grey, and as Asquith maintained his fight against co-operation with the Unionists, on a constituency level fortunes appeared little better.[201] In Scotland the Liberals were 'unable to place a candidate in the Kirkcaldy by-election of 1921, failed to win the Inverness by-election of 1922 and then decided not to intervene in the Moray and Nairn by-election later in the year'.[202] Nationally, the Independent Liberals were being consistently beaten into third place by Labour in three-cornered contests, as outside the Nonconformist rural areas 'protest votes were finding their home with Labour rather than with the Asquithian Liberals'.[203]

Yet, the picture was not one of 'irreversible decline'.[204] Following Asquith's victory in 1920, the Scottish Liberal Federation had been successfully 'purged' of Coalition personnel and policy and by the end of the year, both Sir William Robertson (Chairman) and Sir Robert Lockhart (Vice Chairman) had resigned over the federation's new policy to support only Independent Liberal candidates even in the face of constituency opposition.[205] Sir Donald McLean, as its new chairman, thereafter guided the federation along Asquithian lines. On a local level, the Paisley Liberal Association, its enthusiasm having received a boost following the election of Asquith, seems also to 'contradict the thesis of the accelerating disintegration of Liberal machinery'.[206] In 1922, the Paisley Liberal Association boasted a membership of 1,600, rising to 2,000 during the year 1923–4, and in 1920 had reconstituted a strong ward structure through which an active social scene was encouraged, supplemented by the activities of the debating circle established the following year.[207] Furthermore, throughout the period, it recorded an important achievement by attracting many newly enfranchised women members – its female membership always outstripping the male

199 BLO, MS Asquith 35.252, Confidential Memorandum, 4 Oct. 1926.

200 Brown, 'Labour Party and Political Change in Scotland', p. 197.

201 For details of the proposed 'coalition' under Grey, see BLO, MS c.466, fos. 165–8, Sir Donald MacLean to Asquith, 9 Oct. 1922. In same collection, note: c.466, fo. 186, Letter from Asquith to Sir Donald MacLean, 29 Nov. 1922, in which Asquith comments that at a recent meeting 'L. G. almost foamed at the mouth at the mention of Grey's name'.

202 Brown, 'Labour Party and Political Change in Scotland', p. 212.

203 Cook, *Age of Alignment*, p. 12.

204 Hutchison, *Political History of Scotland*, p. 312.

205 EUL, SLA Collection, Minutes, vol. IX: 1908–1925, 22 Nov. 1920. (Note: Sir Thomas Glen Coats also resigned from the federation over this issue.) See also Brown, 'Labour Party and Political Change in Scotland', p. 210.

206 Hutchison, *Political History of Scotland*, p. 315.

207 PCL, 320, Ren–1, PLA Minutes, Annual Reports 1921–22; 1923–24; *PDE*, 17 Mar. 1920.

contingent both in numbers and enthusiasm.[208] Liberal decline, therefore, cannot be entirely explained in terms of organisational disunity.

In 1922 Asquith fought both the national and the local elections from his Paisley platforms. Standing as both leader of the Liberal opposition and as local MP, his campaign focus was thus dislocated by two areas of concern which were neither naturally compatible nor mutually reinforcing. For much of the campaign, moreover, Asquith was absent from Paisley, supporting other Liberal candidates in both England and Scotland. His narrow majority in 1922, therefore, may be partly explained by the recurrence of mistakes made first in East Fife – his neglect of local feeling.[209] In *Memories and Reflections*, Asquith recorded that the Paisley electors 'expect the bulk of the speaking at election times to be done by the candidate'.[210]

Yet, more serious than this practical manifestation of the tension between Asquith's two political roles were the implications such divided loyalties had on his electoral strategy. Throughout the campaign, Asquith focused his anger and his major political attacks on the Coalition government.[211] Going one step further, he aligned the Liberal policy to the labour 'cause'. On 1 November, Asquith announced that he found himself 'almost in complete agreement with by far the larger part of [Mr Biggar's opening campaign speech]'.[212] This tone continued through many more Liberal addresses during the campaign. Consider the following from Lady Bonham Carter:

> There was not going to be so much disagreeing in Paisley this time as formerly. That was unfortunate. Their Labour friends were obliged to agree with them about so many things. She [Lady Bonham Carter] sympathised with them. They were suffering from that too. Liberals agreed with them about foreign policy, and Ireland, and the League of Nations, and the economy and Free Trade. Really their aims were very much the same: the difference between them was a difference of method, a difference of attaining those ends.[213]

Whilst to a national audience, this attempt to win the wavering radical vote, by casting Liberalism as the true alternative to the Unionists, paid dividends – the Independent Liberals gained forty-three seats in 1922,

208 *PDE*, 26 Feb. 1921.

209 Stuart Ball has made clear that Asquith's defeat in East Fife in 1918 may be partly explained in terms of his 'neglect' of the seat, e.g., 'From the formation of the first Coalition government in May 1915 to the Maurice Debate in May 1918 Asquith appeared in his seat for three speeches': Ball, 'Asquith's decline and the General Election of 1918', p. 50. See below, Appendix 4.

210 H. H. Asquith, *Memories and Reflections, 1852–1927* (London, 1928), ii, p. 180.

211 *PDE*, 3 Nov. 1922; 4 Nov. 1922.

212 Ibid., 2 Nov. 1922.

213 Ibid., 3 Nov. 1922.

thirty-two of them from Unionists and Independents – in Paisley, where Asquith faced no Unionist challenger, this strategy succeeded only in blurring the line of differentiation between the Liberal and Labour programmes.[214] Indeed, as no similar protestations were forthcoming from the Labour camp, it seemed evident that it was Labour, rather than the Liberals who held the real initiative. Though unsuccessful in Paisley, 1922 represented a year of significant success for Labour throughout the country, where Labour's share of the vote increased to 29.7% and its MPs to 142.[215]

More so perhaps than in 1920, the Liberal campaign in Paisley in 1922 highlights a Liberal Party without 'a clear and vivid picture of its rival'.[216] In broad terms, the Liberal programme in 1922 offered nothing new: a reaffirmation of the Liberal commitment to free trade, strong criticisms of wasteful military adventures, condemnations of 'class' politics and vague promises of social and educational reform – little to distinguish the party from either of its rivals. Asquith, along with the local Liberal association, however, put his narrow majority down to two factors: the growth of unemployment and the resurrection of the housing question.[217]

In February 1922, a deputation from the Unemployed Committee which had waited on Asquith, left the meeting with the impression that 'Paisley's M.P. is not prepared to do much for the unemployed either in Paisley or elsewhere.'[218] Whilst, as we have seen in municipal contests, the local Labour party failed to harness local discontent caused by unemployment, Biggar put the unemployment question to the forefront of his campaign and targeted the unemployed specifically at meetings and demonstrations. In contrast, Asquith, at a campaign meeting, responded to a request that he address the unemployed of the town, by stating that 'he was addressing his constituents as a whole and not any class'.[219] Later that same day, Biggar followed up a campaign meeting at the Town Hall with an address to 2,000 unemployed. In comparison to Biggar's strategy, Asquith's attempted populism seemed little better than neglect.

The 'Housing Question' entered the election in various guises, in discussions over municipal building programmes, overcrowding and the local housing shortage and, most importantly, increased rents. Paisley experienced 'rapid progress' in its provision of council-funded housing in the 1920s and by 1934, 2,739 houses had been built with the financial assistance provided under the 1919 House, Town Planning (Scotland)

214 Cook, *Age of Alignment*, p. 19.
215 Ibid., p. 18.
216 Kelley, 'Asquith at Paisley', p. 158.
217 PCL, 320 Ren–1, PLA, Executive Committee Meeting, 14 Dec. 1922.
218 PAEU, AEU (Paisley Branch No. 5, Formerly the United Machine Workers Association, Paisley Branch) Minute Book, 20 Feb. 1922.
219 *PDE*, 13 Nov. 1922.

Act ('Addison Act') and later under Wheatley's Act of 1924.[220] Whilst local Labour bodies supported this initiative, frequent complaints were made regarding the high rents charged by the council, and recommendations were made that rents should be set at 1/8 of the lowest wage.[221] Private enterprise failed likewise to solve the local housing shortage in Paisley where, in 1921, 64.6% of the population occupied one- and two-apartment houses and 50% of the 'ticketed' houses on inspection proved to be overcrowded.[222] Whilst it must be emphasised that Scottish tenants in general had, for a long period, exhibited a preference for 'low-rented' and thus 'amenity deficient housing', the rise in rents facilitated by the introduction of the 1920 Rent Act, brought the state of Scottish housing to the fore in the general election of 1922.[223]

Overturning the 1915 rent restrictions, the 1920 act provided for rent increases of 15% of the net rent and an additional 25% where responsibility for repairs lay with the landlord.[224] In Paisley, an average increase of around 10% was applied by local factors and landlords in 1920.[225] Whilst the Industrial Committee of the local Labour party decided in August to make no recommendation regarding the strike call made by the Scottish Labour Housing Association [SLHA] against the increased rents, many local unions – some sending delegates to SLHA conferences in Glasgow – passed resolutions in support of the call for a general strike on the 23rd.[226] Yet the majority of Paisley workers failed to answer the strike call and a 'good start' was reported by most of the public works on the day of the strike.[227] The following week, local factors reported that 'with very few exceptions, rents were promptly paid' and, despite the picketing of many landlords' offices and the display of SLHA posters in tenement windows, local rent strike activists 'admitted that Paisley was far behind in the No-Rent movement'.[228]

220 PCL, W. Gallacher, 'Paisley in the 1930s' (unpublished manuscript, *c.*1980), p. 22. See also D. Niven, *The Development of Housing in Scotland* (London, 1979), pp. 26–9.

221 TLC, 30 Apr. 1919. Note that in 1922 many council tenants had had to give up their new houses because they 'could not afford the rent'. (Statement by Provost Lang [Paisley] to Housing Congress, Glasgow: *PDE*, 21 Apr. 1922.)

222 Gallacher, 'Paisley in the 1930s', p. 22; *PDE*, 16 Mar. 1921.

223 Note: 'Easier summary eviction for the non-payment of rent inclined Scottish tenants to opt for a rental level commensurate with their ability to pay, whatever misfortunes befell them', R. Rodger, 'The Victorian building industry and the housing of the Scottish working class', in M. Doughty (ed.), *Building the Industrial City* (Leicester, 1986), p. 189. See also J. Butt, 'Working-class housing in Glasgow, 1900–1939, in MacDougall, *Essays in Scottish Labour History*, p. 152.

224 McLean, *Legend of Red Clydeside*, p. 167.

225 Note comment made to local Labour party: 'practically all houses occupied by the working classes with the exception of a few owned by the Co-operative Societies had been subjected to increases': TLC, 6 Oct. 1920.

226 TLC, 18 Aug. 1920; PAEU, AEU (Paisley Branch No. 7) Minutes, 6 Jul. 1920; 17 Aug. 1920; AEU (Paisley Branch No. 5) Minutes, 3 May 1920; 12 Jul. 1920; 18 Apr. 1921.

227 *PDE*, 20 Aug. 1920; 23 Aug. 1920.

228 Ibid., 20 Aug. 1920; 23 Aug. 1920; 31 Aug. 1920.

Following the failure of the rent strike in 1920, the initiative in the housing question passed to the SLHA, whose actions in representing the interests of tenants in the test case of Kerr *v.* Bryde as it made its way through the court of session and on to the lords, on the very eve of the 1922 election, produced 'an uncovenanted bonus' for Labour.[229] By a three votes to two majority, the House of Lords defended the judgement of the lord president in the court of session, that under the terms of the 1920 Act a factor had to give a tenant notice of removal *before* any increase in rent could be imposed. As a result, tenants were entitled to have returned to them a sum roughly equal to around twelve months' rent and rates which could be deducted from future rent.[230] The decision was an unqualified success for the SLHA and made a strong impression on the nation-wide Labour campaign at the general election.[231] In Paisley however, Biggar's status as a factor made it far more difficult for Labour to exploit the lords' decision. Biggar instead focused on Labour's municipal and state-financed building programme rather than the rents issue. Thus, while some credit must be given to Asquith's focus on the rents issue as an important aspect influencing his reduced majority, in Paisley this proved a far less important dimension than in Glasgow where, as Johnston remarked, the decision proved to be 'a gift from the gods'.[232]

Described by Wood as 'one of the most decisive factors working to Labour's advantage in 1922' in Scotland, the Irish Catholic vote in Paisley proved a united force behind Labour during the 1922 election to a degree unrealised in the elections of 1918 and 1920.[233] Foremost within Biggar's election committee were local members of the Catholic Socialist Society and other Irish nationalist groups, and the recent experience of co-operation at the Education Authority elections that year prepared the organisational groundwork for combined parliamentary action.[234] At a meeting of Irish electors in November, opposition to a resolution proposing support for Biggar occasioned only one amendment proposal and the resolution in favour of Biggar was declared carried 'unanimously' by the chairman.[235]

The year 1922, therefore, reflects the fragmented state of the once unified Liberal vision which determined the power of Liberal philosophy on a local level. The loss of the Irish vote, and the manner in which unemployment and the rents question made the abstract notion of class

229 Brown, 'Labour Party and Political Change in Scotland', pp. 140–2; McLean, *Legend of Red Clydeside*, p. 171.
230 McLean, *Legend of Red Clydeside*, p. 172.
231 Ibid., p. 173. See also NLS, MS Muirhead, Acc. 3721, Box 139 (215), Cutting from *Glasgow Herald*, 22 Jan. 1923.
232 McLean, *Legend of Red Clydeside*, p. 173.
233 Wood, 'Hope deferred: Labour in Scotland in the 1920s', p. 30.
234 *Glasgow Observer and Catholic Herald*, 4 Nov. 1922.
235 *PDE*, 13 Nov. 1922.

more meaningful as the ordering concept at the root of society, destabilised Asquith's concept of community. His statement to a meeting in the Central Hall that 'the Liberal was the only party which stood for all classes' and that 'Class government was opposed to the best interests of democracy' failed to touch the keenest concerns of a predominantly working-class electorate whose common interests were being starkly illuminated by the experience of unemployment.[236] Gramsci clearly defines how such economic determinants provide a critical context within which an 'organic' change in political perspectives may occur when he writes:

> economic crises ... create a terrain more favourable to the dissemination of certain modes of thought, and certain ways of posing and resolving questions involving the entire subsequent development of national life.[237]

1923: 'unfortunate local circumstances'

In the Executive report of the Scottish Council of the Labour Party of 1923, it was stated that the 'potential Labour seats' of Paisley, Kelvingrove, Greenock and Motherwell 'were not won through unfortunate local circumstances'.[238] In Paisley such circumstances were elemented by long-running Co-operative Party–Labour Party hostilities and the emergence of a strong Communist voice in the local Labour party; this resulted in the nomination of two 'Labour' candidates in the general election of 1923, which again saw Asquith victorious.[239] Whilst it is unhelpful, as McKibbin has done, to postulate that Asquith would have been defeated by 'a Co-operative candidate', 'had it not been for a bitter dispute within the "democratic" forces of the constituency', the causes of the dispute within the Labour ranks beg further consideration.[240]

'Very prolonged negotiations' in Paisley, referred to in the Scottish Council Executive report, began soon after the election of 1922 and were set against local concerns over the apparent decline of Labour fortunes.[241] Following the decision in favour of Communist party affiliation to the local Labour party, passed by eight votes to five on 24 January 1923, a conference was held three days later, involving all affiliated societies to the local Labour party and attended also by Ben Shaw and Robert Murray (MP for West Renfrewshire).[242] At this meeting, David Maxwell, a local Communist activist,

236 Ibid., 4 Nov. 1922.
237 Gramsci, *Selections from the Prison Notebooks*, p. 184.
238 NLS, Labour Party (Scottish Council), *Executive Report* (1923), p. 7.
239 See below, Appendix 4.
240 R. McKibbin, *The Evolution of the Labour Party, 1910–1924* (Oxford, 1974), p. 185.
241 NLS, 5.2707, Labour Party (Scottish Council), *Executive Report* (1923), p. 7.
242 TLC, 27 Jan. 1923.

> stressed the point that one of the main reasons for the decay of the Labour Party in Paisley was the lack of interest being shown by the Industrial delegates to the local Party. He also pointed to the decline in membership in Trade Unions and while matters remained like this even if [they] gained control of various authorities [they] had no guarantee that the workers' standard of living would be raised.[243]

The Plumbers' delegate, in similar vein, criticised calls for a district political organiser as 'futile'. Ultimately, the conference voted unanimously for the following resolution:

> That this Conference recommends to the organised workers of Paisley the necessity of giving all their support to the local Labour Party and Industrial Committee in their efforts to organise the workers of Paisley and obtain proper representation in local Councils and the Imperial Parliament and to assist in the organisation of all workers in their respective Trade Unions in order to obtain control of the Industry where they work.[244]

The failure of the local Labour party to harness the discontent of the unemployed and 'take command of the Unemployment problem' thus determined the return to a call for a form of 'direct action' and an overall philosophical eclecticism which denoted that local political initiative had been allowed to pass to local Communist sympathisers and interest groups – namely the SLHA and the Unemployed Committee.[245]

Against National Executive opposition, Paisley Labour party defended its decision to permit Communist party affiliation to the local branch at a meeting in April, and in September voted by eleven votes to four in support of the Communist nominees at the local municipal elections.[246] Yet it was in the contribution of local Communists to the growing Labour disillusionment with John M. Biggar that the true power of this minority may be gauged. Whilst McKibbin has questioned the influence of local Paisley Communists in the growing discontent with the Co-operative candidate, declaring that 'the fact that the dissidents allowed themselves to be addressed by Harry Pollitt ... and met in the Communist Hall tells us little', a closer examination of the key players who repeatedly challenged the Co-operative right to the seat reveals a distinct Communist presence.[247]

243 Ibid., 27 Jan. 1923.
244 Ibid., 27 Jan. 1923.
245 Ibid., 27 Jan. 1923. Note, the local branch of the SLHA was invited to affiliate to the local Labour party at a party meeting on 31 January: TLC, 31 Jan. 1923. In the Kelvingrove constituency of Glasgow, Communist infiltration of the local Labour party had been facilitated, in a similar manner, by Communist membership of the local Co-operative party: McKibbin, *Evolution of the Labour Party*, p. 188.
246 TLC, 4 Apr. 1923; 12 Sep. 1923.
247 McKibbin, *Evolution of the Labour Party*, pp. 185–6.

In June 1923, it became the finding of the local Labour party executive 'to oppose the name of Mr J. M. Biggar as candidate', as recent investigations had shown that Biggar 'had been very harsh with some tenants in the Sheriff Court trying to evict tenants from their homes'.[248] Thereafter, following months of fruitless negotiation, on 15 November, Co-operators and representatives of the Labour party, the ILP, the Unemployed Committee and the SLHA met to discuss the parliamentary situation. The Labour party deputation included the Communists, Gormley and Maxwell, J. Stewart of the ILP and Thomas Scollan, now Labour party chairman.[249] Gormley made clear that the Unemployed Committee 'could not entertain the idea of a house factor as candidate', and Scollan stated that the Labour party 'would support any other candidate but J. M. Biggar', a stance echoed by the representative of the SLHA.[250] The ILP, represented by Allan McLean, reaffirmed the party's neutrality in the controversy, yet in a private meeting with the Co-operative executive committee, McLean seconded an amendment that the party seek another candidate. This proposal attracted only two votes against a motion in favour of retaining Biggar as the Co-operative candidate which, attracting twenty-four votes, became the recommendation of the committee.[251] In response, the following day the Labour party voted by thirty-four votes to two in favour of running their own Labour candidate, the motion to this effect having been moved by Gormley and seconded by J. McLaughlin of the SLHA.[252] Thereafter, from a list of potential candidates which included G. Hunters[253] (the nominee of the local Bakers' Union), D. D. Cormack of Dumbarton (nominee of the SLHA) and Harry Pollitt, nominated by Gormley and seconded by McLaughlin, D. D. Cormack was adopted as the Labour candidate with a majority of thirty votes – Pollitt's candidature having been ruled 'out of order' by the chairman.[254] Two days later, Cormack's candidature received unanimous approval from a meeting of the Labour party during which an election committee was chosen which included the names of Maxwell, Gormley and McLaughlin.[255]

248 TLC, 6 Jun. 1923.

249 Ibid., 16 Nov. 1923. Note that the SLHA was becoming a prominent force in the burgh, its membership having hit the thousand mark this year: *PDE*, 27 Feb. 1923.

250 CP Minutes, 15 Nov. 1923.

251 *Forward*, 22 Dec. 1923. Note how in this article by J. M. Biggar, the blame for the 1923 defeat is placed at the feet of the local ILP.

252 TLC, 16 Nov. 1923.

253 Note: It is probable that the Bakers' representative given as 'G. Hunters' in the TLC Minutes was in fact W. G. Hunter of the Operative Bakers and Confectioners of Scotland who had served on the Parliamentary Committee of the STUC from 1913 to 1917: A. Tuckett, *The Scottish Trades Union Congress: The First Eighty Years, 1897–1977* (Edinburgh, 1986), p. 120.

254 TLC, 16 Nov. 1923.

255 Ibid., 18 Nov. 1923.

Thus, as in Greenock, Paisley was faced with a split candidature on the left in 1923.[256] In November, Biggar secured the endorsement of the Labour Party's Scottish and National Executives, and, despite the appearance of Cormack's name on a list of candidates endorsed by the ILP, the national ILP declared later that this was a mistake, and the local ILP branch maintained its neutral stance in a policy declaration in December.[257] Whilst Cormack sponsored a last-minute bid for reconciliation – proposing that Ramsay MacDonald be allowed to nominate the Paisley candidate – two 'Labour' candidates eventually stood for election.[258]

In terms of policy, little divided Biggar and Cormack, a lawyer and former army lieutenant during the Great War who had been awarded the Military Cross and who, in addition to his defence of tenants' rights as the lawyer in the first hearings of the Kerr *v.* Bryde case, had recently defended Paisley tenants from eviction in a case sponsored by the local SLHA.[259] Both supported the capital levy; both favoured the opening up of trade with Russia; and both attempted to refocus the campaign away from the question of free trade versus protection to unemployment, housing, education and social reform. Where they differed was in their presentation of the housing problem and their appreciation of the recent party dispute. Biggar, as in 1922, focused on the Labour Party's house-building programme, while Cormack and his supporters exploited the Co-operator's damning record on rents. Yet beyond this fundamental question, the choice of Labour candidate was framed in terms of local rights versus executive authority. In contrast to the 'big names' – Patrick Dollan and Neil McLean, for example – who graced Biggar's platforms, Cormack's support was predominantly local in character. Asserting the 'right' of the local Labour party to select its own candidate, free from the dictation of an unaffiliated association, Cormack's candidature illuminated lasting ambiguities in local Labour relations and wider questions regarding executive power which were to colour the electoral fight in the locality in the following year.

Nationally, however, the 1923 election was one dominated largely by the question of protectionism, Baldwin's challenge to free trade that year having given rise to the reconciliation of Lloyd George and Asquith and necessitating a general election on the issue.[260] The results showed a 'revived' Liberal Party with 29.7% of the vote nation-wide, securing 158 MPs to Labour's 191 and the Unionists' 258.[261] Yet such an optimistic analysis is only accurate in part.

256 Brown, 'Labour Party and Political Change in Scotland', p. 270. Also: Wood, 'Hope deferred: Labour in Scotland in the 1920s', p. 41.

257 *PDE*, 21 Nov. 1923; 26 Nov. 1923; 30 Nov. 1923; 1 Dec. 1923.

258 Ibid., 22 Nov. 1923.

259 Ibid., 28 Nov. 1923.

260 Searle, *Liberal Party*, pp. 142–3.

261 Cook, *Short History of the Liberal Party*, p. 94.

'Reunification when it came in 1923 owed more to Baldwin's incompetence than to any desire for reconciliation ... at a national level the new-found unity of the Party ... was never anything other than superficial.'[262] Indeed, in a confidential memorandum of 1926, Asquith described the reunion as 'a fiction, if not a farce' and referred to Liberal unity as 'an abuse of language'.[263] In Paisley, where Lloyd George and Asquith shared a platform on 24 November, the reunion, whilst attracting great attention, proved a minor feature of the Liberal campaign, the local Lloyd George Liberals having been routed in 1920.[264]

Rather, as nationally, the question of protection dominated the Liberal campaign in Paisley. At the first meeting of his campaign, Asquith reflected on his first visit to Paisley, twenty years before, when he had defended free trade against the Chamberlainite onslaught and reiterated the familiar attacks on the whole-hogger mentality.[265] Yet the Liberal case was framed this time as a conservative measure, as Asquith made clear on 23 November: 'The Liberal Party in this election was on the defensive upon two fronts. It was on the defensive against Protection, and it was on the defensive against Socialism. (Cheers.)'[266] Although attempting further to show that theirs was 'not merely an attitude of resistance and negation', the Liberals, however, failed.[267] Whilst the Liberals claimed tariffs represented no cure for unemployment, contemporary realities proved that neither did free trade, in and of itself, hold the solution to the country's economic problems. The Paisley Liberals presented themselves as the party of 'common sense', defending the 'established right' of free trade but went little beyond such protestations of faith in 'the old battle cry'.[268]

In the light of new political alignments, the echoes of the Edwardian tariff reform controversy, cast Liberalism in the light of a strangely 'old-fashioned' creed and imbued the campaign with the futile air of a battle long since consigned to the pages of history. In his opening address, Cormack recast the campaign as 'a battle between the "auld red lichts" and the "new red lichts"', claiming for himself the legacy of the Paisley weavers who 'while they were weaving those beautiful webs ... were also dreaming dreams of a social fabric as sound and sensible and yet at the same time as homely and harmonious as their beautiful shawls'.[269] 'Labourists today' he challenged, 'were carrying on the tradition of Radicalism.'[270]

262 Searle, *Liberal Party*, p. 145.
263 BLO, MS Asquith 35.252, Confidential Memorandum, 4 Oct. 1926.
264 *PDE*, 26 Nov. 1923.
265 Ibid., 21 Nov. 1923.
266 Ibid., 24 Nov. 1923.
267 Ibid., 24 Nov. 1923.
268 Cook, *Short History of the Liberal Party*, p. 92.
269 *PDE*, 21 Nov. 1923.
270 Ibid., 21 Nov. 1923.

Yet, while the combined Labour vote in 1923 would have comfortably defeated Asquith had it been in the possession of one candidate rather than two, it is likewise important to note that the combined anti-Labour vote presents a far larger majority in favour of the established parties. Unionism still retained a voice.

Rumours circulated early in the contest that moves were afoot to organise a pact between the Liberals and Unionists across Renfrewshire.[271] However, on 23 November, Lt.-Col. Archibald Douglas McInnes Shaw, councillor for the Maryhill ward of Glasgow and son of that city's lord provost, was adopted as the Unionist candidate for Paisley.[272] What is crucial to note is that the Unionists did not agree to contest the seat until *after* Cormack had been adopted by the Labour Party, thus effectively splitting the Labour vote. References, therefore, to 1923 as the Labour victory that never was become meaningless, as it seems likely that without Cormack, there would have been no Unionist challenge to Asquith's position.

Since 1920, local Unionist organisation, in contrast to national developments, had declined, with the main body encouraging a 'Unionist perspective' on contemporary issues in Paisley being the avowedly non-party Women's Guild of Empire who sought to educate local women in the 'combating [of] Socialism and Communism'.[273] Established in 1920 with a membership of forty, the guild, by March 1922, boasted 560 members – a figure which rose to 940 by 1923.[274] Organising social events somewhat in the manner of the late Primrose League, the guild attracted many prominent local women to its ranks, among them Mrs W. H. Coats, its chairwoman in 1922, and Mrs Hamilton of Blackland, who was elected chairwoman of the guild's housing committee in 1923. However, whilst the popularity of the guild clearly highlights Hutchison's claims for a Unionist Party adept at attracting the support of women, his further claim that the young were also being attracted by the Unionist vision demands qualification. It was not until 1924 that a branch of the Junior Imperialist Union was established in Paisley.[275]

Throughout the early 1920s, the local Unionist association appears silent, meetings being held only very irregularly, and even then dominated by a small local clique led by the Coats of Woodside. In this regard Paisley illustrates the general rule elaborated by Gordon Brown of local Unionist constituency organisation being poor in Liberal-held

271 Ibid., 22 Nov. 1923.

272 *PRG*, 24 Nov. 1923. Note that Mrs W. H. Coats had been invited to stand in the Unionist interest in Paisley but had declined.

273 *PDE*, 23 Mar. 1922. For national picture, see Hutchison, *Political History of Scotland*, p. 316; and Brown, 'Labour Party and Political Change in Scotland', pp. 168–77.

274 *PRG*, 7 Oct. 1922; *PDE*, 23 Mar. 1923; 30 Mar. 1923.

275 NLS, SCUA, Acc. 14241/99.i, Minutes of the Central Council and Executive Committee of the Junior Imperialist Union, 4 Mar. 1924.

seats.[276] In 1922, a meeting of the party hierarchy in London had pre-empted local debate by recommending that Paisley should not be contested at the forthcoming election.[277] Thus the local association was bereft of even the impetus of an election fight to encourage organisation following immediately on from the disaster of 1920. Even in 1923, there were many local Unionists who considered it inadvisable to challenge Asquith, whilst other 'timid Tories' threatened to vote for the Liberal candidate regardless of a Unionist challenge.[278] In 1923, the Unionist candidate thus stood without the backing of a strong constituency association, or even a unity of purpose among its members.

Shaw, however, did attract considerable support – 4,000 attending his Drill Hall meeting on the Tuesday before the poll.[279] Courting both the middle- and working-class vote, he recommended smaller, lower-cost rented accommodation provided by local government; promoted protection as a 'bargaining lever' in world markets; attacked the Liberal party as 'weak' and cast Labour in the role of the real opposition; and stressed the advantages of protective tariffs for Scottish business and the health of the empire.[280] In addition, despite the fact that the Orange movement had withdrawn its representatives from the Unionist Party councils in 1922, as a prominent Orangeman – he became the Grand Master for the order in Scotland in 1924 – Shaw undoubtedly activated the Paisley order to a level of political awareness in 1923 unmatched since the pre-war days, and, through his connections with the order, won many working-class votes from Labour.[281] Throughout the campaign, he proved a popular candidate, the *Express* noting that his 'vigorous style, transparent honesty and sincerity of purpose have appealed even to the extremists of the Labour Party'.[282] Yet even such an attractive candidate failed to win the seat for the Unionists.

Ultimately, Shaw polled 2,000 votes less than Asquith, proving the persistent power of Liberalism for middle-class voters – many of whom rejected Shaw, seeing the Liberals as the most powerful alternative to the 'socialist menace' in Paisley. In this manner it is clear that whilst nationally the middle-class vote was 'going' Unionist; in Paisley Liberalism had, by 1923, evolved as the dominant party of the

276 Brown, 'Labour Party and Political Change in Scotland', p. 187.
277 *PDE*, 28 Oct. 1922, 1 Nov. 1922.
278 *PRG*, 24 Nov. 1923, Letters from 'Protection and Prosperity' and 'Safety First'.
279 *PRG*, 8 Dec. 1923.
280 Ibid., 24 Nov. 1923; *PDE*, 27 Nov. 1923; 28 Nov. 1923; 29 Nov. 1923.
281 G. Walker, 'The Orange Order in Scotland between the Wars', *IRSH*, xxxvii (1992), pp. 186–7; *PRG*, 20 Dec. 1924. Note the comment made by Biggar that if Shaw's vote in the 1923 contest was to be analysed 'possibly there might be proved a share of some of those who supported Co-operation and Labour at the last Election: *PDE*, 7 Dec. 1923.
282 *PDE*, 30 Nov. 1923.

'establishment' in the area, granting validity to Labour claims to the radical tradition of the burgh.[283]

Here, critically, we observe a moment of crisis in the organisation of the local party system where, in the dual role of the Liberal party as defender of the establishment and traditional guarantor of local radicalism, an 'organic contradiction' became apparent which, if it were to be resolved, necessitated a transformation in the political structure.[284] Irreducible to the mere economic context of the challenge, the 1923 election marks a fundamental stage in the fragmentation of local Liberalism.

The Labour Challenger

At the ninth annual conference of the Labour Party (Scottish Council) of March 1924, Thomas Scollan, as one of the Paisley Labour party delegates, moved the following resolution:

> That this Conference discuss and define the rights and powers of Local Labour Parties and National Executives relative to the selection of candidates, and that the proceedings in Paisley in December be taken as a basis for discussion, and that the relation of the Co-operative Party to the Labour Party be also defined.[285]

Although, on the recommendation of William Shaw, the chairman, Scollan had to withdraw the resolution, his defence of the actions of the Paisley Labour party in 1923 included an explicit attack on the National Executive, whose decision to endorse Biggar was referred to as 'autocracy, flouting the will of the local Labour Party'. Instead, Scollan declared, he wanted 'democracy from the bottom to the top, so that they would prevent another bungle. Paisley could be won, and would be won, if they had unity in their ranks.'[286]

During the ten months separating the 1923 and 1924 elections, the search for a Paisley Labour candidate threw into relief national dilemmas in the party – the rights of local parties and the position of the Co-operative party and so-called 'Co-operative seats' – and became a test case for policy on such matters at the highest level.

Despite the problems of 1923, at the beginning of 1924 'both the Co-operative Party and the Scottish Executive seem to have assumed that the seat was still to be a Co-operative one'.[287] However, following the local Co-operative party adoption in February of Hugh B. Guthrie, a local school teacher and staunch ILPer who had contested Camlachie in

283 Hutchison, *Political History of Scotland*, p. 321.
284 Sassoon, *Gramsci's Politics*, p. 183.
285 NLS, 5.2707, Labour Party (Scottish Council), *Report of the Ninth Annual Conference*, p. 38.
286 Ibid., p. 38.
287 McKibbin, *Evolution of the Labour Party*, p. 186.

the Labour interest in 1918, it was clear that the local Labour party still did not accept the Co-operative Party's apparent prior claim to the seat.[288]

In January, John Stewart, the ILP delegate to the local Labour party, had blamed the actions of the Labour Party's Scottish and National Executives for the disunity at the 1923 election, and from then on the ILP proved the most vocal opponent of compromise with the Co-operative ranks.[289] In March, whilst Guthrie – chosen ultimately to placate the local Labourists – had been endorsed by the Scottish Co-operative Party, the local Labour party called on affiliated societies to propose nominees for the Labour candidature.[290] Arguing that on Biggar's retiral the Co-operative claim on the constituency had lapsed, on 3 April the Paisley ILP proposed Rosslyn Mitchell, the Glasgow lawyer and former Labour candidate for Glasgow Central, for the Labour candidature.[291] Having already secured the support of the Scottish Advisory Committee of the ILP, Mitchell was duly adopted as Labour candidate for the burgh in May.[292]

Earlier attempts at reconciliation included a 'Unity Conference' of all the parties concerned in March which approved a resolution asserting the equal rights of trade unions, Labour party affiliates and the local Co-operative Defence Committee to nominate a candidate. It also called on the National Executive of the Co-operative Party to 'sanction the formation of a joint selection committee composed of representatives from the Paisley Labour Party and the Paisley Co-operative Defence Committee'.[293] But such moves failed to secure a solution. At a joint meeting later that month, the Labour party made it clear that as far as they were concerned 'the working agreement which was in practice before the dispute could not be resumed'.[294]

By the end of May a stalemate had been reached when the Labour Party National Executive refused to endorse Mitchell until relations with the Co-operative Party had been resolved.[295] Then in June, a delegation appointed by the National Executive headed to Glasgow to hear the cases of the competing factions.[296]

288 CP Minutes, 4 Feb. 1924; *PDE*, 3 Feb. 1924.

289 See also Hutchison, *Political History of Scotland*, p. 302.

290 CP Minutes, 6 Mar. 1924; TLC, 19 Mar. 1924. See also McKibbin, *Evolution of the Labour Party*, p. 186. Note a report to the Labour Party NEC which recorded that 'It was felt that this nomination would be acceptable to the Labour forces': British Labour Party, NEC Minutes, *Report of Joint Meeting held Between NEC and Co-operative Party (14 Apr. 1924)*, 23 Apr. 1924.

291 TLC, 3 Apr. 1924. (This was the closing date for nominations and Mitchell stood as the sole nominee.) See also McKibbin, *Evolution of the Labour Party*, p. 186.

292 TLC, 14 May 1924; LSE, ILP Archive, 1/6, NAC Minutes, 27.19 Jun. 1924. Note that NAC endorsement went ahead despite the protests of the 'Exchange' branch of the Party.

293 *PDE*, 8 Mar. 1924; TLC, 5 Mar. 1924.

294 CP Minutes, 20 Mar. 1924.

295 TLC, 21 May 1924.

296 Ibid., 18 Jun. 1924.

On 21 June, the National Executive deputation, consisting of E. P. Wake (national agent) and C. T. Cramp (chairman of the National Executive), arrived in Glasgow where they were joined by William Shaw, chairman of the executive committee of the Scottish Council, and Ben Shaw, the Scottish secretary.[297] Hearing first the case of the National Executive of the Co-operative Party, the deputation were informed that 'Paisley had been fought at considerable expense by the Co-operative Party on four occasions' and that as a party they 'had a prior claim to the candidature'.[298] Rosslyn Mitchell was interviewed thereafter, however, and claimed to have been 'nominated and selected in the usual constitutional way by the Paisley Divisional Labour Party'. He emphasised that he had had no wish to 'start a rebel movement in the Labour Party', but stressed that 'the National Executive would have a difficult task in getting the Paisley Labour Party to support Mr Hugh Guthrie'. Rather he made clear that the 'Paisley Labour Party claimed its constitutional right under our rules to select a Labour candidate.'[299]

After hearing Hugh Guthrie, a delegation from the ILP was heard, including among their number both national and local representatives. In the course of the interview, W. H. Martin, the chairman of the ILP Scottish Council, like Mitchell, stressed the constitutional position:

> He claimed that to allow the Co-operative Party to keep Paisley as their preserve was to place an unaffiliated organisation in a superior position to any of the constituent parts of the Labour Party ... [He] claimed on behalf of the affiliated branches to the Paisley Labour Party the right of that constituency to select a Labour candidate and to determine for themselves whether the constituency should be regarded as a Labour or Co-operative Division.[300]

The testimony of the local Labour party, delivered by a deputation which included Thomas Scollan and John Stewart – both ILP members – in addition to John Gormley, now the secretary of the new individual members section of the local Labour party, and Allan Young, the Painters' delegate to the party, stressed the character of the working arrangement with the Co-operative party 'on the ground':

297 Andersonian Library, British Labour Party, NEC Minutes, *Report of Deputation Appointed by National Executive to Enquire into the Paisley Position with regard to the Nomination of Mr Hugh Guthrie M.A., as Co-operative Candidate and the Nomination of Mr E. Rosslyn Mitchell, M.A. L.L.B., as the Labour Candidate* (report dated 26 Aug. 1924, to be found in minutes of NEC Meeting dated 2 Sep. 1924).

298 Ibid., 2 Sep. 1924.

299 Ibid., 2 Sep. 1924.

300 Ibid., 2 Sep. 1924, fo. 375. Note Phipps's observation of the Aberdeen Labour movement in these years: 'There was an inherent conflict between a centralizing Labour Party bent on state intervention having to use trades councils, the product and symbol of local working class autonomy, to build up its organization': Phipps, 'Aberdeen Trades Council', p. 215.

the Co-operative Party as an efficient fighting organisation does not exist in Paisley. The political work as far as propaganda and organisation were concerned, had been carried out by the Labour Party even for the Co-operative candidates in the past.[301]

Aside from the immediate local importance of the crisis, however, the national perspective clearly occupied the minds of the National Executive deputation, who, in consultation with the executive of the Scottish Council, referred to the 'very loose' agreement which existed between Co-operative and Labour executives regarding the selection of candidates. Wake emphasised that they 'had to consider whether the Co-operative Party was to be exploited by other elements; or was to work in harmony with us'. Yet he did admit that all decisions made at national level regarding candidatures 'were subject to the good will and consent of the divisional Labour parties'.[302]

The following day, the deputation travelled to Paisley for a general meeting with the local Labour party. Here again Cramp 'emphasised the necessity of consideration being given to the National issue involved and the desirability of maintaining harmonious working between Labour and Co-operation throughout the country'.[303] Yet, whilst the National Executive report here records that Cramp suggested the Labour party consider a further conference with the local Co-operative party, local Labour party minutes in contrast record that Wake, whilst acknowledging the constitutional rights of the local party to nominate a candidate, had remarked that 'the local party could make it easier if they were to accept the position that this was a Co-operative seat and forego their rights as a Labour Party'.[304] Clearly the implications of the Paisley crisis went far beyond 'local passions'.

Following reports that further negotiations had proved fruitless, the report concluded with the recommendation that 'it [was] impossible to resist the claim of the Paisley Labour Party to select and run a Labour candidate for the constituency' and encouraged that 'the terms of the Agreement [with the Co-operative Party] be more clearly defined ... it [being] distinctly understood that the agreement can only operate in cases where mutual arrangement is obtained locally.'[305] However, on consideration of the report of the June meetings, the National Executive resolved to meet again with the Co-operative party and defer the endorsement of Rosslyn Mitchell.[306] Endorsement was finally granted by the NEC in November, following the decision of the local Co-operative

301 Andersonian Library, British Labour Party, NEC Minutes, *Report of Deputation Appointed by National Executive* ... (minutes of NEC Meeting dated 2 Sep. 1924, fo. 375).

302 Ibid., 2 Sep. 1924, fo. 376.

303 Ibid., 2 Sep. 1924, fo. 377.

304 Ibid., 2 Sep. 1924, fo. 377, TLC, 22 Jun. 1924.

305 Ibid., 2 Sep. 1924, fo. 377.

306 Andersonian Library, British Labour Party, NEC Minutes, 2 Sep. 1924.

party not to challenge Mitchell's candidature, in a vote that recorded only one opponent and two abstainers.[307]

Nationally, the Paisley case acted as the focus of debate regarding Labour–Co-operative relations in the months that followed and provided the background to the decision taken at the 1925 Co-operative Congress which passed a resolution in favour of 'a working arrangement with the Labour Party over candidates and elections' and the Cheltenham Agreement of 1927 which encouraged closer relations between the executives of the two parties and 'provided that the local Co-operative parties should be eligible for affiliation to divisional Labour Parties with representation and voting rights corresponding to the affiliation fees paid'.[308]

In Paisley, however, Mitchell's endorsement highlighted the increased strength of the local ILP. As Hutchison has reflected: 'Paisley represents in microcosm the power of the ILP within the Labour Party. In this burgh both the Communist and Co-operative parties had been skilfully outmanoeuvred.'[309] Such a statement, however, must be qualified by the knowledge of the declining national power of the Co-operative Party as an influence on Labour party policy; the rejection earlier that year of local Communist party affiliation following the national Congress decision; and the long-running nature of Co-operative–Labour disharmony in the burgh which the ILP was able to exploit and of which 1924 was only one chapter.[310] Whilst the ILP was 'skilful', its timing was also fortunate.

The Liberal Champion

Writing to W. M. R. Pringle in January 1924, Asquith reflected on the Liberal policy towards the imminent creation of the first Labour government:

> we must give the Labour Government a reasonable chance, at the same time being careful not to arouse the suspicion that we are acting in collusion, and with a new coalition ...
>
> There is moreover a real danger of damping down party enthusiasm, and giving no immediate satisfaction to the fighting spirit.[311]

307 TLC, 5 Nov. 1924; CP Minutes, 13 Oct. 1924.
308 Smith and Ostergaard, *Constitutional Relations Between the Labour and Co-operative Parties*, pp. 7–8; See also Cole, *Century of Co-operation*, p. 323.
309 Hutchison, *Political History of Scotland*, p. 303.
310 Note the following: 'It seems that by the end of 1924 Head Office was much more sceptical about the possible value of an alliance with the Co-operative movement than it had been before the war. It is doubtful whether London was ever as enthusiastic as Glasgow; yet even Glasgow gave the air (at least) of being sadder and wiser for its experience': McKibbin, *Evolution of the Labour Party*, p. 188.
311 BLO, MS Asquith 46, fo. 153, H. H. Asquith to W. M. R. Pringle, 10 Jan. 1924.

In Paisley, Asquith's support of the new MacDonald administration aroused the suspicion he had feared and challenged the loyalty of a number of party activists, among them the former Liberal association president, William Galbraith, who, in association with a group of local businessmen of both parties, in a public call for support in January, commented:

> There appears to be a strong feeling among supporters of both political parties in the town that there is no necessity for causing an immediate political upheaval, the probable result of which would be the establishment of a Labour Government. It is believed by many prominent men of business that the consequences of such an upheaval would be prejudicial to trade and employment.[312]

Following a meeting of concerned local businessmen of both the Unionist and Liberal parties, chaired by Galbraith, a small committee was formed which drew up a representation to Asquith.[313] Having voiced concern at the 'adverse' effect a Labour government would have on trade, they 'asked him as their representative'

> to consider if the national interest does not demand that, putting party politics in the background, some attempt be made by Liberals and Unionists to assist each other in putting the country on a settled course towards national prosperity.[314]

Asquith, however, responded by reaffirming his commitment that the Labour Party were the 'natural and appropriate successors under existing conditions'.[315]

Asquith's support of the Labour government clearly isolated a proportion of his middle-class support in Paisley. However, the evolution of a local Liberal–Unionist election pact ultimately determined the character of his 1924 campaign, and prevented a greater haemorrhage of support through the removal of Asquith's Unionist challenger, McInnes Shaw, who had been courting the constituency since his defeat in 1923.

Following the collapse of the Labour government over the Campbell case and the Zinoviev letter, in October 1924, a small article in the *Express* announced that the Unionist candidate for West Renfrewshire, A. T. Taylor of Kilmacolm, had resigned from his position due to 'pressure of business'.[316] Two days later, it was reported that rumours were circulating that, in Paisley also, the Unionist candidate was to step down, in this instance to allow Asquith a 'straight fight' against

312 *PDE*, 5 Jan. 1924.

313 Ibid., 8 Jan. 1924.

314 Ibid., 9 Jan. 1924.

315 Ibid., 18 Jan. 1924 (extract from speech by Asquith in the House of Commons, 17 Jan. 1924).

316 Ibid., 4 Oct. 1924.

Mitchell.[317] Such rumours, however, were denied locally and on 9 October, McInnes Shaw appeared in Paisley to make final arrangements for the first meeting of his campaign.[318]

Nevertheless, on 14 October, it was announced that Shaw had stepped down as Unionist candidate for Paisley, only to reappear in the same guise in West Renfrewshire, the seat Taylor had vacated under apparently conventional circumstances less than two weeks before.[319] As the *Express* made clear, the move had been necessitated by an agreement recently entered into in London between the Liberal and Unionist executives to the effect that 'in face of the Socialist menace, the house of the Moderates would cease to be divided against itself and that a united front should be presented to the common "enemy"'.[320] The agreement made way for the removal of the weaker candidate in about eighty-five cases nation-wide where a Liberal and a Unionist faced each other in a constituency contested by Labour, yet it was made clear that the operation of the agreement rested on its approval first in Paisley. At a meeting of Renfrewshire Unionists on the 13th, W. H. Coats had emphasised that 'if Mr Asquith were opposed by a Unionist in Paisley the agreement would be scrapped'.[321] The Paisley Unionists agreed to the pact.

In Scotland, though the terms of the pact are uncertain, it is clear that following Paisley's approval, ultimately twenty-eight constituencies in the west were covered, thus ensuring that the 1924 campaign would be one in which Labour faced a 'combined enemy'.[322]

'The savour of an almost old-world courtesy ...'[323]

An entry in the diary of Lady Violet Bonham Carter on the 1924 Paisley election reflected that 'a new generation of young men who had ripened into voters, almost it seemed since the last election, were determined to give a solid class vote to Labour, no matter what we said ... or what we did.'[324] Going one step further, Asquith explained his defeat in 1924 in terms of the 'steady and open growth of the Socialistic poison which had entered into the body politic in that part of Scotland ... [which] had

317 Ibid., 6 Oct. 1924.

318 Ibid., 6 Oct. 1924; 10 Oct. 1924; 13 Oct. 1924.

319 Ibid., 14 Oct. 1924.

320 Ibid., 14 Oct. 1924.

321 Ibid., 14 Oct. 1914. Note: Gordon Brown has highlighted that 'Paisley was the key seat of the Pact': Brown, 'Labour Party and Political Change in Scotland', p. 339. See also *Forward*, 18 Oct. 1924.

322 Brown, 'Labour Party and Political Change in Scotland', pp. 331–44.

323 *Forward*, 8 Nov. 1924, E. R. Mitchell, 'Paisley'.

324 D. Bennett, *Margot: A Life of the Countess of Oxford and Asquith* (London, 1986), p. 340. Such a perspective reinforces the conclusions of M. Childs, 'Labour grows up: the electoral system, political generations, and British politics, 1890–1929', *TCBH*, vi (1995), pp. 123–44. Here, Childs makes clear: 'an important and growing proportion of new voters would be those who reached their majority between 1910 and 1929': p. 138.

gained the ascendancy ... over the sentiments and emotions of the people'.[325] Both perspectives point to crucial causal factors in Labour's success – the strength of popular enthusiasm for the Labour candidate and Labour's appeal to sentiment and morality.[326]

Edward Rosslyn Mitchell, born in Wiltshire, the son of a celebrated evangelical preacher, became active in Liberal politics during his years studying law at Glasgow University, where he was a prominent member of the Liberal Club, and in 1902 organised Lord Rosebery's rectorial campaign.[327] Despite co-operating with Wheatley in the creation of a national slum clearance and rebuilding programme between 1905 and 1912, his 'conversion' to Labour, however, did not come until 1918, by which time he had become well known as an 'Independent Radical' councillor for Glasgow's Springburn Ward, attaining the position of magistrate in 1915 and occupying the chairmanship of the Parks Committee, the Committee on Galleries and Museums and the governorship of Glasgow School of Art.[328] During the war he had fought the tenants' case on the council against local landlords and co-operated in the defence of the Clyde deportees, organising a petition demanding their release.[329]

In 1918, he joined the ILP, believing that the 'future of radicalism lay in the Labour and not in the Liberal Party [where] it would have a broader base from which to work'.[330] In 1919 he stood against Bonar Law as Labour candidate for the Central Division of Glasgow, and reduced the Conservative majority from 12,877 to 2,514. Then in 1923, he contested the seat again, this time against Sir W. Alexander, and reduced the Conservative majority to only 416 votes.[331]

Mitchell thus entered the Paisley contest in 1924 as an experienced Labour campaigner and, perhaps more importantly, one who had operated successfully in a constituency with a high business profile against a prominent parliamentarian. Following his defeat in 1924, Asquith commented on the Labour campaign in Paisley in a speech to the Reform Club in London:

> He believed that the large growth [in the Labour vote] was due to the indefatigable and intensive use, almost entirely by volunteers – he might say entirely by volunteers – of all the weapons in the arsenal of propaganda – speaking in the highways and by-ways, teaching at school and in class, but not least by the dissemination of handy and readable literature, terse and perhaps full-blooded, but

325 *PDE*, 30 Oct. 1924. See also Asquith, *Memories and Reflections*, p. 179.
326 See below, Appendix 4.
327 Knox, *Scottish Labour Leaders*, pp. 212–14.
328 Ibid., pp. 212–14. Also: Middlemas, *Clydesiders*, p. 53; and *Forward*, 10 Nov. 1923.
329 Middlemas, *Clydesiders*, p. 61.
330 Knox, *Scottish Labour Leaders*, p. 212.
331 Ibid., p. 213.

> easily read and easily remembered, and almost incalculably persuasive in propagandist power. The faith which was so engendered became a real religion – a fanaticism – but when it came to be mobilised it could move mountains.[332]

Clearly, despite the refusal of the Co-operative societies to provide window space, bill-boards and trucks for campaign advertisements, the Labour campaign proved effective. Whilst the Asquith campaign team introduced 'kitchen gatherings', where Lady Bonham Carter attempted to attract the votes of the female electorate, Mitchell's varied meetings programme attracted special attention. Day-time work-gate meetings, trade-union meetings and multiple evening addresses in small and large venues attracted huge crowds. On the polling day, the *Express* recorded that school-children sported Mitchell's photograph in their hats, and the *Gazette* noted that 'the weavers' adorned in Mitchell's colours 'far outnumbered those who sported the Liberal favour'.[333]

The evident enthusiasm engendered by the Labour campaign owed much to the personal qualities and oratory of the Labour candidate. Throughout the campaign, Mitchell's smart appearance, good looks and eloquence attracted the attention of the press and public. This was no 'wild' Clydesider in the Maxton mould. (Indeed, Mitchell joked that David Kirkwood had offered him membership of the Clydeside *fraternité* on condition that he got rid of his spats.)[334] An educated man, and successful lawyer, Mitchell recast the popular image of Labour in Paisley into a form more palatable to the wavering middle-class Liberal voter, and undermined the gruesome imagery of the 'Red Threat' with his evident respectability and prohibitionist stance on the drinks question.[335]

In an article in *Forward* following his success, however, Mitchell focused on philosophy as the critical factor in Labour's success:

> The voters hammered out two conflicting intellectual points of view and decided for the Socialistic as against the individualistic ... The eventual difference between the two sides is that we were affirmative, they were negative; we were creative, they were critical; we were constructive, they were analytical. We tried to explain political principles as ethics. They expressed them as expediency ... We dealt more with human values than money values ...[336]

Mitchell presented a spiritual appreciation of socialism and an ethical interpretation of economic inequalities which in one combined the

332 *PRG*, 15 Nov. 1924.

333 *PDE*, 29 Oct. 1924; *PRG*, 1 Nov. 1924.

334 *PDE*, 27 Dec. 1924. See also Hutchison, *Political History of Scotland*, pp. 279–80.

335 Note comment from Knox: 'the ILP was grateful to receive recruits such as Mitchell as it gave the party a respectable image with the electorate, particularly the middle classes, to whom Mitchell was the Glasgow ILP's 'chief speaker': Knox, *Scottish Labour Leaders*, p. 212.

336 *Forward*, 8 Nov. 1924.

'practical politics' of economic self-interest with a spiritual dimension which encouraged a broader vision of social rights and responsibilities.[337]

In an article in the *New Leader*, he underscored this view by stating that Labour and socialism sought change through 'an Idea'. He wrote:

> this Idea was rather a new apprehending of the Idea of seers and prophets and poets and teachers through the centuries, that love is power, that service is the law of progress, that enrichment of life's quality comes from renunciation, that we gain in social freedom immeasurably more than we surrender in individual liberty, that the heart of man thrives in the home and shrivels in the jungle.[338]

Class politics were thus defined in terms of the evolution of competing plural consciences. In these terms, by appealing to 'rights' rather than to the apparently invisible workings of world trade, the market was effectively 'humanised' and working-class interests acquired the passions of forbidden though justified rights.

Mitchell's election address continued the moral fervour by laying out Labour's principles in the form of mottoes, evoking the character of the lessons of the catechism:

> Labour wants you to fall in love with your country and to love the world.
>
> 'The world is my parish', is the motto of statesman as of preacher.
>
> LOVE and SERVICE are eternally and in all things the laws of life.
>
> The glory of a nation is the splendour of its manhood, the goodness of its womanhood, and the godliness of its government.
>
> LABOUR OFFERS PEACE FOR SAD FOLK EVERYWHERE.[339]

To prove their intrinsic worth, however, Mitchell needed to prove that the responsibilities of love, service and sacrifice, promised a 'new tomorrow'.[340] Here Mitchell emphasised that the 'irresistible progress of democracy' was operating in Labour's favour:

> The old order changes, and with the coming of the new to which the old must yield place, must come also new organisations that can express in action the developed thoughts of the people.[341]

337 In this regard, Mitchell's philosophy mirrored that of the wider ILP as described by Joyce, who sees the party's 'critique of capitalism' as being 'moral' rather than 'economic': Joyce, *Visions of the People*, p. 78.

338 As quoted in *PDE*, 8 Nov. 1924.

339 NLS, MS Muirhead, Acc. 3721, Box 180/7, *Election Address of Mr E. Rosslyn Mitchell* (1924).

340 Similarly, Joyce has highlighted that for most Edwardian Labour activists, the way to power was 'social responsibility overcoming present capitalism ... leading to higher social forms': Joyce, *Visions of the People*, p. 78.

341 NLS, MS Muirhead, Acc. 3721, Box 180/7, *Election Address of Mr E. Rosslyn Mitchell.*

According to Mitchell,

> There are no new Liberals being born. There are no young Conservatives cradled in stability. The new generation emerging from school-room to maturity are with us. God makes a new world for every generation.[342]

In practical terms, the proof that the future lay with Labour was identified in the Liberal–Tory pact through which the Liberal political identity was shown to be contradictory, and in the failure of Liberalism to resolve crucial social and housing problems.[343] In this regard, Labour at last claimed the radical tradition and the progressive legacy as their own. At Mitchell's opening demonstration, Hugh S. Roberton, founder of the Glasgow Orpheus Choir, noted.

> The Labour Party was not a new party, and it carried on the old traditions of the Chartists, the Radicals and the Land Leaguers, and was the lineal descendant of the Paisley weavers of 100 years ago. (Cheers.) Radicalism kept Liberalism alive, the old passionate desire for progress, but Liberalism was not only dead today, but was going to be buried in the bowels of Conservatism.[344]

Supported by the force of history, infused with the fervour of moral obligations and operating in a climate of economic uncertainty which undermined the claims of the established parties, the Labour challenge was elemented by concerns which paralleled and provided an alternative to those of the crumbling local Liberal hegemony. Labour offered an economic vision (nationalisation), a moral code rooted in the stability of a co-operative community, a recognisable local leadership, promises of future well-being grounded in the experience of achievable reforms (the Wheatley Act figured prominently in many of Mitchell's addresses), an analysis of power relationships and a popular interpretation of the past.

Following Asquith's defeat, the *Gazette* contemplated the cause of his failure:

> Did the Unionists faithfully observe the spirit of co-operation between the anti-socialist forces, and did the Liberals, on their side make their fullest contribution? How far was the result influenced by the Roman Catholic vote? And did the old Radical traits of the constituency so far disapprove of Toryism as to refuse to have any co-operation with it at all, if not indeed helping to swell the vote for

342 *PDE*, 8 Nov. 1924.

343 The failure of many electors in the Dundee election of 1922 to make a distinction between Liberal and Tory has been cited by William M. Walker as a crucial factor in Churchill's defeat: see Walker, 'Dundee's disenchantment with Churchill', p. 88.

344 *PDE*, 17 Oct. 1924.

Rosslyn Mitchell? Or does the result simply give justification for the claim that Socialism is growing in popularity in Paisley?[345]

The 84% turn-out at the poll – a figure around 10% higher than the national Scottish average – undermines claims of significant abstentions contributing to Liberal failure in the 1924 election in Paisley. Rather, basing one's analysis on the 1923 result, it appears clear that Asquith failed to retain the anti-Labour vote of the previous year and that Mitchell proved successful in absorbing much of that haemorrhage of support.[346] Indeed, Mitchell's ability to attract progressive Liberal support was evident soon after his election to office.[347] However, were such votes a positive endorsement of 'socialism', or was it rather the case that in Paisley it was Liberalism that was ultimately 'on trial'?

Mitchell's brand of ethical socialism had more in common with the philosophy of citizenship which underpinned pre-war Liberal programmes than the class war diatribes of the Labour Party's inter-war militant wing. It is therefore questionable whether Mitchell's victory should be interpreted as a vote for something 'new' rather than the affirmation of the claim that Labour now more accurately articulated the popular radical agenda. Measured against the constants of basic radical principles, Liberalism, in its post-war mutation as a party of the establishment, had lost its claim on the radical continuum. As Marquand has established, 'Liberal England' died 'because the Liberals did not move quite fast enough along the path they had tentatively begun to follow'.[348] The transition to Labour was neither revolutionary nor entirely complete in 1924, yet Paisley had reached a critical stage in the redefinition and reconstitution of the 'Radical' vote.

The year 1924 represents the 'organic crisis' of the Paisley Liberal party in the post-war political environment, when, as the 'traditional party', it ceased to be recognised by the classes who once elemented it as the vehicle of their political aspirations.[349] At a special meeting of the Liberal Association following Asquith's defeat, the chairman, Dr McKenna, identified the pact with the Unionists as the principle cause of Asquith's defeat and concluded: 'never again, so far as the present generation was concerned, would anything in the nature of a "Pact" be

345 *PRG*, 1 Nov. 1924. Note that women Unionists in Paisley on the announcement of the pact had issued a strong declaration against the 'high handed tactics' of the Unionist Party and had put the case for a Unionist candidate in the interests of 'clean politics and political integrity': *PDE*, 15 Oct. 1924.

346 The founding of the local Labour Party's Individual Members Section this year proved important in this regard. Its chairman commented in a letter to the press that April, that the new section would attempt to attract middle class voters who, in the past, had been Labour's 'Secret Disciples'. He emphasised: 'There is no class which has less real freedom under our present social system than the middle class': *PDE*, 22 Feb. 1924.

347 *PDE*, 29 Mar. 1929; 1 Apr. 1929.

348 D. Marquand, *The Progressive Dilemma* (London, 1991), p. 18.

349 Gramsci, *Selections from the Prison Notebooks*, p. 210.

entertained'. His recommendation received the unanimous support of the meeting.[350] In the annual report of that year, the pact was identified as 'that unwanted child of doubtful parentage'.[351] At root, as Gramsci makes clear, this ultimately reflects the crisis of the governing hegemony – a 'crisis of authority' – which facilitates the creation of counter-hegemonies.[352] In Paisley, the tension between the *substance* of the radical tradition – representative democracy – and the *principle* which made it the critical electoral weapon for Liberals since 1832 – loyalty – had become starkly apparent. By 1924, in the light of the new Liberal–Unionist pact, the tradition – as articulated by Asquith – seemed to be elemented by little more than the inherently conservative notion of loyalty to the past – a distinctly 'un-radical' concept.

Yet, what 'replaced' Liberalism was far from its antithesis.[353] Rather, the form of Mitchell's labourism underlines the observations of many sociologists; namely that the shift from communal to class consciousness attenuated social bonds and encouraged reformism and radicalism rather than Socialism.[354] Anti-capitalist protests were rooted in 'local traditions undermined by industrialisation' – in Paisley's case, its Radical heritage.[355] In 1924, Labour had won by 'owning' its past.

350 PCL, 320 Ren–1, PLA, 20 Nov. 1924.
351 PCL, 320 Ren–1, PLA, Annual Report 1924.
352 Gramsci, *Selections from the Prison Notebooks*, p. 210.
353 This point echoes Doyle's conclusions on the 1924 general election in Norwich: 'The "Red Letter" election of 1924 may have annihilated Liberalism as a parliamentary force, but it took rather longer for the effects of the culture which had created it to be extinguished at the local level': B. M. Doyle, 'Urban Liberalism and the "lost generation": politics and middle-class culture in Norwich, 1900–1935', *HJ*, xxxviii (1995), p. 634. See also Yeo and Yeo, 'On the uses of "community"', pp. 247–8.
354 See also Hutchison, *Political History of Scotland*, p. 285.
355 Lears, 'Concept of cultural hegemony', p. 582. Here Lears is referring to the work of the sociologist Craig Calhoun, esp. *The Question of Class Struggle* (Chicago, 1982).

CHAPTER SIX

Conclusion: The Radical Thread

Looking Forward: 'a strange mix up ... in Paisley'

> The doubtful blessing of a Tory Government, combined with the year's experience of Government by the Socialist Party is gradually turning the country towards Liberalism once more ... It only needs enthusiasm and adherence to Liberal principles to bring about a change in the representation of the country in Parliament. Liberalism still remains in spite of many and determined efforts on the part of Tory and Socialists to destroy it. They both recognise that the Liberal Party is their chief enemy and the fact of their constant reference to its death reveals an uneasiness easily explained. The greater danger to the Liberal Party is internal dissension ...
>
> Paisley Liberal Association, Annual Report 1926.

In 1924, only eight Liberal MPs were elected to Scottish seats and although this number increased to thirteen in 1929, in both general elections the Liberals failed to secure more than 18% of the total votes cast.[1] Yet it would be wrong to analyse such results as the ultimate proof of Liberal weakness in the face of the pressures of the modern, urban class-based electorate. Whilst Lloyd George's Land Inquiry Committee of 1925 seemed to point to a Liberal Party still campaigning in the shadow of Henry George and a late Victorian agenda, the 'Yellow Book' of 1928 (*Britain's Industrial Future*) and the subsequent policy statement of 1929, 'We Can Conquer Unemployment', highlight that the Liberal Party remained adept at gauging the needs of the modern capitalist community.[2]

In Paisley, however, the energy which infused the local Liberal association in the Asquith years soon dissipated and the weak organisational roots which had supported the increase in members in the early 1920s soon became apparent. By February 1929, the association was recording a deficit of £50 and in March 1935 new recruits to the association were failing to make up even one third of those lost through resignations and death.[3] Later that year, difficulties

1 F. W. S. Craig, *British Electoral Facts, 1832–1980* (Chichester, 1981), pp. 27–9.

2 J. Campbell, 'The renewal of Liberalism: Liberalism without Liberals', in Peele and Cook, *Politics of Reappraisal*, p. 110.

3 PCL, 320 Ren–1, PLA, 27 Feb. 1929; 1 Mar. 1935.

were encountered in recruiting a new president for the association and the local branch of the Scottish League of Young Liberals, virtually moribund in 1935, was declared 'defunct' in 1937. [4] The singular bright spot in Liberal organisation was the success of the Women's Section which maintained the social life of the association through a busy calendar of whist drives and dances and hosted the majority of public lectures in the 1920s. In the early 1930s it remained 'the pivot of the general activity of the Association' and mirrored the success of the Women's National Liberal Federation in the inter-war period by retaining active support despite general Liberal decline.[5] Yet continual wistful references in the association minute books to 'the brilliant period when the late Lord Oxford was member for this constituency' betray the outlook of a party which sought solace in its past rather than in its future.[6]

This impression is further enhanced when one looks at the ideology at the heart of the movement in the 1930s. Paisley Liberals maintained a loyalty to free trade despite the socio-economic pressures of the inter-war years. In 1933 the annual report reflected:

> Nothing in these years of trial weakened the case for Free Trade. On the contrary, on all hands and from all quarters we are told that one of the causes of the world-wide dislocation of trade is the existence of tariffs. Britain has unfortunately added to the dislocation but it may be that this intensification of folly of tariffs will turn the nations to wiser courses. It still is Britain's duty to give a lead in this, and it remains the Liberal Party's duty to bring Great Britain back to Free Trade.[7]

Yet, to regain the parliamentary seat for Liberalism, free trade was compromised.

The disappointment of 1924 and the resolve of local party leaders not to become involved in further 'deals with the Tories' made the 1929 election a critical one for the future course of Liberalism in the burgh. The Liberals had adopted W. M. R. Pringle, the former MP for North-West Lanarkshire, as their candidate in January 1928, but his death in April of that year necessitated a prolonged search for an alternative nominee. Invitations to accept the Liberal nomination were rejected by at least nine individuals before the association appealed to the Liberal Federation to assist them in securing a candidate.[8] In the end, James McCulloch, a manufacturer's agent from Langholm and 'an out-and-out free trader', was adopted by the Liberals in April 1929.[9]

4 Ibid., 1 Apr. 1935; 2 Sep. 1935; 15 Mar. 1937.
5 Ibid., Annual Report 1935. See also Thane, 'Women, Liberalism and Citizenship', p. 68.
6 Ibid., Annual Report, 1933.
7 Ibid., Annual Report, 1933.
8 Ibid., 27 Sep. 1928; 21 Nov. 1928; 27 Feb. 1929; 14 Mar. 1929.
9 *PDE*, 19 Apr. 1929.

In an election which found the anti-Labour vote split between McCulloch and the 'last minute' Unionist candidate Miss Minna G. Cowan[10] (daughter of Sheriff Substitute Hugh Cowan), Labour secured the seat with a majority of nearly 12,000. The electorate had increased by over 35% since 1924 and the bulk of that increase seems to have opted for Labour's new champion, James Welsh.[11] McCulloch's war record – he had been exempt from service due to ill health but had been an active member of the Anti-conscription Fellowship and a member of the UDC – came in for attack during the campaign. Also, despite the support of the *Paisley Daily Express,* McCulloch's free trade programme convinced few to desert Labour. Welsh's victory, however, owed much to the legacy which Mitchell had left behind him. Anticipating the forthcoming election in 1929, the *Express* reflected on the contest five years before:

> [Mitchell's] reputation as a man of business, a scholar, a thinker of the most progressive type, an orator, and an occupant of high office in the Glasgow Town Council had preceded him to Paisley ... Once elected Mr Mitchell declared that he wished to be known as all Paisley's member.[12]

Welsh, a cinema manager, a colleague of Mitchell's on Glasgow Town Council and Mitchell's successor as chairman of the Parks Committee in that town, seemed to promise more of the same progressivism which Paisley had experienced under Mitchell. Indeed, the *Express* continued to run Mitchell's column 'From a Politician's Log Book' throughout the election contest. Yet in the strained economic climate which marked the opening of the new decade, Welsh would not prove as moderate nor as conciliatory as his predecessor.

McCulloch's defeat and Welsh's determined opposition to MacDonald's National Government in 1931 shocked the Liberal Association out of its complacency and back into the arms of the Unionists, despite its previous protestations against 'trading' its principles.[13] In October 1931 James McCulloch, who had remained the prospective Liberal candidate for Paisley despite his defeat in 1929, was turned down as Liberal candidate for the forthcoming election after a ballot at a meeting of around 100 Paisley Liberals.[14] The meeting in the Clark Town Hall was marked by internal Liberal wrangling. McCulloch had made it clear that he would not sacrifice his free trade principles by

10 Cowan, in styling herself as a 'progressive Unionist', reinforces Hutchison's claim that 'the Unionist party re-tailored its strategy in a more progressive and at the same time a more middle-class direction': Hutchison, *Political History of Scotland*, p. 322.

11 See below, Appendix 4. This trend supports Michael Childs emphasis on the Labour sympathies of the new generation of voters who emerged in the inter-war period: Childs, 'Labour grows up', pp. 137–8.

12 *PDE*, 13 Mar. 1929.

13 PCL, 320 Ren–1, PLA, Annual Report 1927.

14 *PDE*, 10 Oct. 1931.

supporting the National Government manifesto and seemed to have significant support for this position within the local party, as a section of the audience left the hall in protest following the announcement of the ballot. Outside the hall, these Liberal discontents 'discussed the turn events had taken':

> some declaring that the Association was finished, and when challenged added: 'Well, if it's not, it won't be long till it is.' Many of the women were obviously excited, and when one gentleman tried to pour oil on the troubled waters the reply came promptly – 'I'm finished with the lot of you.' Others were inclined to advise Mr McCulloch to fight independently, while one expressed the opinion that Mr McCulloch was 'making the mistake of fighting the Conservatives instead of the Socialists'.[15]

The following day, the Liberal and Unionist Associations met to decide on a candidate whom both parties could support.[16] McCulloch, meanwhile, held meetings in the Liberal Club with his supporters, whose youth was the focus of comment in the local press. Yet despite holding a crowded meeting the following week, McCulloch failed to attract the 300 volunteers which would have convinced him to persist in an independent candidature.[17]

In October only two candidates went to the polls in Paisley: Welsh for Labour and, with the backing of both the Liberals and the Conservatives, the Hon. Joseph Paton Maclay of Kilmalcolm, the eldest son of Lord Maclay of the firm Messrs Maclay & Macintyre, shipowners, Glasgow, and the president of the West Renfrewshire Liberal Association. Maclay, like Mitchell and Welsh, had been a town councillor in Glasgow and had also served as a Magistrate and JP in that city. In contrast to McCulloch, his war record was 'impeccable': he had served as Controller of Shipping during the crisis.

Echoing the cries of Gladstonian Liberals against the Liberal Unionists of the late nineteenth century, Welsh claimed that Maclay's adoption proved the emptiness of his opponents' Liberalism:

> By that action the Liberal Party had ceased to exist so far as Paisley was concerned. If the Liberal Party were not prepared to stand up for their own principles and put forward candidates who would honour these principles then there would be no room for them in the political future of this country.[18]

15 Ibid., 10 Oct. 1931.

16 Ibid., 12 Oct. 1931.

17 TLC, 13 Jan. 1933: McCulloch later joined the Labour Party and declared to a meeting in Paisley in 1933 that 'he had no apology to offer for leaving the Liberal Party as they could never come back as a Democratic Party'.

18 *PDE*, 15 Oct. 1931.

Yet Maclay won the seat for Liberalism following a campaign dominated by the economic crisis which was gripping the country.[19] The *Express* concluded: 'Paisley has returned to its old allegiance with a vengeance.'[20]

Maclay's 10,000-vote majority would seem to reinforce the conclusion of the *Express*. Maclay campaigned successfully among the female electorate and the unemployed. Indeed, after the poll his agent concluded that, 'It was the women of Paisley who had put Maclay into Parliament.'[21] This conclusion goes some way to reinforcing John Turner's proposition that the female vote in certain constituencies was critical in returning anti-Labour candidates in the inter-war period.[22] The majority of voters in Paisley were women, and in the 1920s the rise in the number of women in professional and clerking occupations would seem to indicate that their socio-economic profile was changing, making them more likely to vote for the established parties.[23] Nevertheless, it is doubtful whether Maclay would have been as successful had he faced Unionist opposition or indeed a National Labour candidate. Whilst the attendance at Welsh's meetings seemed to decline as the campaign reached its conclusion, the 1931 election reflected less the rebirth of Liberalism than the expression of a widely accepted short-term political expedient. The fear of continued economic crisis invested electoral capital in tariff reform and a return to inter-party co-operation rather than the principles of Liberal individualism which had comforted the Liberal association during its period in the electoral wilderness.

Maclay's victory, however, failed to reinvigorate the local Liberal association. In June 1932 the financial state of the association was declared 'unsatisfactory', and in October ward committees were encouraged to take steps to 'dispel the prevalent apathy' at the grass roots.[24] Moreover, the Liberals were becoming increasingly disappointed with their party's role in the new National Government. The 1933 annual report of the Paisley Liberal association records: 'A full year's experience of the policy pursued by the National Government has given point to the criticism expressed regarding it at its inception.'[25] Since the election a very small number of propaganda meetings had been held and only a few Young Liberals turned out in January 1933 to hear a 'rousing address' from Major E. Donaldson on 'the necessity for a free and unfettered Liberal Party in the country.'[26] By June, concerns were

19 See below, Appendix 4.
20 Ibid., 28 Oct. 1931.
21 Ibid., 28 Oct. 1931.
22 Turner, 'Sex, age and the Labour vote in the 1920s', p. 251.
23 The Paisley parliamentary electorate was made up of 23,106 male and 28,279 female voters in 1929 and 26,642 male and 34,483 female voters in 1945; see also below, Appendix 2.
24 PCL, 320 Ren–1, PLA, 30 Jun. 1932; 10 Oct. 1932.
25 Ibid., Annual Report 1933.
26 Ibid., Annual Report 1933.

being raised as to the Liberal association's ability to attract new male members.[27]

In November, despite Liberal desires to free themselves from their understanding with local Unionists, Maclay reported to the executive committee that he would not be following the Liberal Party into opposition.[28] The annual report noted: 'While remaining a Liberal he judged himself bound by his election promises to stand by the National Government as long as he conscientiously could.'[29] The executive, whilst supporting their member, passed a resolution confirming their allegiance to Sir Herbert Samuel and encouraged the circulation the following year of the opposition Liberals' political programme.[30] In September 1934, they declined the offer from Renfrewshire Conservatives to co-host a National Government meeting.[31]

Maclay entered the 1935 election campaign as 'a liberal candidate prepared to support the government on all lines of progressive policy consistent with Liberal principles'. According to the association's annual report, it proved a platform which 'united all sections of Liberals'.[32] It was also a fitting platform for Paisley, where the local association had refused to 'take sides' in the disputes in the Scottish Liberal Federation which had riven the party elite in two since 1932.[33]

Maclay again faced no opposition from local Unionists in 1935. Only the Labour candidate, Oliver Baldwin – the premier's son – blocked the way to a second inter-war Liberal victory. Rosslyn Mitchell commented in the *Express*:

> What a strange mix up we are going to have in Paisley. It shows how surely the lines of demarcation have been subdued. The Liberal son of a Liberal peer stands as a supporter of a National Party, led by a Conservative Prime Minister; while the Socialist son of the same Conservative Prime Minister stands as a supporter of the Labour Party in antagonism to the party led by his father.[34]

After a campaign marked by aggressive heckling at Liberal meetings, Maclay retained Paisley with a significantly reduced majority of less than 400.[35] His continued sympathies with the National Government had undoubtedly lost him the votes of a significant number of progressive

27 Ibid., 19 Jun. 1933.
28 Ibid., 10 Nov. 1933.
29 Ibid., Annual Report 1934.
30 Ibid., 6 Apr. 1934. The commitment to Liberal unity evidenced in such a compromise mirrors that of the early 1920s when, in Scotland, many Asquithian Liberal Associations retained the membership of Coalition Liberals: Hutchison, *Political History of Scotland*, p. 314.
31 PCL, 320 Ren–1, PLA, 14 Sep. 1934.
32 Ibid., Annual Report 1936.
33 Fry, *Patronage and Principle*, p. 179.
34 Rosslyn Mitchell, 'From a Friend's Log-book': *PDE*, 28 Oct. 1935.
35 See below, Appendix 4.

Liberals who were looking for an independent voice in a Commons becoming increasingly dominated by the Conservatives. Likewise, Baldwin's oratory and celebrity must surely have played a part in attracting wavering Liberals and retrieving votes lost by Labour in the exceptional conditions of 1931. Yet on the eve of the Second World War, Paisley retained its Liberal representation, having returned one of only three independent Liberals elected in Scotland in 1935.

The true test of this apparent Liberal revival, however, took place in 1945. The political truce agreed by all parties on the declaration of war in 1939 called an abrupt halt to the Liberals' search for a new candidate. (Maclay had intimated in 1938 that he would not be seeking re-election.) In the interim, five potential nominees had been approached and none had accepted the offer of the candidature.[36] The search for a prospective candidate was only relaunched in 1944. With apparently no other competitors in the field, Lady Glen Coats – who, despite the truce, had addressed the association in April 1940 – was unanimously adopted at a special general meeting of the Liberal association in July 1944 to stand as Paisley's Liberal candidate.[37]

Facing Unionist, Labour and Independent opposition in the general election of 1945, Lady Glen Coats secured only 10% of the poll, was beaten into third place and forfeited her deposit.[38] Representing in one figure, the Liberal and industrial heritage of the community, Lady Glen Coats's performance was not indicative of Liberalism's final 'time of death', but rather confirmed that the corpse had long since grown cold. Devoid of tactical Unionist support under the umbrella of the National Government, Liberalism's true strength of support was starkly apparent in the result.

Lady Glen Coats's campaign was dominated by the rhetoric of Liberalism's local past and evoked a time in which the socio-economic and political identity of the community had been united through the language of industrial paternalism and progressive Liberalism. In resurrecting a Liberalism long since resigned to memory, she drew on a sense of locality and community which had been eclipsed in the trauma of the Depression and the Second World War by a growing appreciation of the national scope of the political agenda. Attacking Labour's plans for nationalisation, she pointed to Paisley's local mills and the Coats's role in establishing them: 'Don't tell me you would be better off in Paisley without the enterprise that is there.'[39] In response to Labour's Oliver Baldwin (now Viscount Corvedale) and his call on the electorate's support, she asked:

36 PCL, 320 Ren–1, PLA, 5 Apr. 1938; 21 Apr. 1938; 11 Oct. 1938; 21 Nov. 1938; 14 Mar. 1939.
37 Ibid., 20 Jul. 1944.
38 See below, Appendix 4.
39 *PDE*, 19 Jun. 1945.

> if there was no seat in England which Mr Oliver Baldwin could represent. Why not Bewdley, where the name of Baldwin was as well known as the name of Coats in Paisley? Why must this young Englishman seek to represent this town, of whose interests he was unaware and of which he knew very little? Paisley was Liberal by conviction and tradition and would remain so.[40]

However, Corvedale took Paisley for Labour with a majority of almost 23%, beating the Unionist candidate, T. G. D. Galbraith, into second place. Galbraith undoubtedly benefited from the votes of many Liberals who supported him as the best means of preventing a Labour victory and declaring their support for Churchill as the nation's war-time leader. This being so, 1945 represents the ultimate bankruptcy of Liberalism in the burgh and the point when, bereft of much of its middle-class Liberal support, Paisley followed the rest of Scotland in redefining party politics as principally a fight between Labour and Conservatism.

The inter-war decline of the domestic cotton industry and the United Mills take-over of Coats's UK manufacturing units in 1931, the consequent diversification of female employment in the community, and the world-wide economic depression of the 1930s, destroyed the economic basis of the Liberal hegemony in Paisley and shattered its hold on the wider community. In this regard, the events of the inter-war period confirm the existence of the Liberal vision as organic to a specific industrial epoch and social order which had passed.

In this way, the 'experience' of economic instability reasserts its power as a critical causal factor in the transformation of popular politics, located, in terms of physical want and self-interest, 'outside' the discursive constructs in which many historians of the 'linguistic school' would have us restrict the agency of the individual.[41] Yet, as we have seen, such economic determinism can take us only so far in appreciating the complexity of the organic change in Paisley's politics from Liberalism to Labour.

With the gift of hindsight, it is clear that the dye had been cast in 1924, in the pact secured between the Liberals and Unionists. Liberalism's poor showing in 1929 seemed to confirm to all but the staunchest independent Liberals, that a split anti-Labour vote would demolish what was left of Liberalism's electoral potential. Thereafter, victory in 1931 and 1935 was secured only through compromises with the Liberals' former Unionist opponents at a time of national economic crisis. Throughout, a far more accurate barometer of Liberalism's potency was to be found in the declining membership, revenue and activities of the local Liberal association. The year 1945 confirmed what most already knew: Liberalism was a feature of Scotland's past.

40 Ibid., 23 Jun. 1945.
41 See Scott, 'Evidence of experience', p. 777.

However, the unity of the Labour ascendancy, apparently confirmed by the election of Rosslyn Mitchell in 1924, masked continued divisions in the local movement which would assert themselves forcefully throughout the later inter-war period. In municipal politics, Labour boasted only four councillors in Paisley in 1935 and had to wait until 1945 before securing a majority in the local council.[42] Such slow progress was symptomatic of long-lasting division and disagreement among the groups which made up the labour movement in the burgh and reflects the persistent fragmented nature of the labour voice in politics throughout this period.

As with the Scottish Labour movement as a whole, the Paisley Labour party throughout the 1930s failed to attract female activists in significant numbers.[43] Indeed, in June 1931 the Paisley Labour party's women's section disbanded due to 'lack of membership'.[44] Whilst the individual members' section experienced a growth in numbers during these years, by June 1932 recording 200 on its role, the local party's neglect of the female voter highlights the continued failure of the movement to articulate an ideology which took account of 'alternative' visions of 'class'.[45] Though the support of the women of the Co-operative party and Women's Guilds suggested a possible way forward in attracting the female vote in an appeal to their interests as consumers rather than producers, Labour's inability to integrate the female experience in its articulation of 'class' politics highlights Labour's continued reliance on its gendered radical roots.

The complex legacy of Paisley's radical tradition which had been 'bequeathed' to the Labour party in the 1920s generated ideological and organisational confusion within the movement throughout the inter-war years. Labour remained a broad church affair and as a result attempted to accommodate the frequently conflicting perspectives of its component groups. The 1930s and early 1940s would see the 'working-out' of the various strands of the radical tradition and the coalescence of support around a more explicitly socialist programme.

42 *PDE*, 6 Nov. 1935; CP Minutes, 14 Mar. 1946.

43 In 1930 there were only twenty three Women's Sections affiliated to the Labour Party in Scotland: Brown, 'The Labour Party and Political Change in Scotland', Table 7.1. Recent research also indicates that Labour's poor record in organising women in the inter-war period may also have its parallel in many English constituencies. See S. Davies, 'Class, religion and gender: Liverpool Labour Party and women, 1918–1939', in J. Belchem (ed.), *Popular Politics, Riot and Labour: Essays in Liverpool History, 1790–1940* (Liverpool, 1992), pp. 217–46.

44 TLC, 24. Jan. 1931, 17 Jun. 1931.

45 Ibid., 10 Apr. 1935. Chris Waters's criticism of Joyce's depiction of 'popular discourse', i.e. that it fails to take account of how it may have meant 'very different things to women and men in working class communities' is here addressed, and its consequences highlighted in a Labour Party which, on the eve of the Second World War was still dominated by a *male* vision of history and society: C. Waters, 'Review', *SH*, xvii (1992), p. 516.

In Paisley the TLC, for the most part, *was* the Labour party in the burgh in the early inter-war period and by 1935 boasted 3,775 members in its political section, representing thirty-two branches and twenty-two organisations.[46] The disaffiliation of the ILP from the Labour Party in 1932, however, led to organisational confusion in Paisley, where a significant proportion of former ILP members remained within the Labour party and affiliated to the Scottish Socialist Party [SSP]. However, the Paisley Labour party managed to co-operate with both the SSP and the ILP. In December 1933 a letter to the local Labour party from the ILP (Paisley Branch), requesting that their name be removed from the list of affiliated organisations, was rebuffed when the Labour party replied that they had delegates from the ILP regularly in attendance at meetings.[47] That month the Labour party sent three delegates to a youth conference organised by the ILP in Paisley and also sent two delegates to the SSP's 'Peace Conference' in Glasgow.[48] Whilst the Scottish Labour conference in Edinburgh in 1938 largely resolved such confusion by separating TLCs from local party organisation, the 1930s found Labour in organisational 'limbo' in Scotland, where the SSP took the lead in presenting the labour message.[49]

In Paisley, however, a further source of tension remained in the continued activities of the local Co-operative party. The treasurer of the Paisley Co-operative party proposed 'winding up' the business of the party soon after the 1924 election and debates to this effect dominated the late 1920s. The representative of the Paisley Provident argued in 1926 that 'the members of various societies had lost faith in the Defence Committee and it should be done away with'. But the Paisley Co-operative party persisted well into the post-war period.[50]

Throughout this time, although relations with the local Labour party improved, the Co-operative party on occasion asserted an independence from the demands of Labour party organisers and attempted to maintain the party's separate identity and prove its worth to the local subscribing societies. In 1929, as the ILP led the search for a candidate to replace Mitchell, the Co-operative party sought to pre-empt discussion by proposing J. M. Biggar as the Labour candidate for the

46 TLC, 10 Apr. 1935. Throughout this period, it is difficult to recognise when the TLC is acting as a trades council and when as the local Labour party in the burgh. Without any formal negotiation or signs of dispute, in 1934, the TLC simply changed the name of its Individual Members' Section to the Paisley Labour Party Independent Members' Section: ibid., 11 Apr. 1911. Likewise, local press reports use the terms interchangeably. In the interests of continuity, I have persisted in identifying the TLC as the local Labour party in this chapter.

47 Ibid., 13 Dec. 1933.

48 Ibid., 13 Dec. 1933.

49 W. W. Knox and A. McKinlay, 'The re-making of Scottish Labour in the 1930s', *TCBH*, vi (1995), pp. 174–93.

50 CP Minutes, 13 Nov. 1924; 27 Dec. 1926. See also PCL, PC3354, Paisley CP Minutes, 1939–1947.

burgh.[51] However, following a card vote of all societies affiliated to the Labour party, Welsh was adopted unanimously.[52] The *Scottish Co-operator* commented:

> Paisley has chosen Councillor Welsh and we hope Councillor Welsh wins Paisley. but we must frankly confess that we are keenly disappointed with the decision ... a Labour withdrawal in favour of the Co-operative nominee would have given a semblance of reality to the Labour–Co-operative agreement. At present that agreement is a particularly transparent sham.[53]

Although Welsh's candidature in 1931 seemed to pass without significant Co-operative opposition, Oliver Baldwin's nomination in 1935 attracted muted criticism from Co-operative quarters. In October 1932, perhaps owing to the disaffiliation of the ILP earlier that year, the Co-operative candidate – Mrs Margaret Small from Perth – was the only nominee presented for Labour's endorsement.[54] In December, Small was adopted as Paisley's Labour candidate, despite strong opposition from the AEU.[55] Small, however, never contested Paisley, resigning before the 1935 election.[56] In her place, the Paisley Co-operators proposed J. M. Williams, a sub-editor of *Forward,* as the new Labour candidate in October 1935. Even at this stage, however, rumours were circulating of Baldwin's possible candidacy in Paisley.[57] On 21 October, Baldwin and Williams addressed the local party. The selection of Baldwin was unanimous.[58] Whilst the Co-operative party proved conciliatory and recommended that their members support Baldwin during the election, they discontinued publication of the *Pioneer* – a propaganda sheet which had supported Small's candidature in Paisley.[59] Immediately after Baldwin's defeat, the local Co-operative party established a sub-committee to select a new candidate for the burgh and whilst their candidate, John Downie, went on to accept the nomination of the Greenock Co-operative party in September 1936, the Co-operators lost no time in setting mechanisms in place to find a new candidate.[60] In 1937, however, a selection meeting confirmed Baldwin as the Labour Party's choice for Paisley.[61] Although the Co-operative party challenged this decision in the period from 1943 to 1944, Baldwin in the end won Paisley with the Co-operators' support, their annual report of 1945

51 *PDE*, 12 Apr. 1929.
52 Ibid., 25 Apr. 1929.
53 Ibid., 30 Apr. 1929 (as quoted).
54 TLC, 12 Oct. 1932.
55 Ibid., 14 Dec. 1932.
56 *PDE*, 7 Oct. 1935; CP Minutes, 26 Sep. 1935.
57 Ibid., 21 Oct. 1935.
58 Ibid., 22 Oct. 1935.
59 CP Minutes, 24 Oct. 1935.
60 Ibid., 6 Sep. 1935; 12 Nov. 1935.
61 Ibid., May 1943.

noting the 'friendly relations' between the Co-operative and Labour parties which had marked both the parliamentary and municipal campaigns.[62]

The further 'internal' threat to the Labour ascendancy posed by the Communist Party of Great Britain had also been neutralised by 1945, but it had proved a prolonged battle. Whilst the 1925 Labour Party conference voted in favour of prohibiting individual membership to Communists, the Communist presence in the Paisley Labour party was such that the local party had to be reconstructed in 1926, following a recommendation from the Scottish Executive. However, problems persisted. The Communist, John Gormley, was ejected from the party as late as 1930 and in 1932 the Labour party affiliated to the local United Front. The limits of such Labour sympathies with United Front activities were, nevertheless, evident in 1933 when the local Labour party voted by eight votes to four against co-operation with the local Communist party in a May Day demonstration and when, later that year, the executive committee voted by seven votes to two against any proposal at the annual conference to unite with the Communist Party.[63] In 1934, the local Labour party's annual report blamed the local Communists for the break-up of the United Front in Paisley and the following year, despite the intransigence of their Communist delegates, the NUTW was declared disaffiliated from the TLC.[64]

Yet despite increased centralisation in the Labour Party, a developing commitment to corporatism and welfarism and stricter party regulation, the heterogeneity which Labour's absorption of the radical inheritance had encouraged was not entirely quashed in the 1930s. As can be seen in the Paisley Labour party's response to ILP disaffiliation, Co-operative party collaboration and United Front involvement, local intransigence often meant the discipline of national bodies was seldom achieved at a local level.[65] Labour continued to be the repository of complex and conflicting radical interests.

Looking Back: 'this plebeian invention of tradition'

Labour's success in 1924 did not represent the birth of a 'new' vision of the social order, but the recapitulation of a community's genuinely plebeian sense of its own radical dissenting past which had been 'domesticated' by Liberalism.[66] As Joyce has made clear:

> The significance of this plebeian invention of tradition cannot be too much emphasised, not least in attaching the sentiments of

[62] Ibid., 23 Aug. 1945.
[63] TLC, 11 Jan. 1933; 12 Sep. 1933
[64] Ibid., 11 Apr. 1934; 13 Mar. 1935.
[65] Knox and McKinlay, 'Re-making of Scottish Labour in the 1930s', pp. 182–3.
[66] See Joyce, *Visions of the People*, p. 77.

> working people to the socialist cause by fusing their own traditions and socialist thought. However, the social outlook evident in these mythologies, and in the literary means that gave these ... expression, was rooted in the radical and popular tradition rather than in class.[67]

Labour victory was thus achieved, not through the denial of the Liberal ethos, but through the appropriation of its vocabulary of popular collectivism *in its local form*. 'Class' politics, in this regard, had little to do with a universal doctrine and *everything* to do with the experience of the individual locality.

The transformation of the local labour market in the mid-nineteenth century laid local political traditions in Paisley open to competing and frequently incompatible interpretations. Yet, until the early 1920s, the Liberal version proved ascendant. Through the operation of paternalism within the work-place and the perpetuation of a patriarchal code throughout the wider community which generated a deferential political perspective, the industrial Liberal elite fostered an appreciation of the past and a vision of the future which sought to guarantee the pre-eminence of their philosophy, despite the vagaries of a changing social and economic climate. In this they were largely successful.

The year 1886, however, shattered the philosophical and organisational unity of the Liberal hegemony by fracturing the popular interpretation of the community's radical identity and positing competing 'Liberal' versions of radical principles – a conjunctural crisis anticipated by earlier local political dilemmas. Revolutionised by the absorption of many Liberal progressives, the 'right' challenged Liberalism as the guarantor of the radical continuum through its interweaving of a dissenting rhetoric, the ideals of Tory Democracy and a popular vision of 'Union', and proved to be the major challenger for the Liberal mantle until the late Edwardian period. Unionists, by absorbing the radical tradition retold the meta-narrative of Liberalism in a way which worked against its popular 'meaning'. Yet, throughout the 1890s, in terms of electoral performance, the Liberal party showed little sign of 'decline' and every indication that its progressive voices – if not its elite – could 'read' the emerging social agenda in politics. The year 1886, therefore, did not point to an organic change in the political identity of the community, but represents a period of conjunctural change in the evolution of the local Liberal party.

The Labour challenge which evolved after 1900 simultaneously drew strength from, and was restricted by, the Liberal ethos which at once preceded and elemented it. Its concept of class was locally generated and its social vision included little to differentiate it from wider progressive politics, failing as it did to absorb alternative experiences of class, gender

[67] Ibid., p. 77.

and work-place identity. Whilst gaining in support, progress was slow and the emergence of an exclusive identity proved more a focus of dissension than a united expression of purpose. On the eve of war, therefore, ideological challenges from both left and right generated by economic, social and political changes within society, threatened to undermine the unity of purpose and the popularity of Paisley Liberalism and the stable core of the local Liberal hegemony. Yet, in electoral terms, Liberalism remained pre-eminent.

The battle of words, which at once reflected and created the challenges from both Labour and the Unionists, however, pointed to dilemmas at the heart of Liberalism which electoral results only served to mask. The 'class' agenda which was seeking to assert itself was, however, like the identities which had generated it, 'a product of arguments about meanings, arguments which were primarily political in character'.[68] The language of Liberalism and a historical appreciation of its principles provided the political vocabulary for the arguments around which 'classes' began to form. In this way, the manner in which political identities emerged proved as important (if not more so) than the actions and experiences of these identities on the political stage. The Liberals, by denying class interests, Labour, by failing to incorporate the female experience of work and the Unionists, by rejecting free trade as an integral component of radicalism, defined the parameters within which politics were articulated, determined the character of the crises which Liberalism would face, and conditioned the potential which successive reinterpretations of the radical tradition would possess.

Thus, whilst war proved the occasion for the emergence of new alliances on the left in 1918, it proved neither an electoral turning-point nor a period of ideological resolution. War failed to provide a new political vocabulary for Paisley's Labour movement. Labour's performance in municipal elections in the 1920s continued to be disappointing, indicating little change in the priorities of the local community upon which it relied for support. While division continued among Co-operators, Labourists, Trade Unionists and Socialists, the politics of 'community' – as opposed to 'class' – proved enduring. Asquith's victory in 1920 encouraged and revived activism within the local Liberal party as Liberalism survived another conjunctural crisis.

The Liberal party's identity as a party of reform, however, was being strongly contested. Challenged by the experience of economic depression, the Labour party in 1924 highlighted an organic contradiction at the core of the local Liberal party – a party which emerged in the 1920s as the prominent party of the establishment in Paisley. Its policy, motivated increasingly by reactive gestures against its political opponents, the Liberal party was shown to be a party whose radical ancestry was no

[68] Joyce, *Democratic Subjects*, p. 161.

longer confirmed by either its contemporary ideology or by its supporters. The radical tradition had been betrayed and the rhetoric of reform had become the language of Labour – the coded expressions of the ethical roots of a counter-hegemony. An organic change had been effected in the political identity of the community.

Language was fundamental in the evolution of Labour in Paisley. Its ideology, conceived in the Gramscian sense as 'a process in which different kinds of meanings are produced and reproduced through the establishment of a mental attitude toward the world', relied on the power of its language to impart meaning to its 'Idea'.[69] Yet, as Gramsci notes, 'in "language", there is contained a specific conception of the world' – a conception which pre-dates its appropriation by a counter-hegemonic force.[70] The *meaning* of 'rights', 'justice', 'equality', the 'radicalism' of the community and the obligations of its leaders were understood historically in Paisley as the product of the independent 'weaver' tradition, the legacy of the Charter, the moral passions of Gladstonian Liberalism and popular versions of a moral economy. Such linguistic discourse was imbued with meaning through the operation of history and the evolution of tradition. Labour, therefore, had little choice but to express its interests through such historicised discourse. In doing so, however, it simultaneously reinforced the cultural hegemony of Liberalism. This linguistic cycle was only broken when the socio-economic relations which determined its meaning were destroyed – when the industrial paternalism of the threadocracy came under strain in the inter-war period and the Liberal party sought power through political 'deals' with the Unionists.

Liberal electoral success in the later 1920s and 1930s, therefore, ironically exemplified the party's local political bankruptcy. Victory was purchased at the expense of its history and as a result Liberalism divorced itself from its past. As 'the philosophy of an historical epoch is ... nothing other than the history of that epoch itself, nothing other than the mass of variations that the leading group has succeeded in imposing on preceding reality', it was a dangerous expedient.[71] The Liberal party never again reached the level of success it had achieved in Paisley at the turn of the century.

Labour's experience in the 1930s, however, confirmed the volatility of the radical tradition. Whilst 'Socialism' was spoken of with greater confidence on its platforms by 1945, it remained a vague and ambiguous set of principles, owing more to ethics than economics. At the general election of that year, Viscount Corvedale emphasised:

69 Gramsci, *Selections from the Prison Notebooks*, p. 590.
70 Ibid., p. 201.
71 Ibid., p. 345.

> He believed their purpose in life was to help other people. He found Socialism a higher ideal than he found in capitalism. In Socialism there was something really to hope for and to live for, a greater ideal and a greater hope.[72]

Labour's continued inability to attract the female vote, its susceptibility to internal division and its reliance on an ethical appreciation of economic inequalities reflected the legacy of the radical inheritance which Labour only partly absorbed at the turn of the century.

As the meta-narrative of Paisley as a political community, the radical tradition – the means by which it understood its past and appreciated its future – could never be the exclusive property of one party. Rather, it was the 'site' upon which political battles were enacted, the language through which change was articulated, the discourse through which socio-economic power relations were reflected. At any one time such factors could coalesce to determine the transcendence of one party or group, yet their 'ownership' would be temporary. Meanings were always conditional and the radical thread had many strands.

72 *PDE*, 11 Jun. 1945.

Appendix 1

Table 1.1: *Population of Paisley, 1695–1781*

	Abbey Parish		Town Parish		TOTAL
Year	Families	Souls	Families	Souls	Abbey & Town
1695	435			2,200	
1755		2,509		4,290	6,799
1781	1,536			11,100	

Source: *New Statistical Account for Scotland*, vol. VII, p. 248

Table 1.2: *Population of Paisley, 1791–1831*

	Abbey Parish				Town of Paisley				
Year	Fam.	Males	Fem.	TOTAL	Fam.	Males	Fem.	TOTAL	Abbey & Town
1791	2,255	5,259	5,533	10,792	3,232	6,577	7,223	13,800	24,592
1801	2,991	6,592	7,561	14,153	3,945	7,821	9,205	17,026	31,179
1811	3,612	7,614	9,171	16,785	4,446	8,843	11,094	19,937	36,722
1821	4,210	9,609	10,966	20,575	5,730	12,133	14,295	26,428	47,003
1831	5,306	12,062	13,944	26,006	7,002	14,460	17,000	31,460	57,466

Source: *New Statistical Account for Scotland*, vol. VII, p. 249

Table 1.3: *Population of Paisley, 1861, 1881–1931*

Year	Males	Males as % of Total Population	Females	Females as % of Total Population	TOTAL
1861	—	—	—	—	47,427
1881	25,838	46.44	29,800	53.56	55,638
1891	30,679	46.19	35,746	53.81	66,425
1901	37,271	46.96	42,092	53.04	79,363
1911	39,706	47.01	44,749	52.99	84,455
1921	39,945	47.08	44,892	52.92	84,837
1931	40,673	47.05	45,772	52.95	86,445

Source: *Census Reports* (Scotland) 1881, 1891, 1901, 1911, 1921, 1931. Figures for 1861 from: *Third Statistical Account for Scotland – County of Renfrew* (1962), p. 314

Table 1.4: *Occupied Population working in Industry, 1881–1911*

Year	Total Males occupied in industry	As % of occupied Male Population	Total Females occupied in industry	As % of occupied Female Population	Total Population occupied in industry	As % of occupied Population
1881	12,838	79.99	8,263	81.63	21,101	80.63
1891	14,806	77.15	10,152	81.92	24,958	79.02
1901*	18,197	77.50	10,803	79.17	29,000	78.11
1911	19,788	76.84	10,940	77.53	30,728	77.09

Note: For the purposes of collating data, the occupational categories taken to represent industrial pursuits as utilised in the 1881 Census, 'Class V' have been used. These include occupations which are not directly involved in the production, processing or extraction of raw materials or manufactured goods (e.g. dealers and lodging house keepers), but which, being of an 'urban' character have been used in this table to emphasise the decidedly industrial focus of Paisley's occupational profile.

Source: *Census Reports* (Scotland) 1881, 1891, 1901, 1911

* For figures for both 1901 and 1911, Category XXII items in section 1, 'About Animals', including cattle dealers, drovers and animal dealers/keepers have been removed.

Table 1.5: *Population occupied in the Textile Industry, 1881–1931*

Year	Total Males occupied in textiles	As % of occupied Male Population	Total Females occupied in textiles	As % of occupied Female Population	Total Population occupied in textiles	As % of occupied Population
1881	2,914	18.15	6,518	64.39	9,432	36.04
1891	3,008	15.67	7,453	60.14	10,461	33.12
1901	2,947	12.55	8,279	60.67	11,226	30.24
1911	3,744	14.54	8,127	57.59	11,871	29.78
1921*	2,589	9.47	7,025	46.80	9,614	22.71
1931	2,173	7.96	4,071	27.24	6,244	14.78

Source: *Census Reports* (Scotland) 1881, 1891, 1901, 1911, 1921, 1931.

* Figures for all years include canvas, sack, tarpaulin and sail makers.

Table 1.6: *Age composition of Women working in textiles, 1881–1911*

Year	Under 5 Years	5+	15+	20+	25+	45+	65+	TOTAL
1881	—	489	2,226	1,607	1,528	544	124	6,518
1891	—	824	2,473	1,729	1,822	509	96	7,453
1901	—	725[1]	2,719	1,987	2,261[2]	492[3]	95	8,279
1911	—	365[4]	2,590[5]	2,064	2,432	632	44[6]	8,127

Source: *Census Reports* (Scotland) 1881, 1891, 1901, 1911

1 Figure represents total for employees aged 10 & over (252) + employees aged 14 & over (473).
2 Figure represents total for employees aged 25 & over (1,625) + employees 35 & over (636).
3 Figure represents total for employees aged 45 & over (325) + employees aged 55 & over (167).
4 Figure represents total for employees aged 10–13 (27) + employees aged 14 (338).
5 Figure represents total for employees aged 15 (504), 16 (526), 17 (562), + 18–19 (998).
6 Figure represents total for employees aged 65–69 (32) + employees aged 70 & over (12).

Table 1.7: *Conjugal status of female workers in textiles: Paisley, 1881, 1911*

Year	Modal Age Group in Textiles (yrs)	Number of Women in this group inTextiles	As % of women over 15 occupied in Textiles	As % of those occupied aged 15–24	% of women aged 15–24 married/widowed
1881	15–24	3,833	63.58	72.65	14.00
1911	15–24	4,654	59.96	62.19	9.60

Source: *Census Reports* (Scotland) 1881, 1911

Table 1.8: *Women in Domestic Service (Indoor), 1881–1931*

Year	Number of Women Employed	Number employed as % of total occupied female population
1881	1,068	10.55
1891	1,076	8.68
1901	991	7.26
1911	959	6.80
1921	799	5.32
1931	1,049	7.02

Source: *Census Reports* (Scotland) 1881, 1891, 1901, 1911, 1921, 1931

Appendix 2

Table 2.1: *Women in Professional Occupations (Teaching), 1881–1931*

Year	Number of Women Employed	Number employed as % of total occupied female population
1881	111	1.10
1891	152	1.23
1901	247	1.81
1911	292	2.07
1921	313	2.08
1931	321	2.15

Source: *Census Reports* (Scotland) 1881, 1891, 1901, 1911, 1921, 1931

Table 2.2: *Commercial Clerks, 1881–1931*

Year	Males	Females
1881	464	18
1891	652	51
1901	884	246
1911	1,105	537
1921	1,179	1,185
1931	1,430	1,224

Source: *Census Reports* (Scotland) 1881, 1891, 1901, 1911, 1921, 1931

Graph 2.3: *Occupied male population in metals, metalwork and machines, 1881–1921*

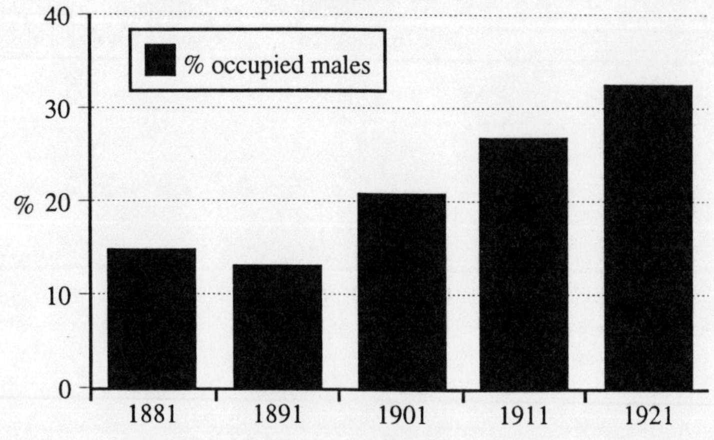

Source: *Census Reports* (Scotland) 1881, 1891, 1901, 1911, 1921

Appendix 3

Table 3.1: *Coats's Pensioners, 1886*

Name of Pensioner	Year entered Coats's Service	Pension: Amount per week
Cath Mcara	1825	12/-
Archibald Gibb	1826	22/-
Margaret Stein	1827	8/-
Helen Morris	1827	8/-
Marshall Graham	1833	16/-
Elizabeth Love	1836	8/-
Margaret Logan	1836	8/-
Isabella Earl	1839	8/-
Ann Stewart	1840	8/-
Andrew Gibson	1849	20/-
Elizabeth Forsyth	1853	8/-
James Landes	1853	10/-
Mary McKinnon	1853	8/-
Maggie Patterson	1867	5/-
Elizabeth Dick	—	8/-
Thomas Arroll (late manager)	1847	(£170 per annum)

Source: UGABRC, JPC Collection, UGD, 199/1/1/1, Minute Book 1884–1890, 18 Jan. 1886

Table 3.2: *Clark & Co. Workers' Assistance Payments, 1910–1920*

Year	Amount paid out of thread manufacturing and profit and loss accounts for workers' assistance payments £	s	d
1910	241	15	—
1911	384	9	6
1912	318	17	10
1913	305	7	8
1914	222	12	—
1915	270	15	1
1916	266	4	9
1917	291	19	1
1918	419	11	2
1919	543	8	2
1920	399	14	11

Source: UGABRC, JPC Collection, UGD 199/6/11/1, Clark & Co. Private Journal, 1897–1928

Table 3.3: ***Clark & Co. Contributions to Charities and Other Organisations, 1900–1919***

Year	Charity contributions and donations from the thread manufacturing and profit and loss accounts £	s	d
1900	588	—	1
1901	unknown	unknown	unknown
1902	unknown	unknown	unknown
1903	447	2	—
1904	447	2	—
1905	457	2	—
1906	449	2	—
1907	447	2	—
1908	447	2	—
1909	447	2	—
1910	447	2	—
1911	447	2	—
1912	222	2	—
1913	272	2	—
1914	272	2	—
1915	346	5	6
1916	361	6	6
1917	401	12	6
1918	456	17	—
1919	565	—	—

Source: UGABRC, JPC Collection, UGD, 199/6/11/1, Clark & Co. Private Journal, 1897–1928

Table 3.4: ***Girls' Club, Physical Culture and Dressmaking Classes, 1907–1921: Membership Figures***

Session	Physical Culture Class Membership	Dressmaking Class Membership
1907–1908	35	65
1908–1909	12	104
1909–1910	22	72
1910–1911	18	106
1911–1912	42	57
1912–1913	42	65
1913–1914	66	55
1914–1915	41	39
1915–1916	24	36
1916–1917	63	23
1917–1918	38	no class
1918–1919	45	no class
1919–1920	57	29
1920–1921	48	49

Source: PM, JPC Collection, 1/5/72, Notes on Welfare of Workers (1920), p. 11.

Appendix 4

Parliamentary Election Results: Paisley, 1832–1945

Election	Electors	T-out (%)	Candidate	Party	Votes	%
1832	1,242	76.9	Sir J. Maxwell, Bt.	L	775	81.2
			J. McKerrell	C	10	18.8
					765	*62.4*
[Resignation]						
1834	1,261	85.6	Sir D. K. Sandford	L	542	50.2
(24/3)			J. Crawfurd	L	509	47.1
			J. E. Gordon	C	29	2.7
					33	*3.1*
1835	1,510	75.4	A. G. Spiers	L	661	58.1
			H. Ross	C	477	41.9
					184	*16.2*
[Resignation]						
1836	1,465	82.5	A. Hastie	L	680	56.2
(17/3)			J. Aytoun	L	529	43.8
					151	*12.4*
1837	1,610	—	A. Hastie	L	Unopp.	—
1841	1,324	11.86	A. Hastie	L	157	11.86
			W. Thomason	Ch	0	0
					157	*11.86*
1847	1,060	—	A. Hastie	L	Unopp.	—
1852	1,342	58.1	A. Hastie	L	406	52.1
			W. T. Haly	L	374	47.9
					32	*4.2*
1857	1,305	87.3	A. Hastie	L	611	53.6
			H. E. C. Ewing	L	524	46.0
			C. F. F. Wordsworth	Ch	*4*	*0.4*
[Death]						
1857	1,349	64.1	H. E. C. Ewing	L	767	88.7
(11/12)			W. T. Haly	L	98	11.3
					669	*77.4*
1859	1,370	—	H.E.C. Ewing	L	Unopp.	—
1865	1,361	—	H.E.C. Ewing	L	Unopp.	—
1868	3,264	89.4	H. E. C. Ewing	L	1,576	54.0
			A. C. Campbell	C	921	31.6
			A. Kintrea	L	421	14.4
					655	*22.4*
1874	5,083	—	W. Holms	L	Unopp.	—

Election	Electors	T-out (%)	Candidate	Party	Votes	%
1880	4,979	—	W. Holms	L	Unopp.	—
[Resignation]						
1884	5,688	85.4	S. Clark	L	3,049	62.8
(18/2)			Lord Ernest Hamilton	C	1,806	37.2
					1,243	*25.6*
1885	6,794	87.0	W. B. Barbour	L	3,390	57.3
			R. M. McKerrell	C	2,523	42.7
					867	*14.6*
1886	6,794	81.7	W. B. Barbour	L	3,057	55.1
			J. P. Smith	LU	2,491	44.9
					566	*10.2*
[Death]						
1891	8,107	85.8	W. Dunn	L	4,145	59.6
(1/6)			R. M. McKerrell	C	2,807	40.4
					1,338	*19.2*
1892	8,223	81.5	W. Dunn	L	4,262	63.6
			C. N. Johnston	C	2,441	36.4
					1,821	*27.2*
1895	9,105	82.0	Sir W. Dunn, Bt.	L	4,404	59.0
			A. Moffat	C	3,062	41.0
					1,342	*18.0*
1900	10,758	74.4	Sir W. Dunn, Bt.	L	4,532	56.6
			G. S. C. Swinton	C	3,474	43.4
					1,058	*13.2*
1906	12,179	88.2	J. M. McCallum	L	5,664	52.7
			J. A. D. MacKean	LU	2,594	24.2
			R. Smillie	SWRC	2,482	23.1
					3,070	*28.5*
1910 (J)	12,331	86.8	J. M. McCallum	L	6,812	63.7
			D. F. Campbell	C	3,890	36.3
					2,922	*27.4*
1910 (D)	12,541	74.9	J. M. McCallum	L	6,039	64.3
			A. R. Jephcott	C	3,350	35.7
					2,689	*28.6*
1918	38,508	57.6	Sir J. M. McCallum	L	7,542	34.0
			J. M. Biggar	Co-op	7,436	33.5
			J. Taylor	Co NDP	7,201	32.5
					106	*0.5*
[Death]						
1920	39,235	77.6	Rt. Hon. H. H. Asquith	L	14,736	48.4
(12/2)			J. M. Biggar	Lab/Co-op	11,902	39.1
			J. A. D. MacKean	Co C	3,795	12.5
					2,834	*9.3*

Election	Electors	T-out (%)	Candidate	Party	Votes	%
1922	38,093	78.0	Rt. Hon. H. H. Asquith	L	15,005	50.5
			J. M. Biggar	Lab/Co-op	14,689	49.5
					316	*49.5*
1923	37,792	77.1	Rt. Hon. H. H. Asquith	L	9,723	33.4
			J. M. Biggar	Lab/Co-op	7,977	27.4
			A. D. M. Shaw	C	7,758	26.6
			D. D. Cormack	Ind Lab	3,685	12.6
					1,746	*6.0*
1924	37,901	84.1	E. R. Mitchell	Lab	17,057	53.5
			Rt. Hon. H. H. Asquith	L	14,829	46.5
					2,228	*7.0*
1929	51,385	78.2	J. Welsh	Lab	22,425	55.8
			J. McCulloch	L	10,640	26.5
			Miss M. G. Cowan	C	7,094	17.7
					11,785	*29.3*
1931	53,373	79.4	Hon. J. P. Maclay	L	26,187	61.8
			J. Welsh	Lab	16,183	38.2
					10,004	*23.6*
1935	55,473	80.3	Hon. J. P. Maclay	L	22,466	50.4
			O. R. Baldwin	Lab	22,077	49.6
					389	*0.8*
1945	61,286	73.9	Viscount Corvedale	Lab	25,156	55.6
			T. G. D. Galbraith	C	14,826	32.7
			Lady Glen-Coats	L	4,532	10.0
			A. R. Eagles	Ind	765	1.7
					10,330	*22.9*

Appendix 5

5.1: *Questions Issued to Town Council Candidates by Paisley Trades Council, 1892*

1. Will you insist, as regards all persons employed by the Council upon them receiving not less than trade union rates of wages for each occupation?
2. Will you promote the direct employment of labour by the Council, wherever possible, in preference to contracting?
3. Where contracting is necessary, such as in making police clothing &c. will you do all in your power to prevent subcontracting, which tends to sweating, and rigidly enforce the rule of employing only firms which pay trade union rates of wages, and observe the standard hours of labour, where such standard exists?
4. Will you support the construction and maintenance by the council itself of improved dwellings and common lodging houses, as the private common lodging houses for the most part are detrimental to the health and morals of the community?
5. Are you favourable to granting the council power to provide public markets where required?
6. Will you press for a fair division of the rates between owner and occupier?
7. Are you in favour of levying special taxation upon the owners of ground rents and other land values, and of collecting half-rates from the owners of empty houses and vacant land?
8. Will you endeavour to secure special contributions, by way of 'betterment' from the owners of property benefitted by public improvements?
9. Will you vote for the opening on Sundays of public baths and parks?

Source: *PDE*, 9 Nov. 1892

5.2: *Questions Issued to Town Council Candidates by Paisley Trades Council, 1893*

1. Will you insist as regards all persons employed by the Council upon (a) a normal eight hours' day? (b) not less than trade union rate of wages for each occupation? (c) full liberty of combination? (d) one day's rest in seven and sufficient annual holidays? (e) the prohibition of overtime except in unexpected emergencies?
2. Will you promote the direct employment of labour by the Council, wherever possible, in preference to contracting?
3. Where contracting is necessary, will you try to put down all sweating, and rigidly enforce the rule of employing only firms which (a) pay the trade union rate of wages for the particular occupation? (b) observe the standard hours of labour, where such standard exists?
4. Are you in favour of a minimum wage of 20s. per week for municipal employees?

5. Are you in favour of a clause being inserted in all municipal contracts to prevent subcontracting?

6. Will you vote against increase of salaries over £800 per annum to any municipal employee?

7. Will you press for the immediate undertaking by the Council of such works as are required in the public interest in order to increase the demand for labour in the coming slack season?

8. Are you in favour of allowing the use of a hall in the Municipal Buildings for Trades' Council Meetings?

9. Will you vote in favour of the establishment of a Municipal Labour Bureau?

10. Will you press for prompt and extensive action by the Council for the condemnation of unsanitary buildings?

11. Will you support the construction and maintenance, by the Council itself, of an adequate number of improved artizan's dwellings?

12. Will you press for the employment by the Council of an adequate staff to compel the enforcement of sanitary laws relating to house property?

13. Will you press for a fair division of the rates between owner and occupier?

14. Are you in favour of levying special taxation upon the owners of ground rents and other land values, and of collecting half-rates from the owners of empty houses and vacant land?

15. Will you endeavour to secure special contributions, by way of 'betterment' from the owners of property benefitted by public improvements?

16. Will you support a 'Municipal Death Duty' on local real estate, as a way of absorbing the 'unearned increment'?

17. Will you support any reasonable proposal for evening meetings of the Council and its committees, so that men at work in the day can become effective members?

18. Are you in favour of (a) the formation of the Council exclusively by direct election? (b) free use, for candidates' meetings of all suitable school rooms receiving educational grants and other public buildings? (c) payment of the members of the Council, with a special salary for the Provost? (d) making women eligible for election?

19. Will you, in order to secure for the public the unearned increment, oppose the sale of the freehold of any land owned by the Council, and endeavour to obtain an alteration of any law making necessary the sale of 'surplus land'?

20. Will you insist on the rigid enforcement, without respect of person, of the laws relating to the smoke nuisance, the pollution of rivers, and noxious trades; and endeavour to obtain adequate further powers to prevent the creation of nuisances?

Source: *PRG*, 30 Sep. 1893

Appendix 6

Table 6.1: *Number of Persons and Percentage of Total Population Living in One, Two, Three and Four Roomed Houses in Scotland (1901)*

	Scotland (Towns)	Leith	Paisley
Total Population	3,120,241	77,439	79,353
One-room houses	394,023	6,727	10,738
As %	*12.63*	*8.69*	*13.53*
Two-room houses	1,302,762	32,805	39,580
As %	*41.75*	*42.36*	*49.87*
Three-room houses	627,994	17,876	15,614
As %	*20.13*	*23.09*	*19.68*
Four-room houses	263,403	7,050	5,191
As %	*8.44*	*9.10*	*6.54*
Five-room & over houses	532,059	12,981	8,240
As %	*17.05*	*16.76*	*10.38*

Source: *PP*, 1908, XCIII, Cd. 4016: *Return Showing the Housing Conditions of the Population of Scotland (1908)*

Table 6.2: *Housing Condition of the Population of Scotland (1901)*

	Scotland (Burghs over 10,000)	Glasgow	Paisley
Total Population	2,369,705	761,709	79,363
Not more than 2 per room	1,196,103	345,035	32,732
As %	*50.47*	*45.30*	*41.24*
More than 2 per room	1,173,602	416,674	46,631
As %	*49.53*	*54.70*	*58.76*
Not more than 3 per room	1,789,519	547,710	54,568
As %	*75.52*	*71.91*	*68.76*
More than 3 per room	580,186	213,999	24,795
As %	*24.48*	*28.09*	*31.24*
Not more than 4 per room	2,140	678,512	70,026
As %	*90.33*	*89.08*	*88.24*
More than 4 per room	229,242	83,197	9,337
As %	*9.67*	*10.92*	*11.76*

Source: *PP*, 1908, XCIII, Cd. 4016: *Return Showing the Housing Conditions of the Population of Scotland (1908)*

Table 6.3: *Housing Provision and Percentage of Total Population Living in One, Two and Three-Roomed Houses (1911)*

	% of total houses having			% of total population living in houses of		
Town	**One room**	**Two rooms**	**Three rooms**	**One room**	**Two rooms**	**Three rooms**
Paisley	18.9	50.7	17.5	12.0	53.0	20.8
Leith	8.2	45.2	24.1	5.4	44.5	26.0
Greenock	14.1	47.7	21.6	10.0	48.9	23.5
Glasgow	20.1	46.3	18.9	13.8	48.4	21.1

Source: *PP*, 1917–18, XIV, Cd. 8731: *Report of the Royal Commission on the Housing of the Industrial Population of Scotland, Rural and Urban*

Appendix 7

7.1: *Unionist Campaign Literature, 1910*

ELECTORS OF PAISLEY

(1) The **LIBERAL** Policy would **MAINTAIN THE HEREDITARY PRINCIPLE** in the House of Lords.

The **UNIONIST** Policy would **ABOLISH THAT HEREDITARY PRICIPLE.**

(2) The **LIBERAL** Policy would introduce **SINGLE CHAMBER GOVERNMENT.**

The **UNIONIST** Policy would maintain an **ELECTED SECOND CHAMBER** to prevent hasty and ill-considered legislation.

(3) The **LIBERAL** Policy would enable a temporary **COALITION of MINORITIES,** such as now exists, to over-ride the will of the people.

The **UNIONIST** Policy would not allow a **REAL MAJORITY** of the people to be dominated by a temporary combination of minorities.

(4) The **LIBERAL** Party is **AFRAID** to trust the people with the **REFERENDUM.**

The **UNIONIST** Party recognises the **SOVEREIGN WILL** of the **PEOPLE** through the **REFERENDUM.**

(5) The **LIBERAL** Policy would make the **Party Leaders** the **Masters** of the People.

The **UNIONIST** Policy would make the **PEOPLE** their own **MASTERS.**

(6) The **LIBERAL** Policy would give **HOME RULE** to **IRELAND** without further reference to the People.

The **Unionist** Policy would insist that Home Rule be definitely decided by the **People's Referendum.**

(7) **THE LIBERAL POLICY is calculated to destroy the Freedom of the People.**

THE UNIONIST POLICY would give them absolute control over the affairs of the Nation.

The House of Lords has never thwarted the clearly declared will of the People as expressed at a General Election; but, on the other hand, has preserved the Liberties of the People against oppressive legislation and the dismemberment of the United Kingdom.

THEREFORE

VOTE FOR JEPHCOTT

THE WORKING MAN'S UNIONIST CANDIDATE

Source: *PRG*, 3 Dec. 1910

Bibliography

Manuscript Sources

A. Government Records

Edinburgh, Scottish Record Office
Various, including:
Housing Files, DD6
Paisley Central Working Men's Club and Institute, FS 4/842
Progressive Bookstall, Paisley, FS 12/257
Census Reports (Scotland), 1881, 1891, 1901, 1911, 1921, 1931.

B. Political Archives

Edinburgh, National Library of Scotland
Elibank Collection
Haldane Collection
Labour Party, Scottish Council Annual, *Conference Reports*
Labour Party, Scottish Council, *Executive Reports*
Liberal Party Pamphlets and Leaflets (various)
Muirhead Collection
Paisley Trades and Labour Council, *Fifth Annual Report* (1916) (micro-fiche)
Rosebery Collection
Scottish Conservative and Unionist Association Archives, (includes Archives of the Liberal Unionist Association)
Scottish Workers' Parliamentary Elections Committee (Scottish Workers' Representation Committee from 1902), Annual Conference Reports (1901–1906)

Edinburgh, University of Edinburgh [Special Collections Dept.]
Scottish Liberal Association Archives

Glasgow, Andersonian Library, University of Strathclyde
Labour Party, National Executive Committee Minutes, 1900–1924 (micro-fiche)

Glasgow, William Gallacher Library, STUC Headquarters
Gallacher Collection
William McQuilkin Collection

Glasgow, Mitchell Library, Glasgow City Archives
Parker Smith Collection
Social Democratic Federation, Pamphlets and Leaflets, 1871–1931

Glasgow, University of Glasgow [Special Collections Dept.]
McCallum Scott Collection

Paisley, Central Library
Liberal Association Minutes: Paisley Branch (1922–1947)
Paisley Conservative Association, Misc. Files
Paisley Parliamentary Elections Committee: Minutes (1901–1905)
Paisley Trades and Labour Council (United Trades Council/Paisley Labour Party and Industrial Committee): Minutes (1911–1935)
West Renfrewshire Conservative Association, Letter Book 1909–1911.
Women's Liberal Association Minutes: Paisley and District Branch (1890–1902)

Paisley, Paisley Museum
Co-operative Party Minutes: Paisley Branch (1922–1947)

London, School of Economics
Independent Labour Party Archives

Oxford, Bodleian Library
Asquith, H. H.: Papers
Gilbert Murray Collection
Harcourt Collection
National Party, Grand Council Minute Book, 1917–1923
Sir Donald McLean Collection
Vivian Phillips Collection

C. INDUSTRY AND LABOUR ARCHIVES

Glasgow, Mitchell Library, Glasgow City Archives
Laighpark Dyeworks, Misc. Files
Scottish Union of Bakers and Confectioners, Paisley and District Council: Minutes (1924–1934) – Department of Social Sciences
Society of Amalgamated Toolmakers, Paisley Branch: Minutes (1914–1915)
United Machine Workers Association, Paisley Branch: Minutes (1907–1918), TD 1137/1–6

Glasgow, Archives and Business Records, Thurso Street
A. F. Craig & Co. Ltd. Archives
J. & P. Coats Collection
Fullerton, Hodgart & Barclay Ltd. Archives
William Fulton & Sons Ltd. Archives

Paisley, Central Library

Adelphi Starch Works, Misc. Files

Amalgamated Engineering Union (Glasgow, Kilbirnie, Kilmarnock, Mid-Lanark and Paisley District Committees), *Silver Jubilee 1920–1945: Twenty Five Years' Progress* (Paisley, 1945)

Amalgamated Engineering Union, Paisley District, Misc. Files

Babcock & Wilcox (Renfrew), Misc. Files

Brown & Polson, Misc. Files

Clark & Co., Misc. Files

Doulton & Co., Misc. Files

Eadie Brothers, Misc. Files

Henderson, Hogg & Co. Ltd., Misc. Files

Isdale & McCallum, Misc. Files

J. & P. Coats, Misc. Files

Kilpatricks (Electrical Engineers), Misc. Files

Operative Bricklayers Association, Paisley Branch: Minutes (1895–1902)

Paisley Distress Committee Minutes (1905–1914)

Paisley Distress Committee, Letters to the Distress Committee (1905–1908)

Messrs William Paton Ltd, Johnstone: Misc. Files

William Peacock, Rope Manufacturers, Misc. Files

Stoddards, Glenpatrick Carpet Factory, Misc. Files

Underwood Mill, Misc. Files

United Patternmakers Association (Paisley Branch, No. 37): Minutes (1881–1891; 1933–1941)

United Plumbers of Great Britain and Ireland (Paisley District Lodge): Minutes (1888–1900; 1911–1917; 1922–1925; 1925–1930)

Wotherspoon Starch Works, Misc. Files

Paisley, AEU District Offices, Inkle Street

Amalgamated Society of Engineers: 2nd Paisley Branch: Minutes (1891–1945); 3rd Paisley Branch: Minutes (1897–1903)

Society of Amalgamated Toolmakers, Paisley Branch: Minutes (1919–1921)

United Machine Workers Association, Paisley Branch: Minutes (1918–1924)

Paisley, Paisley Museum

J. & P. Coats Collection

Printed Primary Sources

A. Parliamentary Papers

1876, LXIX (Cd 440): *Report by the Assistant Registrar of Friendly Societies for Scotland, As Register of Trade Unions, 1875.*

1884–5, XXI (Cd 4547): *Royal Commission for Inquiry into the Housing of the Working Classes, Second Report (Scotland).*

1889, LXX (Cd 5807): *Return of Rates of Wages in Principle Textile Trades in the United Kingdom.*

1899, XII (Cd 9456): *Report by Inspectors on the Prevention of Accidents from Machinery in the Manufacture of Cotton.*

1890, LXVIII (Cd 6161): *Report and Return of Rates of Wages in Minor Textile Trades of the United Kingdom.*

1892, XXXIV–XXXV (Cd 6708): *Royal Commission on Labour: First Report.*

1892, XXXVI (Cd 6795): *Royal Commission on Labour: Second Report.*

1889, LXX (Cd 5809); 1890, LXVIII (Cd 6176); 1890–91, LXXVIII (Cd 6476); 1893–94, LXXXIII (Cd 6890); 1894, LXXXI (Cd 7566); 1895, XCII (Cd 7901); 1896, LXXX (Cd 8231); 1897, LXXXIV (Cd 8643); 1898, LXXXVIII (Cd 9012); 1899, XCII (Cd 9437); 1900, LXXXIII (Cd 316): *Reports on Strikes and Lockouts by the Labour Correspondent of the Board of Trade* (1888–1899).

1901, LXXIII (Cd 689); 1902, XCVII (Cd 1236); 1903, LXVI (Cd 1623); 1904, LXXXIX (Cd 2112); 1905, LXXVI (Cd 2631); 1906, CXII (Cd 3065); 1907, LXXX (Cd 3711); 1908, XCVIII (Cd 4254); 1909, XLIX (Cd 4680); 1910, LVIII (Cd 5325); 1911, XLI (Cd 5850); 1912–13, XLVII (Cd 6472); 1914, XLVIII (Cd 7089); 1914–1916, XXXVI (Cd 7658): *Report of the Commissioners: Trade Boards, Strikes and Lock-outs.*

1903, LXVI (Cd 110): *Return Showing Statistics of Strikes and Lock-outs in each of the ten years, 1893–1902.*

1906, LVI (Cd 2825): *Report of the Royal Commission on Trade Disputes and Trade Combinations.*

1905, LXVIII (Cd 2524): *Report of the Local Government Board of Scotland on the Methods of Administering Poor Relief in Certain Large Town Parishes of Scotland.*

1908, XCIII (Cd 4016): *Return Showing the Housing Conditions of the Population of Scotland (1908).*

1909, LXXX (Cd 4545): *Report of an Inquiry by the Board of Trade into the Earnings and Hours of Labour of Work-people of the United Kingdom. (Textile Trades in 1906).*

1909, XLIII (Cd 4653): *Royal Commission on the Poor Law: vol. xvi, Reports on the Relation of Industrial and Sanitary Conditions to Pauperism by Mr Steel Maitland and Miss R. E. Squire.*

1910, XLVI (Cd 4978): *Royal Commission on the Poor Law: vol. vi, Evidence (with Appendices) Relating to Scotland.*

1910, LII (Cd 5073): *Royal Commission on the Poor Law: vol. xixa, Reports on the Effects of Employment or Assistance Given to the Unemployed since 1886 as a Means of relieving Distress outside the Poor Law in Scotland (Rev. J. C. Pringle).*

1910, LIV (Cd 5243): *Royal Commission on the Poor Law: vol. xxix, Report on the Methods of Administering Charitable Assistance and the Extent and Intensity of Poverty in Scotland, prepared by the Committee on Church Interests, appt. General Assembly of the Church of Scotland.*

1910, LIV (Cd 5440): *Royal Commission on the Poor Law: vol. xxx, Documents relating specially to Scotland.*

1914–16, XXXVII (Cd 7848): *Interim Report of the Central Committee on Women's Employment.*

1914–16, XXIX (Cd 8136): *Report by Lord Balfour of Burleigh and Mr L. Macassey, K. C. on the Causes and Circumstances of the Apprehended Difficulties affecting Munition Workers in the Clyde District.*

1917–18, XIV (Cd 8731): *Report of the Royal Commission on the Housing of the Industrial Population of Scotland, Rural and Urban.*

1924–1925, XIV (Cd 2481): *Annual Report of the Ministry of Labour for the Years 1923 and 1924.*

1929–30, XII (Cd 3615): *Report of the Committee on the Cotton Industry.*

1933–34, XIII (Cd 4728): *Reports of Investigations into the Industrial Conditions in Certain Depressed Areas.*

1933–34, XII (Cd 4469): *Report of the Scottish Departmental Committee on Housing.*

1937–38, XIV (Cd 5803): *Report of the Departmental Committee on the Poor Law in Scotland.*

B. NEWSPAPERS

British Citizen and Empire Worker
Daily Record
Forward
Glasgow Echo
Glasgow Herald
Glasgow Observer and Catholic Herald
Paisley and Renfrewshire Gazette
Paisley Chronicle (1885–1887); thereafter, *Radical Times*
Paisley Daily Express
Paisley Daily Standard
Paisley Magazine

Paisley Observer (1905–1906); thereafter, *Scottish Observer*
Renfrewshire Independent
Scottish Co-operator
Scottish Worker

C. CONTEMPORARY COMMENTARIES, ETC.

ASQUITH, H. H., *The Paisley Policy* (London, 1920).

——, *Memories and Reflections, 1852–1927* (London, 1928).

BLAIR, M., *The Paisley Shawl and the Men who Created and Developed It* (Paisley, 1907).

——, *The Paisley Thread Industry and the Men who Created and Developed It with Notes Concerning Paisley, Old and New* (Paisley, 1907).

BREWSTER, REV. P., *His Chartist and Socialist Sermons* (Glasgow, 1910).

BROWN, R., *The History of Paisley From the Roman Period Down to 1884* (Paisley, 1886).

——, *Paisley Burns Club (1805–1893)* (Paisley, 1893).

BUCHAN, A., *History of the Scottish Co-operative Women's Guild* (SCWS, Glasgow, 1913).

CHALMERS, G., *Caledonia: Or, a Historical and Topographical Account of North Britain from the Most Ancient to the Present Times, with a Dictionary of Places Chorographical and Philological* (Paisley, 1890).

CRAIG, J. W., *Historical Notes on Paisley and its Neighbourhood* (Paisley, 1881).

DOLLAN, P. J., 'The Clyde Rent War' (Glasgow, 1925).

DAVIS, E. W., and FLOCKHART, A., *Paisley War Emergency Committee (1914–1919): Its History, Objects and Achievements* (Paisley, 1920).

FLANAGAN, J. A., *Wholesale Co-operation in Scotland: The Fruits of Fifty Years' Efforts (1868–1918), An Account of the Scottish Co-operative Wholesale Society Compiled to Commemorate the Society's Golden Jubilee* (SCWS, Glasgow, 1920).

GALLACHER, W., and PATON, J., *Towards Industrial Democracy: A Memorandum on Workshop Control* (Paisley, 1917).

GASKELL, E., *Renfrewshire and Ayrshire Leaders* (publ. for private circulation, *c.*1908).

GILMOUR, D., *Paisley Weavers of Other Days* (Paisley, 1876).

HECTOR, W., *Vanuara:Or Odds and Ends, Personal, Social and Local, From Recollections of By-Past Times* (Paisley, 1880).

JOHNSTON, T. (ed.), *Rev. Patrick Brewster: His Chartist and Socialist Sermons* (Glasgow, 1910).

KELSO, W. W., *Sanitation in Paisley: A Record of Progress, 1488–1920* (Paisley, 1922).

KENNEDY, H., *On Some Recollections and Suggestions in Connection with the Baking Trade from 1845 till 1905, with Special Reference to the Paisley Branch* (Paisley, 1905).

KERR, L., *Glenshiels* (London, 1932).

——, *Woman of Glenshiels* (London, 1935).

——, *The Eager Years: An Autobiography* (London, 1940).

LOWE, D., *Souvenirs of Scottish Labour* (Glasgow, 1919).

MACDONALD, J. R., 'Mr Chamberlain as a social reformer', in Rt. Hon. Viscount Milner *et al.*, *Life of Joseph Chamberlain* (London, *c.*1914).

MCINTYRE, J., *Canal Street Church, Paisley (1780–1930)* (Paisley, 1930).

MARTIN, F., *Lecture on Fifty Years Progress of the Corporation* (Paisley, 1902).

MARWICK, SIR JAMES D., *The River Clyde and the Clyde Burghs* (Glasgow, 1909).

METCALFE, W. M., *A History of Renfrew from the Earliest Times* (Paisley, 1905).

——, *History of Paisley* (Paisley, 1909).

MITCHELL, R., *Passing By* (Edinburgh, 1935).

——, *Many Phases* (Glasgow, 1937).

MORT, F., *Renfrewshire* (Cambridge, 1912).

MURRAY, R., *Politics and Co-operative Production* (Glasgow, n.d.).

MURRAY, W. S., *Captains of Industry* (Glasgow, 1901).

OLIVER, A., *Life of George Clark Hutton D.D.: Minister of Canal Street United Free Church, Paisley* (Paisley, 1910).

ROWAT, D., *Jubilee of the Paisley Provident Co-operative Society Limited, 1860–1910* (Paisley, 1910).

SCOTT, W. R., and CUNNISON, J., *The Industries of the Clyde Valley During the War* (Oxford, 1924).

SMILLIE, R., *My Life for Labour* (1924).

Statistical Account for Scotland (Old), vol. VII, ed. Sir John Sinclair (1791–99).

Statistical Account of Scotland (New), vol. VII (Edinburgh, 1845).

STURROCK, J. B., *Looking Back: A Series of Reminiscences, Sketches and Studies* (Paisley, 1910).

URIE, J., *Reminiscences of Eighty Years* (Paisley, 1908).

WHEATLEY, J., *Homes or Hutches?* (Glasgow, 1923).

[——], *The Crisis in the Cotton Industry: Report of the Proceedings of the Provisional Emergency Cotton Committee, September 27 1922 to March 13 1923* (Manchester, 1923).

[——], 'The Decay of Scottish Unionism', by 'A Scottish Unionist', *Independent Review*, 3, 1904.

[——], *Glasgow and District Railwaymen's Strike Bulletin* (Glasgow, 1919).

[——], *Guide to Paisley and Surrounding Districts with Fifty Photographic Views of Places and Persons of Interest* (Paisley, 1896).

[——], *Handbook to the 37th Annual Co-operative Congress, Paisley, Renfrewshire* (SCWS, Glasgow, 1905).

[——], *The Inauguration of the George A. Clark Town Hall, Paisley* (Paisley, 1882).

[——], *Minute of the Proceedings of the Town Council of Paisley connected with the visit of Her Majesty the Queen and Celebration of the Fourth Centenary of the Burgh, 23.August 1888* (Paisley, 1888).

[——], *The Pageant of Paisley* (Paisley, 1929).

[——], *Paisley Comic Serials (Hoo'let, Hawk, Eclipse)* (Paisley, 1868).

[——], *Paisley Co-operative Manufacturing Society Ltd.: Jubilee Souvenir of the PCMS Ltd. 1862–1912* (Glasgow, 1912).

[——], *Paisley Corporation Diary* (Paisley, 1923).

[——], *Paisley Tramways Order Confirmation Act, 1911* , ch. cxxviii (18 Aug. 1911).

[——], *Record of the Visit of His Majesty King George V to the Burgh of Paisley* (Paisley, 1917).

[——], *Scottish Co-operative Wholesale Society Ltd. 1868–1929: A Historical and Descriptive Handbook* (SCWS, Glasgow, 1929?).

SECONDARY SOURCES

ADAMS, T., 'Co-operators and politics: a rejoinder', *IRSH*, xxxii (1987).

——, 'The formation of the Co-operative Party reconsidered', *IRSH,* xxxi (1987).

AGNEW, J. A., *Place and Politics: The Geographical Mediation of State and Society* (Boston, 1987).

——, 'Place and politics in post-war Italy: a cultural geography of local identity in the provinces of Lucca and Pistoia', in K. Anderson and F. Gale (eds.), *Inventing Places: Studies in Cultural Geography* (n.p., 1992).

ALEXANDER, S., 'Women, class and sexual differences in the 1830s and 1840s: some reflections on the writing of a feminist history', *History Workshop,* xvii (1984).

ASHCRAFT, R., 'Liberal political theory and working-class radicalism in nineteenth-century England', *Political Theory*, xxi (1993).

BALL, S. R., 'Asquith's decline and the General Election of 1918', *SHR,* lxi (1982).

BELCHEM, J., *Class, Party and the Political System in Britain, 1867–1914* (Oxford, 1990).

——, *Popular Radicalism in Nineteenth-Century Britain* (Basingstoke, 1996).

BENNETT, D., *Margot: A Life of the Countess of Oxford and Asquith* (London, 1986).

BERLANSTEIN, L. R. (ed.), *The Industrial Revolution and Work in Nineteenth-Century Europe* (London, 1992).

BIAGINI, E. F., *Liberty, Retrenchment and Reform – Popular Liberalism in the Age of Gladstone, 1860–1880* (Cambridge, 1992).

BIAGINI, E. F. (ed.), *Citizenship and Community: Liberals, Radicals and Collective Identities in the British Isles, 1865–1931* (Cambridge, 1996).

——, and REID, A. J. (eds.), *Currents of Radicalism, Organised Labour and Party Politics in Britain, 1850–1914* (Cambridge, 1991).

BLACK, C. S., *The Story of Paisley* (Paisley, 1949).

BLEWETT, N., 'The franchise in the United Kingdom, 1885–1918', *P&P*, xxxii (1965).

BROWN, C. G., *The Social History of Religion in Scotland Since 1730* (London, 1987).

BROWN, G., 'The Labour Party and Political Change in Scotland, 1918–1929: The Politics of Five Elections' (Edinburgh University, Ph.D. thesis, 1981).

BROWN, J., *From Radicalism to Socialism: Paisley Engineers, 1890–1920, Pamphlet 71, History Group of the Communist Party* (n.d.).

BROWN, Joyce, 'Attercliffe, 1894: how one local Liberal party failed to meet the challenge of Labour', *JBS*, xiv (1975).

BROWN, S., '"Echoes of Midlothian": Scottish Liberalism and the South African War, 1899–1902', *SHR,* lxxi (1992).

BRUCE, S., *No Pope of Rome: Anti-Catholicism in Modern Scotland* (Edinburgh, 1985).

BUCKLEY, K. D., *Trade Unionism in Aberdeen, 1878–1900* (Aberdeen, 1955).

BULMER THOMAS, I., *The Growth of the British Party System*, vol. I: *1640–1923* (London, 1965).

BURAWOY, M., *The Politics of Production: Facory Regimes Under Capitalism and Socialism* (London, 1985).

BURGESS, K., *The Challenge of Labour* (London, 1980).

BUSFIELD, D., 'Skill and the sexual division of labour in the West Riding textile industry, 1850–1914', in Jowitt and McIvor, *Employers and Labour in the English Textile Industries*.

BUTLER, D., and FREEMAN, J., *British Political Facts, 1900–1968* (3rd edn, London, 1969).

BUTT, J., 'Working-class housing in Glasgow, 1900–1939', in MacDougall, *Essays in Scottish Labour History*.

CAIN, P., 'The Conservative Party and "Radical Conservatism", 1880–1914: incubus or necessity?', *TCBH,* vii (1996).

CAIRNCROSS, A. K., and HUNTER, J. B. K., 'The early growth of Messrs J. & P. Coats, 1830–83', *Business History,* xxix (1987).

CALHOUN, C. J., 'Community: toward a variable conceptualization for comparative research', *SH*, v (1980).

CALLINICOS, A., *Theories and Narratives: Reflections on the Philosophy of History* (Cambridge, 1995).

CAMPBELL, J., 'The renewal of Liberalism: Liberalism without Liberals', in Peele and Cook, *Politics of Reappraisal.*

CAMPBELL, R. H., *Scotland Since 1707: The Rise of an Industrial Society* (Edinburgh, 1985).

CAMPBELL, R. H., and DOW, J. B. A. (eds.), *Source Book of Scottish Economic and Social History* (Oxford, 1968).

CARBERRY, T. F., 'An Examination and Evaluation of the Co-operative Party of the Co-operative Union Ltd' (London University, Ph.D. thesis, 1966).

CHAMBERLAIN, C., 'The growth in support for the Labour Party in Britain', *BJS*, xxiv (1973).

CHECKLAND, S., and CHECKLAND, O., *Industry and Ethos: Scotland 1832–1914* (London, 1984).

CHILDS, M., 'Labour grows up: the electoral system, political generations, and British politics, 1890–1929', *TCBH*, vi (1995).

CLARK, D. B., 'The concept of community: a re-examination', *The Sociological Review*, xxi (1973).

CLARK, S., *Paisley: A History* (Edinburgh, 1988).

CLARKE, P. F., *Lancashire and the New Liberalism* (Cambridge, 1971).

——, 'Electoral sociology of modern Britain', *History*, lvii (1972).

——, 'Liberals, Labour and the franchise', *EHR*, xcii (1977).

——, *Liberals and Social Democrats* (Cambridge, 1978).

CLARKE, T., and DICKSON, T., 'Class consciousness in early industrial capitalism: Paisley 1770–1850', in T. Dickson (ed.), *Capital and Class in Scotland* (Edinburgh, 1982).

COETZEE, F., *For Party or Country: Nationalism and the Dilemmas of Popular Conservatism in Edwardian England* (New York, 1990).

COLE, G. D. H., *A Century of Co-operation* (Manchester, 1944).

——, *British Working-Class Politics, 1832–1914* (London, 1946).

COLLINS, B., 'Irish emigration to Dundee and Paisley during the first half of the nineteenth century', in J. M. Goldstrom and L. A. Clarkson (eds.), *Irish Population, Economy and Society* (Oxford, 1981).

CONEYS, M., 'The Labour Movement and the Liberal Party in Rochdale, 1890–1906' (Huddersfield Polytechnic, M.A. thesis, 1982).

COOK, C., *The Age of Alignment: Electoral Politics in Britain, 1922–1929* (London, 1975).

——, 'Liberals, Labour and local elections', in Peele and Cook, *Politics of Reappraisal*.

——, *A Short History of the Liberal Party, 1900–1976* (London, 1976).

CRAIG, F. W. S., *British Electoral Facts, 1832–1980* (Chichester, 1981).

CRAWFORD, R. L., 'Literary Activity in Paisley in the Early Nineteenth Century' (Glasgow University, B.Litt. thesis, 1965).

CROUCHER, R., *We Refuse to Starve in Silence: A History of the National Unemployed Workers; Movement, 1920–1946* (London, 1987).

CUNNINGHAM, H., 'The language of patriotism: from radical opposition to Tory jingoism, 1750–1914', *History Workshop*, xii (1981).

DAMER, S., 'State, class and housing: Glasgow 1885–1919', in Melling, J. (ed.), *Housing, Social Policy and the State* (London, 1980).

DANGERFIELD, G., *The Strange Death of Liberal England* (London, 1935).

DAVIES, S., 'Class, religion and gender: Liverpool Labour Party and women, 1918–1939', in J. Belchem (ed.), *Popular Politics, Riot and Labour: Essays in Liverpool History, 1790–1940* (Liverpool, 1992).

DAWSON, M., 'Money and the real impact of the Fourth Reform Act', *HJ*, xxxv (1992).

DEN OTTER, S., '"Thinking in communities": late nineteenth-century Liberals, idealists and the retrieval of community', in Green, *Age of Transition*.

DEVINE, M., *History of Paisley* (Unpublished draft manuscript, 1977).

DEVINE, T. M. (ed.), *Irish Immigrants and Scottish Society in the Nineteenth and Twentieth Centuries* (Edinburgh, 1991).

DICKSON, T., and CLARKE, T., 'Social concern and social control in nineteenth-century Scotland: Paisley, 1841–1843', *SHR*, lxv (1986).

DICKSON, A., and SPEIRS, W., 'Changes in class structure in Paisley, 1750–1845', *SHR*, lix (1980).

DICKSON, A., and TREBLE, J. H. (eds.), *People and Society in Scotland*, vol. III: *1914–1990* (Edinburgh, 1992).

DONNACHIE, I., 'Scottish Labour in Depression: the 1930s', in Donnachie, Harvie and Wood, *Forward! Labour Politics in Scotland*.

——, HARVIE, C., and WOOD, I. S. (eds.), *Forward! Labour Politics in Scotland, 1888–1988* (Edinburgh, 1989).

DOUGHTY, M. (ed.), *Building the Industrial City* (Leicester, 1986).

DOUGLAS, F., 'The Scottish Tories' (Pamphlet) (Glasgow, 1945).

DOUGLAS, R., 'The National Democratic Party and the British Workers' League', *HJ*, xv (1972).

DOWNS, L. L., 'Reply to Joan Scott', *CSSH*, xxxv (1993).

——, 'If "Woman" is just an empty category, then why am I afraid to walk alone at night?: identity politics meets the post-modern subject', *CSSH*, xxxv (1993).

DOYLE, B. M., 'Urban Liberalism and the "lost generation": politics and middle-class culture in Norwich, 1900–1935', *HJ*, xxxviii (1995).

DUNBABIN, J. P. D., 'Parliamentary elections in Great Britain, 1868–1900: a psephological note', *EHR*, lxxxi (1966).

——, 'British elections in the nineteenth and twentieth centuries: a regional approach', *EHR*, xcv (1980).

——, 'Some implications of the 1885 British shift towards single-member constituencies: a note', *EHR*, cix (1994).

DUNCAN, R., *Wishaw: Life and Labour in a Lanarkshire Industrial Community, 1790–1914* (Motherwell, 1986).

——, *Steelopolis: The Making of Motherwell, c.1750–1939* (Motherwell, 1991).

DUTTON, D. J., 'Unionist politics and the aftermath of the General Election of 1906: a reassessment', *HJ*, xxii (1979).

——, 'The Unionist Party and social policy, 1906–1914', *HJ*, xxiv (1981).

DYER, M. C., 'The Politics of Kincardineshire' (Aberdeen University, Ph.D. thesis, 1973).

EASTHOPE, A., 'Romancing the stone: history-writing and rhetoric', *SH*, xviii (1993).

——, 'The Unionist Party and social policy, 1906–1914', *HJ*, xxiv (1981).

ELEY, G., and NIELD, K., 'Starting over: the present, the post-modern and the moment of social history', *SH*, xx (1995).

FFORDE, M., *Conservatism and Collectivism, 1886–1914* (Edinburgh, 1990).

FINN, M. C., *After Chartism: Class and Nation in English Radical Politics, 1848–1874* (Cambridge, 1993).

FORGACS, D. (ed.), *A Gramsci Reader: Selected Writings, 1916–1935* (London, 1988).

FOSTER, J., 'Red Clyde, Red Scotland', in I. Donnachie and C. Whatley (eds.), *The Manufacture of Scottish History* (Edinburgh, 1992).

FOWLER, A., 'Lancashire cotton trade unionism in the Iinter-war Years', in Jowitt and McIvor, *Employers and Labour in the English Textile Industries*.

FRASER, W. H., 'Trades Councils in the Labour movement in nineteenth-century Scotland', in MacDougall, *Essays in Scottish Labour History*.

——, and MORRIS, R. J., *People and Society in Scotland*, vol. II: *1830–1914* (Edinburgh, 1990).

FRY, M., *Patronage and Principle: A Political History of Modern Scotland* (Aberdeen, 1991 edn).

GALLACHER, W., *Last Memoirs* (London, 1966).

GALLACHER, W., 'Paisley in the 1930s' (Unpublished manuscript, *c.*1980).

GILLEY, S., 'Catholics and Socialists in Glasgow, 1906–1912', in K. Lunn (ed.), *Hosts, Immigrants and Minorities: Historical Responses to Newcomers in British Society, 1870–1914* (Folkestone, 1980).

GLASER, J. F., 'English nonconformity and the decline of Liberalism', *AHR*, lxiii (1958).

GLASGOW LABOUR HISTORY WORKSHOP, 'Roots of Red Clydeside: the labour unrest in West Scotland, 1910–1914', in A. J. McIvor and R. Duncan (eds.), *Militant Workers: Labour and Class Conflict on the Clyde, 1900–1950* (Edinburgh, 1992).

GLASS, S. T., *The Responsible Society: The Ideas of the English Guild Socialists* (Reading, 1983).

GOODLAD, G., 'Gladstone and his rivals: popular Liberal perceptions of the party leadership in the political crisis of 1885–6', in Biagini and Reid, *Currents of Radicalism*.

GORDON, E., *Women and the Labour Movement in Scotland, 1850–1914* (Oxford, 1991).

GRAMSCI, A., *Selections from the Prison Notebooks of Antonio Gramsci*, ed. and trans. Q. Hoare and G. N. Smith (London, 1971).

GRAY, R., 'The deconstruction of the English working class' (Review Article), *SH*, xi (1986).

——, 'Class, politics and historical "revisionism"', *SH*, xix (1994).

GREEN, E. H. H., 'Radical Conservatism: the electoral genesis of tariff reform', *HJ*, xxviii (1985).

——, *The Crisis of Conservatism: The Politics, Economics and Ideology of the British Conservative Party, 1880–1914* (London, 1995).

—— (ed.), *An Age of Transition: British Politics, 1880–1914* (Edinburgh, 1997).

HART, M., 'The Liberals, the war and the franchise', *EHR*, xcvii (1982).

HARVIE, C., *No Gods and Precious Few Heroes: Scotland, 1914–1980* (London, 1981).

——, 'Before the breakthrough, 1888–1922', in Donnachie, Harvie, and Wood, *Forward! Labour Politics in Scotland*.

——, 'Scottish politics', in Dickson and Treble, *People and Society in Scotland*, vol. III.

HAWARTH, R., 'The Development of the Bolton ILP, 1885–1895' (Huddersfield Polytechnic, M.A. thesis, 1982).

HIGGS, E., 'Women, occupations and work in the nineteenth-century censuses', *History Workshop*, xxiii (1987).

HILL, J., 'Manchester and Salford politics and the early development of the Independent Labour Party', *IRSH*, xxvi (1981).

HIMEIMY, I. A., 'The Development and Organisation of the Scottish Co-operative Movement' (Edinburgh University, Ph.D. thesis, 1955).

HOBSBAWM, E., and RANGER, T. (eds.), *The Invention of Tradition* (Cambridge, 1983).

HOLFORD, J., *Reshaping Labour: Organisation, Work and Politics. Edinburgh in the Great War and After* (London, 1988).

HOPKINS, E., *The Rise and decline of the English Working Classes, 1918–1990: A Social History* (New York, 1991).

HOWARD, C., 'Expectations born to death: local Labour Party expansion in the 1920s', in J. Winter (ed.), *The Working Class in Modern British History: Essays in Honour of Henry Pelling* (Cambridge, 1983).

HOWE, A., 'Towards the "hungry forties": free trade in Britain, *c.*1880–1906', in Biagini, *Citizenship and Community*.

HOWELL, D., *British Workers and the Independent Labour Party, 1888–1906* (Manchester, 1983).

HUBERMAN, M., 'The economic origins of paternalism: Lancashire cotton spinning in the first half of the nineteenth century', *SH*, xii (1987).

——, 'The economic origins of paternalism: reply to Rose, Taylor and Winstanley', *SH*, xiv (1989).

HUNTER, T., *History of Paisley Burns Club* (Paisley, 1939).

HUTCHISON, I. G. C., *A Political History of Scotland, 1832–1924: Parties, Elections and Issues* (Edinburgh, 1986).

——, 'Glasgow working-class politics', in R. A. Cage (ed.), *The Working Class in Glasgow, 1750–1914* (London, 1987).

INNES, J., *Housing in Paisley 1959* (Paisley, 1960).

JACKSON LEARS, T. J., 'The concept of cultural hegemony: problems and possibilities', *AHR*, xc (1985).

JARVIS, D., 'British Conservatism and class politics in the 1920s', *EHR*, cxi (1996).

JENKINS, K. (ed.), *The Post-modern History Reader* (1997).

JONES, G. S., *Outcast London: A Study in the Relationship between Classes in Victorian Society* (Oxford, 1971).

——, 'Engels and the genesis of Marxism', *New Left Review*, cvi (1977).

——, *Languages of Class: Studies in English Working-Class History, 1832–1982* (Cambridge, 1993).

JONES, R., 'Consumers' co-operation in Victorian Edinburgh: the evolution of a location pattern', *Institute of British Geographers: Transactions*, iv (1979).

JOWITT, J. A., and MCIVOR, A. J. (eds.), *Employers and Labour in the English Textile Industries, 1850–1939* (London, 1988).

JOYCE, P., 'The factory politics of Lancashire in the later nineteenth century', *HJ*, xviii (1975).

——, *Work, Society and Politics: The Culture of the Factory in Later Victorian England* (London, 1980).

——, 'History and Post-Modernism', *P&P*, cxxxiii (1991).

——, *Visions of the People: Industrial England and the Question of Class, 1840–1914* (Cambridge, 1991).

——, 'The imaginary discontents of social history: a note of response to Mayfield and Thorne, and Lawrence and Taylor – a comment', *SH*, xviii (1993).

——, *Democratic Subjects: The Self and the Social in Nineteenth-Century England* (Cambridge, 1994).

——, 'The end of social history?', *SH*, xx (1995).

——, 'The end of social history? A brief reply to Eley and Nield', *SH*, xxi (1996).

KANSTEINER, W., 'Searching for an Audience: the historical profession in the media age: a comment on Arthur Marwick and Hayden White', *JCH*, xxxi (1996).

KEATING, M., and BLEIMAN, D., *Labour and Scottish Nationalism* (London, 1979).

KELLAS, J. G., 'The Liberal Party and the Scottish Church Disestablishment Crisis', *EHR*, lxxix (1964).

——, 'The Liberal Party in Scotland, 1876–1895', *SHR*, xliv (1965).

——, *Modern Scotland* (London, 1980).

KELLEY, R., 'Asquith at Paisley: the content of British Liberalism at the end of its era', *JBS*, iv (1964).

KELLNER, H., *Language and Historical Representation: Getting the Story Crooked* (Madison, 1989).

KELLY, C., 'History and Post-Modernism', *P&P*, cxxxiii (1991).

KILLINGBACK, N., 'Limits to mutuality: economic and political attacks on co-operation during the 1920s and 1930s', in S. Yeo (ed.), *New Views of Co-operation* (London, 1988).

KING, E., *The Scottish Women's Suffrage Movement* (Glasgow, 1978).

——, 'Popular culture in Glasgow', in R. A. Cage (ed.), *The Working Class in Glasgow, 1750–1914* (London, 1987).

KINLOCH, J., and BUTT, J., *History of the Scottish Co-operative Wholesale Society Ltd* (Glasgow, 1981).

KIRK, N., *The Growth of Working Class Reformism in Mid-Victorian England* (London, 1985).

——, ''Traditional working class culture and"The rise of Labour": some preliminary questions and observations', *SH*, xvi (1991).

——, 'History, language, ideas and post-modernism: a materialist view', *SH,* xix (1994).

KNOX, W. W., *Scottish Labour Leaders, 1918–1939: A Biographical Dictionary* (Edinburgh, 1984).

——, 'The political and workplace culture of the Scottish working class, 1832–1914', in Fraser and Morris, *People and Society in Scotland*, vol. II.

——, 'Ours is not an ordinary parliamentary movement: 1922–1926', in McKinlay and Morris, *ILP on Clydeside*.

——, 'Whatever happened to radical Scotland?: the economic and social origins of the mid-Victorian political consensus in Scotland', in R. Mason and N. Macdougall (eds.), *People and Power in Scotland: Essays in Honour of T. C. Smout* (Edinburgh, 1992).

——, *Hanging by a Thread: The Scottish Cotton Industry, c.1850–1914* (Preston, 1995).

——, and MCKINLAY, A., 'The re-making of Scottish Labour in the 1930s', *TCBH*, vi (1995).

KODITSCHEK, T., 'The gendering of the British working class', *Gender and History*, ix (1997).

KOSS, S. E., *Lord Haldane: Scapegoat for Liberalism* (London, 1969).

——, *Asquith* (London, 1976).

LAMBERTZ, J., 'Sexual harassment in the nineteenth-century English cotton industry', *History Workshop*, xix (1985).

LANCASTER, W., *Radicalism, Co-operation and Socialism: Leicester Working-Class Politics, 1860–1906* (Leicester, 1987).

——, and MASON, A. (eds.), *Life and Labour in a Twentieth Century City: The Experience of Coventry* (Coventry, 1986).

LANE, A., and ROBERTS, K., *Strike at Pilkingtons* (London, 1971).

LAWRENCE, J., 'Popular radicalism and the socialist revival in Britain', *JBS*, xxxi (1992).

——, 'Class and gender in the making of urban Toryism, 1880–1914', *EHR*, cviii (1993).

——, and ELLIOT, J., 'Parliamentary Election results reconsidered: an analysis of Borough Elections, 1885–1910', in Green, *Age of Transition*.

LAWRENCE, J., and TAYLOR, M., 'The poverty of protest: Gareth Stedmen Jones and the politics of language – a reply', *SH*, xviii (1993).

LAWSON, J. M., SAVAGE, M., and WARDE, A., 'Gender and local politics: struggles over welfare policies 1918–1939', in L. Murgatroyd, *et. al.* (eds.), *Localities, Class and Gender* (London, 1985).

LAYBOURN, K., 'The rise of Labour and the decline of Liberalism: the state of the debate', *History*, lxxx (1995).

——, and REYNOLDS, J., *Liberalism and the Rise of Labour, 1890–1918* (London, 1984).

LAZONICK, W., 'Industrial relations and technical change: the case of the self-acting mule', *Cambridge Journal of Economics,* iii (1979).

LEE, A. J., 'Conservatism, traditionalism and the British working class, 1880–1918', in D. E. Martin and D. Rubinstein (eds.), *Ideology and the Labour Movement: Essays presented to John Saville* (London, 1979).

LEITCH, A., 'Radicalism in Paisley, 1830–1848 and its Economic, Political, Cultural Background' (Glasgow University, M.Litt. thesis, 1993).

LENMAN, B. P., *The Eclipse of Parliament: Appearance and Reality in British Politics Since 1914* (London, 1992).

LEONARD, T. (ed.), *Radical Renfrew: Poetry from the French Revolution to the First World War* (Edinburgh, 1990).

LESLIE, N. W., 'Trends in the Industrial Geography of Paisley in the Twentieth Century' (Aberdeen University, Undergraduate Dissertation, 1966).

LINDSAY, T. F., and HARRINGTON, M., *The Conservative Party, 1918–1970* (London, 1974).

LLOYD, C., 'For realism and against the inadequacies of common sense: a response to Arthur Marwick', *JCH*, xxxi (1996).

LOWN, J., 'Not so much a factory, more a form of patriarchy: gender and class during Industrialisation', in E. Gamarnikov, D. H. J. Morgan, J. Purvis, and D. E. Taylorson (eds.), *Gender, Class and Work* (London, 1983).

LYNCH, M., *Scotland: A New History* (London, 1992).

MCCAFFREY, J., 'The origins of Liberal Unionism in the West of Scotland', *SHR*, l (1971).

MCCARTHY, M., *A Social Geography of Paisley* (Paisley, 1969).

MACDONALD, C. M. M., 'The Radical Thread: Political Change in Scotland: Paisley Politics, 1885–1924' (Strathclyde University, Ph.D. thesis, 1996).

MACDOUGALL, I. (ed.), *Essays in Scottish Labour History: A Tribute to W. H. Marwick* (Edinburgh, 1978).

MCFARLAND, E. W., 'The Loyal Orange Institution in Scotland 1799–1900' (Glasgow University, Ph.D. thesis, 1986).

——, *Protestants First: Orangeism in Nineteenth-Century Scotland* (Edinburgh, 1990).

MACFARLANE, A., 'History, anthropology and the study of communities, *SH*, v (1977).

MCGREGOR, J., *Paisley Pattern – A Preview* (Paisley, 1947).

MCGUIRE, J., 'Chartism in the Paisley Area' (Strathclyde University, Undergraduate Dissertation, November 1974).

MACHIN, I., 'Disestablishment and democracy, *c.*1840–1930', in Biagini, *Citizenship and Community*.

MCIVOR, A. J., 'Work, wages and industrial relations in cotton finishing, 1880–1914', in Jowitt and McIvor, *Employers and Labour in the English Textile Industries*.

MCKENZIE, R., and SILVER, A., *Angels in Marble: Working Class Conservatives in Urban England* (London, 1968).

MCKIBBIN, R., *The Evolution of the Labour Party, 1910–1924* (Oxford, 1974).

——, 'Why was there no Marxism in Great Britain?', *EHR*, xcix (1984).

——, *The Ideologies of Class: Social Relations in Britain 1880–1950* (Oxford, 1990).

MCKINLAY, A., 'Labour and locality: Labour politics on Clydeside, 1900–1939', *Journal of Regional and Local Studies,* x (1990).

——, '"Doubtful wisdom and uncertain promise": strategy, ideology and organisation, 1918–1922', in McKinlay and Morris, *ILP on Clydeside*.

—— and MORRIS, R. J. (eds.), *The ILP on Clydeside, 1893–1932: From Foundation to Disintegration* (Manchester, 1991).

MCLEAN, I., *The Legend of Red Clydeside* (Edinburgh, 1983).

MAGUIRE, P., 'Co-operation and crisis: government, co-operation, and politics, 1917–1922', in S. Yeo (ed.), *New Views of Co-operation* (London, 1988).

MARQUAND, D., *The Progressive Dilemma* (London, 1991).

MARWICK, A., 'Two approaches to historical study: the Metaphysical (including 'Postmodernism') and the Historical', *JCH*, xxx (1995).

MATTHEW, H. C. G., MCKIBBIN, R. I., and KAY, J. A., 'The franchise factor in the rise of the Labour Party', *EHR*, xci (1976).

MAYFIELD, D., 'Language and social history', *SH*, xvi (1991).

——, and THORNE, S., 'Social history and its discontents: Gareth Stedman Jones and the politics of language', *SH*, xvii (1992).

——, and THORNE, S., 'Reply to "The poverty of protest" and "The imaginery discontents"', *SH*, xviii (1993).

MELLING, J., '"Non-Commissioned Officers": British employers and their supervisory workers, 1880–1920', *SH,* v (1980).

——, 'Scottish industrialists and the changing character of class relations in the Clyde region, *c.*1880–1918', in T. Dickson (ed.), *Capital and Class in Scotland* (Edinburgh, 1982).

——, 'Welfare capitalism and the origins of welfare states: British industry, workplace welfare and social reform 1870–1914', *SH*, xvii (1992).

MIDDLEMASS, R. K., *The Clydesiders: A Left Wing Struggle for Parliamentary Power* (London, 1965).

MITCHELL, J., *Conservatives and the Union: A Study of Conservative Party Attitudes to Scotland* (Edinburgh, 1990).

MITCHELL, M., 'Irish participation in Scottish radicalism', Glasgow Labour History Workshop Seminar, 1994 (unpublished paper).

MILLER, J., 'The factors contributing to the decline of the hand-loom weaving in the West of Scotland, 1815–1850' (Unpublished Manuscript Paisley Central Library, undated).

MOISLEY, H. A., and THAIN, A. G., *Third Statistical Account of Scotland – County of Renfrew* (Glasgow, 1962).

MORAN, J., 'Scottish Conservatism and the Primrose League, 1885–1904' (Strathclyde University, Under-graduate Dissertation, 1993).

MORGAN, K. O., *The Age of Lloyd George: The Liberal Party and British Politics, 1890–1929* (London, 1971).

——, 'The New Liberalism and the challenge of Labour: the Welsh experience, 1885–1929', *Welsh History Review*, v (1972).

MORRIS, R. J., and SMYTH, J. J., *Paternalism as an Employer Strategy, 1880–1960* (ESRC Pamphlet, London, 1989).

MOSS, B. H., 'Republican Socialism and the making of the working class in Britain, France and the United States: a critique of Thompsonian culturalism', *CSSH*, xxxv (1993).

NEMETH, T., *Gramsci's Philosophy: A Critical Study* (Brighton, 1980).

NEWBY, H., 'The deferential dialectic', *CSSH*, xvii (1975).

——, 'Paternalism and capitalism', in R. Scase (ed.), *Industrial Society: Class, Cleavage and Control* (London, 1977).

NICHOLLS, D., 'The New Liberalism – after Chartism?', *SH*, xxi (1996).

NISBET, O., 'A Short Study in Social and Economic History in the County of Renfrewshire, *c.*1800–1850: The Decline of the Renfrewshire Weavers' (Strathclyde University, Undergraduate Dissertation, 1972).

NIVEN, D., *The Development of Housing in Scotland* (London, 1979).

NORRIS, G. M., 'Industrial paternalist capitalism and local labour markets', *Sociology*, xii (1978).

OSTERUD, N. G., 'Gender divisions and the organization of work in the Leicester hosiery industry', in A. V. John (ed.), *Unequal Opportunities: Women's Employment in England, 1800–1918* (Oxford, 1986).

PALMER, B. D., *Descent into Discourse: The Reification of Language and the Writing of Social History* (Philadelphia, 1990).

PARKIN, F., 'Working Class Conservatism: a theory of political deviance', *BJS*, xviii (1967).

PATTERSON, T. C., 'Post-structuralism, post-modernism: implications for historians', *SH*, xiv (1989).

PAYNE, P. (ed.), *Studies in Scottish Business History* (London, 1967).

PEELE, G., and COOK, C. (eds.), *The Politics of Reappraisal, 1918–1939* (London, 1975).

PELLING, H., *Social Geography of British Elections, 1885–1910* (Aldershot, 1967).

——, *Popular Politics and Society in Late Victorian Britain* (London, 1979).

PENN, R., 'Trade Union organization and skill in the cotton and engineering industries in Britain, 1850–1960', *SH*, viii (1983).

PHIPPS, C. W. M., 'The Aberdeen Trades Council and Politics, 1900–1939: The Development of a Local Labour Party in Aberdeen' (Aberdeen University, M.Litt. thesis, 1980).

PIMLOTT, B., and COOK, C. (eds.), *Trade Unions in British Politics* (London, 1982).

POIRIER, P. P., *The Advent of the Labour Party* (London, 1958).

POLLARD, S., 'The foundation of the Co-operative Party', in A. Briggs and J. Saville (eds.), *Essays in Labour History, 1886–1923* (London, 1971).

——,'The Co-operative Party: reflections on a re-consideration', *IRSH*, xxxii (1987).

POPE, R., *War and Society in Britain, 1899–1948* (Harlow, 1991).

PRICE, R., *Labour in British Society: An Interpretative History* (London, 1986).

——, 'Historiography, narrative and the nineteenth century', *JBS*, xxxv (1996).

PUGH, M., *The Making of Modern British Politics, 1867–1939* (Oxford, 1982).

——, *The Tories and the People, 1880–1935* (Oxford, 1985).

PURDUE, A. W., 'The Liberal and Labour Parties in north-east politics, 1900–1914: the struggle for supremacy', *IRSH*, xxvi (1981).

QUINAULT, R., 'Asquith's Liberalism', *History*, lxxvii (1992).

RAWLINSON, G., 'Mobilising the unemployed: the National Unemployed Workers' Movement in the West of Scotland', in A. J. McIvor and R. Duncan (eds.), *Militant Workers: Labour and Class Conflict on the Clyde, 1900–1950* (Edinburgh, 1992).

READ, D. (ed.), *Edwardian England* (1982).

RIDLEY, J., 'The Unionist Social Reform Committee, 1911–1914: wets before the deluge', *HJ*, xxx (1987).

ROBERTSON, A. J., 'The decline of the Scottish cotton industry', *Business History*, xii (1970).

RODGER, R., 'The Victorian building industry and the housing of the Scottish working class', in Doughty, *Building the Industrial City*.

—— 'Mid-Victorian Employers' Attitudes', *SH*, xi (1986).

ROLLO, D. A. T., 'Comparative Aspects of Irish politics in Boston, New York and Glasgow' (Edinburgh University, M.Litt. thesis, 1971).

ROSE, G., 'From "Locality, politics, and culture: Poplar in the 1920s", 1988', in C. Hamnett (ed.), *Social Geography: A Reader* (London, 1996).

ROSE, M., TAYLOR, P., and WINSTANLEY, M., 'The economic origins of paternalism: some objections', *SH*, xiv (1989).

ROSE, R., 'Class and Party divisions: Britain as a test case', *Sociology*, ii (1968).

ROSE, S. O., '"Gender at work": sex, class and industrial capitalism', *History Workshop*, xxi (1986).

——, 'Gender and Labour History: The nineteenth-century legacy', *IRSH*, xxxviii (1993).

SASSOON, A. S., *Gramsci's Politics* (London, 1987).

SAVAGE, M., 'Capitalist and patriarchal relations at work: Preston cotton weaving, 1890–1940', in L. Murgatroyd, *et al.* (eds.), *Localities, Class and Gender* (London, 1985).

——, *The Dynamics of Working-Class Politics: The Labour Movement in Preston, 1880–1940* (Cambridge, 1987).

——, 'Women and work in the Lancashire cotton industry, 1890–1939', in Jowitt and McIvor, *Employers and Labour in the English Textile Industries*.

——, 'Whatever happened to Red Clydeside?', in J. Anderson and A. Cochrane (eds.), *A State of Crisis* (London, 1989).

——, 'Urban history and social class: two paradigms', *Urban History*, xx (1993).

——, 'Social mobility and class analysis: a new agenda for social history', *SH*, xix (1994).

——, and MILES, A., *The Remaking of the British Working Class, 1840–1940* (London, 1994).

SAVILLE, J., 'The ideology of Labourism', in R. Benewick, R. N. Berki and B. Parekh (eds.), *Knowledge and Belief in Politics: The Problem of Ideology* (London, 1973).

SCOTT, A. M., 'Industrialization, gender segregation and stratification theory', in R. Crompton and M. Mann (eds.), *Gender and Stratification* (Cambridge, 1986).

SCOTT, J. W., *Gender and the Politics of History* (Columbia, 1988).

——, 'The evidence of experience', *Critical Inquiry*, xvii (Summer, 1991).

——, 'On language, gender and working-class history', in Berlanstein, *Industrial Revolution and Work*.

——, 'The tip of the volcano', *CSSH*, xxxv (1993).

SEARLE, G. R., *The Liberal Party: Triumph and Disintegration, 1886–1929* (Basingstoke, 1992).

SELF, R., 'Conservative Reunion and the General Election of 1923: a reassessment', *TCBH*, iii (1992).

SEWELL, W. H., 'How Classes are made: critical reflections on E. P. Thompson's Theory of Working Class Formation', in H. J. Kaye and K. McClelland (eds.), *E. P. Thompson: Critical Perspectives* (Cambridge, 1990).

SINCLAIR, A., *Sewing it Up: Coats Patons Multinational Practices*, Scottish Education and Action for Development (Edinburgh, 1982).

SLAVEN, A., and CHECKLAND, S. (eds.), *Dictionary of Scottish Business Biography 1860–1960: Vol.2, Processing, Distribution, Services* (Aberdeen, 1990).

SLAVEN, A., *The Development of the West of Scotland, 1750–1960* (London, 1975).

SMITH, B., and OSTERGAARD, G., *Constitutional Relations Between the Labour and Co-operative Parties: An Historical Review* (London, 1960).

SMITH, J., 'Commonsense Thought and Working-Class Consciousness: Some Aspects of the Glasgow and Liverpool Labour Movements in the Early Years of the Twentieth Century' (Edinburgh University, Ph.D. thesis, 1980).

——, 'Labour tradition in Glasgow and Liverpool, 1880–1914', *History Workshop Journal*, xvii (1984).

——, 'Class, skill and sectarianism in Glasgow and Liverpool, 1880–1914', in R. J. Morris (ed.), *Class, Power and Social Structure in British Nineteenth-Century Towns* (Leicester, 1986).

——, 'Taking the leadership of the Labour movement: the ILP in Glasgow, 1906–1914', in McKinlay and Morris, *ILP on Clydeside*.

SMOUT, T. C., *A Century of the Scottish People* (London, 1986).

——, *A History of the Scottish People, 1560–1830* (London, 1989).

——, '"Writing Scotland's history": preface', *SHR*, lxxvi (1997).

SMYTH, J. J., 'Labour and Socialism in Glasgow, 1880–1914: The Electoral Challenge Prior to Democracy' (Edinburgh University, Ph.D. thesis, 1987.)

——, 'The ILP in Glasgow, 1888–1906: the struggle for Identity', in McKinlay and Morris, *ILP on Clydeside*.

SOUTHGATE, B., 'History and metahistory: Marwick versus White', *JCH*, xxxi (1996).

STEINBERG, M. W. '"The Great End of All Government ...": working people's construction of citizenship claims in early nineteenth-century England and the matter of class', *IRSH*, xl, Supplement 3 (1995).

——, 'Culturally speaking: finding a commons between post-structuralism and the Thompsonian perspective', *SH* xxi (1996).

STONE, L., 'History and post-modernism', *P&P*, cxxxi (1991).

STUBBS, J., 'The impact of the Great War on the Conservative Party', in Peele and Cook, *Politics of Reappraisal*.

TANNER, D., *Political Change and the Labour Party, 1900–1918* (Cambridge, 1990).

——, 'Elections, statistics, and the rise of the Labour Party, 1906–1931', *HJ*, xxxiv (1991).

——, 'The development of British socialism, 1900–1918', in Green, *Age of Transition*.

THANE, P., 'Women, Liberalism and Citizenship, 1918–1930', in Biagini, *Citizenship and Community*.

THOMPSON, E. P., 'On history, sociology and historical relevance', *BJS*, xxvii (1976).

——, *The Poverty of Theory and Other Essays* (London, 1978).

THOMPSON, P., 'Liberals, Radicals and Labour in London, 1880–1900', *P&P*, xxvii (1964).

——, *Socialists, Liberals and Labour: The Struggle for London, 1885–1914* (London, 1967).

TONNIES, F., *Gemeinschaft und Gesellschaft*, trans. C. P. Loomis (London, 1955).

TRENTMANN, F., 'The strange death of free trade: the erosion of "liberal concensus" in Great Britain, *c.*1903–1932', in Biagini, *Citizenship and Community*.

TUCKETT, A., *The Scottish Trades Union Congress: The First Eighty Years, 1897–1977* (Edinburgh, 1986).

TURNER, J., 'Sex, age and the Labour vote in the 1920s', in P. Denley, S. Fogelvik and C. Harvey (eds.), *History and Computing II* (Manchester, 1989).

——, *British Politics and the Great War: Coalition and Conflict, 1915–1918* (London, 1992).

TURNER, R., 'Gala day as an expression of community identity', in A. Jackson (ed.), *Way of Life and Identity*, SSRC, North Sea Oil Panel Occasional Paper, no. 4 (London, 1981).

URWIN, D. W., 'The development of the Conservative Party Organisation in Scotland, until 1912', *SHR*, xxxviii (1965).

VERNON, J., *Politics and the People: A Study in English Political Culture, c.1815–1867* (Cambridge, 1993).

——, 'Who's afraid of the "linguistic turn"? The politics of social history and its discontents', *SH*, xix (1994).

WAITES, B., *A Class Society at War: England, 1914–1918* (Leamington Spa, 1987).

WALD, K. D., 'Class and the vote before the First World War', *British Journal of Political Science*, viii (1978).

WALKER, G., 'The Orange Order in Scotland between the Wars', *IRSH*, xxxvii (1992).

WALKER, W. M., 'Dundee's disenchantment with Churchill: a comment upon the downfall of the Liberal Party', *SHR*, xlix (1970).

WARD, J. T., 'Tory Socialist: a preliminary note on Michael Maltman Barry (1842–1909)', *Journal of Scottish Labour History* (1970).

——, *West Renfrewshire Conservative and Unionist Association (1912–1972)* (Paisley, 1972).

WARDE, A., 'Spatial change, politics and the division of labour', in D. Gregory and J. Urry (eds.), *Social Relations and Spatial Structures* (Basingstoke, 1985).

WATERS, C., 'Review', *SH*, xvii (1992).

WATT, J. M., 'Distress in Paisley, 1841–3' (Dundee University, Undergraduate Dissertation, 1982).

WHITE, H., 'Response to Arthur Marwick', *JCH*, xxx (1995).

WILLIAMS, G., 'The concept of "Egemonia" in the thought of Antonio Gramsci', *Journal of the History of Ideas*, xxi (1960).

WILLIAMS, R., *Keywords: A Vocabulary of Culture and Society* (rev. edn, London, 1983).

WILSON, T., *The Downfall of the Liberal Party, 1914–1935* (London, 1966).

WOOD, I. S., 'Irish immigrants and Scottish radicalism, 1880–1906', in MacDougall, *Essays in Scottish Labour History*.

——, 'Hope deferred: Labour in Scotland in the 1920s', in Donnachie, Harvie and Wood, *Forward! Labour Politics in Scotland*.

WRIGHT, L., *Scottish Chartism* (Edinburgh, 1953).

YEO, E., and YEO, S., 'On the uses of "community": from Owenism to the present', in S. Yeo (ed.), *New Views of Co-operation* (London, 1988).

YEO, S., *Religion and Voluntary Organisations in Crisis* (London, 1976).

ZWAHR, H., 'Class formation and the Labor movement as the subject of dialectic social history', *IRSH*, xxxviii (1993), Supplement.

[——], *Eadie Brothers, 1871–1971* (Glasgow, 1971).

Index

Abercrombie, W. 87, 111–12
Aberdeen 28–9, 118, 132, 138, 200, 239n.
Adam, R. 237
Adams, T. 216–17
Agnew, J. 1–2
Allan Line Steamer Co. 60
Anderson, T. 163–4
Arthur, J. (Mrs) 78, 189
Asquith, H. H. 28, 187, 207, 225, 227–32, 241–3, 246–7, 250–1, 253, 258–62, 267–8, 280; *see also* Paisley
Attercliffe 146–7
Ayr 107n.
Babcock & Wilcox 49, 208
Baird, H. 125, 127, 129–31, 168, 171, 236–7
Baldwin, O. R. (Viscount Corvedale) 272–4, 277, 281–2
Balfour, A. J. 109, 190, 192
Barbour, M. (Mrs) 214–15
Barbour, W. B. 80–4, 89–90, 93, 136
Barclay, G. 60
Barr, P. 119–20
Beardmore's 48, 208
Belchem, J. 18–19
Biggar, J.M. 219, 222–4, 227, 229–33, 235, 244, 246, 248–50, 255, 276
Birmingham 202
Blackfriars' Liberal Association 101
Blackie, J. 126
Blewett, N. 19
Bonham Carter, Lady Violet 231, 243, 260, 262
Bow, McLachlan & Co. 48, 77
Bow, W. 106, 111
Boyd, James & Sons 48
Brewster, P. 136
British Workers' League (BWL) 224
Brook, J. 54–5
Brown & Polson 49–51
Brown, G. 24, 223, 242, 252
Brown, J. 50
Brown, J. A. 51
Brown, Joyce 146–7
Brown, Rev. Dr 85, 107
Brown, W. (Labour councillor) 119–25, 127, 129–30, 132–4, 171
Brown, W. 50
Bruce Glasier, J. 135–6
Buckley, K. 28–9, 132
Cairns, Alexander & Sons 49
Caldwell, W. 49
Campbell, A. C. (of Blythswood) 88, 112
Campbell, D. F. 200–2
Campbell, J. 215
Campbell Swinton, G. S. 184–5
Carlile, W. 42
Carson, G. 139
Central Agency 54
Chadwick, J. & Bro. 55
Chamberlain, J. 89, 109, 141, 142n., 186–7, 190, 192, 195
Champion, H. H. 138
Christie, W. & Sons 48
Clark & Co. 54–5, 127
Clark, G. A. 54, 67
Clark, J. & J. 54
Clark, J. & R. 54
Clark, James (b. 1783) 54
Clark, James (b. 1821) 54
Clark, James (b. 1831) 78, 80–2, 84, 122, 166, 192
Clark, John (b. 1791) 54
Clark, John (b. 1827) 54, 76, 78, 107
Clark, Stewart 54, 56, 60, 72, 80, 84–5, 87, 107, 192
Clarke, P. F. 14, 17–18, 20, 145
class 6, 18–19, 22, 26, 32, 267; and ethnicity 26; and gender 155, 157–9, 162; and locality 21, 27, 31, 145; and war 207; *see also* language, Paisley
Clyde Workers Committee 210–13
Coats, Allan (Mrs) 94
Coats, Archd. 84, 87, 107–9, 189, 192
Coats, J. & P. 54–8
Coats, James (b. 1774) 53
Coats, James (b. 1803) 54
Coats, J. & P. Co. Ltd. 47, 55, 158; and education 65; and First World War 209; and health 65; and recreation 65–7; and United Mills 274; as 'family firm' 53, 59, 61, 164; company housing 64; deference 68–70, 205; excursions 58; Girls' Home 65; half-time workers 56, 151; Half-Timers' School 64–5; paternalism 52, 55–72, 151, 154, 158–9, 181, 205, 273; patriarchy 59–60, 149–52, 160–1; pensions 63–4; short-time work 239; soirées 56–60; sports galas 66; strikes (1897) 126; (1900) 154; (1904) 156; (1905) 156–7; (1907) 160–1; (1908) 161; (1912) 204–5; supervisory workers 151–2, 154–5; women workers 149–51, 209, 239; *see also* Paisley, paternalism
Coats, Lady Glen 273
Coats, Peter (b. 1808) 54, 56, 60, 67
Coats, Peter Jr. 107, 192
Coats, Thomas (b. 1809) 55, 60
Coats, Thomas Glen 57, 60–1, 78, 81, 84, 94, 104, 118, 137n., 138, 242n.
Coats, Thomas Glen (Mrs) 94
Coats, W. H. 189, 260
Coats, W. H. (Mrs) 252
Cochran, R. 78, 80–1, 84, 89–93, 114, 117, 135, 153
Cole, G. D. H. 15–16
Collins, B. 95
community 1, 36, 38, 57; *see also* Paisley .
Coneys, M. 132, 146
Conservative Party (–1912): and social reform 141–3; National Union of Conservative Associations for Scotland 106–8, 143, 194; Scottish Conservative Association 88; 'Tory Democracy' 75, 110, 112, 114–15; *see also* Paisley, Liberal Unionist Party (1885–1912); Unionist Party (1912–)

Co-operative movement: affiliation to Labour Party 177–8, 216, 219, 233–4; and First World War 216–17; and political representation 176–8, 216–17, 233–4; Co-operative Party 216–17, 233–4, 255–8; Scottish Co-operative and Labour Council 218–19; Scottish militancy 176–7, 234n.; *see also* Paisley
Cormack, D. D. 249–52
Cowan, M. G. (Miss) 269
Craig, A. 106
Craig, A. F. & Co. 48, 63, 208, 239
Cramp, C. T. 256–7
Crawfurd, H. (Mrs) 215
Crofters' Holdings Act (1886) 93
Cunningham, H. 184
Dangerfield, G. 14–16
Dickson, A. *et al.* 40–5
Dillon Lewis, E. 138
disestablishment 23, 46, 81–3; *see also* Paisley
Dollan, P. 214, 250
Downie, J. 277
Downs, L. L. 6
Druce, E. 190–1
Dunbabin, J. P. D. 19, 21
Duncan, R. 29
Dundee 29, 95, 99n., 147n., 152, 200, 264n.
Dunn, W. 100, 102, 105, 131–2, 137, 139–40, 145–6, 169, 184–6
Dunn, W. (Mrs) 94
Eadie Bros. 48
Eadie, P. 61, 84–5, 93, 98, 141
economy 154; 1908 recession 27, 199; inter-war 237, 269, 271, 274; *see also* J. & P. Coats Co. Ltd., Paisley
Edinburgh 30, 213n.
'Eight Hour Day' 28–9, 123, 132, 146, 185
elections (parliamentary) 1; (1900) 21, 184, 186; (1906) 202; (1918) 222–4; (1918–9, by-elections) 225, 261; (1920, Paisley by-election) 227–8; (1921, Kirkcaldy by-election) 242; (1922, Inverness by-election) 242; (1922, Moray and Nairn by-election) 242; (1922, Dundee) 29; (1922) 244; (1923) 250, 261; (1924) 266n., 267; (1929) 267; *see also* Paisley
Elliot, J. 224, 236–7
empire 137, 140, 183–6; *see also* Paisley, war
experience (evidence of) 4–5
Ferguson, J. 96–7, 103
Fforde, M. 141–3
Fisher & Co. 48, 84, 99
Fleming & Ferguson 49
Flett, Rev. Dr 57
Flockhart, W. B. 121, 177, 195
franchise: 1884 Franchise Act 142, 144; 1918 Representation of the People Act 19–20, 25, 29; *see also* Paisley
Free Church 23, 28
Fry, M. 24–5
Fullerton, A. 106
Fullerton, Hodgart & Barclay 48, 60, 63, 84, 208, 214, 239–40
Fullerton, John & Co. 48, 77
Fulton, W. & Sons 49, 63
Fyfe, A. 169
Galbraith, T. G. D. 144, 229n., 259
Galbraith, W. 144, 229n., 259
Gallacher, W. 171, 178–80, 188, 198n., 210–11, 215, 218, 225, 240
gender 149–50, 154–6, 162; *see also* Paisley
Giffen, J. 118, 131
Gladstone, W. E. 46, 85, 89
Glasgow: Forty Hours Strike 225; historiography 26–7; housing 169, 238n., 246; industry 199; local government 103, 236, 238, 261, 270; tramways 165–6; unemployment 239
Glover, H. 126
Goodlad, G. 85
Gormley, J. 226, 240, 249, 256, 278
Gramsci, A. 8–12, 87, 247, 281
Gregg, C. J. 115, 166, 177, 194–5
Greig, W. 123–4, 130–1, 133, 144, 171
guild socialism 212; *see also* Paisley
Guthrie, H. B. 254–6
Hair, A. 171
Hamilton, E. (Lord) 80, 141n.
Hamilton, G. 106
Hamilton, J. 123, 173
Hammond, A. 121–3, 133
Hanna, Donald & Sons 49
Hardie, J. Keir 126, 133, 135, 139, 160, 174
Hart, M. 20–1
Harvie, C. 22–4
Hastie, A. 46
Henderson, J. 171
Henderson, R. 121
Hobsbawm, E. 38–9
Holford, J. 30
Holms, J. 121–2
Home Rule: Ireland 15, 22, 27, 75, 80–2, 84–91, 206, 223, 229; Scotland 81; *see also* Irish, Paisley
Howell 80
Hutchesontown Liberal Association 101n.
Hutchison, I. G. C. 23–4, 89, 181
Hutton, Rev. Dr 79, 94
Independent Labour Party (ILP) 27; and candidatures (parliamentary) 135, 219, 250, 255–8; and Liberal Party 102, 146, 147n.; ethical socialism 182–3; membership 181, 196–7; social networks 27, 170, 180–3; *see also* Labour Party, Paisley, Scottish United Trades Council Labour Party, Scottish Workers' Parliamentary Elections Committee, Scottish Workers' Representation Committee
Irish: 'Catholic vote' 26, 223; in Scotland 23, 223; *see also* Home Rule, Paisley
Isdale, J. 51
Isdale, R. 51
Isdale & McCallum 49, 51
Jamieson, Messrs & Sons 51
Jephcott, A. R. 202–3
Johnston, C. N. 141, 143–4
Joyce, P. 31–2, 57, 86, 145, 149, 153, 181n., 203, 275n., 278–9

Kellas, J. G. 22, 82
Kelso, W. W. 168
Kent, J. 129–30, 171
Kerr & Clark 54
Kerr & Co. 54
Kerr, J. P. 54, 107
Kerr, L. 47–8, 61, 178, 241
Kerr, P. 54
Kincardineshire 28
Knox, W. W. 152, 210

Labour Party: and Co-operative movement 176, 233; and Co-operative Party 233–4, 254–8; and Irish community 26; and local government 236; and Scottish Workers' Representation Committee 174–5; historiography (UK) 20; inter-war 244, 278; Labour government (1924) 258–9; Labour government (1930) 269; Scottish organisation 175, 233–5, 247, 250, 254–8; *see also* Independent Labour Party, Paisley, Scottish Workers' Parliamentary Elections Committee, Scottish Workers' Representation Committee, Scottish United Trades Council Labour Party
Lancashire 17–18, 31–2
land reform 93, 96–7, 102; *see also* Paisley
language 3–4, 36, 90; 'linguistic turn' 3–7, 32; meta-narratives 11–12, 86, 279; of Labour 121–2, 129, 135–6, 174, 262–4, 280–1; of Liberalism 75–6, 85, 89–92, 136–8, 140–1, 197, 228–9, 243, 279–80; of paternalism 57–8, 205; of Unionism 85, 89–90, 139–41, 200–1, 203, 279–80; political poetry 136, 139; *see also* class, Paisley
Lawrence, J. 86
Lee, A. J. 86
Liberal Party: and disestablishment 82; and First World War 224; and labour interests 132; and Independent Labour Party 102, 186, 196–7; and National Government (1931) 271–3; and Presbyterianism 23; and protection 251; and Unionist Party 242, 259–60; historiography (UK) 13–21; (Scotland) 21–30; inter-war 229–30, 242, 251, 267–8; Liberal Imperialism 184–6; National Liberal Club 101–2; National Liberal Federation of Scotland 93; New Liberalism 23–4, 27, 99n., 203–4, 206; Scottish Liberal Association 93, 101–2, 186; Scottish Liberal Federation 242, 268, 272; Young Scots 188; *see also* language, Liberal Unionist Party (1886–1912), Paisley
Liberal Unionist Party (1886–1912) 75, 89; and labour interests 142; and social reform 142–3; and tariff reform 190; West of Scotland Liberal Unionist Association 87–8, 107n., 142, 189–90; *see also* Conservative Party (–1912), Paisley, Unionist Party (1912–)
Lib-Lab'ism 103–4
Lloyd George, D. 187, 250–1, 267
Lobnitz & Co. 49
local government: *see* Glasgow, Paisley
London 32
Loudon, T. 124, 134, 199n.
Love, J. 163, 182
Lyle, A. 56–7
Lynch, H. 234–5
Lynch, M. 26

McArthur, J. & Co. 49, 77
MacArthur, M. 159–60, 162n.
McCaffrey, J. 84, 88
McCallum, J. M. 51, 62, 84, 93, 169, 188, 197, 201–2, 220–5
McCallum, J. M. (Mrs) 94
McCarthy, M. 128
McCulloch, J. 268–70
Macdonald, J. 182
MacDonald, J. R. 233, 250, 269
McFarland, E. W. 112–14
MacFarlane, A. 114, 123
McGee, Walter & Son 48
McGhee, B. 123
McGown, J. (Treasurer) 78, 84
McInnes Shaw, A. D. 252–3, 259–60
McIntyre, H. & Co. 77
MacKean, J. A. D. 84, 192, 197, 227–9, 232
MacKean, W. 49–51, 74, 107
MacKean, W. M. 50, 74, 84
MacKenzie Bros 49, 106
MacKenzie, A. 78, 120–1, 165
McKerrell, R. M. 82, 87, 108–9, 114, 137, 139
McKibbin, R. 247–8
McKinlay, A. 27, 170, 182
Maclay, J. P. 270–3
McLean, A. 249
McLean, Donald (Sir) 225, 231, 242
Maclean, J. 177, 179–80
McLeod Fullarton, R. W. 109
McPhee, A. 171
McPhee, J. 133–4
Maltman Barry, M. 138
Marjoribanks, E. 138
Martin, W. H. 256
Mason, J. S. 182
Maxwell, A. B. 111
Maxwell, D. 247–9
Middlesborough 138
Millar, J. 84, 92
Mitchell, E. R. 255–6, 258, 261–5, 269, 272
Mitchell, G. 139
Moffat, J. 189–93
Moffatt, A. 144
Morgan, K. O. 18
Munro, J. 133
Murphy, W. M. 165–7

National Democratic Party (NDP) 220–1
National Federation of Women Workers (NFWW) 161
National Guilds League 211
Neil, J. 219
Neilston 161, 195
Newby, H. 52
New Jersey 54
Norris, G. M. 52, 55

Orange movement 113–14, 253; *see also* Paisley

Paisley
as community 36–8, 53, 57, 61, 140, 147, 188, 230, 273, 280; *see also* class

Beaconsfield Club 87–8, 110–12, 192, 194, 202–3
Boys' Welfare Scheme 63
British Socialist Party (BSP, Paisley branch) 170, 180, 215–16, 218–19, 226; *see also* Social Democratic Federation, Social Democratic Party
Brough Educational Institute 62
Cart Navigation Bill 76–8, 81
Cart Trust 78, 118
civic identity 67–8
class 40–4, 47, 50, 66, 69, 96, 106, 123, 126, 129, 145–7, 152, 157–9, 161–3, 181, 188, 197, 230, 232, 244, 246–7, 265, 279–80
Coats Observatory 67
Coffee Room 74–5
Communist Party (Paisley branch): and Co-operative Party 248; and Labour Party 241, 247–8, 278; and local government 237, 240; and Unemployed Committee 240; and United Front 278
Conservative Party (Paisley, –1908)
Conservatism 114–16, 194
Conservative Association 75, 106–7, 141, 192, 194; and Liberal Unionist Party 107–9, 141, 193; and social reform 143–4; and tariff reform 189; Central Association 109; East End (Eastern) Association 109, 176, 192; 'Tory Democracy' 110, 112, 114–15; *see also* elections, Liberal Unionist Party (1886– 1908), national parties, Unionist Party (1908–)
Co-operative movement 116–17, 125, 176–7, 217; and candidatures (parliamentary) 219; and First World War 216–18; and housing 170, 245; and Independent Labour Party 123, 219, 224; and Liberal Party 117, 224; and local government 119–21, 123, 130–1, 171, 178; and municipalisation 167, 170; and Scottish Workers' Representation Committee 172, 176; and tariff reform 177, 187; and Trades Council 119–21, 123–5, 131, 134; and Trades and Labour Council 218–19, 233; and unemployment 240, 244; Colinslee Strike (1897) 123–5; Equitable Society 117, 119, 124–5, 167, 172, 176, 219; Food Vigilance Committee 218; Manufacturing Society 117, 123, 176; politicisation of 177, 216–19; Provident Society 117, 121, 167, 172, 176–7, 219, 276; Renfrewshire Co-operative Conference Association 177; Underwood Coal Society 117, 167, 176; Women's Guilds 117, 214, 218–19, 231, 275; *see also* Co-operative Party, elections, Labour movement, national movement
Co-operative Party (Co-operative Defence Committee) 219, 234, 276; and candidatures (parliamentary) 234–5, 238, 248–9, 254–8, 262, 276–7; and Independent Labour Party 235, 255; and Labour Party 234–6, 238, 247, 254, 276; and local government 236–8; *see also* Co-operative movement, elections, Labour movement
cornflour 50–1
disestablishment 81–3, 100, 137–8, 146, 198
Distress Committee 199–200; *see also* industry, unemployment
Dunn Square 62
dyeing 47
elections (parliamentary): (1841) 46; (1885) 80–3, 114; (1886) 90–1; (1891) 131, 136–41; (1892) 115, 141, 143–6, 148; (1900) 184–6; (1906) 158, 173, 197–8; (1910, Jan.) 200–2; (1910, Dec.) 202–4; (1918) 220–4; (1920) 226–32; (1922) 243–7; (1923) 247–55; (1924) 260–6; (1929) 268–9; (1931) 270–1; (1935) 272–3; (1945) 273–4; *see also* local political parties, national political parties and candidates
elites 43–4, 47, 50, 61–2, 77, 80, 82, 84, 90, 92, 94, 99–100, 105–6, 119, 121–2, 135, 146, 191–2
engineering 48–9, 150, 199, 239; *see also* industry
Fair Trade League 110–12
Fountain Gardens 67
franchise 45–6, 144, 222
gender 149–59, 162; *see also* women
George A. Clark Town Hall 67, 70–2
Gleniffer Home 67
Home Rule: 'All Round' 100, 102; Ireland 83–91, 93, 137, 139, 198, 222–3, 229; Scotland 93, 97, 139, 203; *see also* Irish community, Irish National League
housing: and First World War 213–14, 223; Labour policy 123, 168, 188; municipal provision 168–9, 244–6, 253; overcrowding 168, 244, 245; Paisley Tenants' Protection Association 169–70, 215, 223; rent levels 244–6; rent strike (1920) 245; Scottish Labour Housing Association (Paisley) 248–50; *see also* Labour movement
immigration 41
Industrial School 65
industry 37, 39–41, 45–50, 53–5, 150, 161, 191, 279; (1908 recession) 198–200; inter-war 237, 239, 274; *see also* engineering, J. & P. Coats Co. Ltd., paternalism, specific firms, industries and trade unions
Infirmary Board 122
Irish community 41, 94–5, 137; as voters 221, 223, 230–1, 237, 246; Catholic Socialist Society 226, 230, 246; *see also* Home Rule, Irish National League
Irish National League (later United Irish League) 83, 94–7, 100, 103, 170, 187, 222–3, 230–1; *see also* Home Rule, Irish community
Junior Imperialist Union 252
Labour movement 175, 180, 200, 215, 275
Independent Labour Party (ILP, Paisley branch) 99, 121–3, 179; and Advanced Radical Association 103; and British Socialist Party 215–16; and candidatures (parliamentary) 173, 181,

219n., 238, 248, 250, 255–8; and Catholic Socialist Society 226; and Co-operative movement 123, 218–19; and Co-operative Party 235, 255–8; and First World War 224; and housing 170, 182; and Labour Party 276, 255–8; and local government 120, 122–3, 129, 171, 199, 238; and parliamentary politics 134; and tariff reform 187, 198; and trade unions 126, 134; and Trades and Labour Council 181–2, 212, 219; and Trades Council 122–3, 125, 131–4, 173; and women 151, 153, 155, 160–3; membership 135, 181, 215; social activities 180–2, 188

Labour Party (Paisley branch, 1918–): and candidatures (parliamentary) 233–5, 249, 254–8; and Communist Party 241, 247–8, 278; and Co-operative movement 233–4; and Co-operative Party 234–8, 247, 254–8, 277; and housing 245–6; and Independent Labour Party 234–5, 237–8, 255, 276; and Irish vote 246; and local government 236–8, 248, 275, 280; and middle-class vote 265; and national organisation 226, 250, 256–8; and Unemployed Committee 240–1, 244, 248; and United Front 278; membership 276; *see also* Trades Council (1891–1911), Trades and Labour Council (1911–18)

Labour Representation Committee (local) 173–4, 179, 199n.

Scottish Labour Party (Paisley branch) 119–20, 132–3

Socialist Sunday School 163–4

Trades Council (1891–1911) 94, 99, 104, 118; and Co-operative movement 119–21, 123–5, 131, 134, 167; and housing 169–70; and Independent Labour Party 122–3, 125, 131–4; and Labour Representation Committee (local) 174; and Liberal Party 118, 120, 131, 133–4, 139; and local government 118–23, 129, 164, 171, 199; and municipalisation 164, 167, 170–1; and Scottish Labour Party 132–3; and Scottish National Labour League 133; and Scottish United Trades Council Labour Party 132–3; and Scottish Workers' Representation Committee 173; and Social Democratic Federation 171, 179; and Social Democratic Party 179; and unemployment 199–200; and Unionist Party 201; and women 124–5, 153, 158–9, 161–3; and Workers' Elections Committee (local) 172–3; membership 127, 134, 167; *see also* Trades and Labour Council (1911–1918), Labour Party (1918–)

Trades and Labour Council (1911–1918): and British Socialist Party 180, 215, 219; and candidatures (parliamentary) 219; and Co-operative movement 176, 178, 218–19; and First World War 208–15, 218–19, 280; and guild socialism 210–13; and housing 214–15; and Independent Labour Party 181–2, 212, 219; and Labour Party 174; and propaganda 175; and Social Democratic Party 179–80; foundation 174; membership 175; *see also* Trades Council (1891–1911), Labour Party (1918–)

Workers' Elections Committee (local) 167, 171–3

Workers' Municipal Elections Committee (local) 130–1, 167, 172

Workers' Parliamentary Elections Committee (local) 167, 172; *see also* British Socialist Party, Co-operative movement, elections, local government, Social Democratic Federation, Social Democratic Party, Socialist Labour Party, and national elections and parties

land reform 100, 102, 104, 123, 132, 137–8, 143, 185, 196, 198, 203, 229

Liberal Party (Paisley) 46, 75–6; Advanced Radical Association 92–3, 97, 99–106, 136, 144–5, 147; and Boer War 184; and the Irish vote 223, 246; and the 'Labour Question' 145–6, 170, 185, 187–8; and social reform 185; and tariff reform 186–7, 196–8, 201–2, 229, 244, 251, 268–9, 271; and unemployment 244, 247, 271; electoral pacts 252, 259–60, 264–6, 268–74, 281; Liberal Association 79–80, 93–4, 97, 99, 104, 137, 184, 227, 242, 259, 265, 267–73; Liberal Club 79, 84, 91–2, 94, 98, 109, 188; Liberalism 46, 75–6, 92, 99, 106, 135–7, 187, 228–30, 244, 247, 251, 253, 265, 270, 273, 279–80; Scottish League of Young Liberals 268, 271; Women's Liberal Association 94, 188, 231n., 268; *see also* Liberal Unionist Party (1886–1908), radical tradition, elections and national party

Liberal Unionist Party (Paisley, 1886–1908): and Conservative Party 107–9, 141, 193–4; and tariff reform 189; Liberal and Radical Unionist Association 107, 141, 190–2; Liberal Unionism 80, 87, 89, 91–3, 114–16, 140–2, 190–1, 193–4, 197, 279; Women's Liberal Unionist Association 107, 193; *see also* Conservative Party (–1908), elections, Liberal Party, Unionist Party (1908–) and national parties

local government

Education Authority: elections (1919) 236; (1922) 237, 246

Parish Council: and unemployment 240; elections (1895) 121–2; (1910) 171; (1913) 182; (1919) 236; (1922) 237

School Board 65, 67; elections (1873) 189; (1885) 78–9; (1891) 118; (1894) 119; (1900, 1906, 1909, 1911) 171

Town Council: and Cart development 76–8; and housing 168; and

municipalisation 165–7, 171; and public health 128–9; and thread industry 159–60; and tramways 165–6; and unemployment 240; and ward structure 121–2; elections (1894) 120; (1895) 122; (1896) 123; (1897) 125–6; (1898) 126, 129–30; (1899) 131; (1900–7) 171; (1907) 179; (1908–9) 171; (1912) 180; (1913) 171; (1919–20) 236; (1921) 235–6; (1922) 236; (1923) 237, 248; (1924) 237; franchise 23
marmalade 49
Memorial Baptist Church 67
Museum and Art Gallery 51, 67
Orange movement 83, 110–14, 170, 253
Paisley Observer 155, 158
Poor Association 63, 67, 200
population 39
Primrose League 110, 115, 193–4
public benefactions 62–3, 67–8
public health: death rate 128; enteric fever outbreak (1898) 128–9; water supply 128–9; *see also* housing
radical tradition 13, 44–6, 75, 80, 83–6, 90, 92, 95, 100, 122, 127, 130, 135–7, 140–2, 147, 162, 170–1, 174, 180, 183, 191, 195–7, 200–3, 228, 251, 261, 263–4, 266, 270–1, 273–5, 278–82
skill 150–1, 205, 207–8, 241
Sma' Shot Day 1, 59
soap 49, 51, 201
Social Democratic Federation (SDF, Paisley branch) 171, 179; *see also* British Socialist Party, Labour movement, Social Democratic Party and national party
Social Democratic Party (SDP, Paisley branch) 179, 188; and Trades and Labour Council 179–80; social activities 179; *see also* British Socialist Party, Labour movement, Social Democratic Federation and national party
Socialism 130, 178, 180, 223–4, 226, 260, 281; *see also* Labour movement
Socialist Labour Party (Paisley Branch) 210, 227; *see also* Labour movement
starch 49–51, 76–7
strikes and lock-outs: ASE 'lock-out' (1897) 105, 121, 125–8; Colinslee strike (1897) 123–5; spoolers (1897) 126; cop-winders (1900) 154; hank-winders (1904) 156; hank-winders (1905) 156–7; thread operatives (1907) 160–1; cone-winders (1908) 161; (1910–14) 204–6; dyers (1912) 204–5; Forty Hours (1919) 225; engineers 'lock-out' (1922) 240
Tariff Reform League 193, 195
temperance 63, 81, 83, 137, 143, 185, 198, 222, 229, 262
trade unions: Amalgamated Society of Carpenters and Joiners 125, 171; Amalgamated Society of Engineers (later Amalgamated Engineering Union) 105, 118, 121, 125–8, 134, 179, 199, 206, 211, 225–6, 244n., 245n., 277; Amalgamated Society of Joiners and Shipbuilders 123; Amalgamated Society of Wood Turners 133; Amalgamated Toolmakers 208; Amalgamated Union of Co-operative Employees 218; and ILP 133–4; and patriarchy 161, 163; and political representation 128, 131, 173–4, 188, 206, 248; and unemployment 241; Associated Shipwrights Union 133; Bakers' Union 133, 249; Boilermakers Union 134; General Textile Workers' Union 210; Miners' Federation 173; National Society of Dyers and Finishers 204–5; Operative Bricklayers Association 128, 173; Paisley Women's Federal Union 153; Patternmakers' Society 163, 182; Powerloom Carpet Weavers Association 118, 133–4; Scottish Carters' Association 173; Scottish Horse and Motormen's Association 234; Shop Assistants' Union 218; Tailors' Society 123, 125; United Machine Workers' Association 208, 244n.; United Plumbers 128; Women Workers' Union 159–61; Workers' Union 210n.
tramways 165–7
Unemployed Committee 240, 248; and candidatures (parliamentary) 249; and Asquith, H. H. 244; and Labour Party 241; and local government 237; unemployment 239–41, 244; *see also* Distress Committee, industry, Labour movement
Unionist Party (Paisley, 1908–): and labour interests 200–3; and tactical voting 232, 253; and tariff reform 200–1, 203, 224, 253; electoral pacts 252–3, 259–60, 264–6, 269–72, 274, 281; Unionism 194, 200; Unionist Association 194–5, 200, 227, 252–3; *see also* Conservative Party (–1908), elections, Liberal Unionist Party (1886–1908), Junior Imperial Union, Women's Guild of Empire and national parties
United Irish League: *see* Irish National League
war: Boer War 145, 183–6, 220; First World War 153, 207–20
War Emergency Committee 213–14
weaver culture 42–3, 45–7, 59, 100, 135–7, 191, 195–6, 212–13, 251
women: and domesticity 157, 159, 161, 231; and First World War 208–10, 213–15, 222; and housing 213–15; and Labour politics 160, 231, 275; and Liberal politics 94, 146, 231, 242–3, 268, 270–1; and marriage 47–8; and strikes 123–6, 154, 156–7, 160–1; and Unionist politics 107, 110, 115, 252, 265n.; and weaving industry 123–5; as thread workers 41–2, 47–61, 199, 209–10, 239; as voters 221–2, 231–2, 271; *see also* gender
Women's Guild of Empire, 252
Parker Smith, J. 76, 87–90, 107, 114
Parlane, J. 84
paternalism 52–3, 55; and family 59, 71–2; and the franchise 146; and localism 52–3, 57, 61, 67, 209–10, 279; and meritocracy 61; and

patriarchy 149–52; and politics 62, 119, 151, 273, 279; as ritual 58, 61, 66, 70–2; decline of 199, 201, 239; language of 57–8, 61, 71–2; 'the gift' 58–9; *see also* J. & P. Coats Co Ltd., language, Paisley
Paton, J. 211
Pawtucket (Rh.I.) 54
Poirier, P. 15–16
Pollard, S. 216–17
Pollock, A. R. 131
Pollock, C. 51
Pollitt, H. 248–9
Polson, J. 50
Polson, J. (Jr.) 50, 84, 107
Polson, W. 50
Presbyterianism 23
Preston 33, 214
Pringle, W. M. R. 258, 268

Redmond, W. 95
Reid, Thomas & Sons 48
Renshaw, C. B. 108, 110
Roberton, H. S. 264
Robertson, Chisholm 132–3
Robertson, G. 182
Robertson, J. 49
Robin & Houston 49, 51
Rochdale 132, 146
Rollings, W. 111
Rosebery, 5th earl of 184, 261
Ross & Duncan 54
Russell, R. 180, 182, 206, 236–7

Savage, M. 33–4, 68, 164
Scollan, T. 238, 249, 254, 256
Scott, J. W. 4–7, 162
Scottish Home Rule Association 139; *see also* Home Rule, Paisley
Scottish Labour Housing Association 245–6, 248; *see also* Paisley
Scottish Labour Party 131, 133, 138–9; *see also* Labour Party, Paisley, Scottish United Trades Council Labour Party, Scottish Workers' Parliamentary Elections Committee, Scottish Workers' Representation Committee
Scottish National Labour League 133
Scottish Tenants' Association 169; *see also* Paisley
Scottish United Trades Council Labour Party 131–3; *see also* Labour Party, Paisley, Scottish Labour Party, Scottish Workers' Parliamentary Elections Committee, Scottish Workers' Representation Committee
Scottish Workers' Parliamentary Elections Committee 172; *see also* Labour Party, Paisley, Scottish Labour Party, Scottish United Trades Council Labour Party, Scottish Workers' Representation Committee
Scottish Workers' Representation Committee 172–5; *see also* Labour Party, Paisley, Scottish Labour Party, Scottish United Trades Council Labour Party, Scottish Workers' Parliamentary Elections Committee
Searle, G. R. 34
Shaw, B. 234, 247, 256
Shaw, W. 254, 256
shawls 1, 53–4; *see also* Paisley
Shaw Maxwell, J. 134–5
Sim, W. 50–1
skill 150–1; *see also* Paisley
Small, M. (Mrs) 277
Smiley, H. H. 84, 87, 107
Smillie, R. 173, 197–8, 233
Smith, J. 27, 170, 182–3, 199
Smyth, J. 25, 238
Social Democratic Federation 138; *see also* British Socialist Party, Paisley
Socialist Labour Party 210, 212; *see also* Paisley
Souden, Bailie 99–100, 129
Stedman Jones, G. 32–3
Stewart, J. 169, 237, 249, 255–6
supervisory workers 151–2, 154–5; *see also* J. & P. Coats Co Ltd.

Tannahill, R. 163
Tanner, D. 34
tariff reform 142n., 186–7, 189
Tariff Reform League 189, 193, 195; *see also* Paisley
Taylor, A. T. 259–60
Taylor, J. 220–4
Thomason, W. 46
Thompson, E. P. 2–3, 8
Thompson, P. 18
trades councils 29
Trade Union Congress 134
tradition 11–12, 38–9, 140; *see also* Paisley
Tweedale, R. 119–20, 124, 177

Unionist Party (1912–): and social reform 206; East Fife (1918) 28; electoral pacts 253, 259–60; Scottish Unionist Association 194, 252; Unionism 142–3; *see also* Conservative Party (–1912), Liberal Unionist Party (1885–1912), Paisley
Urwin, D. W. 22, 87

Waites, B. 207
Wake, E. P. 226, 256–7
Walker, W. 29
Wallace, J. 99, 103, 105, 145
war: Boer War 15, 145, 184; First World War 15, 18–21, 23–5, 27, 29, 207, 209, 229; *see also* Paisley
Watson, J. C. 227
weaving 1; *see also* Paisley, shawls
Weir, Bailie 78, 84
Welsh, J. 269–71, 277
West Renfrewshire 76, 87
Wheatley, J. 261
Williams, J. M. 277
Williams, R. 7
Wilson, D. 219, 233, 236
Wilson, D. (Treasurer) 58, 84, 94
Wilson, R. & Co. 49
women: *see* gender, Paisley
Women's Protection and Provident League 153
Wood, I. 25
Wotherspoon, W. 49, 58
Wotherspoon, W. (Mrs) 94

Young, A. 256